SHUCK UNMASKED

RICK SMITH &
TANIA MENESSE

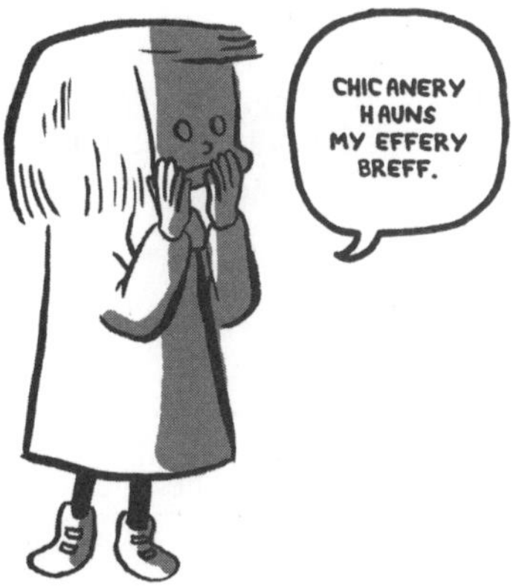
CHICANERY HAUNS MY EFFERY BREFF.

TOP SHELF PRODUCTIONS
MARIETTA, GEORGIA

SHUCK UNMASKED

Written by Rick Smith and Tania Menesse
Drawn by Rick Smith
Entire contents copyright © by Rick Smith and Tania Menesse

Published by:

Top Shelf Productions
PO Box 1282
Marietta, Georgia 30016-1282
USA

Top Shelf Productions and the Top Shelf logo are ® and ™ 2003 by
Top Shelf Productions, Inc.

ISBN # 1-891830-47-3

First Edition: June 2003

Printed in Canada

SHUCK
UNMASKED

Foreword

A good comic is one where the ideas are sophisticated and engaging, and the art cues us how to feel, where to go and how fast to process it. And when a good one comes along we should celebrate it, because among cartoonists it is well known how difficult it is to transfer one's artistic vision onto a two-dimensional drawing surface – a process not unlike crushing a body against the road with a semi-truck. There are few survivors.

As soon as I read Shuck exclaim "Good Ganesh!" I knew everything would be all right. Ganesh is the gentle Hindu god of Hope. Remover of All Obstacles. And the idea that this exclamation should come from the mouth of what appears to be an ancient pagan god (read: demon) conscripted by the church to guard the souls trapped in Purgatory is not only deeply skewed, it's really funny.

Rick Smith and Tania Menesse have managed to create a very original comic, and yet at the same time one that is reminiscent of George Herriman's *Krazy Kat*, or Walt Kelly's *Pogo*. And like those, *Shuck* enjoys mangling the English language. The artwork is easy and pleasing using clean simple shapes, and there seems to be a deliberate sense that we see what we need to see, no more no less. All in all it's a very original, and very gentle book about ghosts, death, and Hell.

Celebrate!

Jeff Smith
Creator of *Bone*

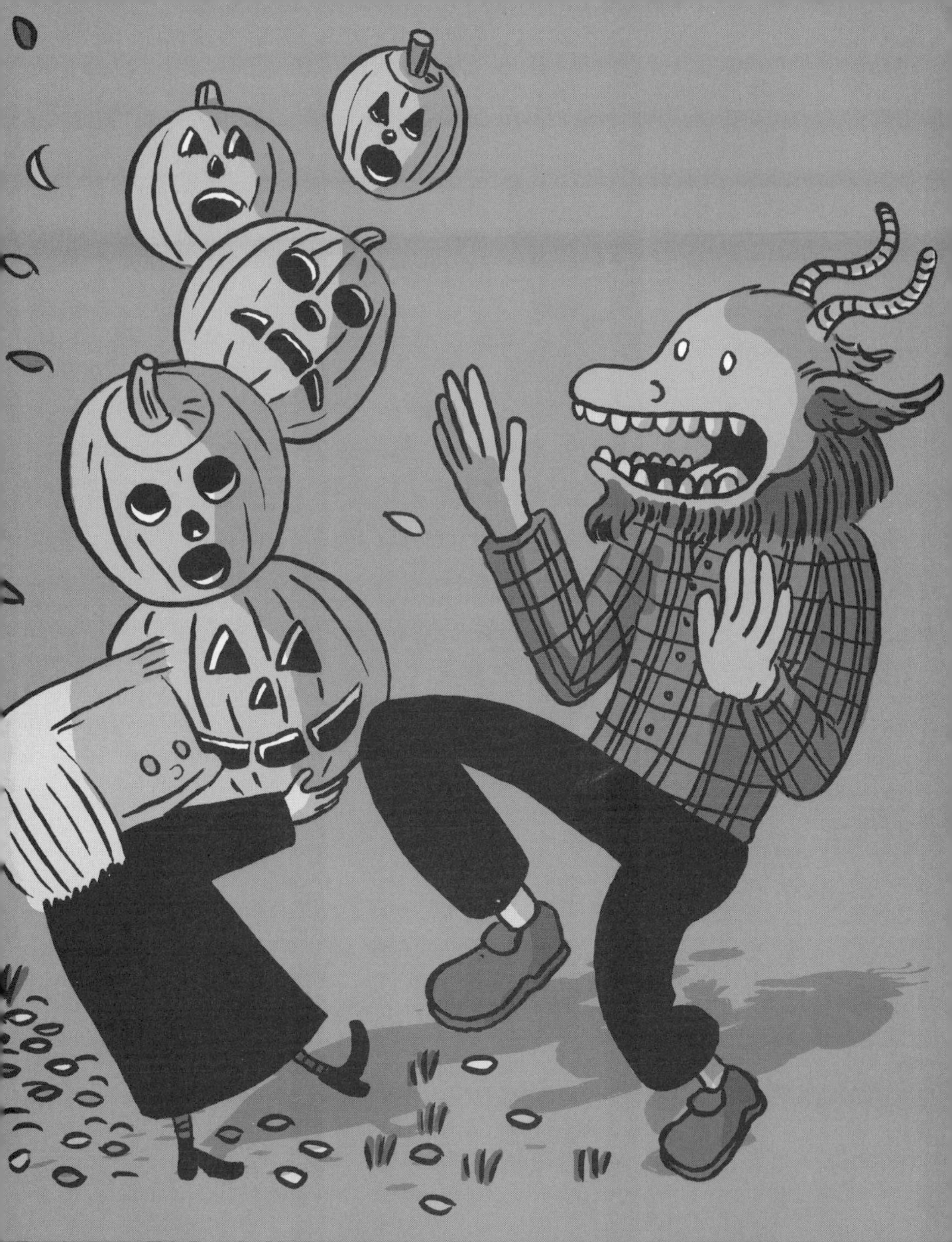

HALLOWED SEASONINGS

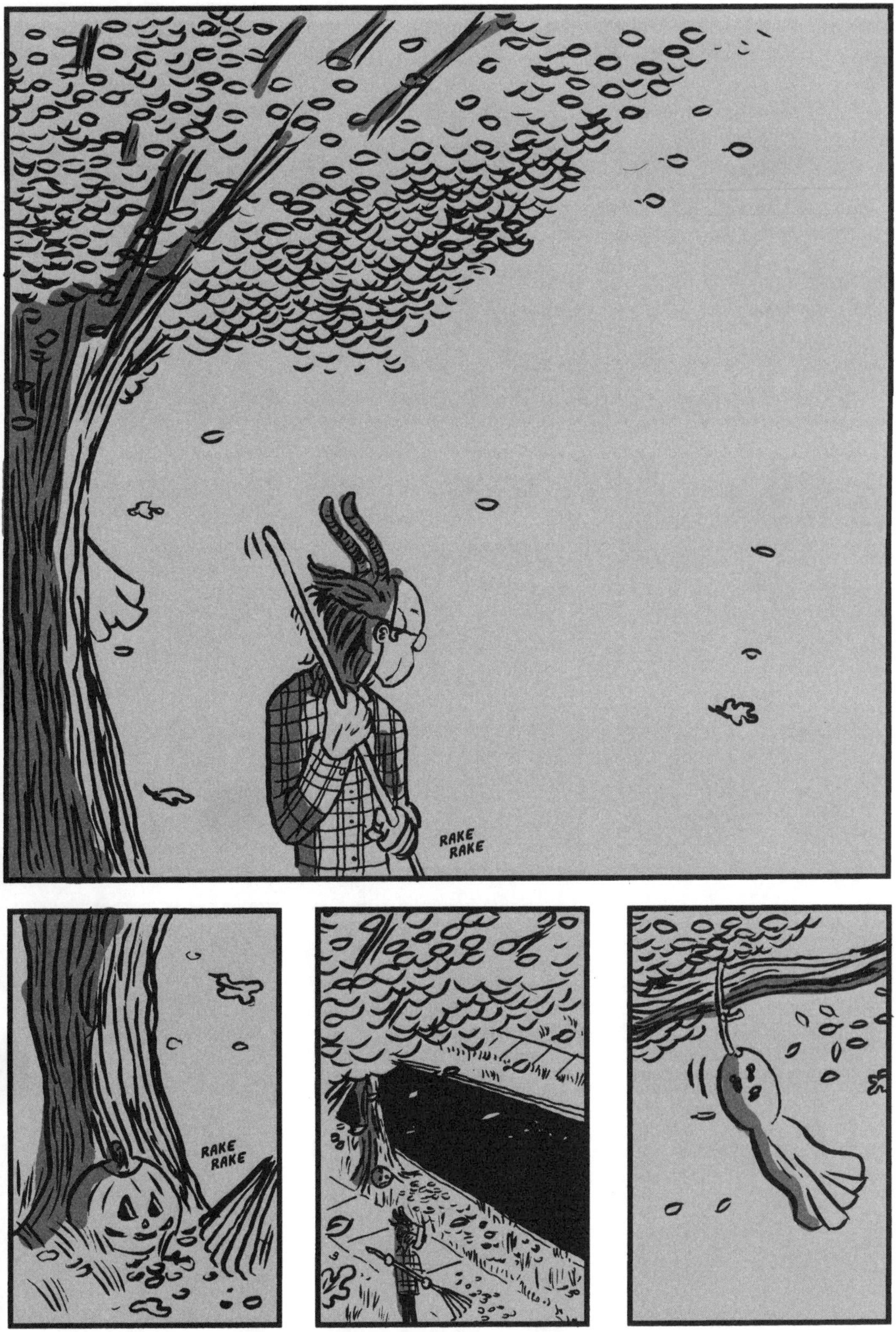
RAKE
RAKE
RAKE
RAKE

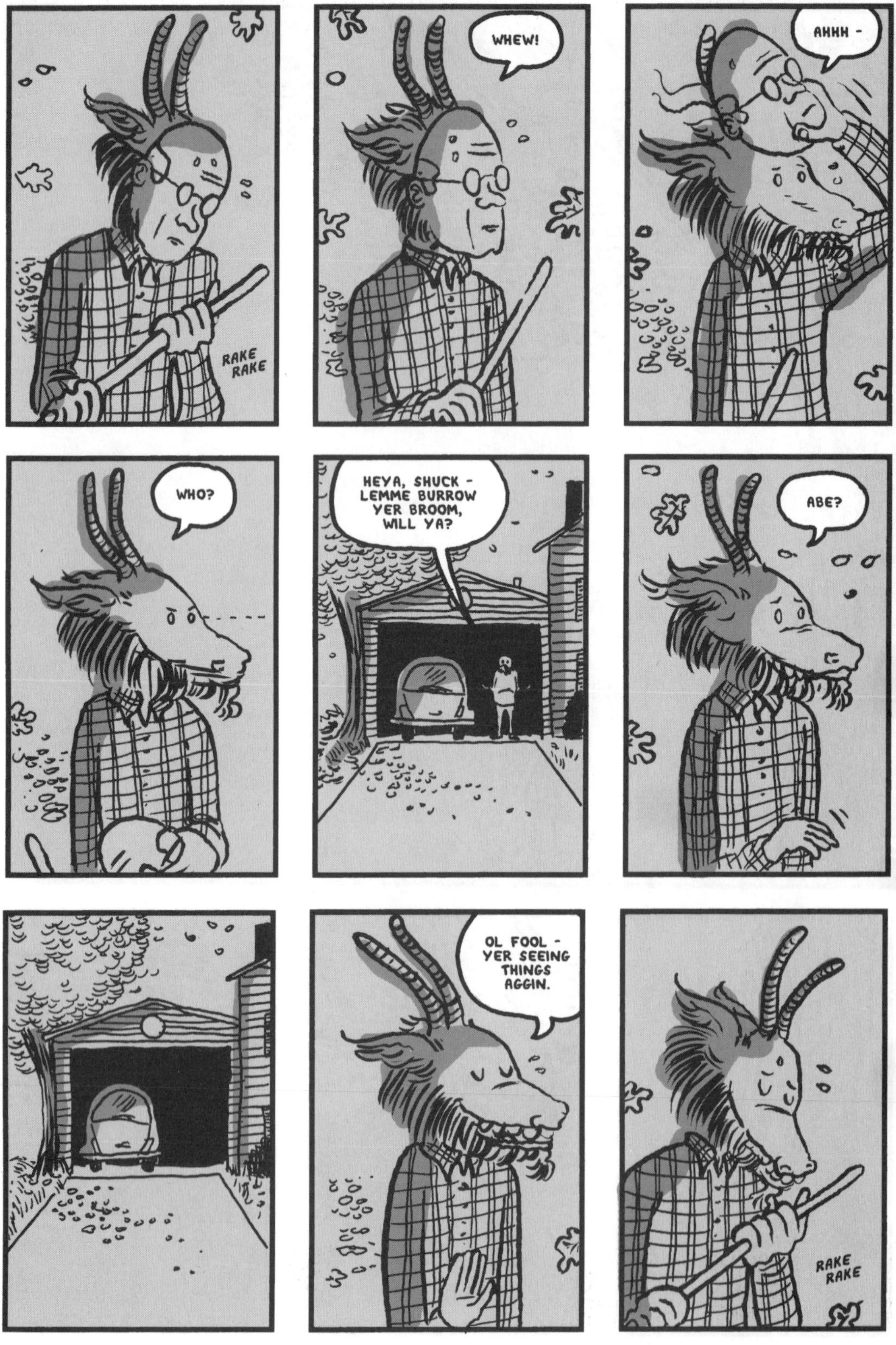
RAKE
RAKE
WHEW!
AHHH -
WHO?
HEYA, SHUCK - LEMME BURROW YER BROOM, WILL YA?
ABE?
OL FOOL - YER SEEING THINGS AGGIN.
RAKE
RAKE

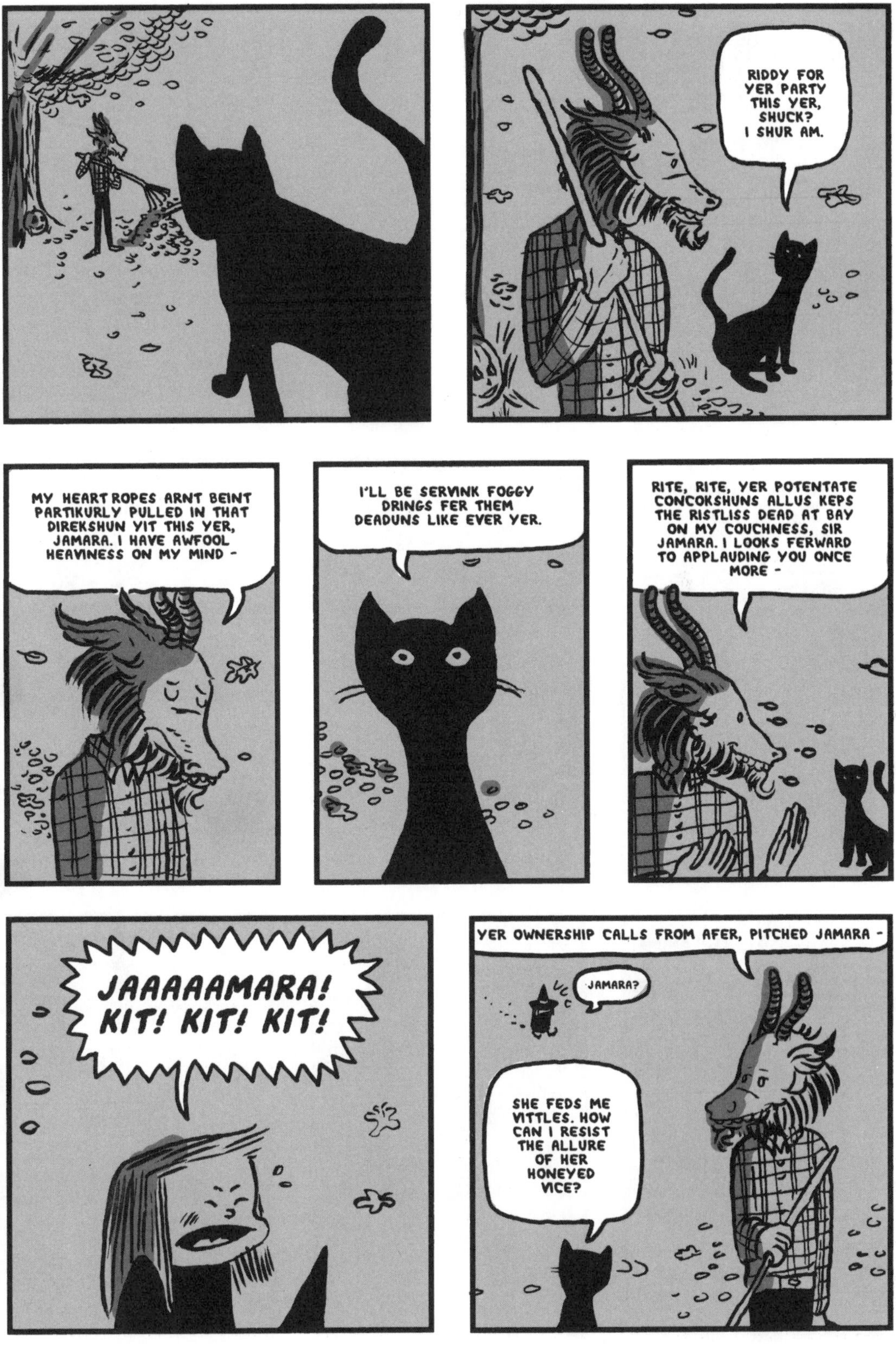
RIDDY FOR YER PARTY THIS YER, SHUCK? I SHUR AM.
MY HEART ROPES ARNT BEINT PARTIKURLY PULLED IN THAT DIREKSHUN YIT THIS YER, JAMARA. I HAVE AWFOOL HEAVINESS ON MY MIND -
I'LL BE SERVINK FOGGY DRINGS FER THEM DEADUNS LIKE EVER YER.
RITE, RITE, YER POTENTATE CONCOKSHUNS ALLUS KEPS THE RISTLISS DEAD AT BAY ON MY COUCHNESS, SIR JAMARA. I LOOKS FERWARD TO APPLAUDING YOU ONCE MORE -
JAAAAAMARA! KIT! KIT! KIT!
YER OWNERSHIP CALLS FROM AFER, PITCHED JAMARA -
JAMARA?
SHE FEDS ME VITTLES. HOW CAN I RESIST THE ALLURE OF HER HONEYED VICE?

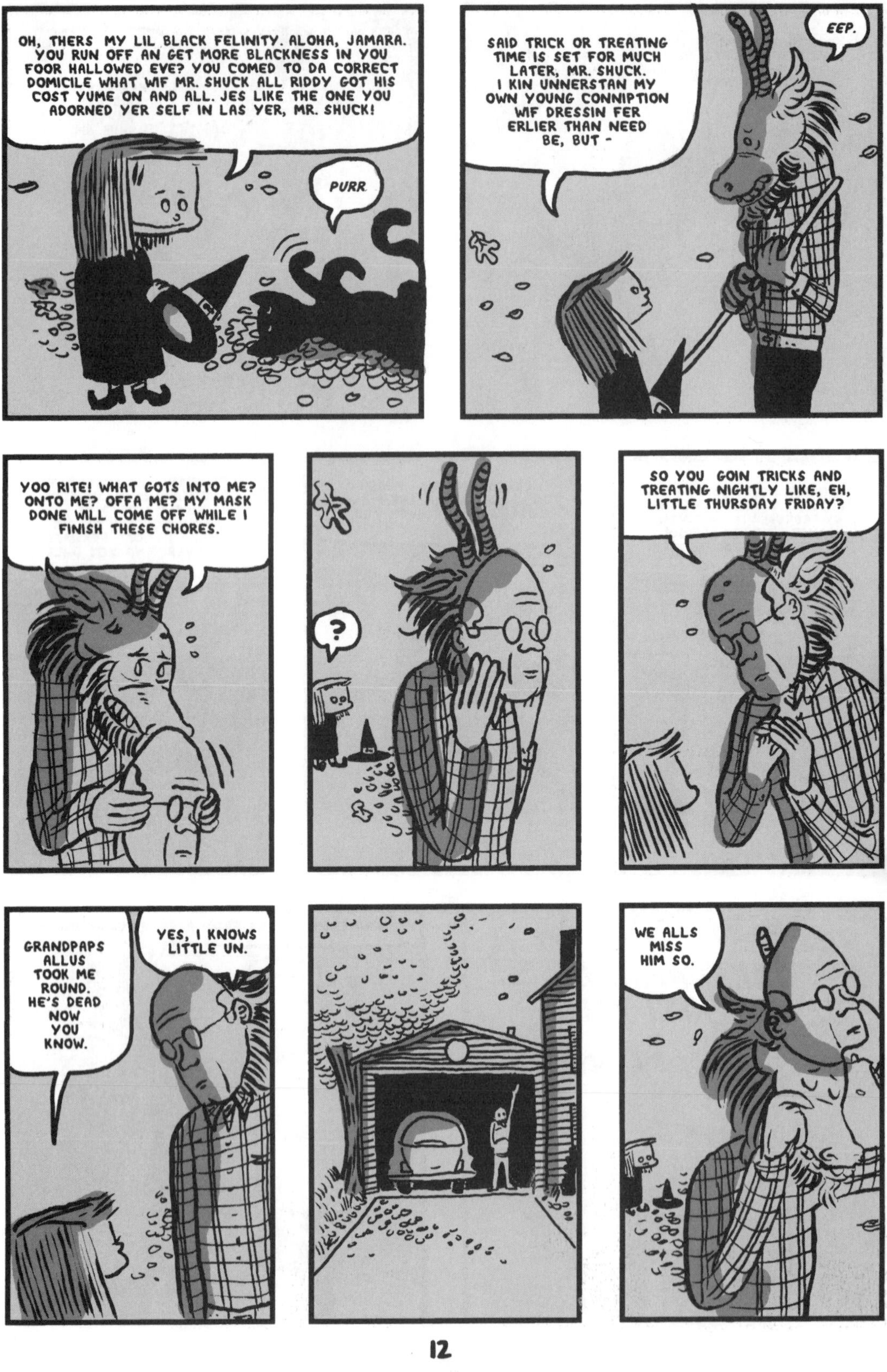
OH, THERS MY LIL BLACK FELINITY. ALOHA, JAMARA. YOU RUN OFF AN GET MORE BLACKNESS IN YOU FOOR HALLOWED EVE? YOU COMED TO DA CORRECT DOMICILE WHAT WIF MR. SHUCK ALL RIDDY GOT HIS COST YUME ON AND ALL. JES LIKE THE ONE YOU ADORNED YER SELF IN LAS YER, MR. SHUCK!
PURR
SAID TRICK OR TREATING TIME IS SET FOR MUCH LATER, MR. SHUCK. I KIN UNNERSTAN MY OWN YOUNG CONNIPTION WIF DRESSIN FER ERLIER THAN NEED BE, BUT -
EEP.
YOO RITE! WHAT GOTS INTO ME? ONTO ME? OFFA ME? MY MASK DONE WILL COME OFF WHILE I FINISH THESE CHORES.
?
SO YOU GOIN TRICKS AND TREATING NIGHTLY LIKE, EH, LITTLE THURSDAY FRIDAY?
GRANDPAPS ALLUS TOOK ME ROUND. HE'S DEAD NOW YOU KNOW.
YES, I KNOWS LITTLE UN.
WE ALLS MISS HIM SO.

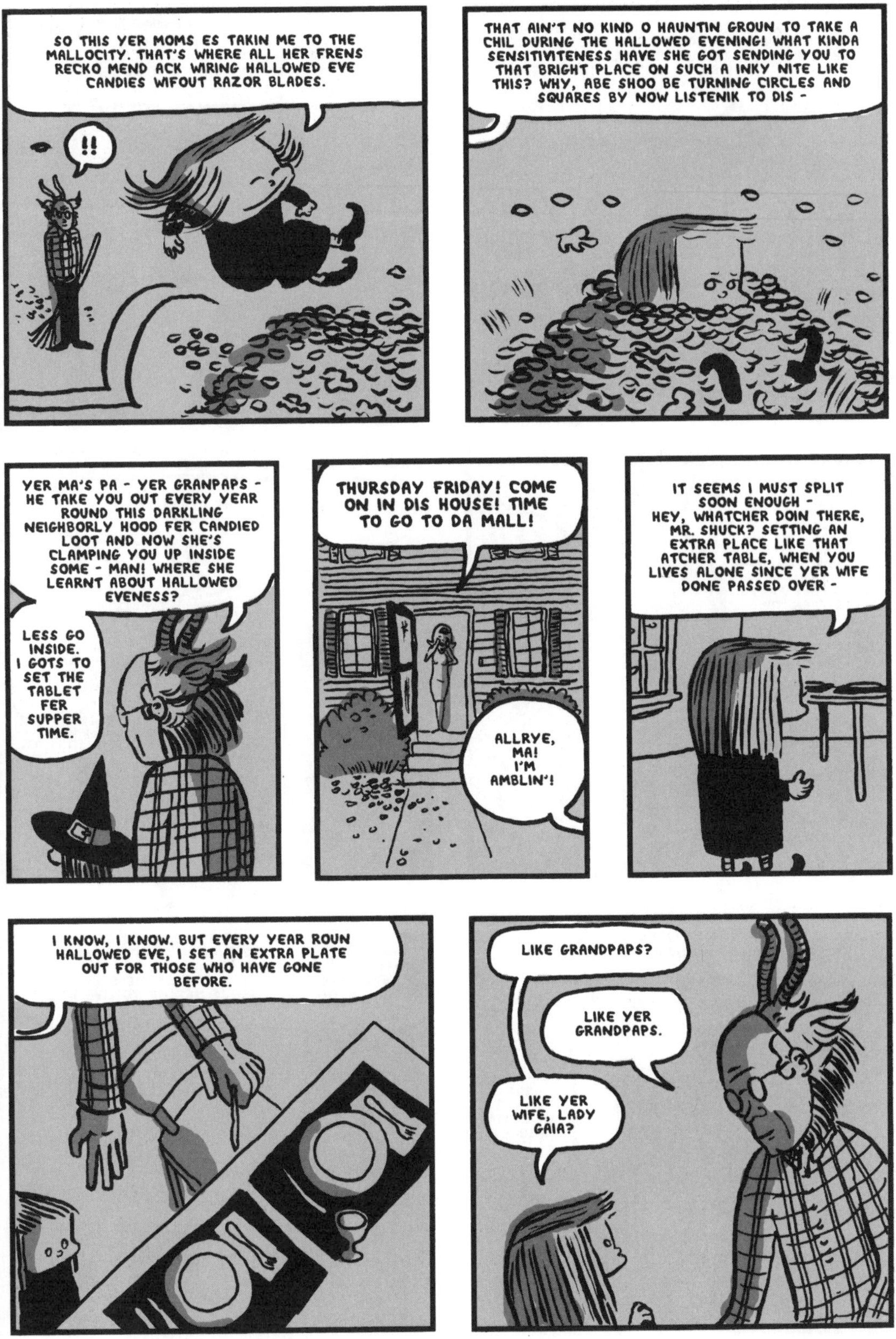

SO THIS YER MOMS ES TAKIN ME TO THE MALLOCITY. THAT'S WHERE ALL HER FRENS RECKO MEND ACK WIRING HALLOWED EVE CANDIES WIFOUT RAZOR BLADES.
!!
THAT AIN'T NO KIND O HAUNTIN GROUN TO TAKE A CHIL DURING THE HALLOWED EVENING! WHAT KINDA SENSITIVITENESS HAVE SHE GOT SENDING YOU TO THAT BRIGHT PLACE ON SUCH A INKY NITE LIKE THIS? WHY, ABE SHOO BE TURNING CIRCLES AND SQUARES BY NOW LISTENIK TO DIS -
YER MA'S PA - YER GRANPAPS - HE TAKE YOU OUT EVERY YEAR ROUND THIS DARKLING NEIGHBORLY HOOD FER CANDIED LOOT AND NOW SHE'S CLAMPING YOU UP INSIDE SOME - MAN! WHERE SHE LEARNT ABOUT HALLOWED EVENESS?
LESS GO INSIDE. I GOTS TO SET THE TABLET FER SUPPER TIME.
THURSDAY FRIDAY! COME ON IN DIS HOUSE! TIME TO GO TO DA MALL!
ALLRYE, MA! I'M AMBLIN'!
IT SEEMS I MUST SPLIT SOON ENOUGH - HEY, WHATCHER DOIN THERE, MR. SHUCK? SETTING AN EXTRA PLACE LIKE THAT ATCHER TABLE, WHEN YOU LIVES ALONE SINCE YER WIFE DONE PASSED OVER -
I KNOW, I KNOW. BUT EVERY YEAR ROUN HALLOWED EVE, I SET AN EXTRA PLATE OUT FOR THOSE WHO HAVE GONE BEFORE.
LIKE GRANDPAPS?
LIKE YER GRANDPAPS.
LIKE YER WIFE, LADY GAIA?

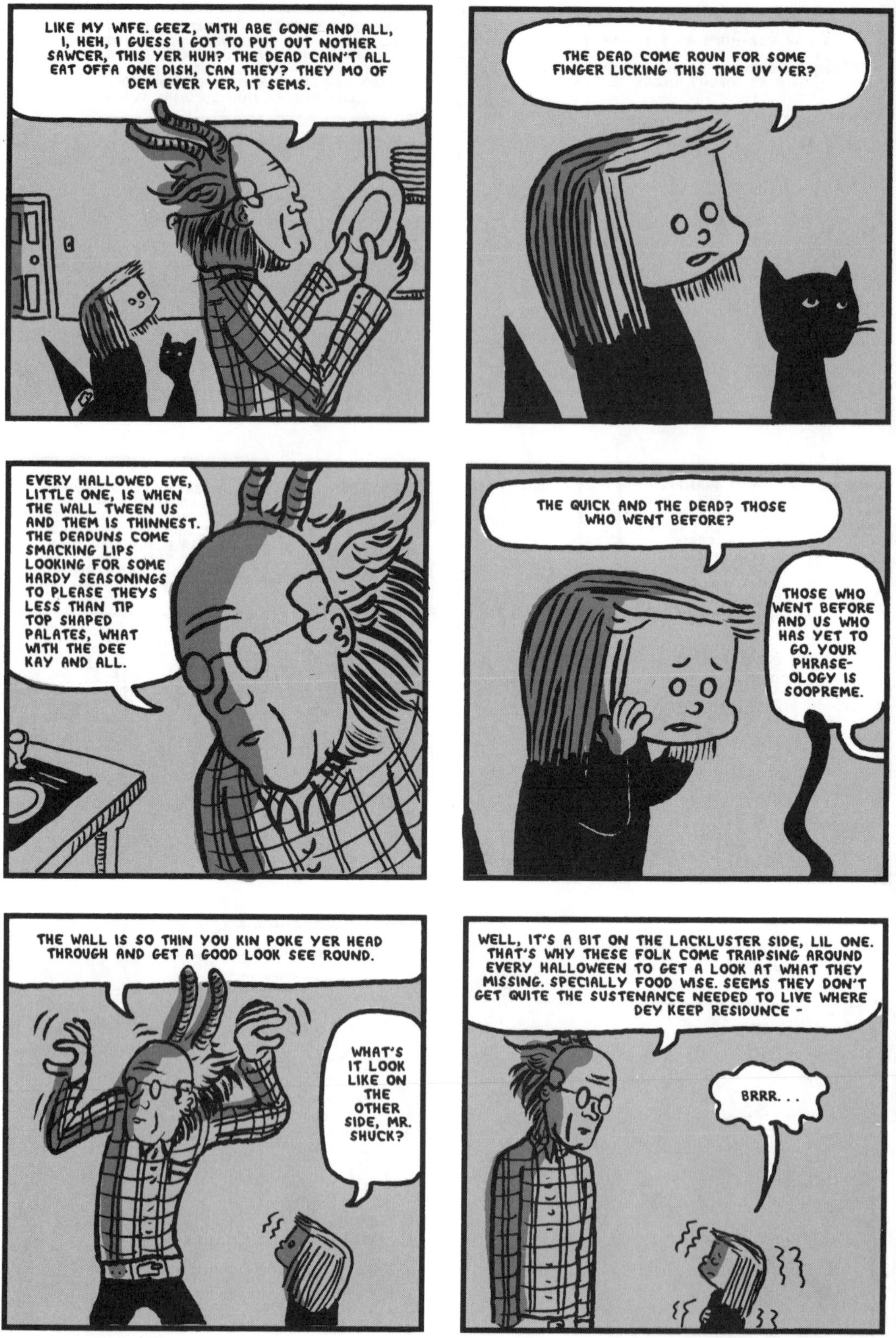
LIKE MY WIFE. GEEZ, WITH ABE GONE AND ALL, I, HEH, I GUESS I GOT TO PUT OUT NOTHER SAWCER, THIS YER HUH? THE DEAD CAIN'T ALL EAT OFFA ONE DISH, CAN THEY? THEY MO OF DEM EVER YER, IT SEMS.
THE DEAD COME ROUN FOR SOME FINGER LICKING THIS TIME UV YER?
EVERY HALLOWED EVE, LITTLE ONE, IS WHEN THE WALL TWEEN US AND THEM IS THINNEST. THE DEADUNS COME SMACKING LIPS LOOKING FOR SOME HARDY SEASONINGS TO PLEASE THEYS LESS THAN TIP TOP SHAPED PALATES, WHAT WITH THE DEE KAY AND ALL.
THE QUICK AND THE DEAD? THOSE WHO WENT BEFORE?
THOSE WHO WENT BEFORE AND US WHO HAS YET TO GO. YOUR PHRASE-OLOGY IS SOOPREME.
THE WALL IS SO THIN YOU KIN POKE YER HEAD THROUGH AND GET A GOOD LOOK SEE ROUND.
WHAT'S IT LOOK LIKE ON THE OTHER SIDE, MR. SHUCK?
WELL, IT'S A BIT ON THE LACKLUSTER SIDE, LIL ONE. THAT'S WHY THESE FOLK COME TRAIPSING AROUND EVERY HALLOWEEN TO GET A LOOK AT WHAT THEY MISSING. SPECIALLY FOOD WISE. SEEMS THEY DON'T GET QUITE THE SUSTENANCE NEEDED TO LIVE WHERE DEY KEEP RESIDUNCE -
BRRR. . .

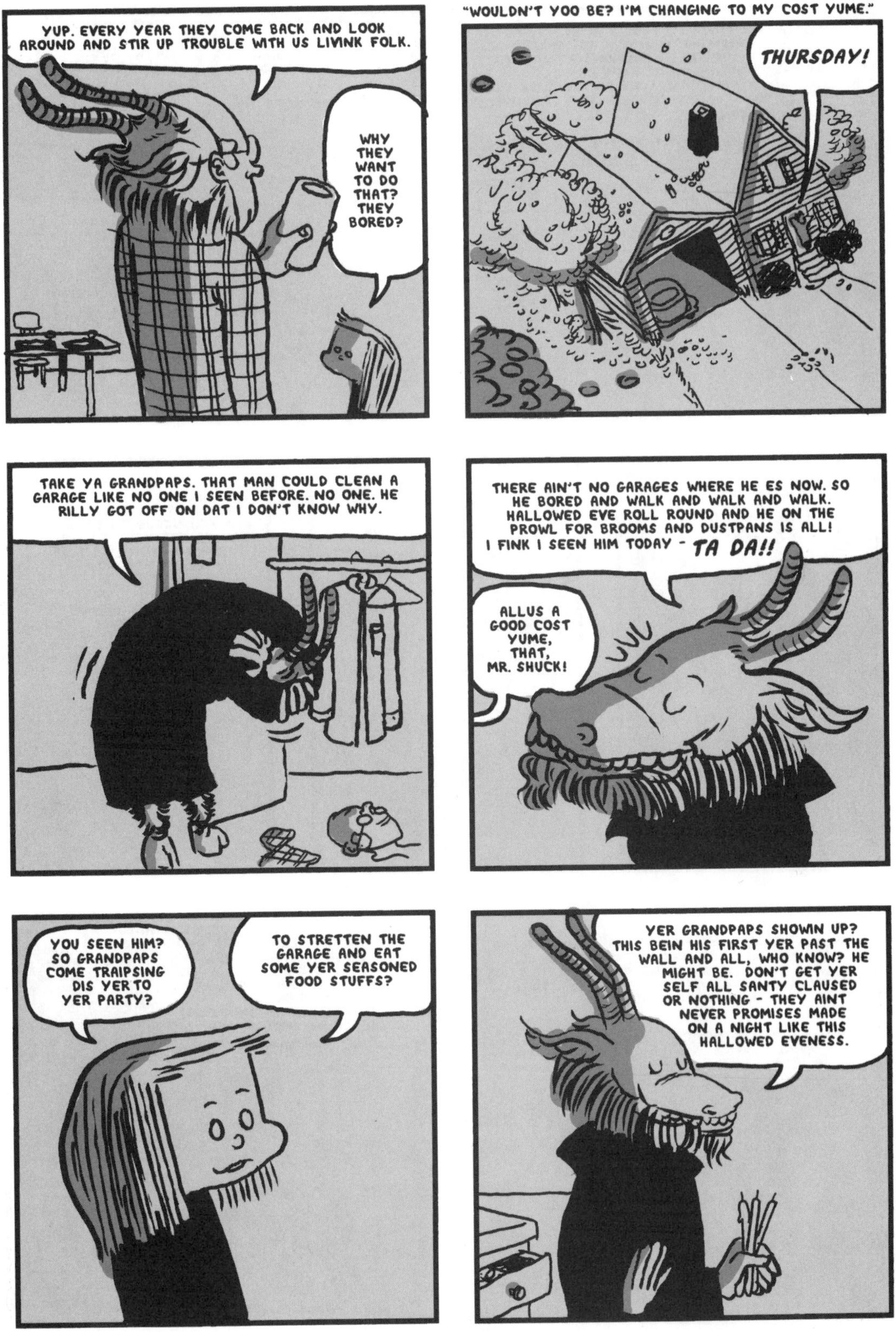
YUP. EVERY YEAR THEY COME BACK AND LOOK AROUND AND STIR UP TROUBLE WITH US LIVINK FOLK.
WHY THEY WANT TO DO THAT? THEY BORED?
"WOULDN'T YOO BE? I'M CHANGING TO MY COST YUME."
THURSDAY!
TAKE YA GRANDPAPS. THAT MAN COULD CLEAN A GARAGE LIKE NO ONE I SEEN BEFORE. NO ONE. HE RILLY GOT OFF ON DAT I DON'T KNOW WHY.
THERE AIN'T NO GARAGES WHERE HE ES NOW. SO HE BORED AND WALK AND WALK AND WALK. HALLOWED EVE ROLL ROUND AND HE ON THE PROWL FOR BROOMS AND DUSTPANS IS ALL! I FINK I SEEN HIM TODAY - TA DA!!
ALLUS A GOOD COST YUME, THAT, MR. SHUCK!
YOU SEEN HIM? SO GRANDPAPS COME TRAIPSING DIS YER TO YER PARTY?
TO STRETTEN THE GARAGE AND EAT SOME YER SEASONED FOOD STUFFS?
YER GRANDPAPS SHOWIN UP? THIS BEIN HIS FIRST YER PAST THE WALL AND ALL, WHO KNOW? HE MIGHT BE. DON'T GET YER SELF ALL SANTY CLAUSED OR NOTHING - THEY AINT NEVER PROMISES MADE ON A NIGHT LIKE THIS HALLOWED EVENESS.

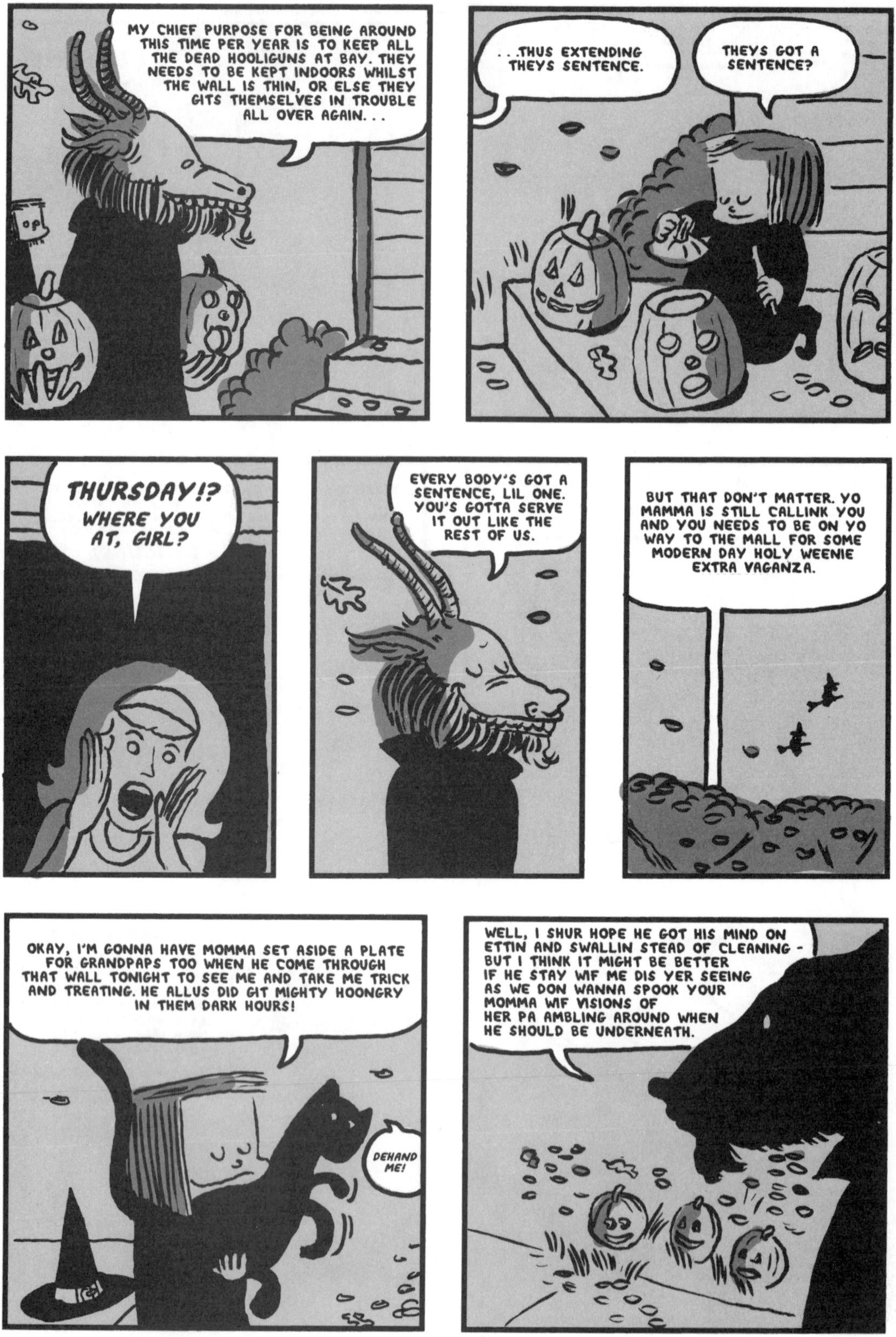
MY CHIEF PURPOSE FOR BEING AROUND THIS TIME PER YEAR IS TO KEEP ALL THE DEAD HOOLIGUNS AT BAY. THEY NEEDS TO BE KEPT INDOORS WHILST THE WALL IS THIN, OR ELSE THEY GITS THEMSELVES IN TROUBLE ALL OVER AGAIN. . .
. . .THUS EXTENDING THEYS SENTENCE.
THEYS GOT A SENTENCE?
THURSDAY!? WHERE YOU AT, GIRL?
EVERY BODY'S GOT A SENTENCE, LIL ONE. YOU'S GOTTA SERVE IT OUT LIKE THE REST OF US.
BUT THAT DON'T MATTER. YO MAMMA IS STILL CALLINK YOU AND YOU NEEDS TO BE ON YO WAY TO THE MALL FOR SOME MODERN DAY HOLY WEENIE EXTRA VAGANZA.
OKAY, I'M GONNA HAVE MOMMA SET ASIDE A PLATE FOR GRANDPAPS TOO WHEN HE COME THROUGH THAT WALL TONIGHT TO SEE ME AND TAKE ME TRICK AND TREATING. HE ALLUS DID GIT MIGHTY HOONGRY IN THEM DARK HOURS!
DEHAND ME!
WELL, I SHUR HOPE HE GOT HIS MIND ON ETTIN AND SWALLIN STEAD OF CLEANING - BUT I THINK IT MIGHT BE BETTER IF HE STAY WIF ME DIS YER SEEING AS WE DON WANNA SPOOK YOUR MOMMA WIF VISIONS OF HER PA AMBLING AROUND WHEN HE SHOULD BE UNDERNEATH.

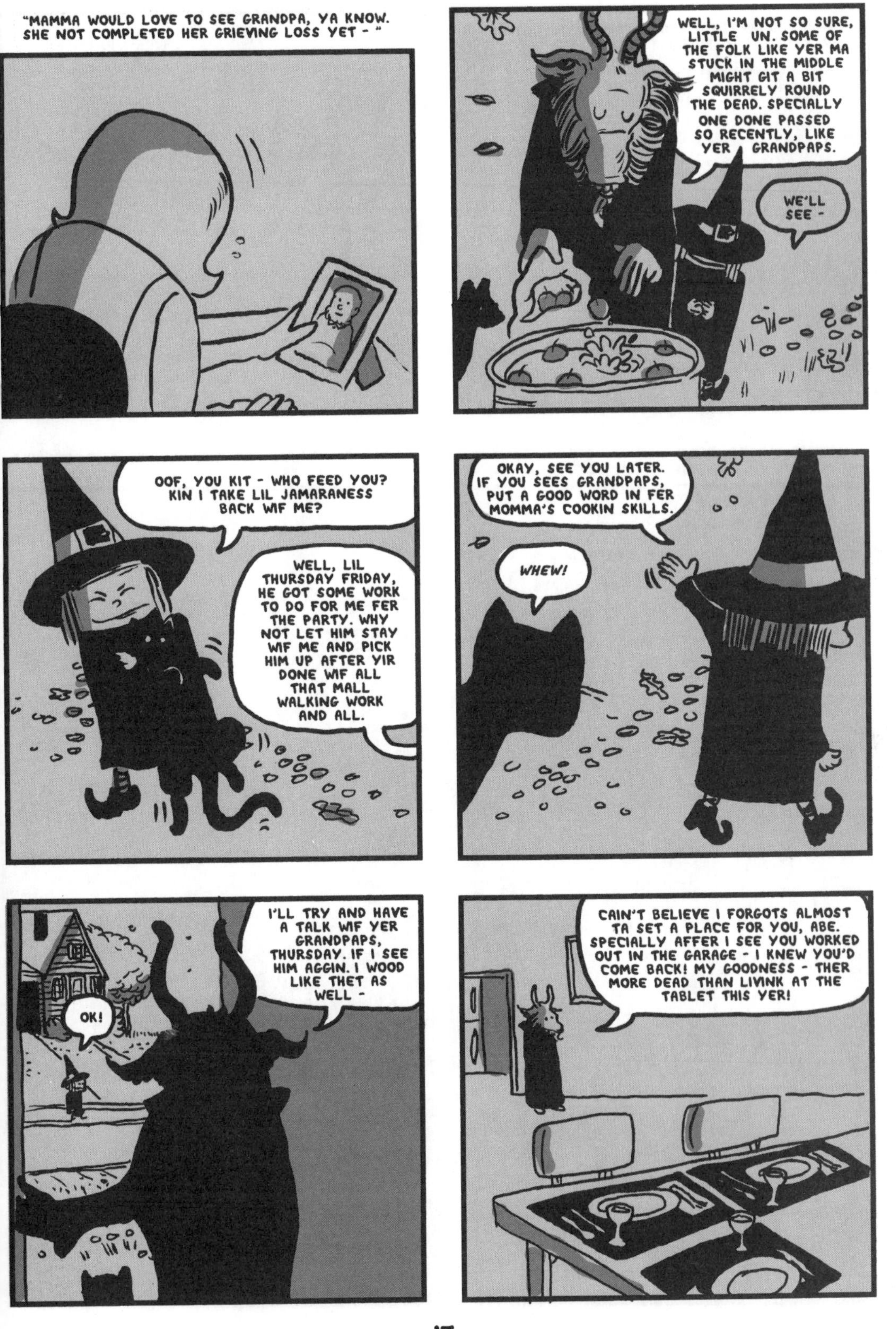
"MAMMA WOULD LOVE TO SEE GRANDPA, YA KNOW. SHE NOT COMPLETED HER GRIEVING LOSS YET - "
WELL, I'M NOT SO SURE, LITTLE UN. SOME OF THE FOLK LIKE YER MA STUCK IN THE MIDDLE MIGHT GIT A BIT SQUIRRELY ROUND THE DEAD. SPECIALLY ONE DONE PASSED SO RECENTLY, LIKE YER GRANDPAPS.
WE'LL SEE -
OOF, YOU KIT - WHO FEED YOU? KIN I TAKE LIL JAMARANESS BACK WIF ME?
WELL, LIL THURSDAY FRIDAY, HE GOT SOME WORK TO DO FOR ME FER THE PARTY. WHY NOT LET HIM STAY WIF ME AND PICK HIM UP AFTER YIR DONE WIF ALL THAT MALL WALKING WORK AND ALL.
OKAY, SEE YOU LATER. IF YOU SEES GRANDPAPS, PUT A GOOD WORD IN FER MOMMA'S COOKIN SKILLS.
WHEW!
I'LL TRY AND HAVE A TALK WIF YER GRANDPAPS, THURSDAY. IF I SEE HIM AGGIN. I WOOD LIKE THET AS WELL -
OK!
CAIN'T BELIEVE I FORGOTS ALMOST TA SET A PLACE FOR YOU, ABE. SPECIALLY AFFER I SEE YOU WORKED OUT IN THE GARAGE - I KNEW YOU'D COME BACK! MY GOODNESS - THER MORE DEAD THAN LIVINK AT THE TABLET THIS YER!

THE DEAD APPEAR NIGHTLIKE FOR SHUCK'S ANNUAL SHINDIG.

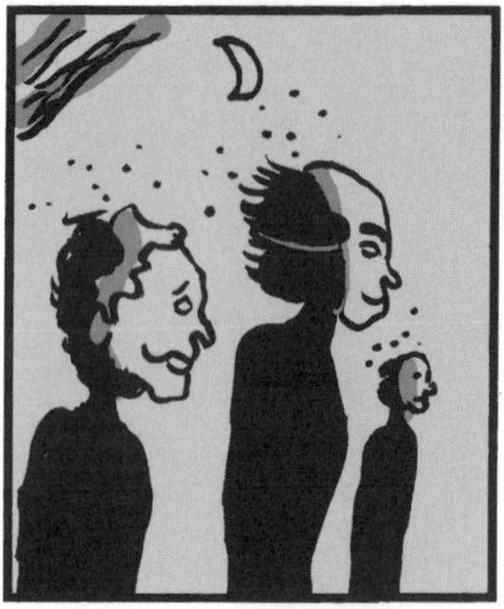

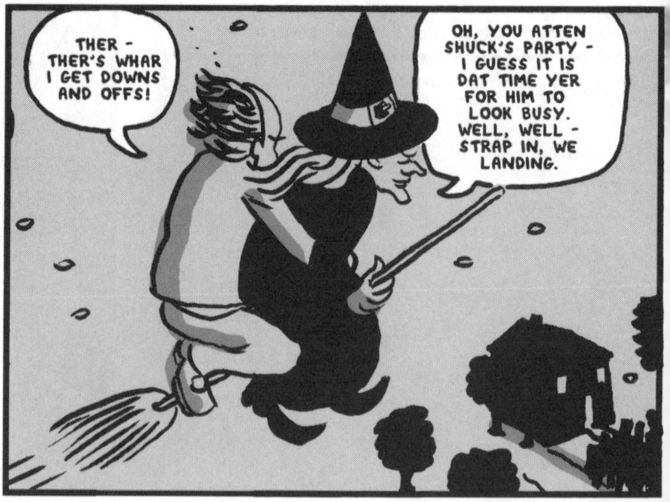
THER - THER'S WHAR I GET DOWNS AND OFFS!
OH, YOU ATTEN SHUCK'S PARTY - I GUESS IT IS DAT TIME YER FOR HIM TO LOOK BUSY. WELL, WELL - STRAP IN, WE LANDING.

WEARING MASKS THAT LET EM COUGH BACK DRINKS WITHOUT GAGGING AT THE SIGHTS AND SOUNDS OF THEY'S ROTTINGNESS, THE DEADUNS COME LOOKIN FOR COCKTAILS.

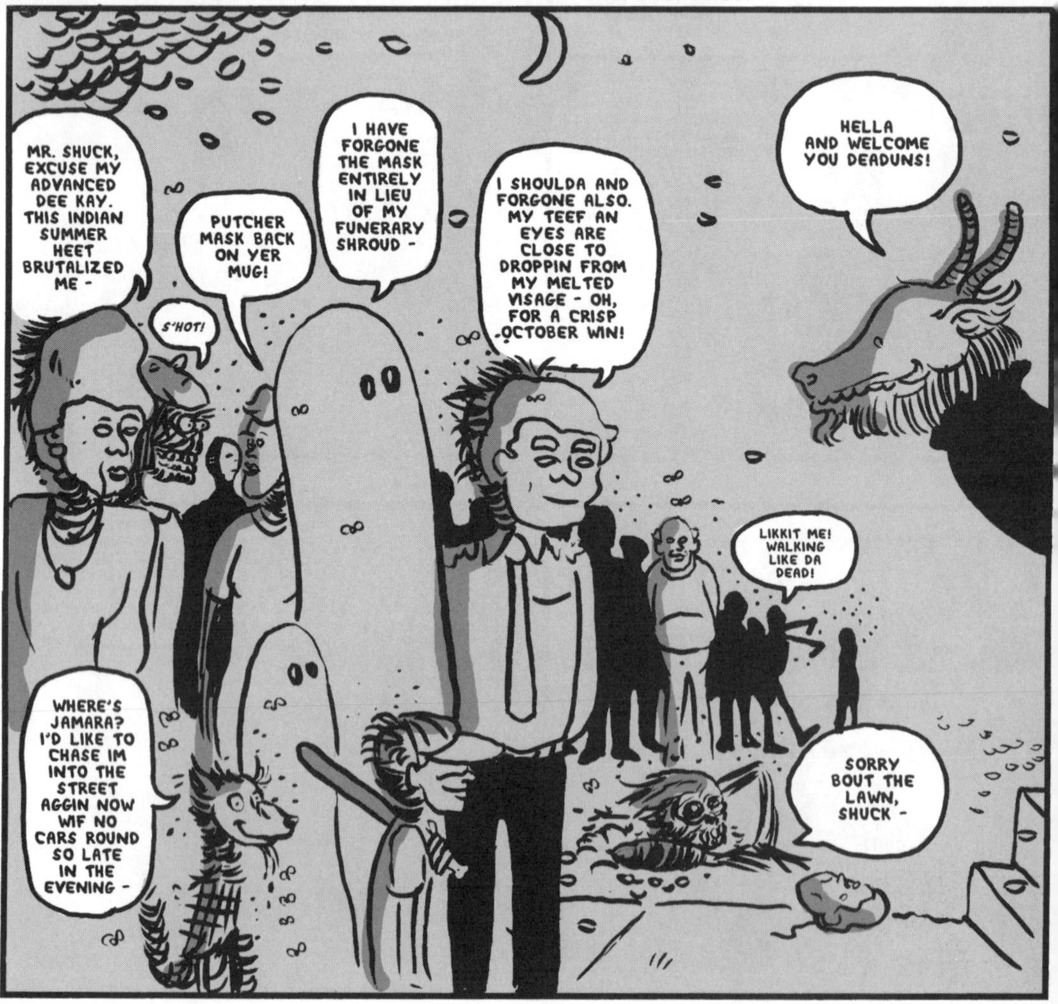
MR. SHUCK, EXCUSE MY ADVANCED DEE KAY. THIS INDIAN SUMMER HEET BRUTALIZED ME -
S'HOT!
PUTCHER MASK BACK ON YER MUG!
I HAVE FORGONE THE MASK ENTIRELY IN LIEU OF MY FUNERARY SHROUD -
I SHOULDA AND FORGONE ALSO. MY TEEF AN EYES ARE CLOSE TO DROPPIN FROM MY MELTED VISAGE - OH, FOR A CRISP OCTOBER WIN!
HELLA AND WELCOME YOU DEADUNS!
LIKKIT ME! WALKING LIKE DA DEAD!
WHERE'S JAMARA? I'D LIKE TO CHASE IM INTO THE STREET AGGIN NOW WIF NO CARS ROUND SO LATE IN THE EVENING -
SORRY BOUT THE LAWN, SHUCK -

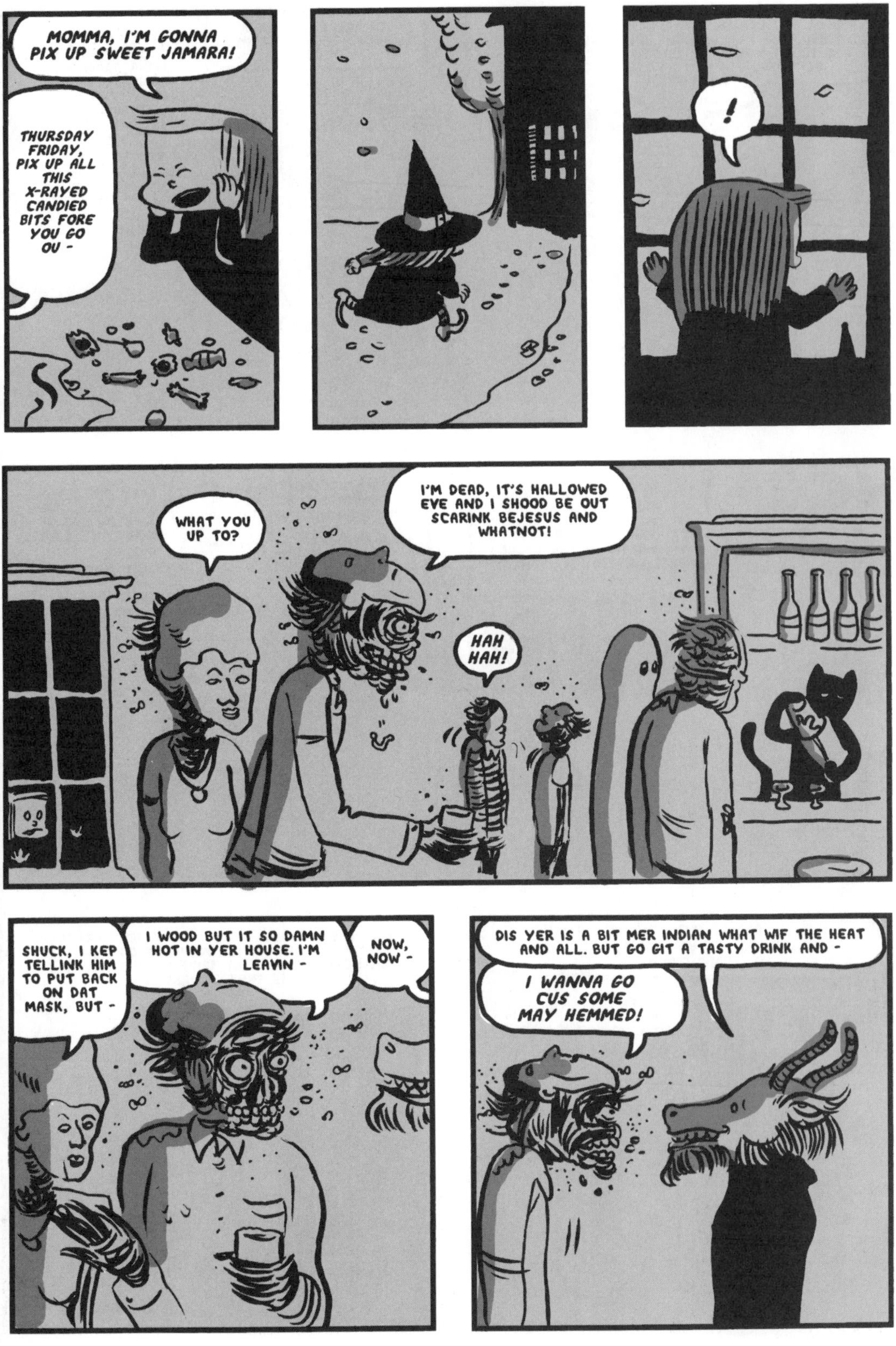
MOMMA, I'M GONNA PIX UP SWEET JAMARA!
THURSDAY FRIDAY, PIX UP ALL THIS X-RAYED CANDIED BITS FORE YOU GO OU -
!
WHAT YOU UP TO?
I'M DEAD, IT'S HALLOWED EVE AND I SHOOD BE OUT SCARINK BEJESUS AND WHATNOT!
HAH HAH!
SHUCK, I KEP TELLINK HIM TO PUT BACK ON DAT MASK, BUT -
I WOOD BUT IT SO DAMN HOT IN YER HOUSE. I'M LEAVIN -
NOW, NOW -
DIS YER IS A BIT MER INDIAN WHAT WIF THE HEAT AND ALL. BUT GO GIT A TASTY DRINK AND -
I WANNA GO CUS SOME MAY HEMMED!

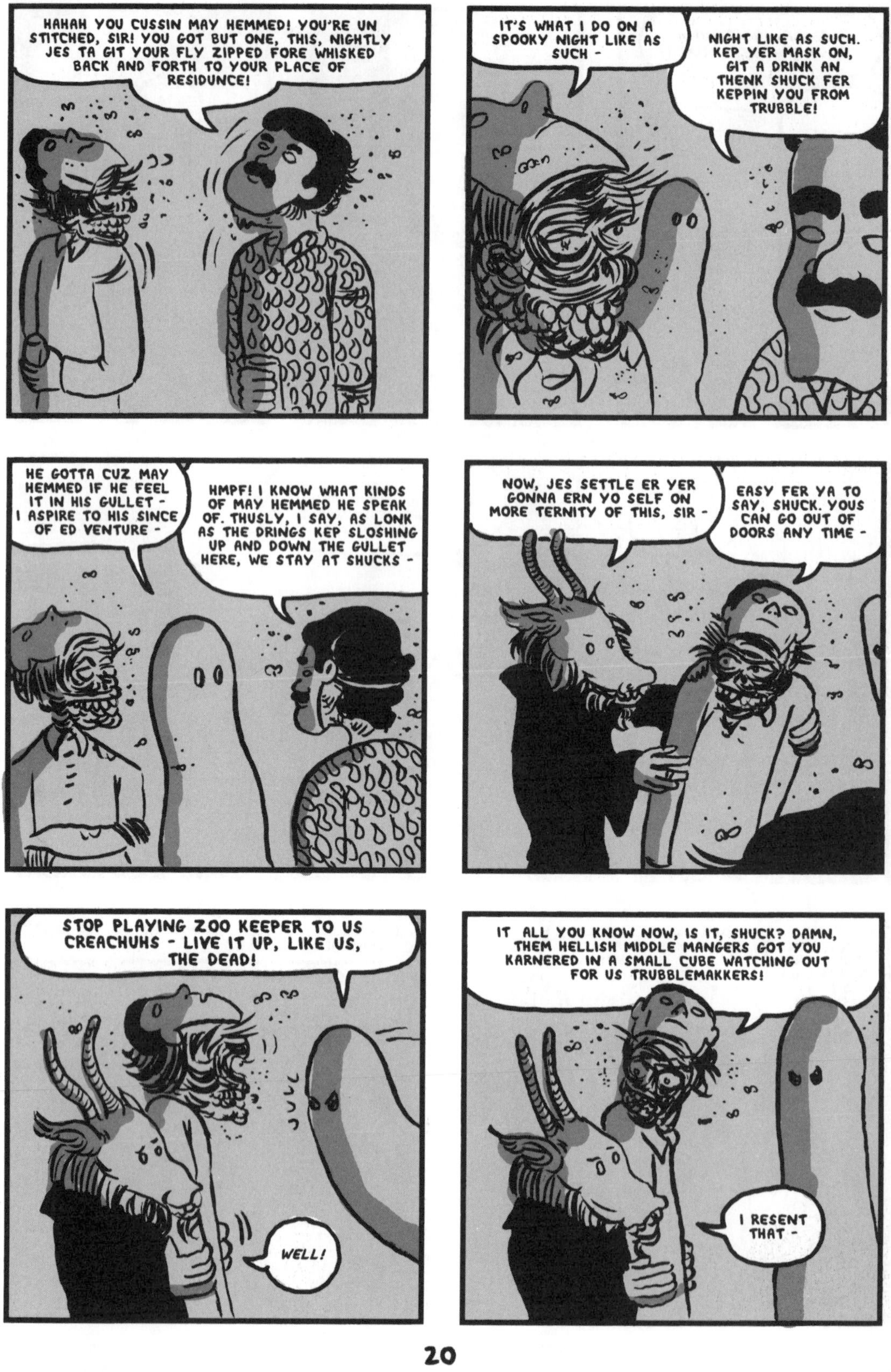
HAHAH YOU CUSSIN MAY HEMMED! YOU'RE UN STITCHED, SIR! YOU GOT BUT ONE, THIS, NIGHTLY JES TA GIT YOUR FLY ZIPPED FORE WHISKED BACK AND FORTH TO YOUR PLACE OF RESIDUNCE!
IT'S WHAT I DO ON A SPOOKY NIGHT LIKE AS SUCH -
NIGHT LIKE AS SUCH. KEP YER MASK ON, GIT A DRINK AN THENK SHUCK FER KEPPIN YOU FROM TRUBBLE!
HE GOTTA CUZ MAY HEMMED IF HE FEEL IT IN HIS GULLET - I ASPIRE TO HIS SINCE OF ED VENTURE -
HMPF! I KNOW WHAT KINDS OF MAY HEMMED HE SPEAK OF. THUSLY, I SAY, AS LONK AS THE DRINGS KEP SLOSHING UP AND DOWN THE GULLET HERE, WE STAY AT SHUCKS -
NOW, JES SETTLE ER YER GONNA ERN YO SELF ON MORE TERNITY OF THIS, SIR -
EASY FER YA TO SAY, SHUCK. YOUS CAN GO OUT OF DOORS ANY TIME -
STOP PLAYING ZOO KEEPER TO US CREACHUHS - LIVE IT UP, LIKE US, THE DEAD!
WELL!
IT ALL YOU KNOW NOW, IS IT, SHUCK? DAMN, THEM HELLISH MIDDLE MANGERS GOT YOU KARNERED IN A SMALL CUBE WATCHING OUT FOR US TRUBBLEMAKKERS!
I RESENT THAT -

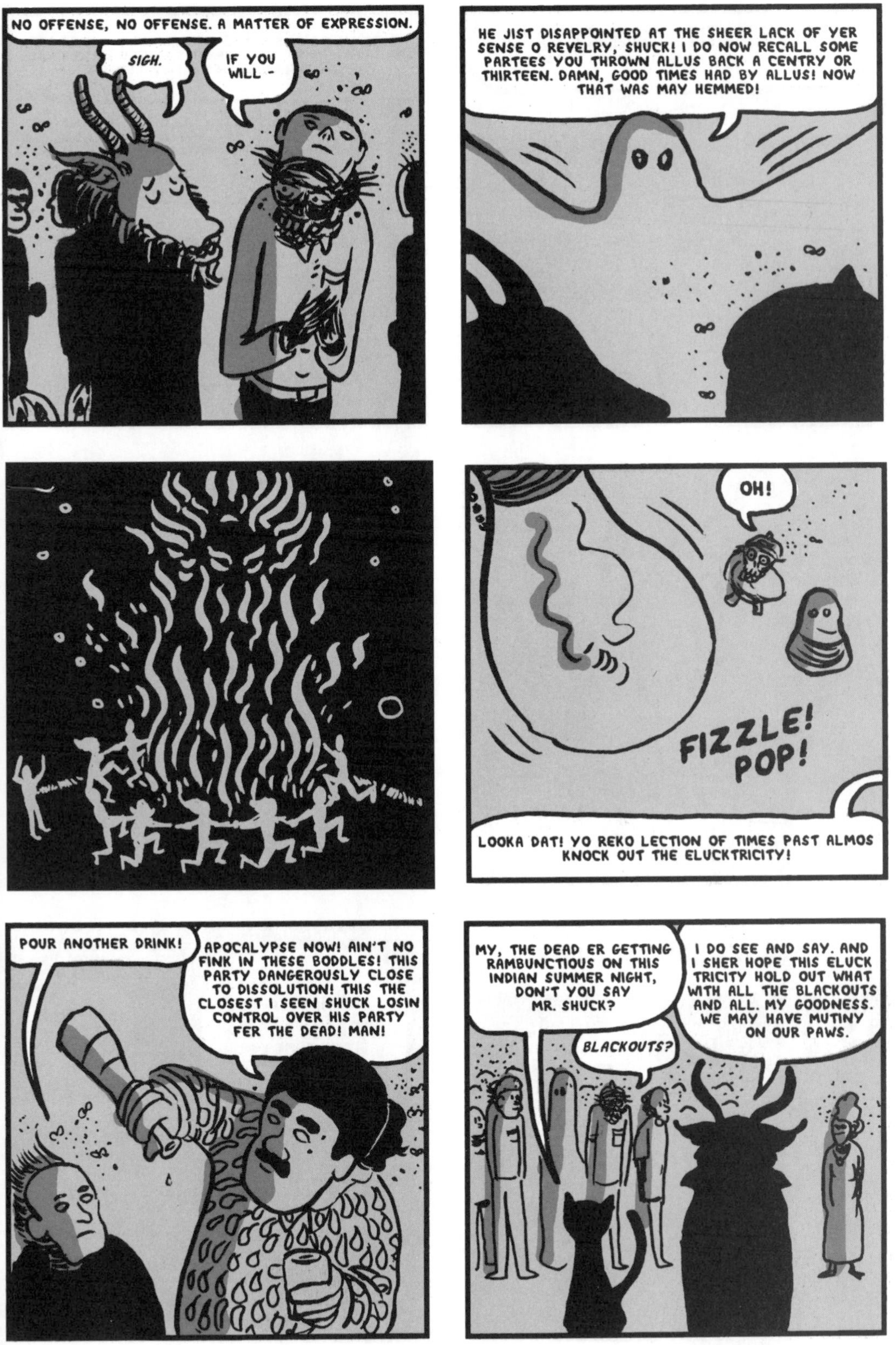
NO OFFENSE, NO OFFENSE. A MATTER OF EXPRESSION.
SIGH.
IF YOU WILL -
HE JIST DISAPPOINTED AT THE SHEER LACK OF YER SENSE O REVELRY, SHUCK! I DO NOW RECALL SOME PARTEES YOU THROWN ALLUS BACK A CENTRY OR THIRTEEN. DAMN, GOOD TIMES HAD BY ALLUS! NOW THAT WAS MAY HEMMED!
OH!
FIZZLE! POP!
LOOKA DAT! YO REKO LECTION OF TIMES PAST ALMOS KNOCK OUT THE ELUCKTRICITY!
POUR ANOTHER DRINK!
APOCALYPSE NOW! AIN'T NO FINK IN THESE BODDLES! THIS PARTY DANGEROUSLY CLOSE TO DISSOLUTION! THIS THE CLOSEST I SEEN SHUCK LOSIN CONTROL OVER HIS PARTY FER THE DEAD! MAN!
MY, THE DEAD ER GETTING RAMBUNCTIOUS ON THIS INDIAN SUMMER NIGHT, DON'T YOU SAY MR. SHUCK?
BLACKOUTS?
I DO SEE AND SAY. AND I SHER HOPE THIS ELUCK TRICITY HOLD OUT WHAT WITH ALL THE BLACKOUTS AND ALL. MY GOODNESS. WE MAY HAVE MUTINY ON OUR PAWS.

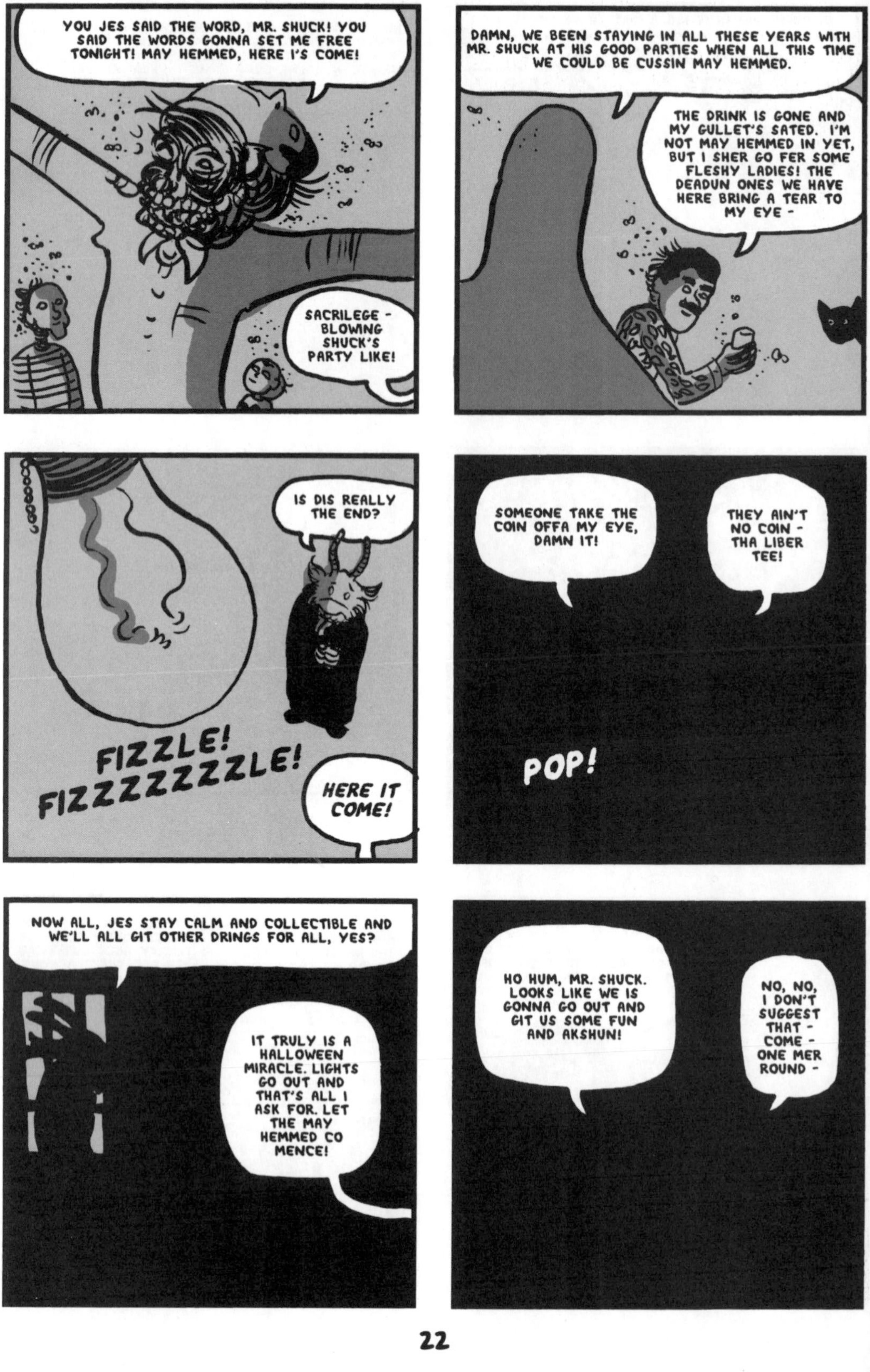
YOU JES SAID THE WORD, MR. SHUCK! YOU SAID THE WORDS GONNA SET ME FREE TONIGHT! MAY HEMMED, HERE I'S COME!
SACRILEGE - BLOWING SHUCK'S PARTY LIKE!
DAMN, WE BEEN STAYING IN ALL THESE YEARS WITH MR. SHUCK AT HIS GOOD PARTIES WHEN ALL THIS TIME WE COULD BE CUSSIN MAY HEMMED.
THE DRINK IS GONE AND MY GULLET'S SATED. I'M NOT MAY HEMMED IN YET, BUT I SHER GO FER SOME FLESHY LADIES! THE DEADUN ONES WE HAVE HERE BRING A TEAR TO MY EYE -
IS DIS REALLY THE END?
FIZZLE! FIZZZZZZZZLE!
HERE IT COME!
SOMEONE TAKE THE COIN OFFA MY EYE, DAMN IT!
THEY AIN'T NO COIN - THA LIBER TEE!
POP!
NOW ALL, JES STAY CALM AND COLLECTIBLE AND WE'LL ALL GIT OTHER DRINGS FOR ALL, YES?
IT TRULY IS A HALLOWEEN MIRACLE. LIGHTS GO OUT AND THAT'S ALL I ASK FOR. LET THE MAY HEMMED CO MENCE!
HO HUM, MR. SHUCK. LOOKS LIKE WE IS GONNA GO OUT AND GIT US SOME FUN AND AKSHUN!
NO, NO, I DON'T SUGGEST THAT - COME - ONE MER ROUND -

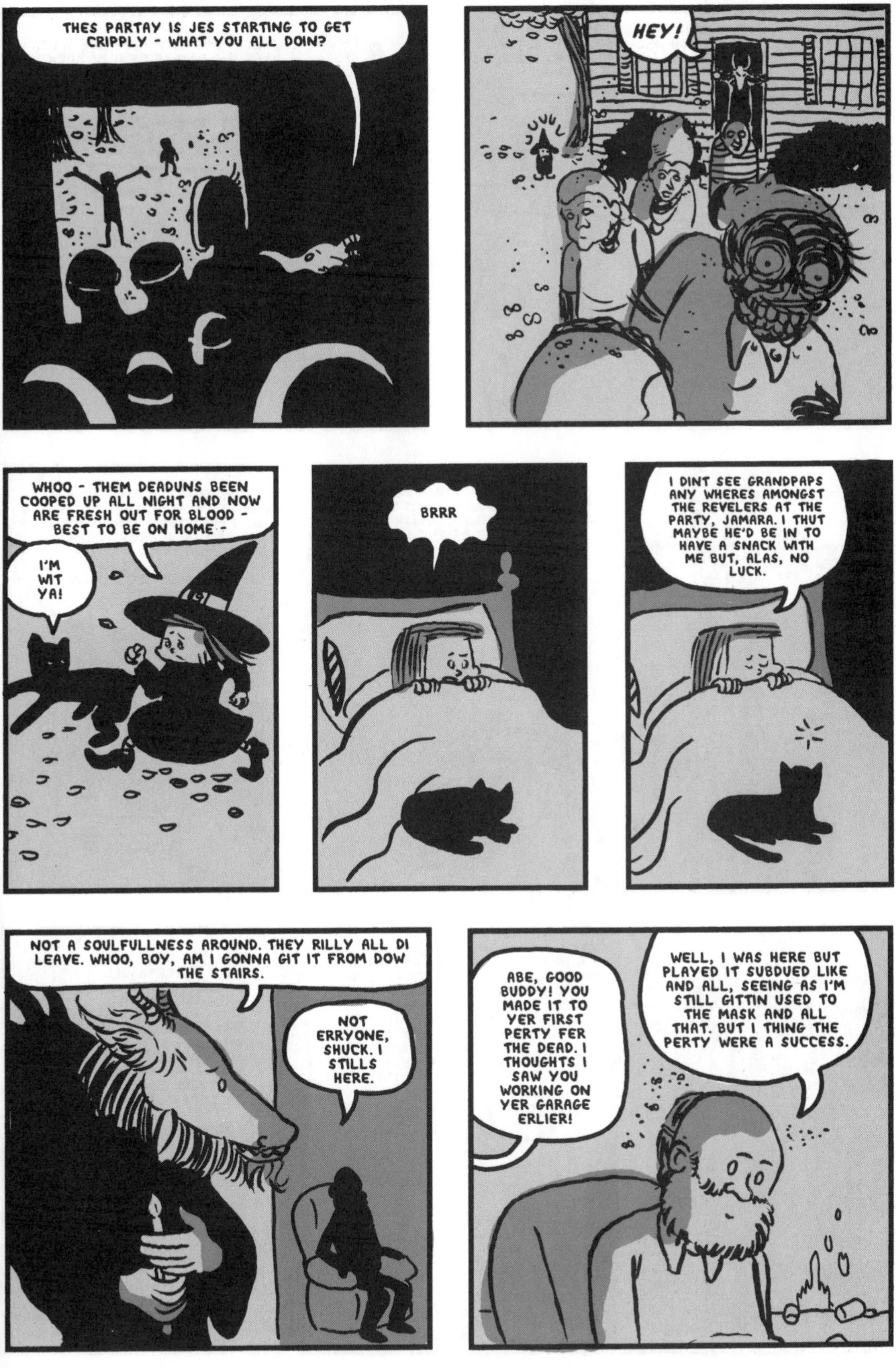
THES PARTAY IS JES STARTING TO GET CRIPPLY - WHAT YOU ALL DOIN?
HEY!
WHOO - THEM DEADUNS BEEN COOPED UP ALL NIGHT AND NOW ARE FRESH OUT FOR BLOOD - BEST TO BE ON HOME -
I'M WIT YA!
BRRR
I DINT SEE GRANDPAPS ANY WHERES AMONGST THE REVELERS AT THE PARTY, JAMARA. I THUT MAYBE HE'D BE IN TO HAVE A SNACK WITH ME BUT, ALAS, NO LUCK.
NOT A SOULFULLNESS AROUND. THEY RILLY ALL DI LEAVE. WHOO, BOY, AM I GONNA GIT IT FROM DOW THE STAIRS.
NOT ERRYONE, SHUCK. I STILLS HERE.
ABE, GOOD BUDDY! YOU MADE IT TO YER FIRST PERTY FER THE DEAD. I THOUGHTS I SAW YOU WORKING ON YER GARAGE ERLIER!
WELL, I WAS HERE BUT PLAYED IT SUBDUED LIKE AND ALL, SEEING AS I'M STILL GITTIN USED TO THE MASK AND ALL THAT. BUT I THING THE PERTY WERE A SUCCESS.

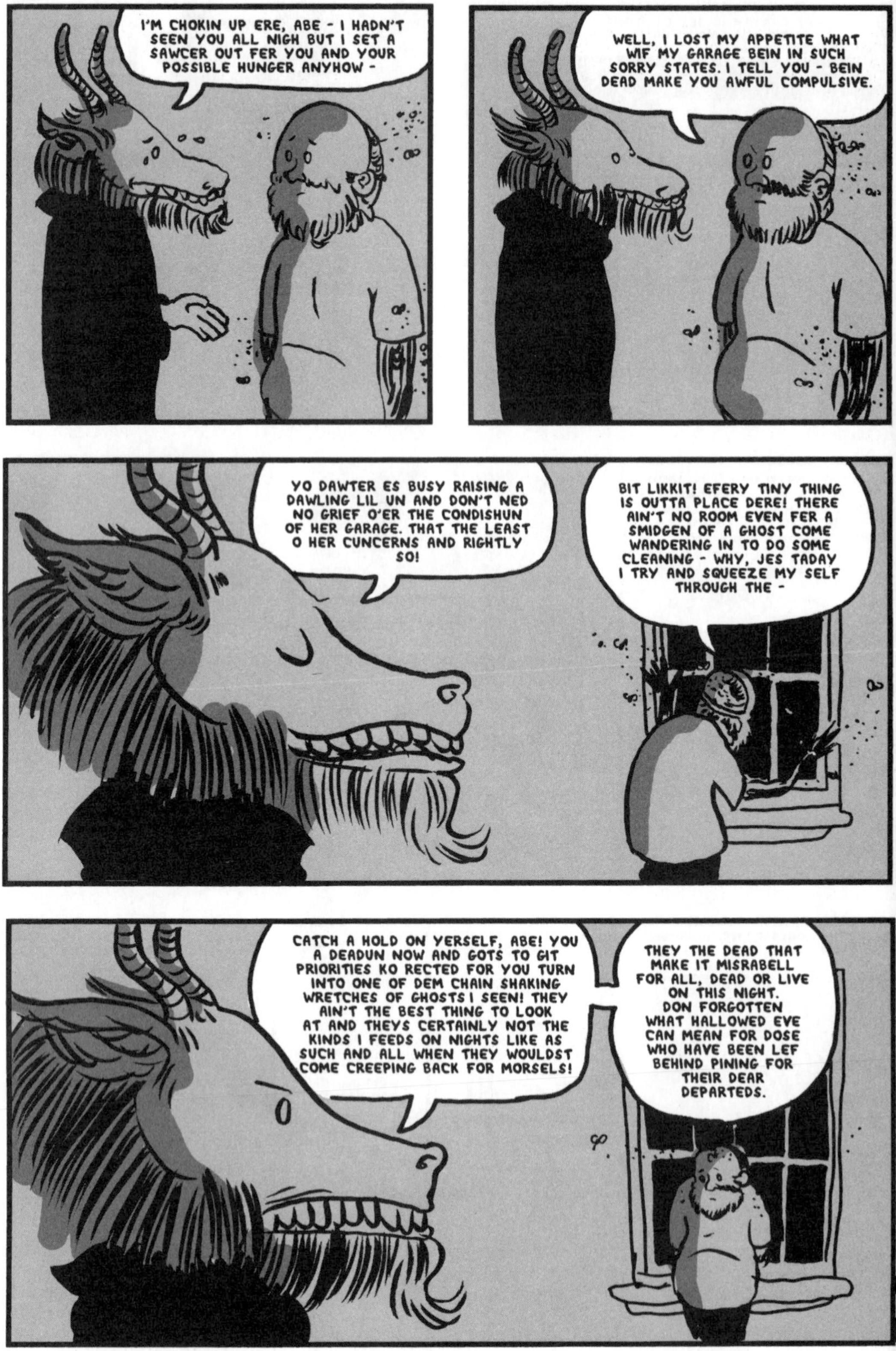
I'M CHOKIN UP ERE, ABE - I HADN'T SEEN YOU ALL NIGH BUT I SET A SAWCER OUT FER YOU AND YOUR POSSIBLE HUNGER ANYHOW -
WELL, I LOST MY APPETITE WHAT WIF MY GARAGE BEIN IN SUCH SORRY STATES. I TELL YOU - BEIN DEAD MAKE YOU AWFUL COMPULSIVE.
YO DAWTER ES BUSY RAISING A DAWLING LIL UN AND DON'T NED NO GRIEF O'ER THE CONDISHUN OF HER GARAGE. THAT THE LEAST O HER CUNCERNS AND RIGHTLY SO!
BIT LIKKIT! EFERY TINY THING IS OUTTA PLACE DERE! THERE AIN'T NO ROOM EVEN FER A SMIDGEN OF A GHOST COME WANDERING IN TO DO SOME CLEANING - WHY, JES TADAY I TRY AND SQUEEZE MY SELF THROUGH THE -
CATCH A HOLD ON YERSELF, ABE! YOU A DEADUN NOW AND GOTS TO GIT PRIORITIES KO RECTED FOR YOU TURN INTO ONE OF DEM CHAIN SHAKING WRETCHES OF GHOSTS I SEEN! THEY AIN'T THE BEST THING TO LOOK AT AND THEYS CERTAINLY NOT THE KINDS I FEEDS ON NIGHTS LIKE AS SUCH AND ALL WHEN THEY WOULDST COME CREEPING BACK FOR MORSELS!
THEY THE DEAD THAT MAKE IT MISRABELL FOR ALL, DEAD OR LIVE ON THIS NIGHT. DON FORGOTTEN WHAT HALLOWED EVE CAN MEAN FOR DOSE WHO HAVE BEEN LEF BEHIND PINING FOR THEIR DEAR DEPARTEDS.

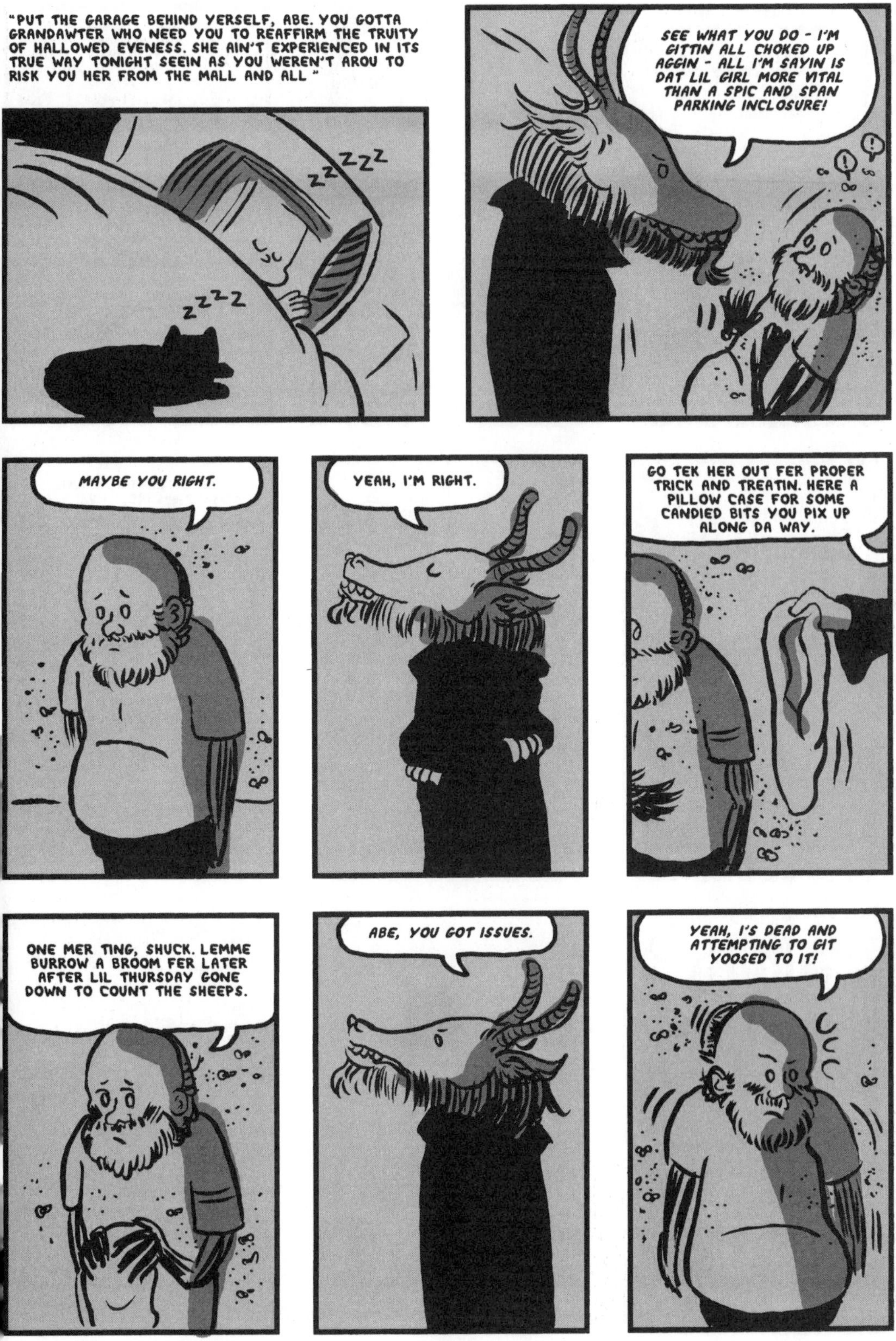
"PUT THE GARAGE BEHIND YERSELF, ABE. YOU GOTTA GRANDAWTER WHO NEED YOU TO REAFFIRM THE TRUITY OF HALLOWED EVENESS. SHE AIN'T EXPERIENCED IN ITS TRUE WAY TONIGHT SEEIN AS YOU WEREN'T AROU TO RISK YOU HER FROM THE MALL AND ALL"
ZZZZ
ZZZZ
SEE WHAT YOU DO - I'M GITTIN ALL CHOKED UP AGGIN - ALL I'M SAYIN IS DAT LIL GIRL MORE VITAL THAN A SPIC AND SPAN PARKING INCLOSURE!
MAYBE YOU RIGHT.
YEAH, I'M RIGHT.
GO TEK HER OUT FER PROPER TRICK AND TREATIN. HERE A PILLOW CASE FOR SOME CANDIED BITS YOU PIX UP ALONG DA WAY.
ONE MER TING, SHUCK. LEMME BURROW A BROOM FER LATER AFTER LIL THURSDAY GONE DOWN TO COUNT THE SHEEPS.
ABE, YOU GOT ISSUES.
YEAH, I'S DEAD AND ATTEMPTING TO GIT YOOSED TO IT!

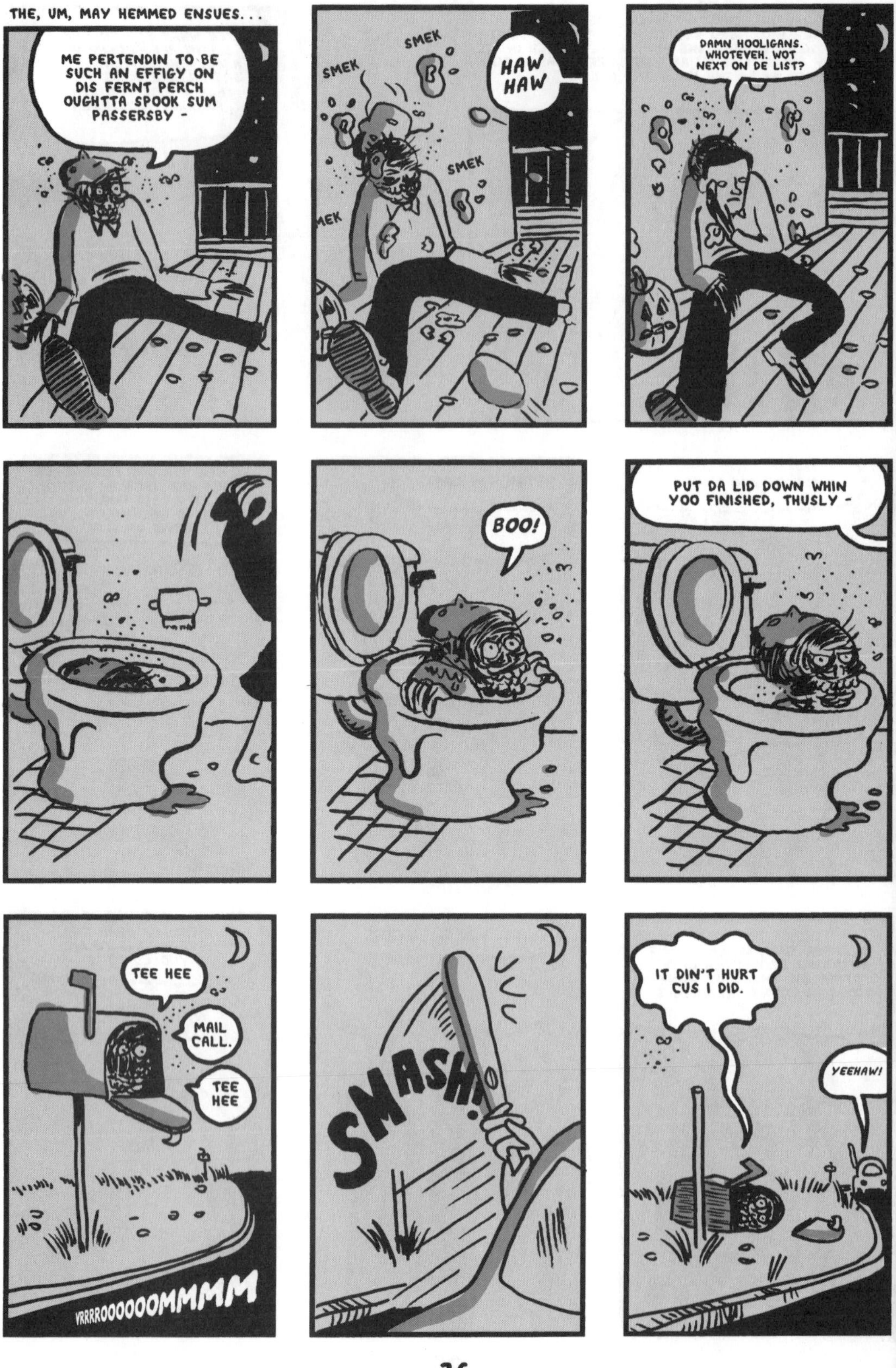
THE, UM, MAY HEMMED ENSUES...
ME PERTENDIN TO BE SUCH AN EFFIGY ON DIS FERNT PERCH OUGHTTA SPOOK SUM PASSERSBY -
SMEK
SMEK
HAW HAW
SMEK
MEK
DAMN HOOLIGANS. WHOTEVEH. WOT NEXT ON DE LIST?
BOO!
PUT DA LID DOWN WHIN YOO FINISHED, THUSLY -
TEE HEE
MAIL CALL.
TEE HEE
VRRRROOOOOOMMMM
SMASH!
IT DIN'T HURT CUS I DID.
YEEHAW!

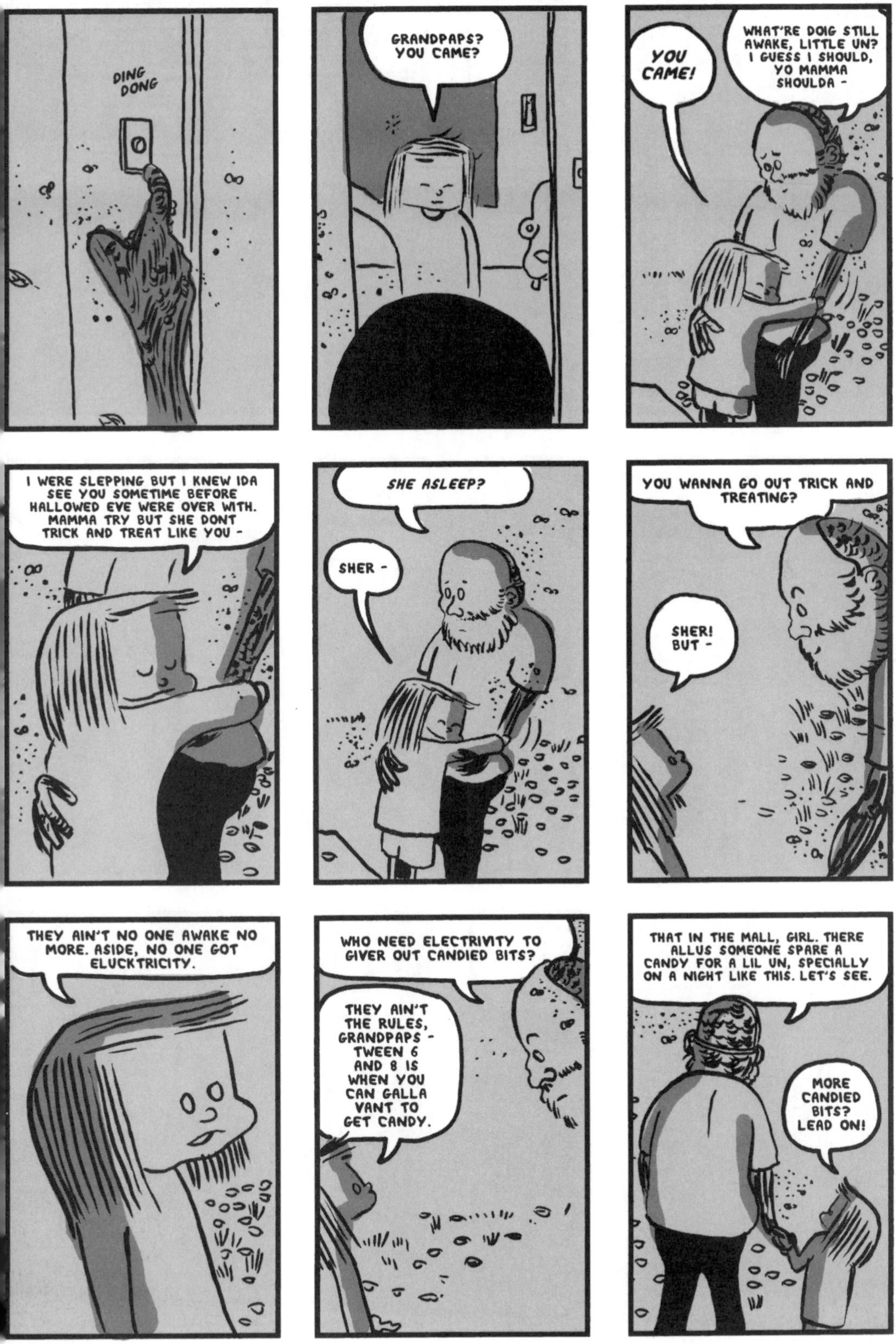
DING DONG
GRANDPAPS? YOU CAME?
YOU CAME!
WHAT'RE DOIG STILL AWAKE, LITTLE UN? I GUESS I SHOULD, YO MAMMA SHOULDA -
I WERE SLEPPING BUT I KNEW IDA SEE YOU SOMETIME BEFORE HALLOWED EVE WERE OVER WITH. MAMMA TRY BUT SHE DONT TRICK AND TREAT LIKE YOU -
SHE ASLEEP?
SHER -
YOU WANNA GO OUT TRICK AND TREATING?
SHER! BUT -
THEY AIN'T NO ONE AWAKE NO MORE. ASIDE, NO ONE GOT ELUCKTRICITY.
WHO NEED ELECTRIVITY TO GIVER OUT CANDIED BITS?
THEY AIN'T THE RULES, GRANDPAPS - TWEEN 6 AND 8 IS WHEN YOU CAN GALLA VANT TO GET CANDY.
THAT IN THE MALL, GIRL. THERE ALLUS SOMEONE SPARE A CANDY FOR A LIL UN, SPECIALLY ON A NIGHT LIKE THIS. LET'S SEE.
MORE CANDIED BITS? LEAD ON!

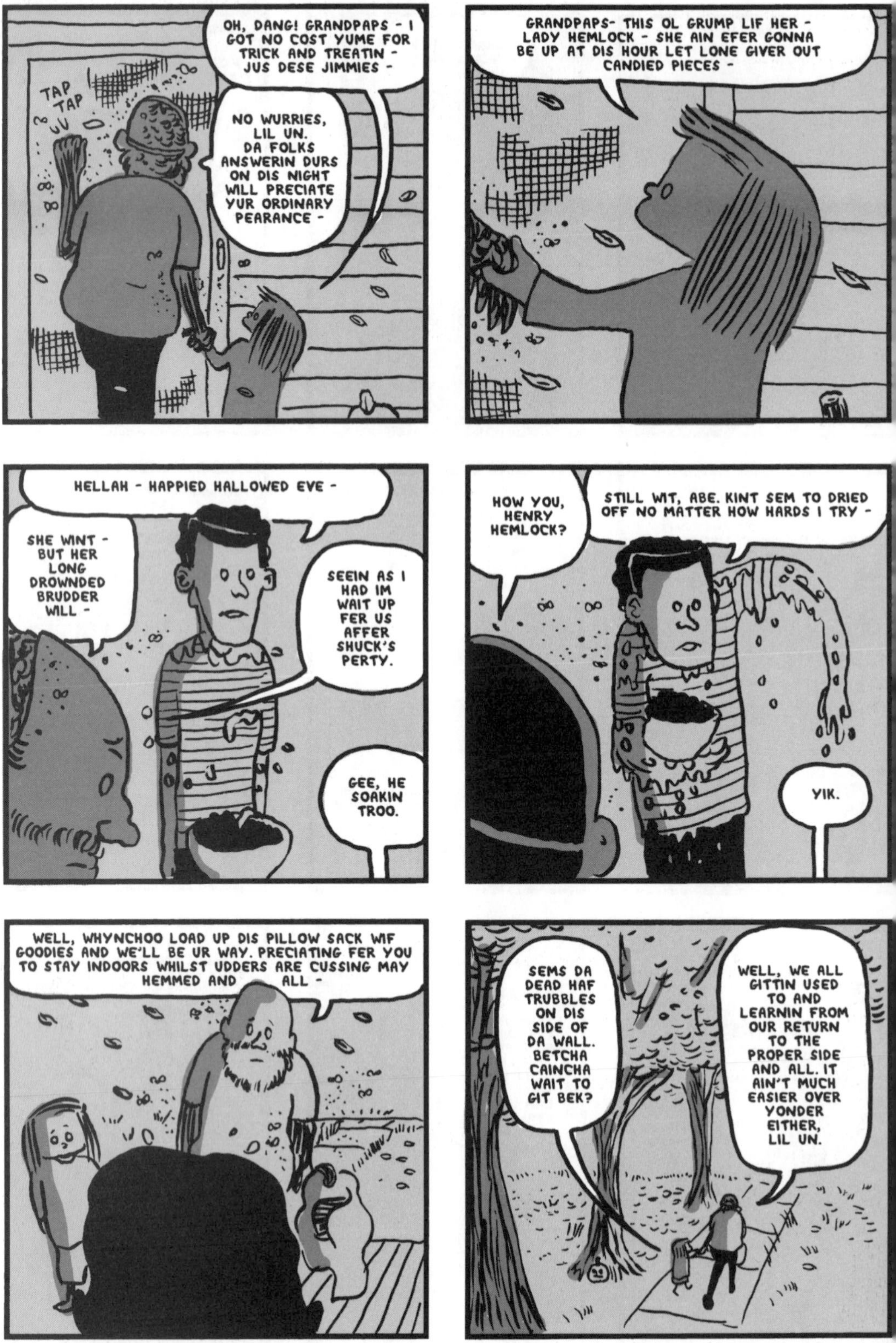
TAP TAP
OH, DANG! GRANDPAPS - I GOT NO COST YUME FOR TRICK AND TREATIN - JUS DESE JIMMIES -
NO WURRIES, LIL UN. DA FOLKS ANSWERIN DURS ON DIS NIGHT WILL PRECIATE YUR ORDINARY PEARANCE -
GRANDPAPS- THIS OL GRUMP LIF HER - LADY HEMLOCK - SHE AIN EFER GONNA BE UP AT DIS HOUR LET LONE GIVER OUT CANDIED PIECES -
HELLAH - HAPPIED HALLOWED EVE -
SHE WINT - BUT HER LONG DROWNDED BRUDDER WILL -
SEEIN AS I HAD IM WAIT UP FER US AFFER SHUCK'S PERTY.
GEE, HE SOAKIN TROO.
HOW YOU, HENRY HEMLOCK?
STILL WIT, ABE. KINT SEM TO DRIED OFF NO MATTER HOW HARDS I TRY -
YIK.
WELL, WHYNCHOO LOAD UP DIS PILLOW SACK WIF GOODIES AND WE'LL BE UR WAY. PRECIATING FER YOU TO STAY INDOORS WHILST UDDERS ARE CUSSING MAY HEMMED AND ALL -
SEMS DA DEAD HAF TRUBBLES ON DIS SIDE OF DA WALL. BETCHA CAINCHA WAIT TO GIT BEK?
WELL, WE ALL GITTIN USED TO AND LEARNIN FROM OUR RETURN TO THE PROPER SIDE AND ALL. IT AIN'T MUCH EASIER OVER YONDER EITHER, LIL UN.

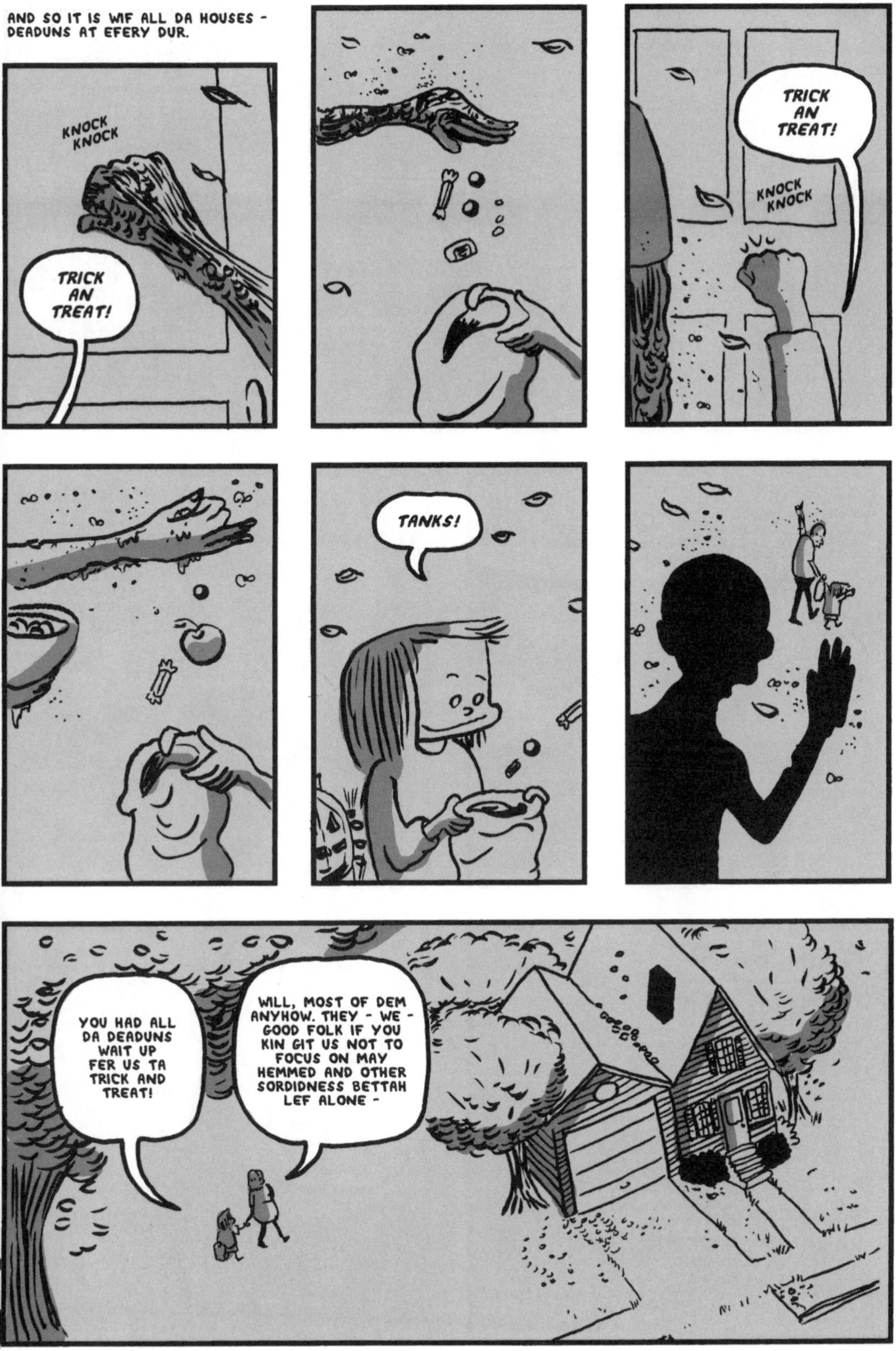
AND SO IT IS WIF ALL DA HOUSES - DEADUNS AT EFERY DUR.
KNOCK KNOCK
TRICK AN TREAT!
TRICK AN TREAT!
KNOCK KNOCK
TANKS!
YOU HAD ALL DA DEADUNS WAIT UP FER US TA TRICK AND TREAT!
WILL, MOST OF DEM ANYHOW. THEY - WE - GOOD FOLK IF YOU KIN GIT US NOT TO FOCUS ON MAY HEMMED AND OTHER SORDIDNESS BETTAH LEF ALONE -

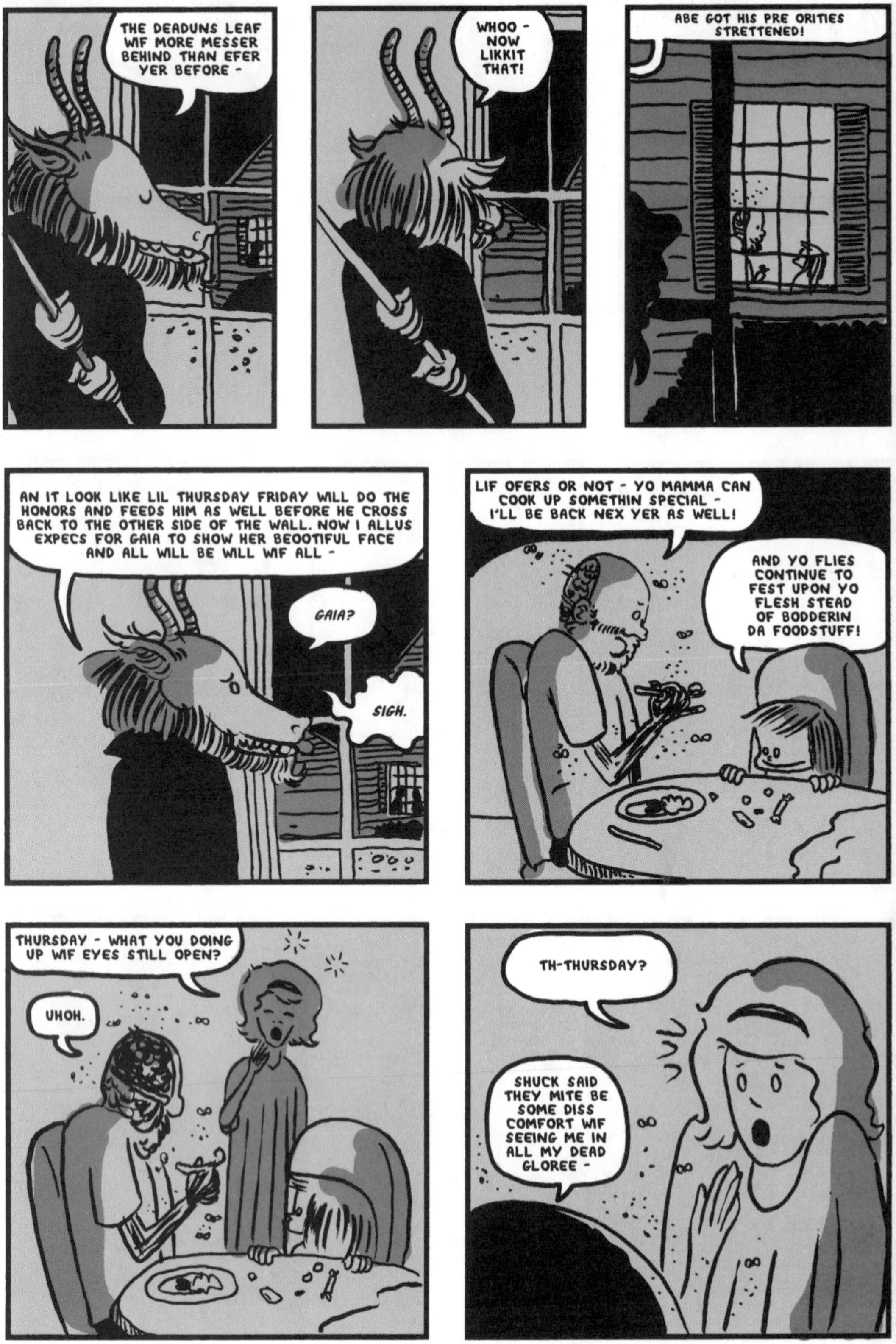
THE DEADUNS LEAF WIF MORE MESSER BEHIND THAN EFER YER BEFORE -
WHOO - NOW LIKKIT THAT!
ABE GOT HIS PRE ORITIES STRETTENED!
AN IT LOOK LIKE LIL THURSDAY FRIDAY WILL DO THE HONORS AND FEEDS HIM AS WELL BEFORE HE CROSS BACK TO THE OTHER SIDE OF THE WALL. NOW I ALLUS EXPECS FOR GAIA TO SHOW HER BEOOTIFUL FACE AND ALL WILL BE WILL WIF ALL -
GAIA?
SIGH.
LIF OFERS OR NOT - YO MAMMA CAN COOK UP SOMETHIN SPECIAL - I'LL BE BACK NEX YER AS WELL!
AND YO FLIES CONTINUE TO FEST UPON YO FLESH STEAD OF BODDERIN DA FOODSTUFF!
THURSDAY - WHAT YOU DOING UP WIF EYES STILL OPEN?
UHOH.
TH-THURSDAY?
SHUCK SAID THEY MITE BE SOME DISS COMFORT WIF SEEING ME IN ALL MY DEAD GLOREE -

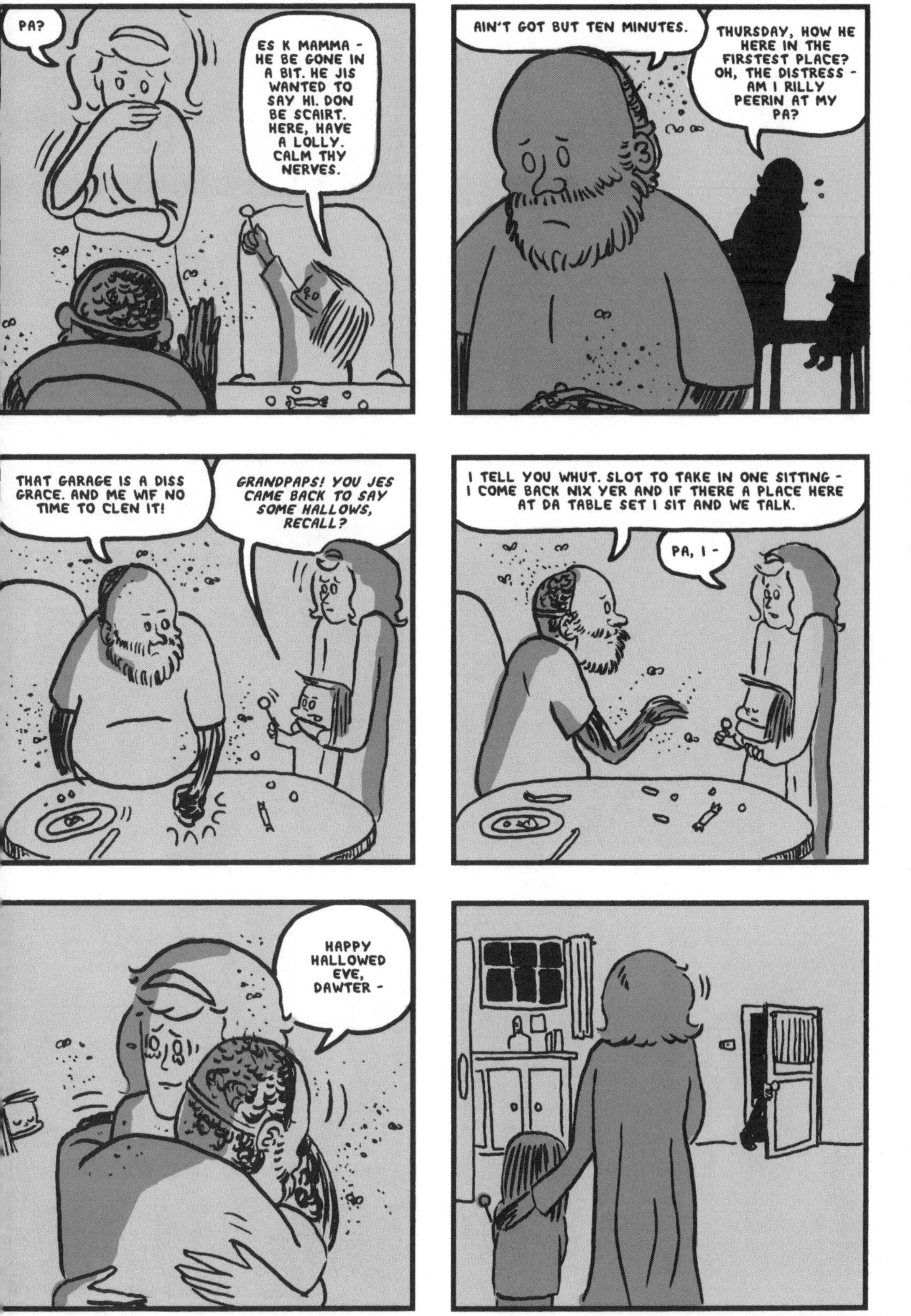
PA?
ES K MAMMA - HE BE GONE IN A BIT. HE JIS WANTED TO SAY HI. DON BE SCAIRT. HERE, HAVE A LOLLY. CALM THY NERVES.
AIN'T GOT BUT TEN MINUTES.
THURSDAY, HOW HE HERE IN THE FIRSTEST PLACE? OH, THE DISTRESS - AM I RILLY PEERIN AT MY PA?
THAT GARAGE IS A DISS GRACE. AND ME WIF NO TIME TO CLEN IT!
GRANDPAPS! YOU JES CAME BACK TO SAY SOME HALLOWS, RECALL?
I TELL YOU WHUT. SLOT TO TAKE IN ONE SITTING - I COME BACK NIX YER AND IF THERE A PLACE HERE AT DA TABLE SET I SIT AND WE TALK.
PA, I -
HAPPY HALLOWED EVE, DAWTER -

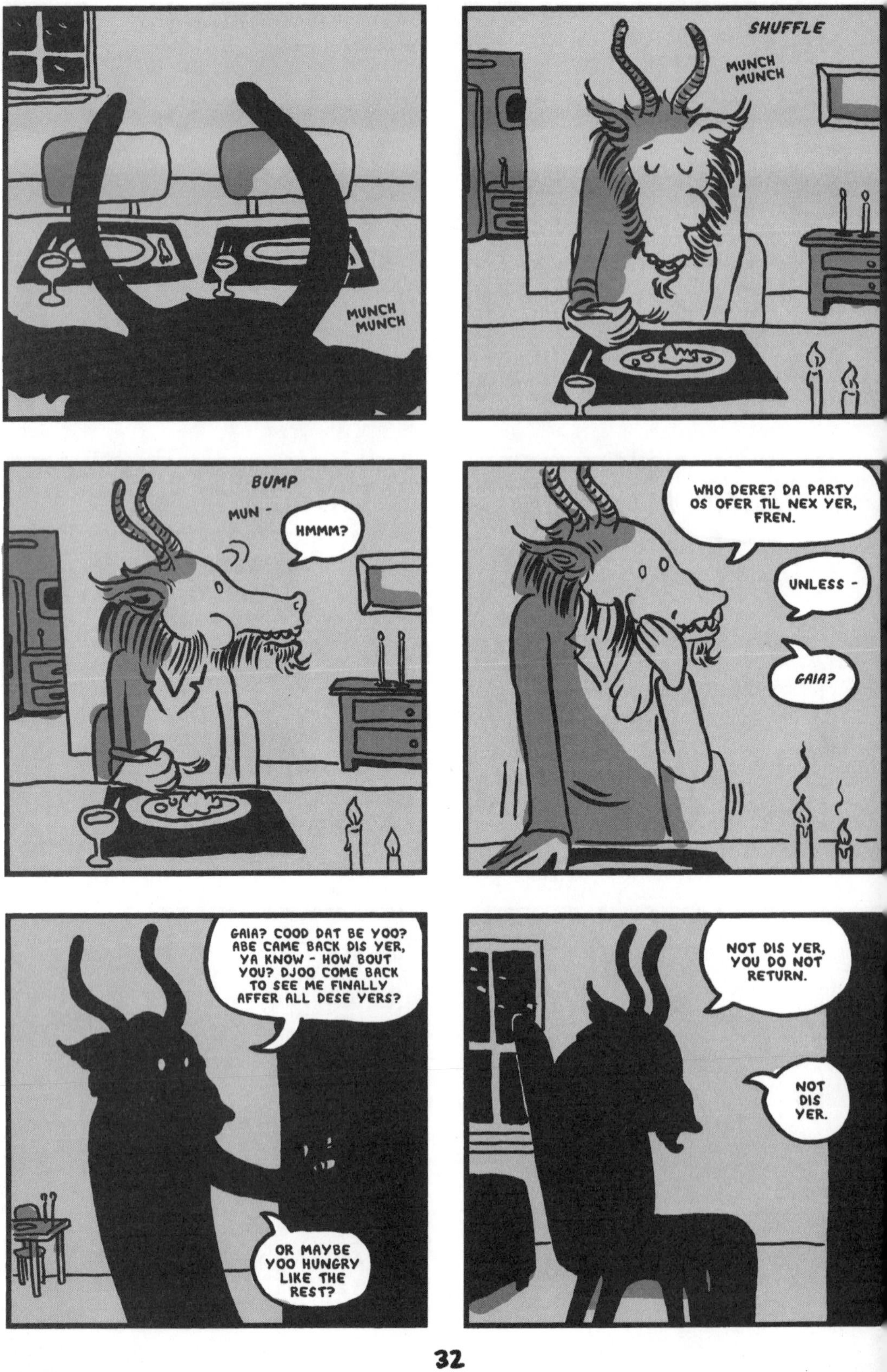
MUNCH
MUNCH
SHUFFLE
MUNCH
MUNCH
BUMP
MUN -
HMMM?
WHO DERE? DA PARTY OS OFER TIL NEX YER, FREN.
UNLESS -
GAIA?
GAIA? COOD DAT BE YOO? ABE CAME BACK DIS YER, YA KNOW - HOW BOUT YOU? DJOO COME BACK TO SEE ME FINALLY AFFER ALL DESE YERS?
OR MAYBE YOO HUNGRY LIKE THE REST?
NOT DIS YER, YOU DO NOT RETURN.
NOT DIS YER.

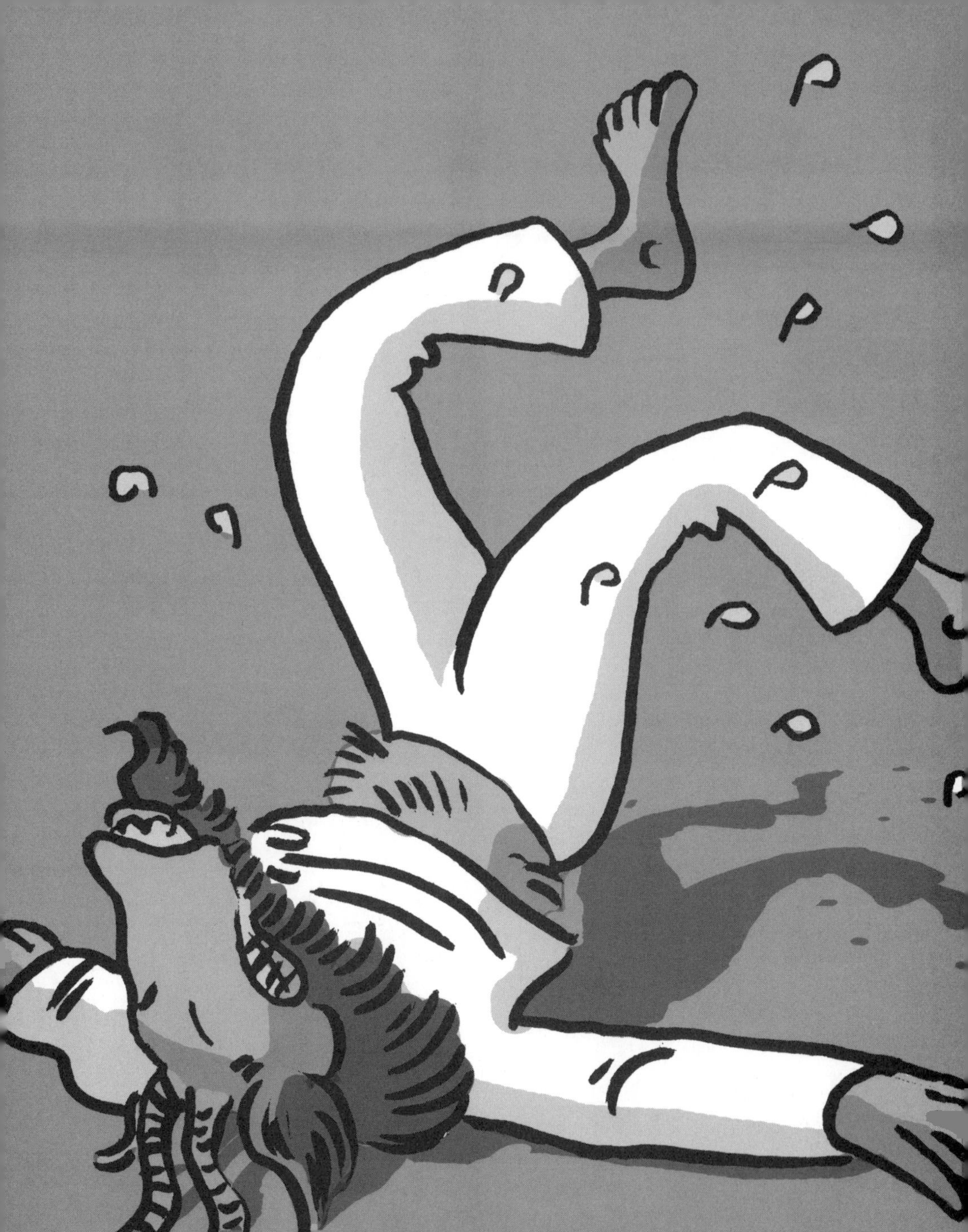

PURGATORY BREWS

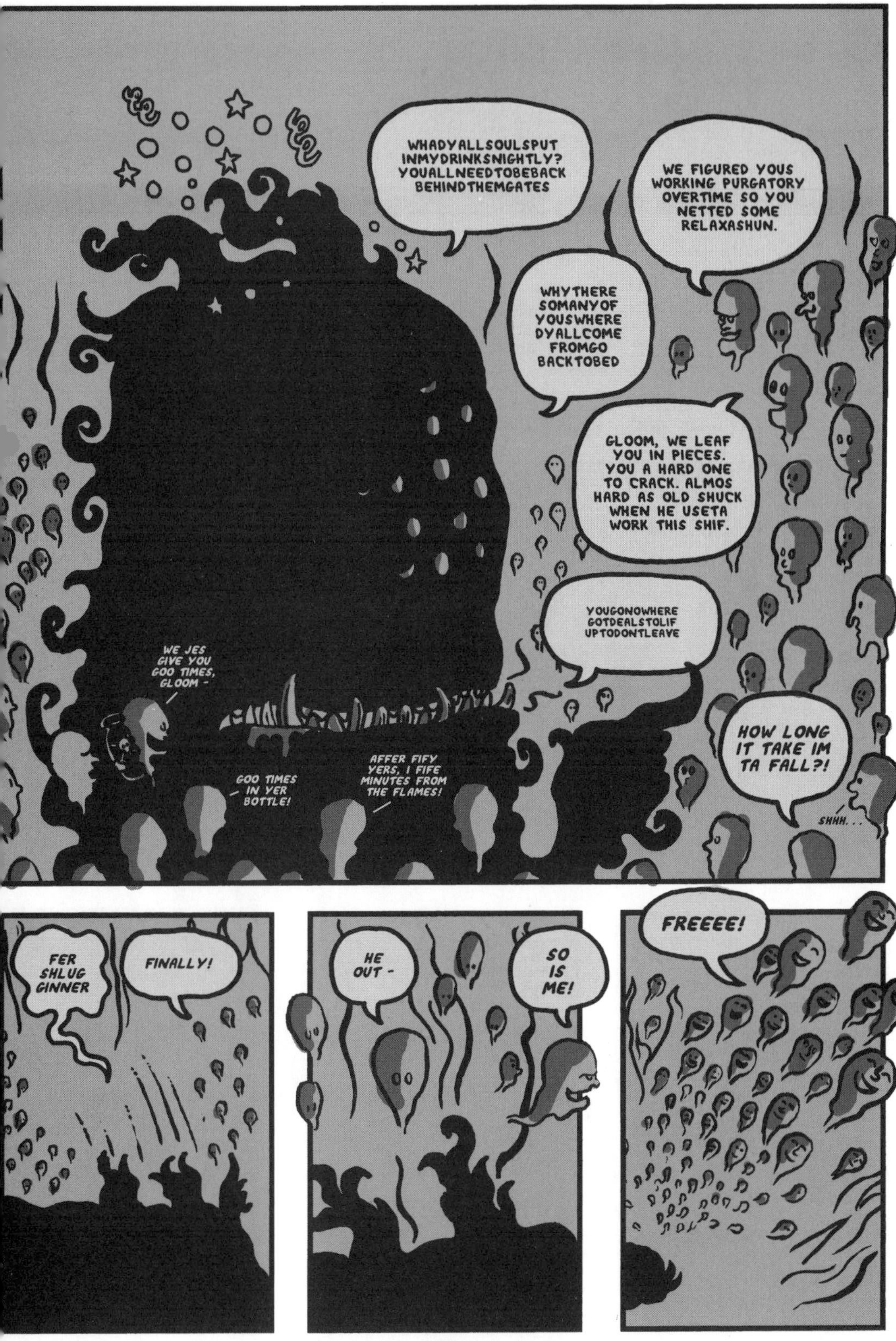
WHADYALLSOULSPUT INMYDRINKSNIGHTLY? YOUALLNEEDTOBEBACK BEHINDTHEMGATES
WE FIGURED YOUS WORKING PURGATORY OVERTIME SO YOU NETTED SOME RELAXASHUN.
WHYTHERE SOMANYOF YOUSWHERE DYALLCOME FROMGO BACKTOBED
GLOOM, WE LEAF YOU IN PIECES. YOU A HARD ONE TO CRACK. ALMOS HARD AS OLD SHUCK WHEN HE USETA WORK THIS SHIF.
YOUGONOWHERE GOTDEALSTOLIF UPTODONTLEAVE
WE JES GIVE YOU GOO TIMES, GLOOM -
GOO TIMES IN YER BOTTLE!
AFFER FIFY YERS, I FIFE MINUTES FROM THE FLAMES!
HOW LONG IT TAKE IM TA FALL?!
SHHH...
FER SHLUG GINNER
FINALLY!
HE OUT -
SO IS ME!
FREEEE!

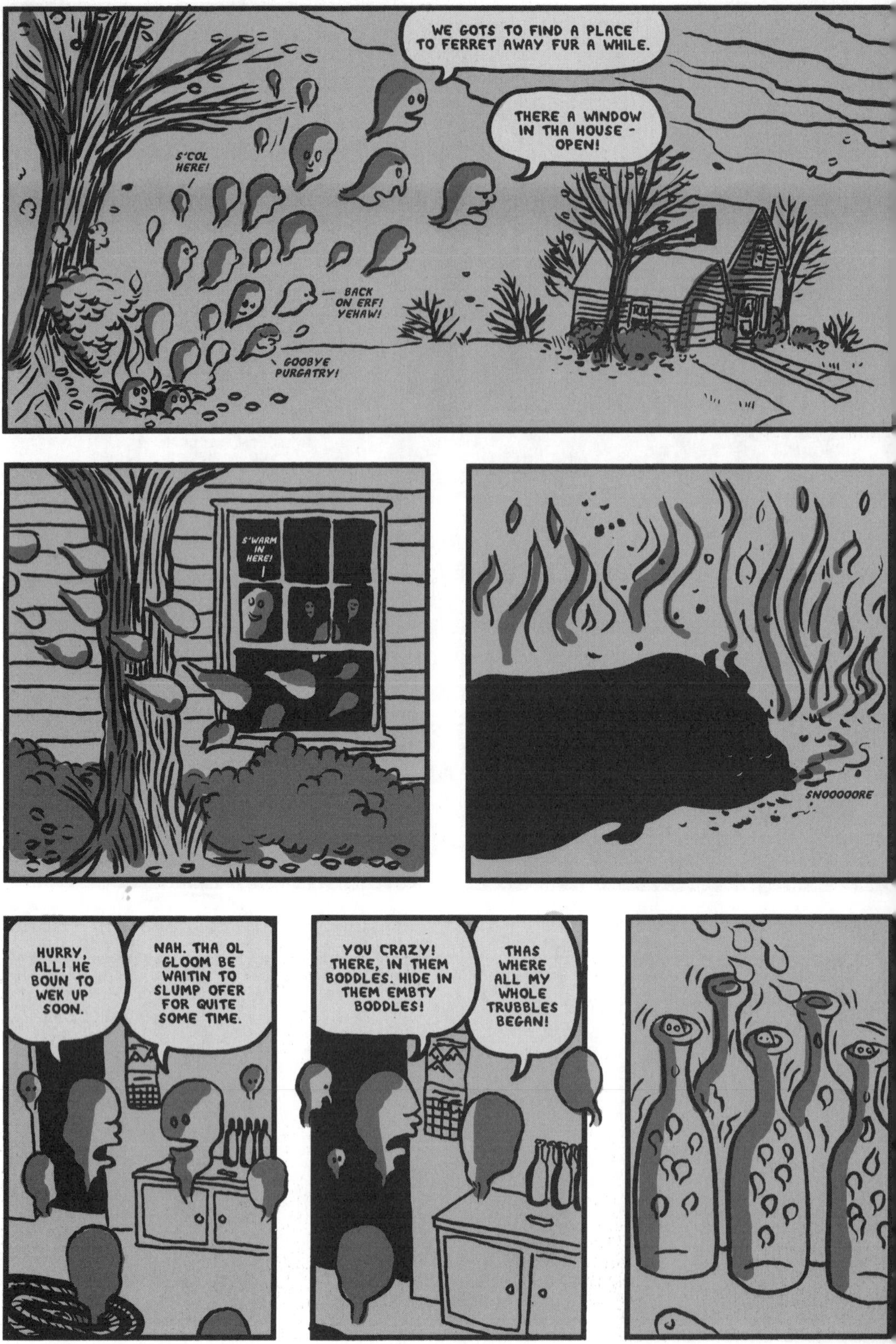

WE GOTS TO FIND A PLACE TO FERRET AWAY FUR A WHILE.
THERE A WINDOW IN THA HOUSE - OPEN!
S'COL HERE!
BACK ON ERF! YEHAW!
GOOBYE PURGATRY!
S'WARM IN HERE!
SNOOOOORE
HURRY, ALL! HE BOUN TO WEK UP SOON.
NAH. THA OL GLOOM BE WAITIN TO SLUMP OFER FOR QUITE SOME TIME.
YOU CRAZY! THERE, IN THEM BODDLES. HIDE IN THEM EMBTY BODDLES!
THAS WHERE ALL MY WHOLE TRUBBLES BEGAN!

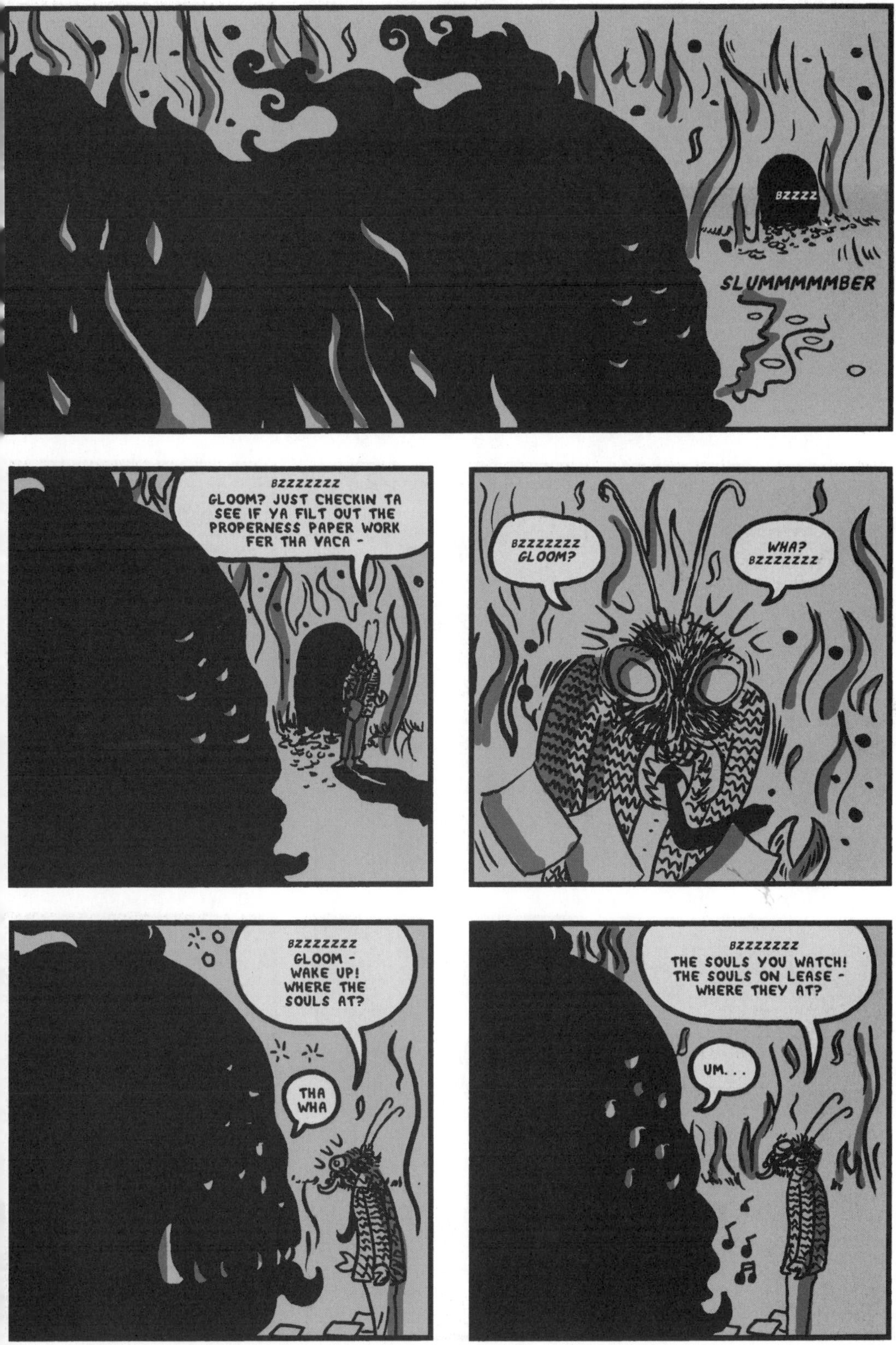
BZZZZ
SLUMMMMMBER
BZZZZZZZ
GLOOM? JUST CHECKIN TA SEE IF YA FILT OUT THE PROPERNESS PAPER WORK FER THA VACA -
BZZZZZZZ GLOOM?
WHA? BZZZZZZZ
BZZZZZZZ
GLOOM - WAKE UP! WHERE THE SOULS AT?
THA WHA
BZZZZZZZ
THE SOULS YOU WATCH! THE SOULS ON LEASE - WHERE THEY AT?
UM. . .

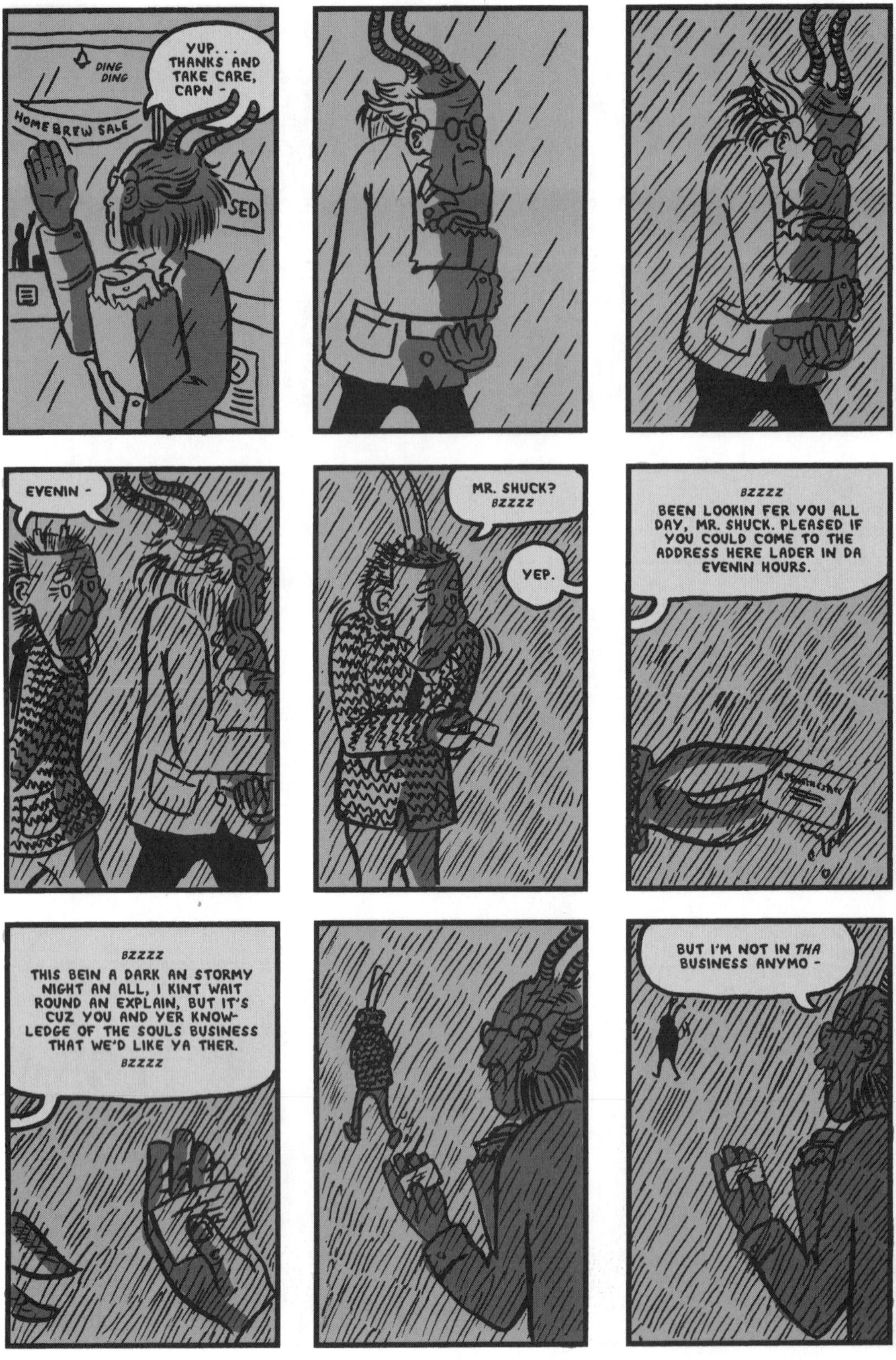
DING DING
YUP... THANKS AND TAKE CARE, CAPN -
HOME BREW SALE
SED
EVENIN -
MR. SHUCK? BZZZZ
YEP.
BZZZZ BEEN LOOKIN FER YOU ALL DAY, MR. SHUCK. PLEASED IF YOU COULD COME TO THE ADDRESS HERE LADER IN DA EVENIN HOURS.
BZZZZ THIS BEIN A DARK AN STORMY NIGHT AN ALL, I KINT WAIT ROUND AN EXPLAIN, BUT IT'S CUZ YOU AND YER KNOW-LEDGE OF THE SOULS BUSINESS THAT WE'D LIKE YA THER. BZZZZ
BUT I'M NOT IN *THA* BUSINESS ANYMO -

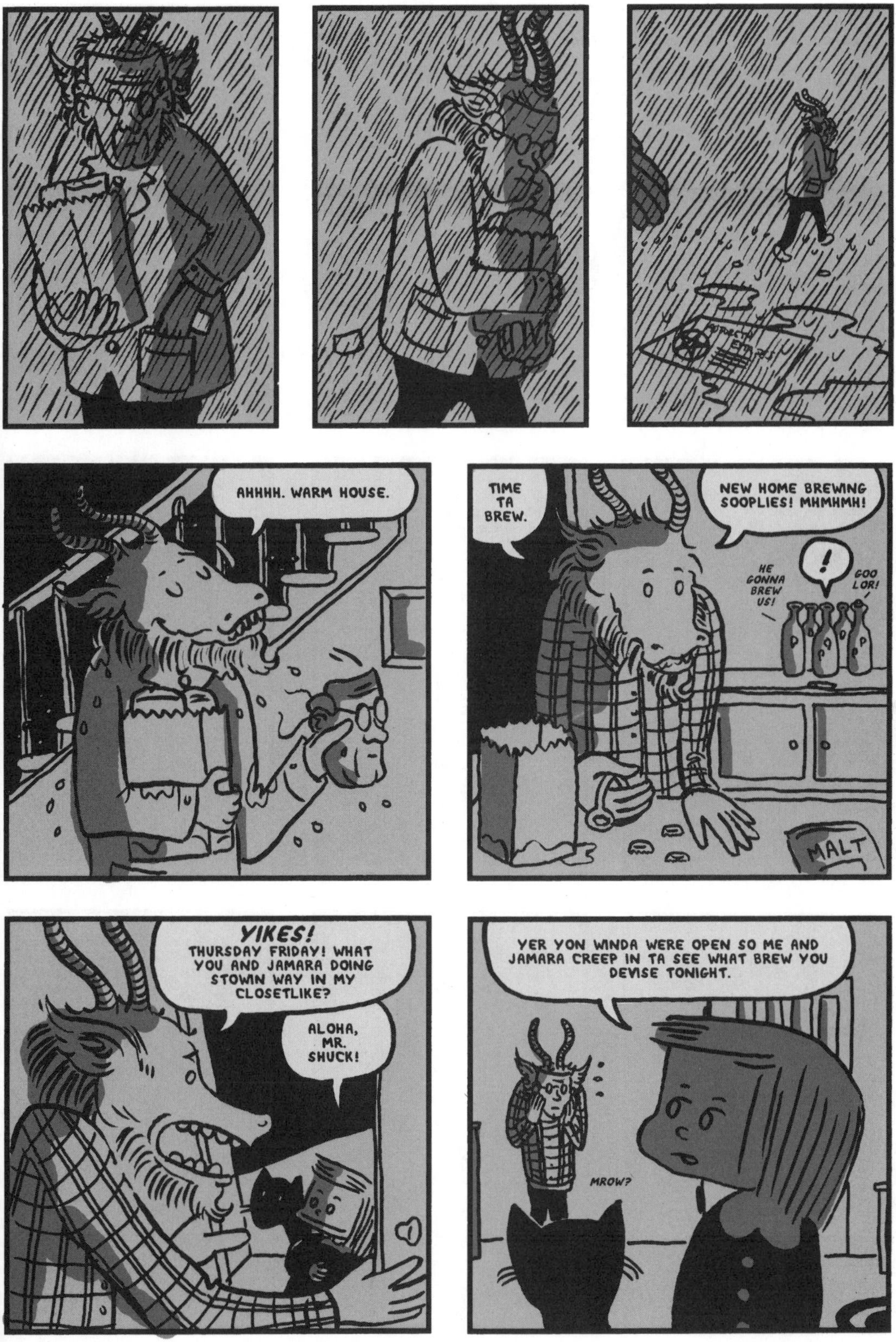
AHHHH. WARM HOUSE.
TIME TA BREW.
NEW HOME BREWING SOOPLIES! MHMHMH!
HE GONNA BREW US!
!
GOO LOR!
MALT
YIKES!
THURSDAY FRIDAY! WHAT YOU AND JAMARA DOING STOWIN WAY IN MY CLOSETLIKE?
ALOHA, MR. SHUCK!
YER YON WINDA WERE OPEN SO ME AND JAMARA CREEP IN TA SEE WHAT BREW YOU DEVISE TONIGHT.
MROW?

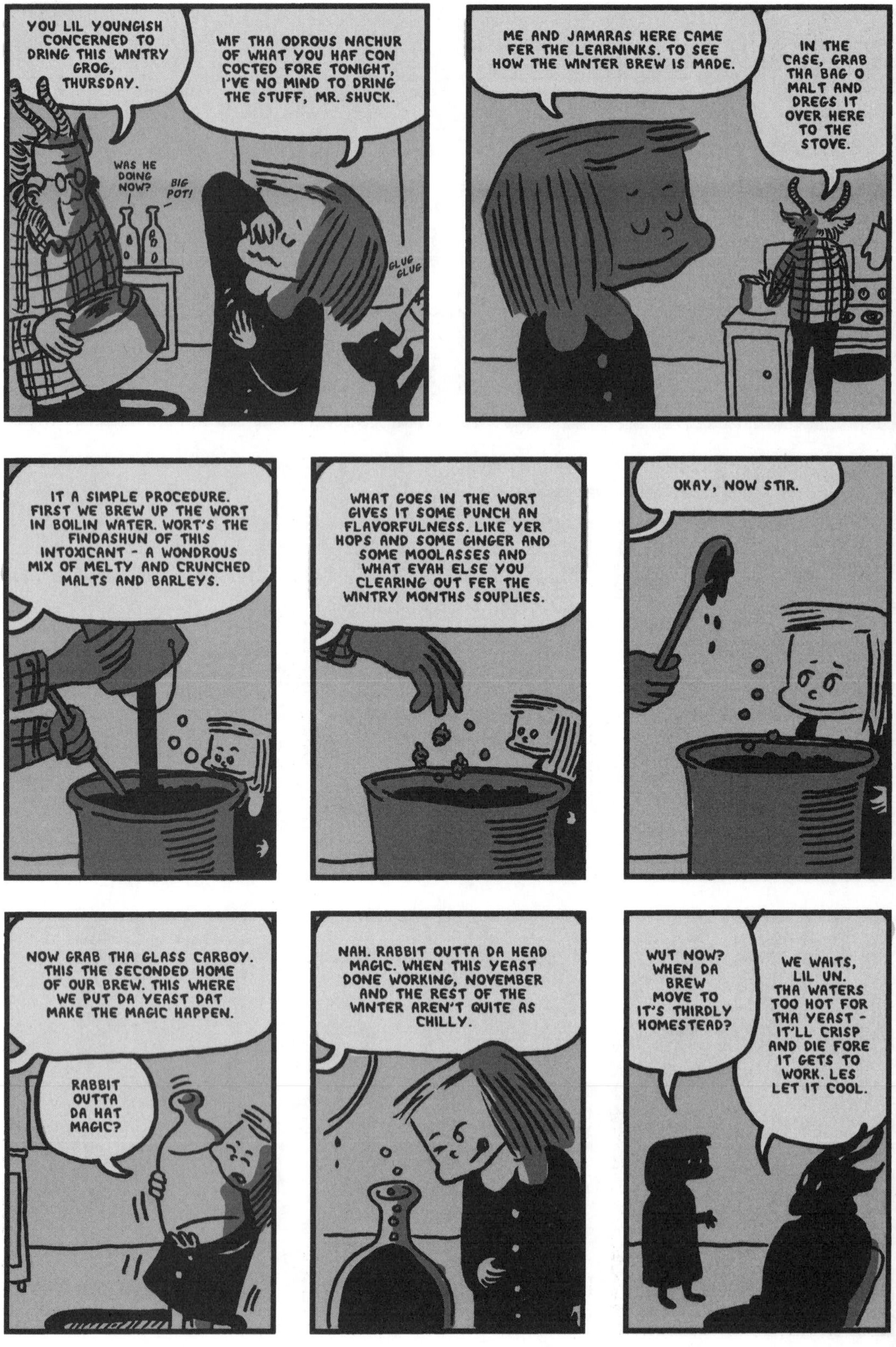
YOU LIL YOUNGISH CONCERNED TO DRING THIS WINTRY GROG, THURSDAY.
WIF THA ODROUS NACHUR OF WHAT YOU HAF CON COCTED FORE TONIGHT, I'VE NO MIND TO DRING THE STUFF, MR. SHUCK.
WAS HE DOING NOW?
BIG POT!
GLUG GLUG
ME AND JAMARAS HERE CAME FER THE LEARNINKS. TO SEE HOW THE WINTER BREW IS MADE.
IN THE CASE, GRAB THA BAG O MALT AND DREGS IT OVER HERE TO THE STOVE.
IT A SIMPLE PROCEDURE. FIRST WE BREW UP THE WORT IN BOILIN WATER. WORT'S THE FINDASHUN OF THIS INTOXICANT - A WONDROUS MIX OF MELTY AND CRUNCHED MALTS AND BARLEYS.
WHAT GOES IN THE WORT GIVES IT SOME PUNCH AN FLAVORFULNESS. LIKE YER HOPS AND SOME GINGER AND SOME MOOLASSES AND WHAT EVAH ELSE YOU CLEARING OUT FER THE WINTRY MONTHS SOUPLIES.
OKAY, NOW STIR.
NOW GRAB THA GLASS CARBOY. THIS THE SECONDED HOME OF OUR BREW. THIS WHERE WE PUT DA YEAST DAT MAKE THE MAGIC HAPPEN.
RABBIT OUTTA DA HAT MAGIC?
NAH. RABBIT OUTTA DA HEAD MAGIC. WHEN THIS YEAST DONE WORKING, NOVEMBER AND THE REST OF THE WINTER AREN'T QUITE AS CHILLY.
WUT NOW? WHEN DA BREW MOVE TO IT'S THIRDLY HOMESTEAD?
WE WAITS, LIL UN. THA WATERS TOO HOT FOR THA YEAST - IT'LL CRISP AND DIE FORE IT GETS TO WORK. LES LET IT COOL.

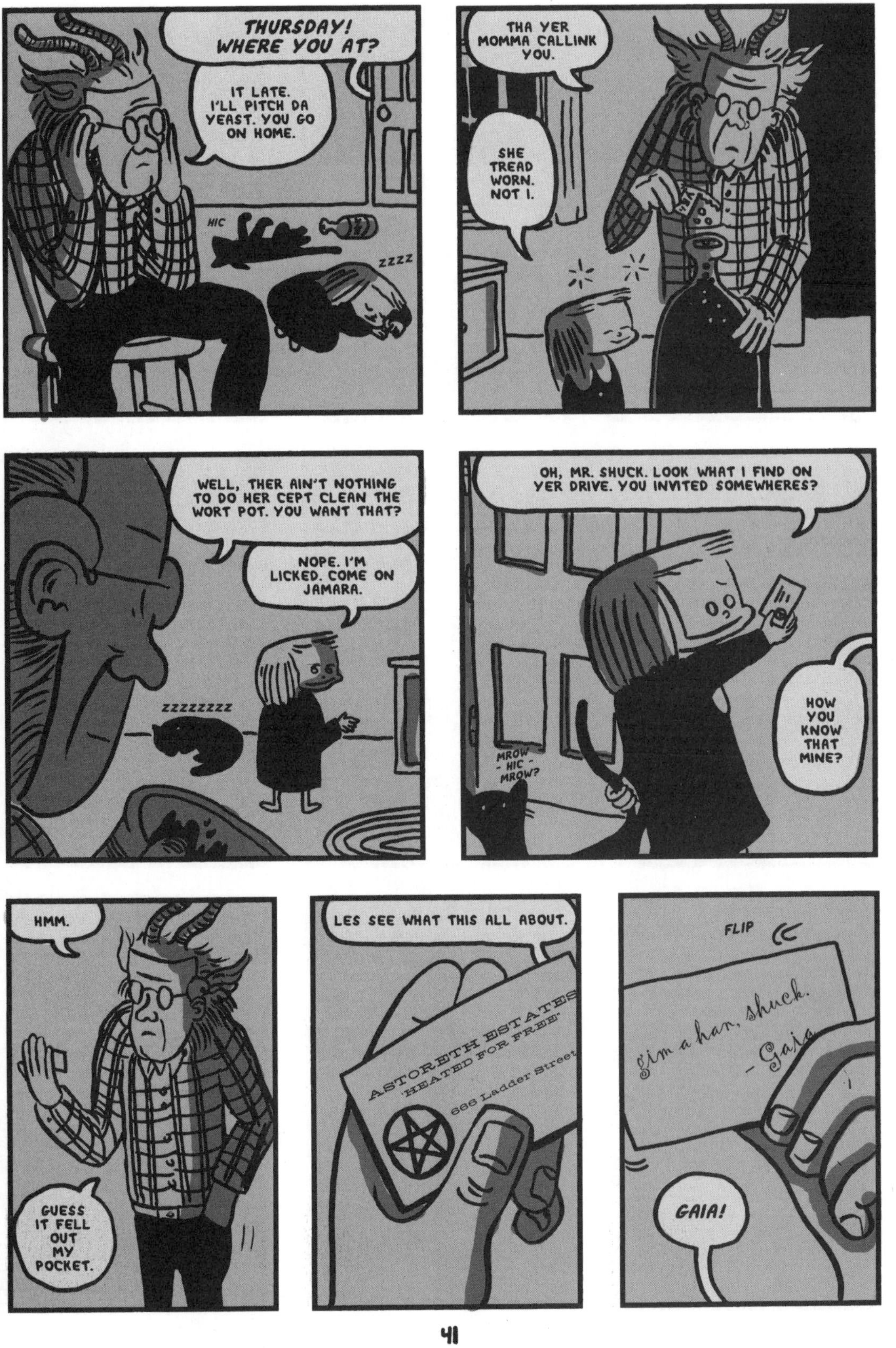
THURSDAY! WHERE YOU AT?
IT LATE. I'LL PITCH DA YEAST. YOU GO ON HOME.
HIC
ZZZZ
THA YER MOMMA CALLINK YOU.
SHE TREAD WORN. NOT I.
WELL, THER AIN'T NOTHING TO DO HER CEPT CLEAN THE WORT POT. YOU WANT THAT?
NOPE. I'M LICKED. COME ON JAMARA.
ZZZZZZZZ
OH, MR. SHUCK. LOOK WHAT I FIND ON YER DRIVE. YOU INVITED SOMEWHERES?
MROW - HIC - MROW?
HOW YOU KNOW THAT MINE?
HMM.
GUESS IT FELL OUT MY POCKET.
LES SEE WHAT THIS ALL ABOUT.
ASTORETH ESTATES
"HEATED FOR FREE"
666 Ladder Street
FLIP
gim a han, shuck.
- Gaia
GAIA!

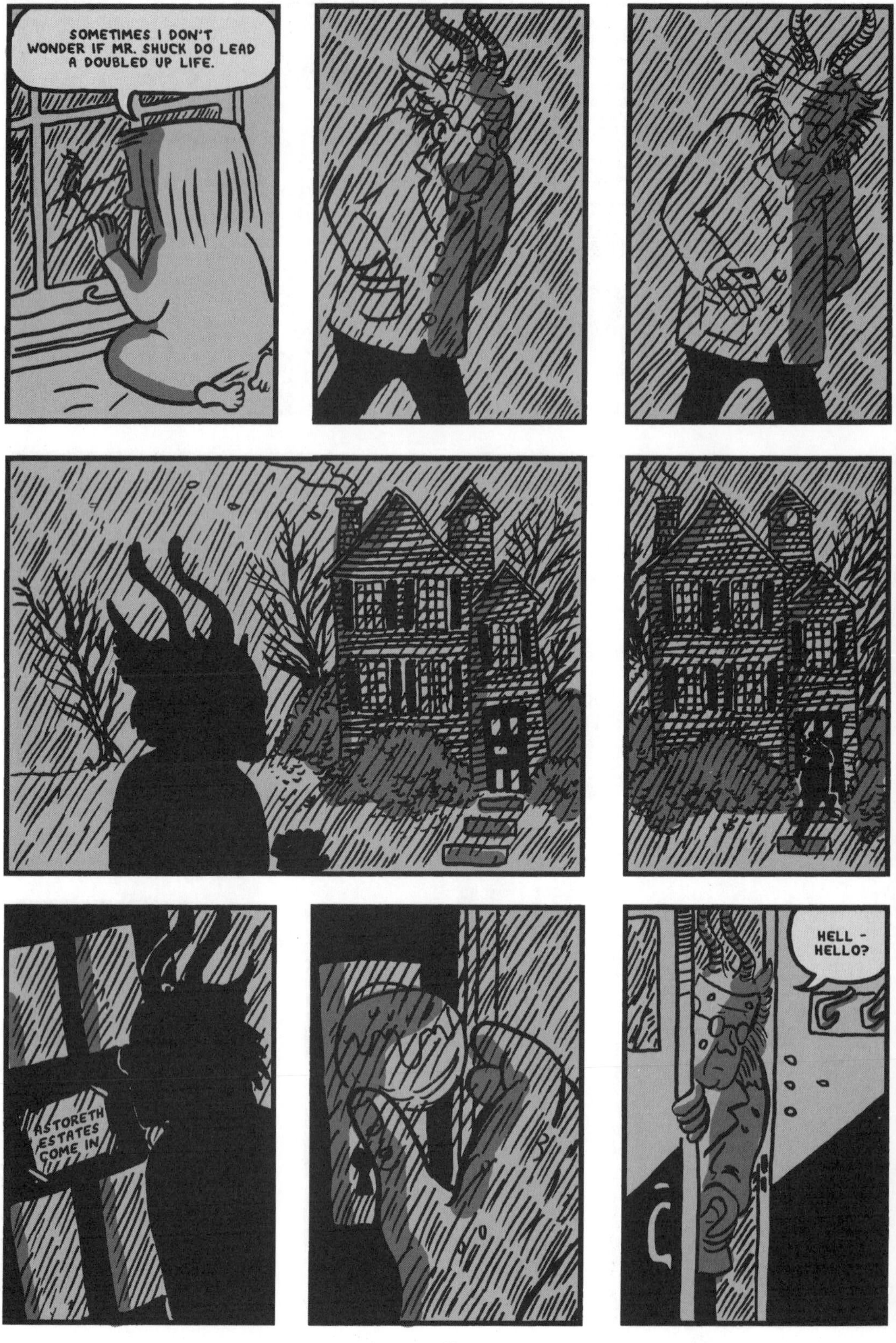
SOMETIMES I DON'T WONDER IF MR. SHUCK DO LEAD A DOUBLED UP LIFE.
ASTORETH ESTATES COME IN
HELL - HELLO?

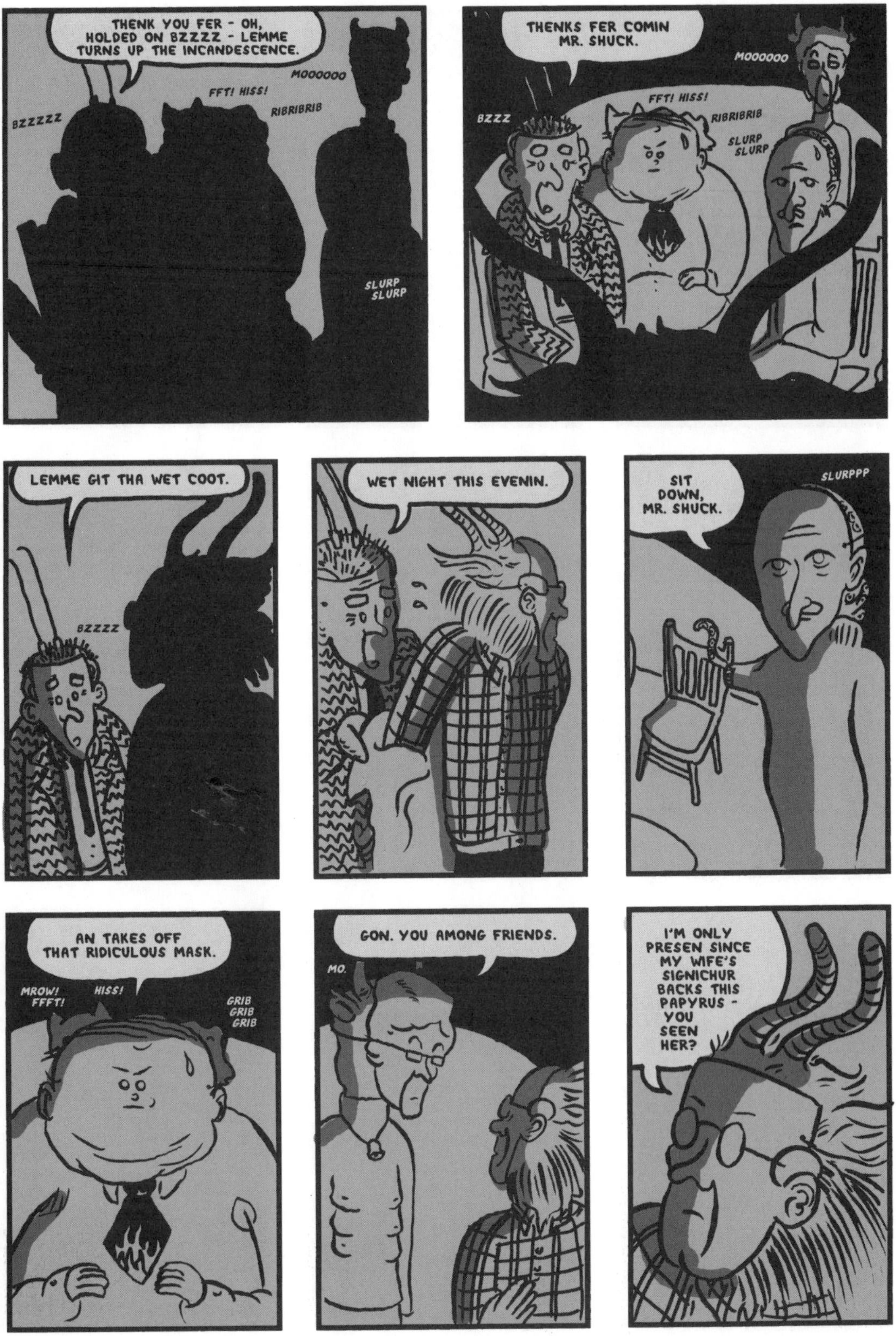
THENK YOU FER - OH, HOLDED ON BZZZZ - LEMME TURNS UP THE INCANDESCENCE.
BZZZZZ
FFT! HISS!
MOOOOOO
RIBRIBRIB
SLURP SLURP
THENKS FER COMIN MR. SHUCK.
MOOOOOO
BZZZ
FFT! HISS!
RIBRIBRIB
SLURP SLURP
LEMME GIT THA WET COOT.
BZZZZ
WET NIGHT THIS EVENIN.
SIT DOWN, MR. SHUCK.
SLURPPP
AN TAKES OFF THAT RIDICULOUS MASK.
MROW! FFFT!
HISS!
GRIB GRIB GRIB
GON. YOU AMONG FRIENDS.
MO.
I'M ONLY PRESEN SINCE MY WIFE'S SIGNICHUR BACKS THIS PAPYRUS - YOU SEEN HER?

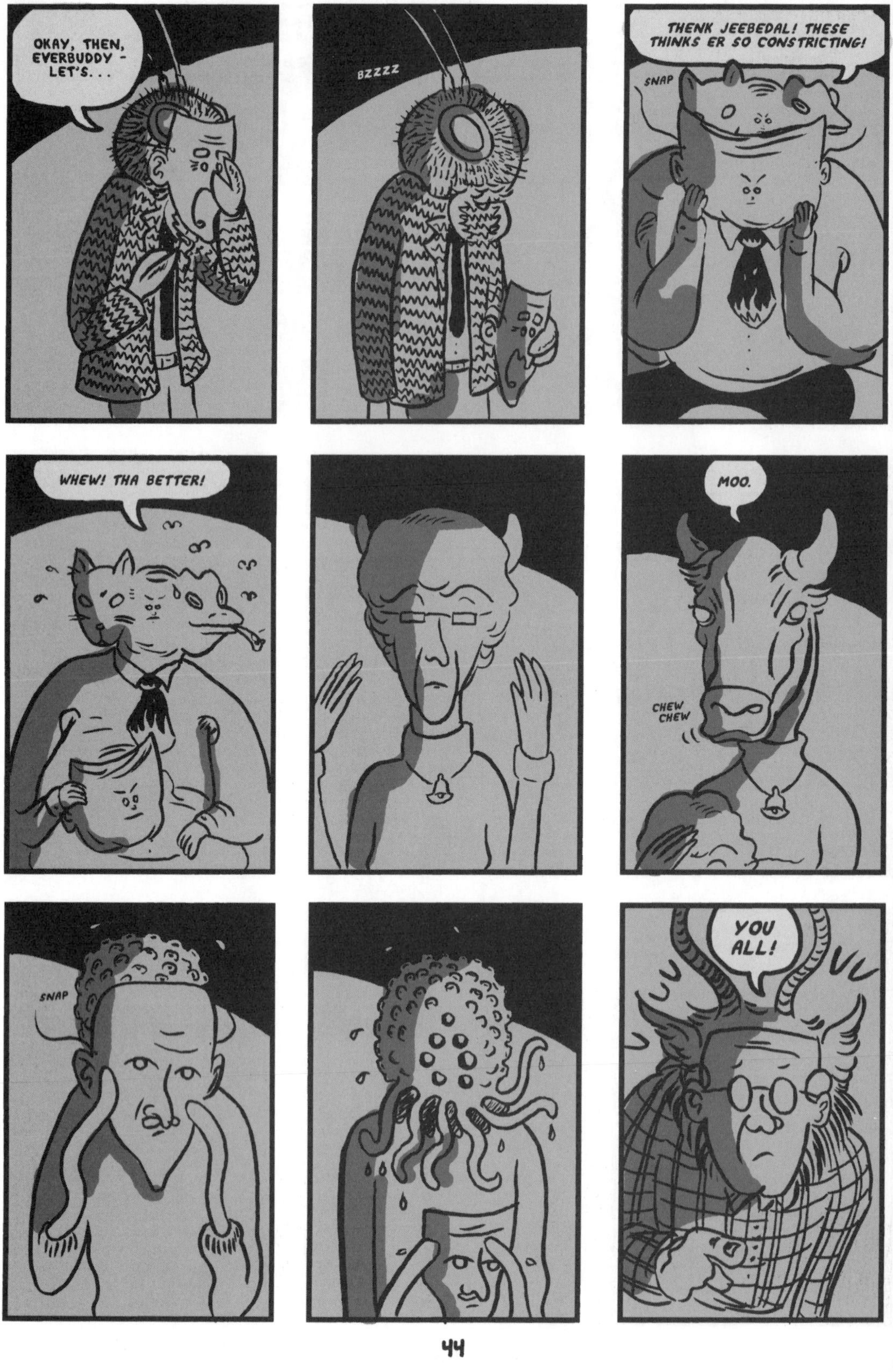
OKAY, THEN, EVERBUDDY - LET'S...
BZZZZ
THENK JEEBEDAL! THESE THINKS ER SO CONSTRICTING!
SNAP
WHEW! THA BETTER!
MOO.
CHEW CHEW
SNAP
YOU ALL!

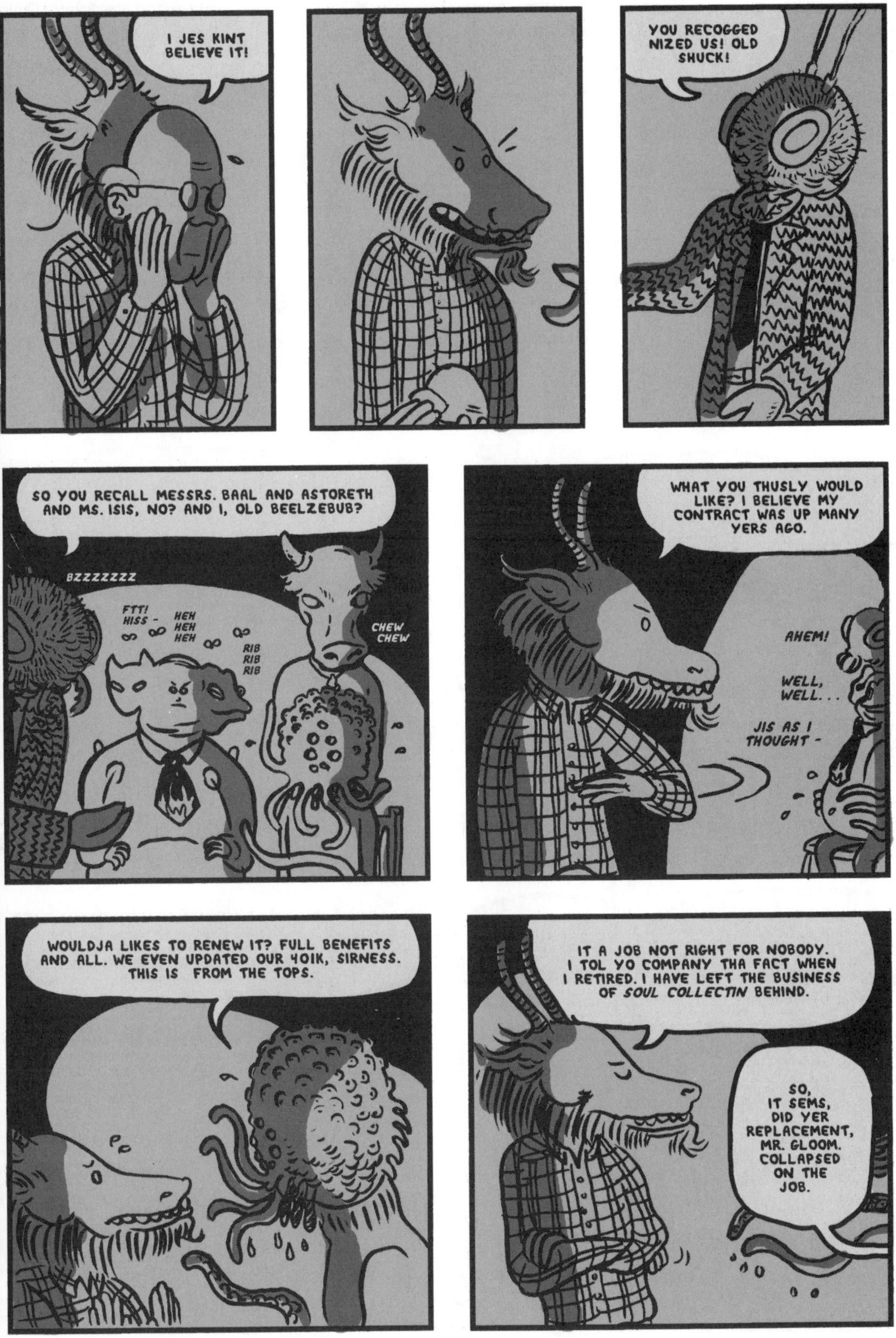
I JES KINT BELIEVE IT!
YOU RECOGGED NIZED US! OLD SHUCK!
SO YOU RECALL MESSRS. BAAL AND ASTORETH AND MS. ISIS, NO? AND I, OLD BEELZEBUB?
BZZZZZZZ
FTT! HISS -
HEH HEH HEH
RIB RIB RIB
CHEW CHEW
WHAT YOU THUSLY WOULD LIKE? I BELIEVE MY CONTRACT WAS UP MANY YERS AGO.
AHEM!
WELL, WELL...
JIS AS I THOUGHT -
WOULDJA LIKES TO RENEW IT? FULL BENEFITS AND ALL. WE EVEN UPDATED OUR 401K, SIRNESS. THIS IS FROM THE TOPS.
IT A JOB NOT RIGHT FOR NOBODY. I TOL YO COMPANY THA FACT WHEN I RETIRED. I HAVE LEFT THE BUSINESS OF *SOUL COLLECTIN* BEHIND.
SO, IT SEMS, DID YER REPLACEMENT, MR. GLOOM. COLLAPSED ON THE JOB.

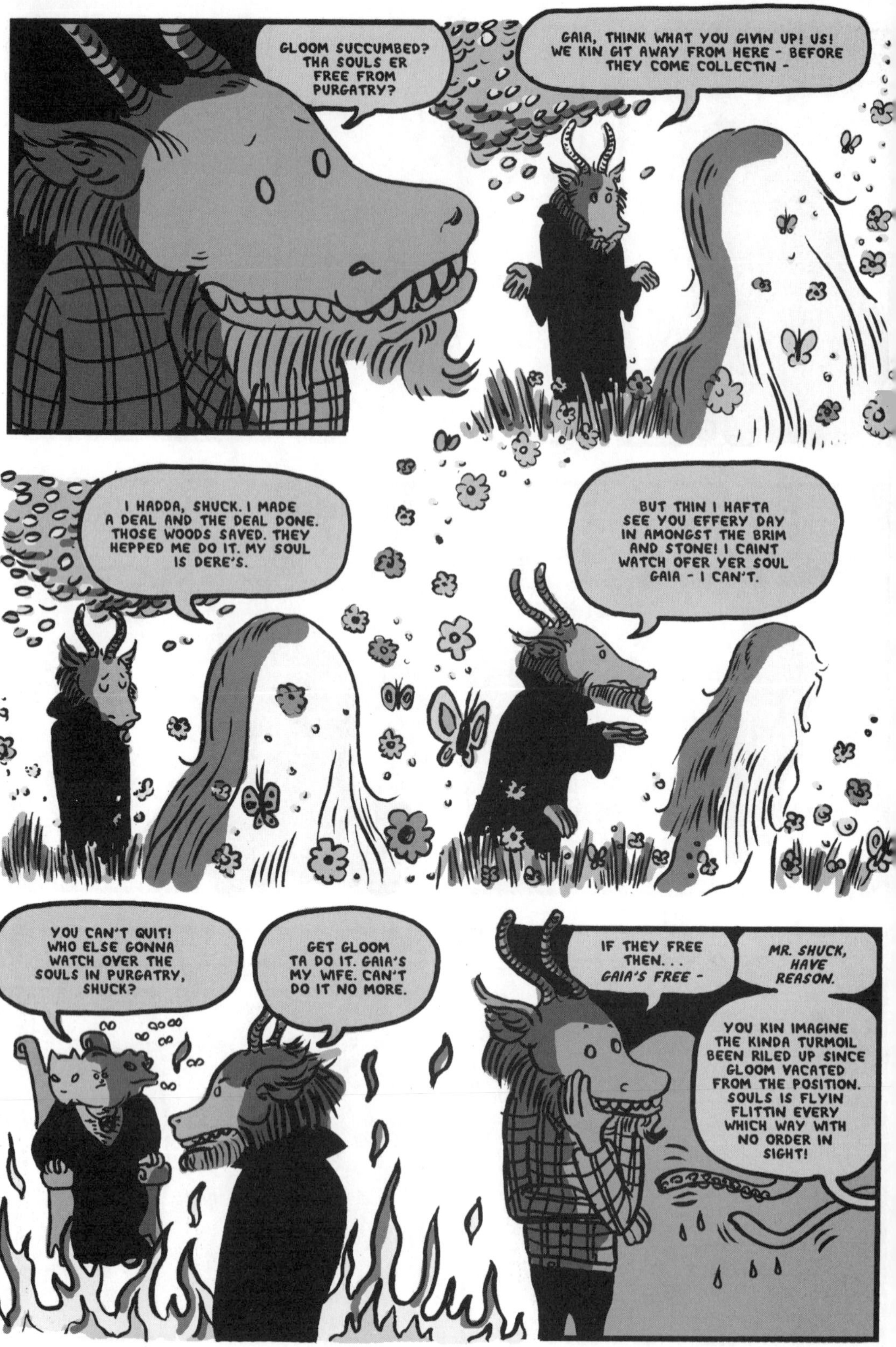
GLOOM SUCCUMBED? THA SOULS ER FREE FROM PURGATRY?
GAIA, THINK WHAT YOU GIVIN UP! US! WE KIN GIT AWAY FROM HERE - BEFORE THEY COME COLLECTIN -
I HADDA, SHUCK. I MADE A DEAL AND THE DEAL DONE. THOSE WOODS SAVED. THEY HEPPED ME DO IT. MY SOUL IS DERE'S.
BUT THIN I HAFTA SEE YOU EFFERY DAY IN AMONGST THE BRIM AND STONE! I CAINT WATCH OFER YER SOUL GAIA - I CAN'T.
YOU CAN'T QUIT! WHO ELSE GONNA WATCH OVER THE SOULS IN PURGATRY, SHUCK?
GET GLOOM TA DO IT. GAIA'S MY WIFE. CAN'T DO IT NO MORE.
IF THEY FREE THEN. . . *GAIA'S FREE* -
MR. SHUCK, HAVE REASON.
YOU KIN IMAGINE THE KINDA TURMOIL BEEN RILED UP SINCE GLOOM VACATED FROM THE POSITION. SOULS IS FLYIN FLITTIN EVERY WHICH WAY WITH NO ORDER IN SIGHT!

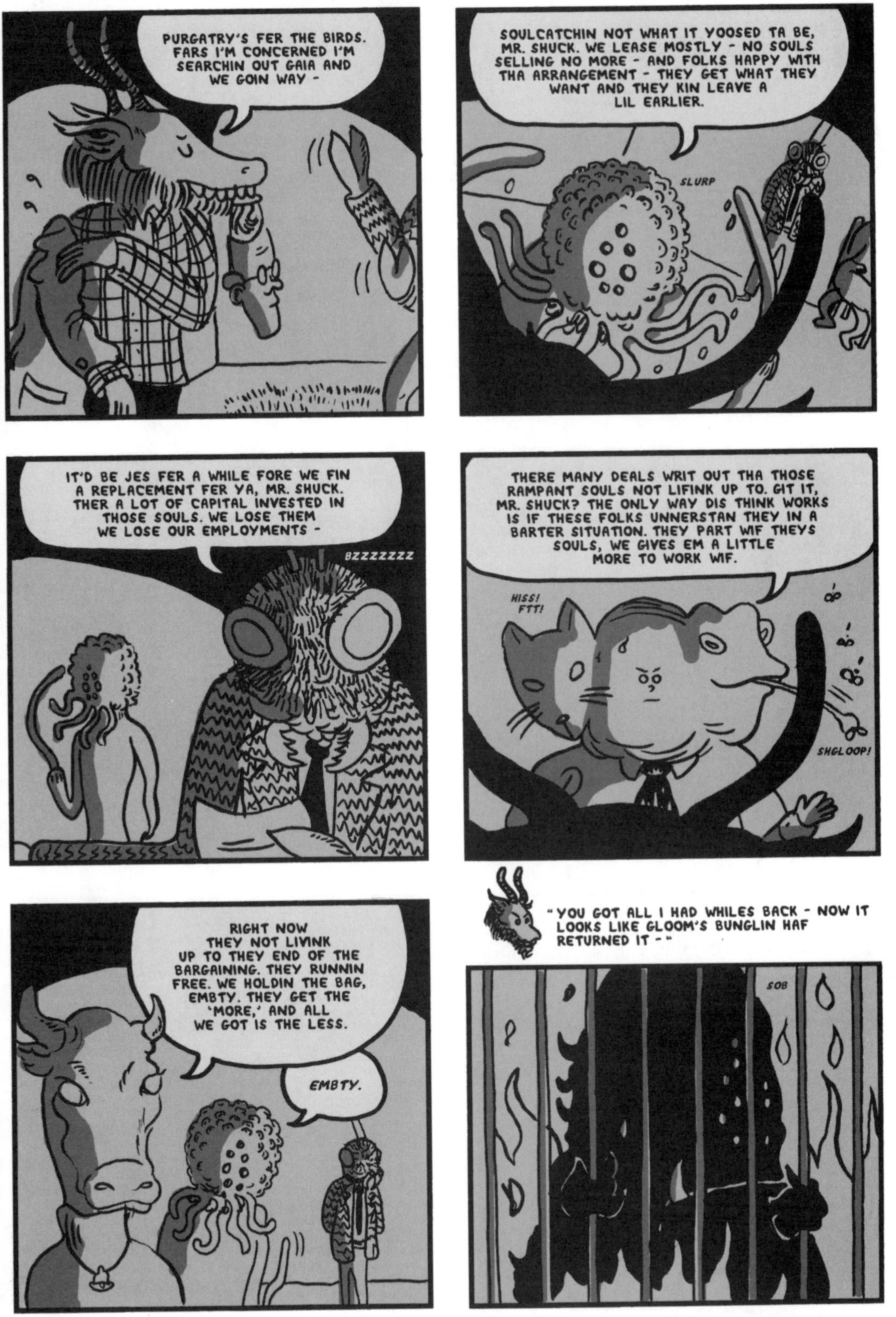
PURGATRY'S FER THE BIRDS. FARS I'M CONCERNED I'M SEARCHIN OUT GAIA AND WE GOIN WAY -
SOULCATCHIN NOT WHAT IT YOOSED TA BE, MR. SHUCK. WE LEASE MOSTLY - NO SOULS SELLING NO MORE - AND FOLKS HAPPY WITH THA ARRANGEMENT - THEY GET WHAT THEY WANT AND THEY KIN LEAVE A LIL EARLIER.
SLURP
IT'D BE JES FER A WHILE FORE WE FIN A REPLACEMENT FER YA, MR. SHUCK. THER A LOT OF CAPITAL INVESTED IN THOSE SOULS. WE LOSE THEM WE LOSE OUR EMPLOYMENTS -
BZZZZZZZ
THERE MANY DEALS WRIT OUT THA THOSE RAMPANT SOULS NOT LIFINK UP TO. GIT IT, MR. SHUCK? THE ONLY WAY DIS THINK WORKS IS IF THESE FOLKS UNNERSTAN THEY IN A BARTER SITUATION. THEY PART WIF THEYS SOULS, WE GIVES EM A LITTLE MORE TO WORK WIF.
HISS! FTT!
SHGLOOP!
RIGHT NOW THEY NOT LIVINK UP TO THEY END OF THE BARGAINING. THEY RUNNIN FREE. WE HOLDIN THE BAG, EMBTY. THEY GET THE 'MORE,' AND ALL WE GOT IS THE LESS.
EMBTY.
"YOU GOT ALL I HAD WHILES BACK - NOW IT LOOKS LIKE GLOOM'S BUNGLIN HAF RETURNED IT --"
SOB

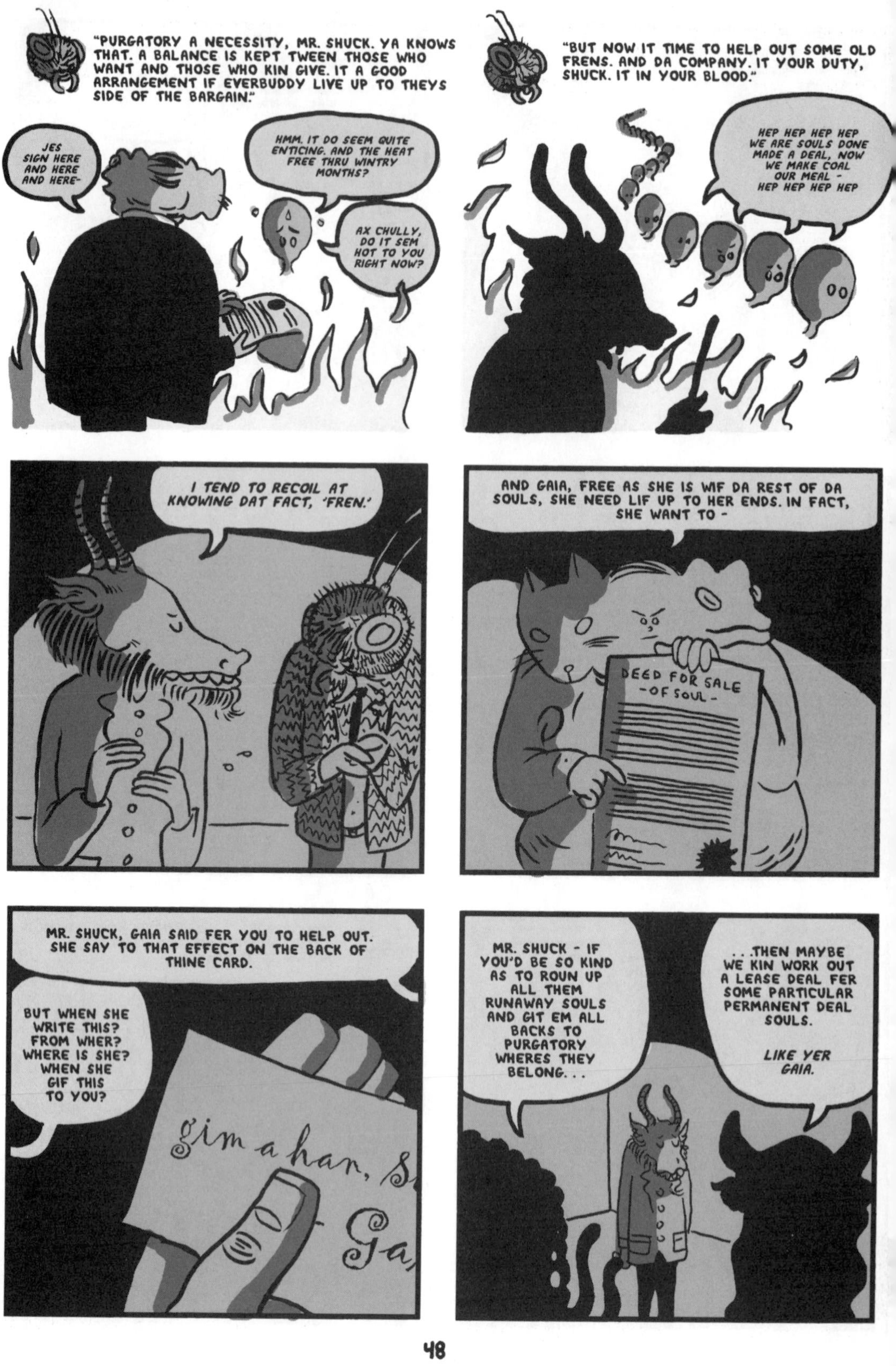

"PURGATORY A NECESSITY, MR. SHUCK. YA KNOWS THAT. A BALANCE IS KEPT TWEEN THOSE WHO WANT AND THOSE WHO KIN GIVE. IT A GOOD ARRANGEMENT IF EVERBUDDY LIVE UP TO THEYS SIDE OF THE BARGAIN."
JES SIGN HERE AND HERE AND HERE-
HMM. IT DO SEEM QUITE ENTICING. AND THE HEAT FREE THRU WINTRY MONTHS?
AX CHULLY, DO IT SEM HOT TO YOU RIGHT NOW?
"BUT NOW IT TIME TO HELP OUT SOME OLD FRENS. AND DA COMPANY. IT YOUR DUTY, SHUCK. IT IN YOUR BLOOD."
HEP HEP HEP HEP WE ARE SOULS DONE MADE A DEAL, NOW WE MAKE COAL OUR MEAL - HEP HEP HEP HEP
I TEND TO RECOIL AT KNOWING DAT FACT, 'FREN.'
AND GAIA, FREE AS SHE IS WIF DA REST OF DA SOULS, SHE NEED LIF UP TO HER ENDS. IN FACT, SHE WANT TO -
DEED FOR SALE -OF SOUL-
MR. SHUCK, GAIA SAID FER YOU TO HELP OUT. SHE SAY TO THAT EFFECT ON THE BACK OF THINE CARD.
BUT WHEN SHE WRITE THIS? FROM WHER? WHERE IS SHE? WHEN SHE GIF THIS TO YOU?
gim a har,
Ga
MR. SHUCK - IF YOU'D BE SO KIND AS TO ROUN UP ALL THEM RUNAWAY SOULS AND GIT EM ALL BACKS TO PURGATORY WHERES THEY BELONG. . .
. . .THEN MAYBE WE KIN WORK OUT A LEASE DEAL FER SOME PARTICULAR PERMANENT DEAL SOULS.
LIKE YER GAIA.

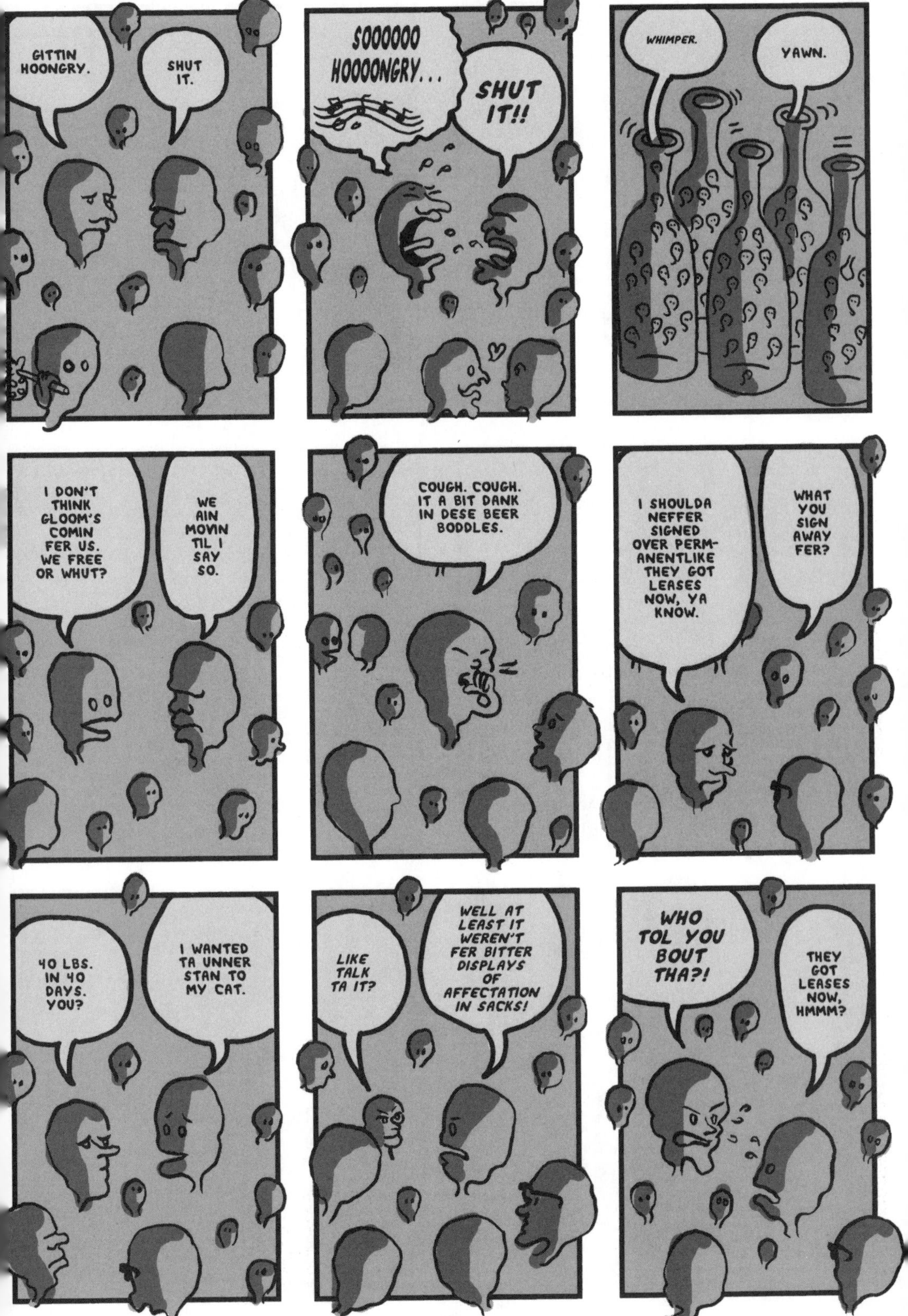
GITTIN HOONGRY.
SHUT IT.
SOOOOOO HOOOONGRY...
SHUT IT!!
WHIMPER.
YAWN.
I DON'T THINK GLOOM'S COMIN FER US. WE FREE OR WHUT?
WE AIN MOVIN TIL I SAY SO.
COUGH. COUGH. IT A BIT DANK IN DESE BEER BODDLES.
I SHOULDA NEFFER SIGNED OVER PERM-ANENTLIKE THEY GOT LEASES NOW, YA KNOW.
WHAT YOU SIGN AWAY FER?
40 LBS. IN 40 DAYS. YOU?
I WANTED TA UNNER STAN TO MY CAT.
LIKE TALK TA IT?
WELL AT LEAST IT WEREN'T FER BITTER DISPLAYS OF AFFECTATION IN SACKS!
WHO TOL YOU BOUT THA?!
THEY GOT LEASES NOW, HMMM?

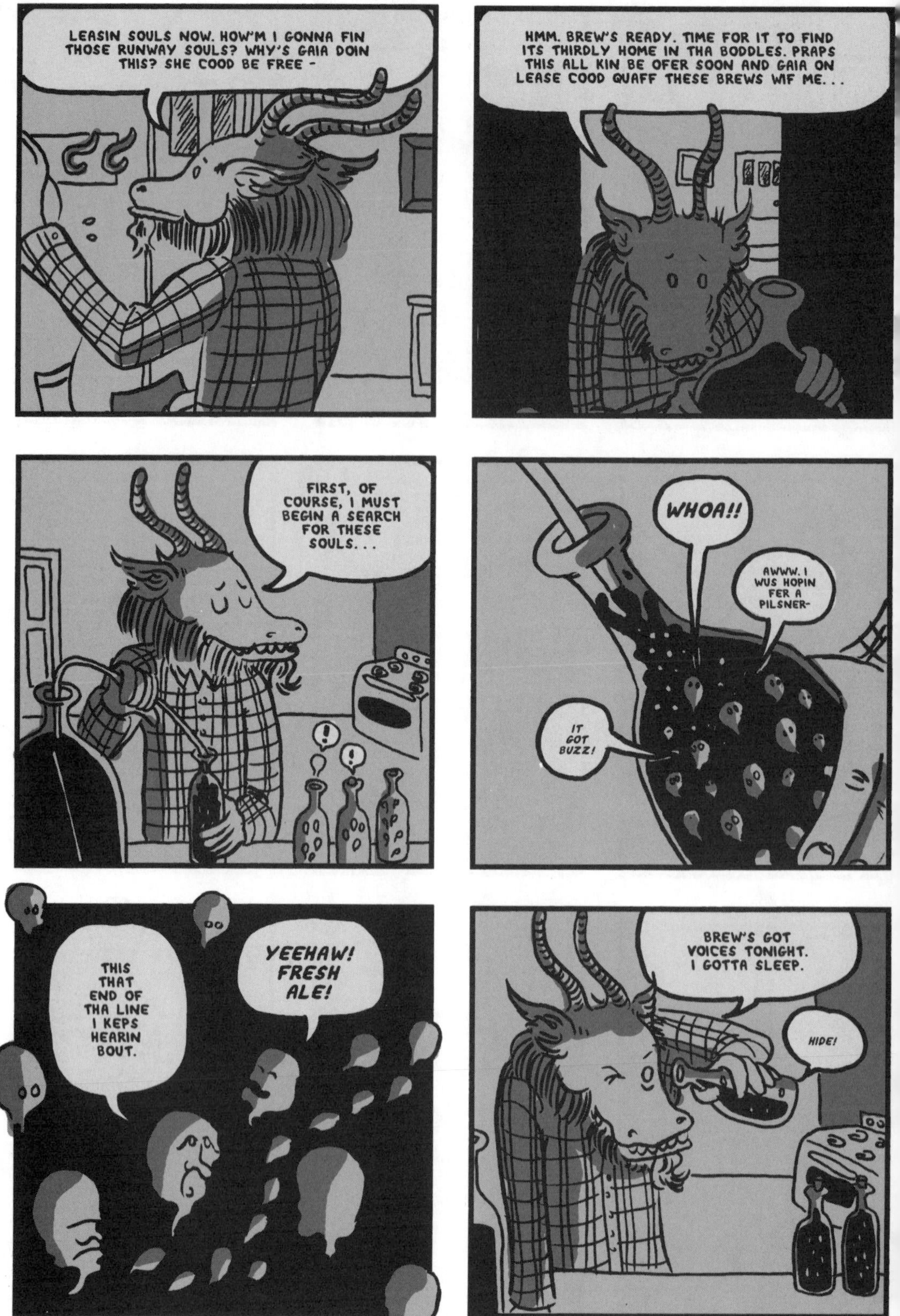
LEASIN SOULS NOW. HOW'M I GONNA FIN THOSE RUNWAY SOULS? WHY'S GAIA DOIN THIS? SHE COOD BE FREE -
HMM. BREW'S READY. TIME FOR IT TO FIND ITS THIRDLY HOME IN THA BODDLES. PRAPS THIS ALL KIN BE OFER SOON AND GAIA ON LEASE COOD QUAFF THESE BREWS WIF ME...
FIRST, OF COURSE, I MUST BEGIN A SEARCH FOR THESE SOULS...
!
!
WHOA!!
AWWW. I WUS HOPIN FER A PILSNER-
IT GOT BUZZ!
THIS THAT END OF THA LINE I KEPS HEARIN BOUT.
YEEHAW! FRESH ALE!
BREW'S GOT VOICES TONIGHT. I GOTTA SLEEP.
HIDE!

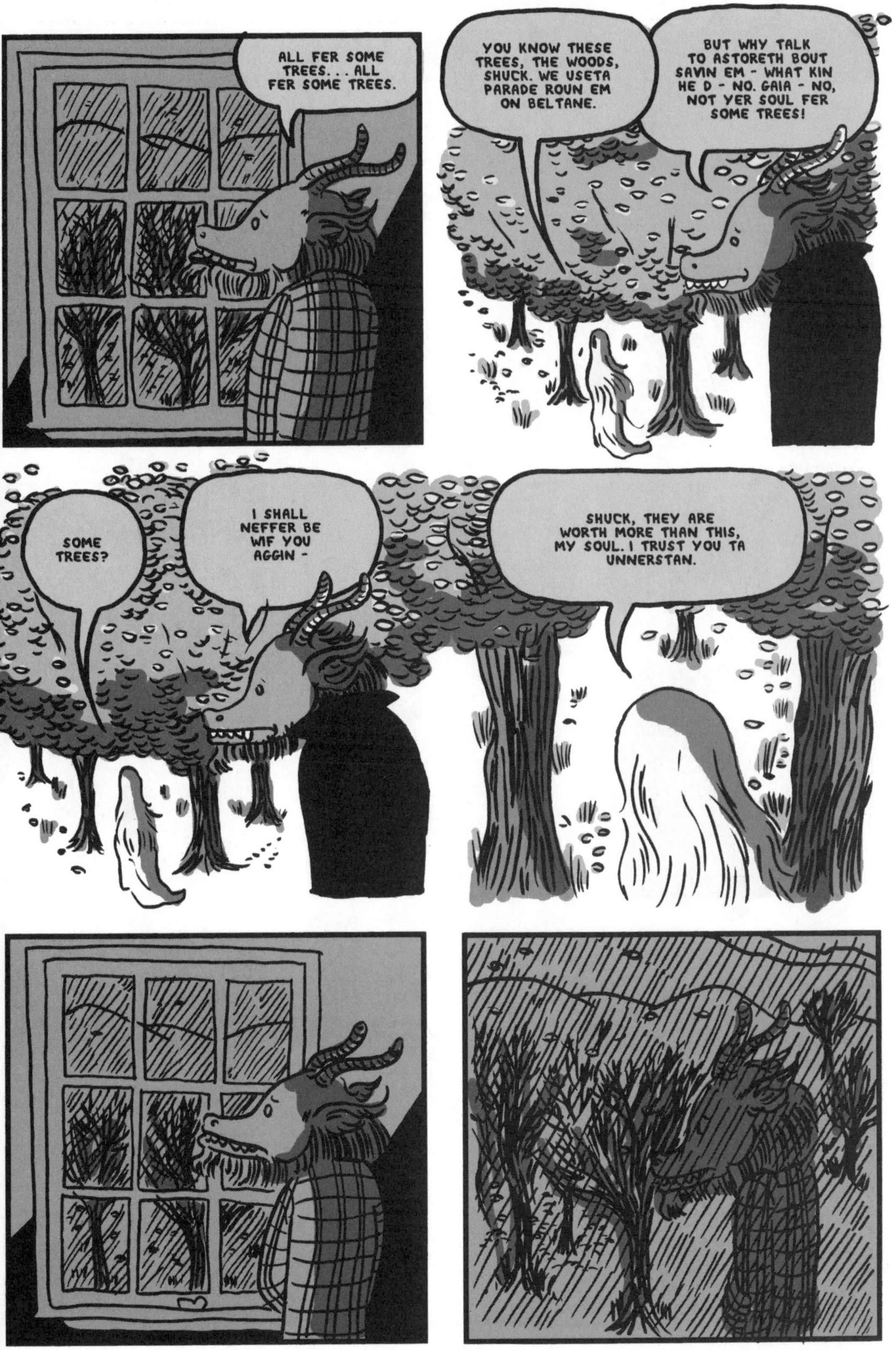
ALL FER SOME TREES. . . ALL FER SOME TREES.
YOU KNOW THESE TREES, THE WOODS, SHUCK. WE USETA PARADE ROUN EM ON BELTANE.
BUT WHY TALK TO ASTORETH BOUT SAVIN EM - WHAT KIN HE D - NO. GAIA - NO, NOT YER SOUL FER SOME TREES!
SOME TREES?
I SHALL NEFFER BE WIF YOU AGGIN -
SHUCK, THEY ARE WORTH MORE THAN THIS, MY SOUL. I TRUST YOU TA UNNERSTAN.

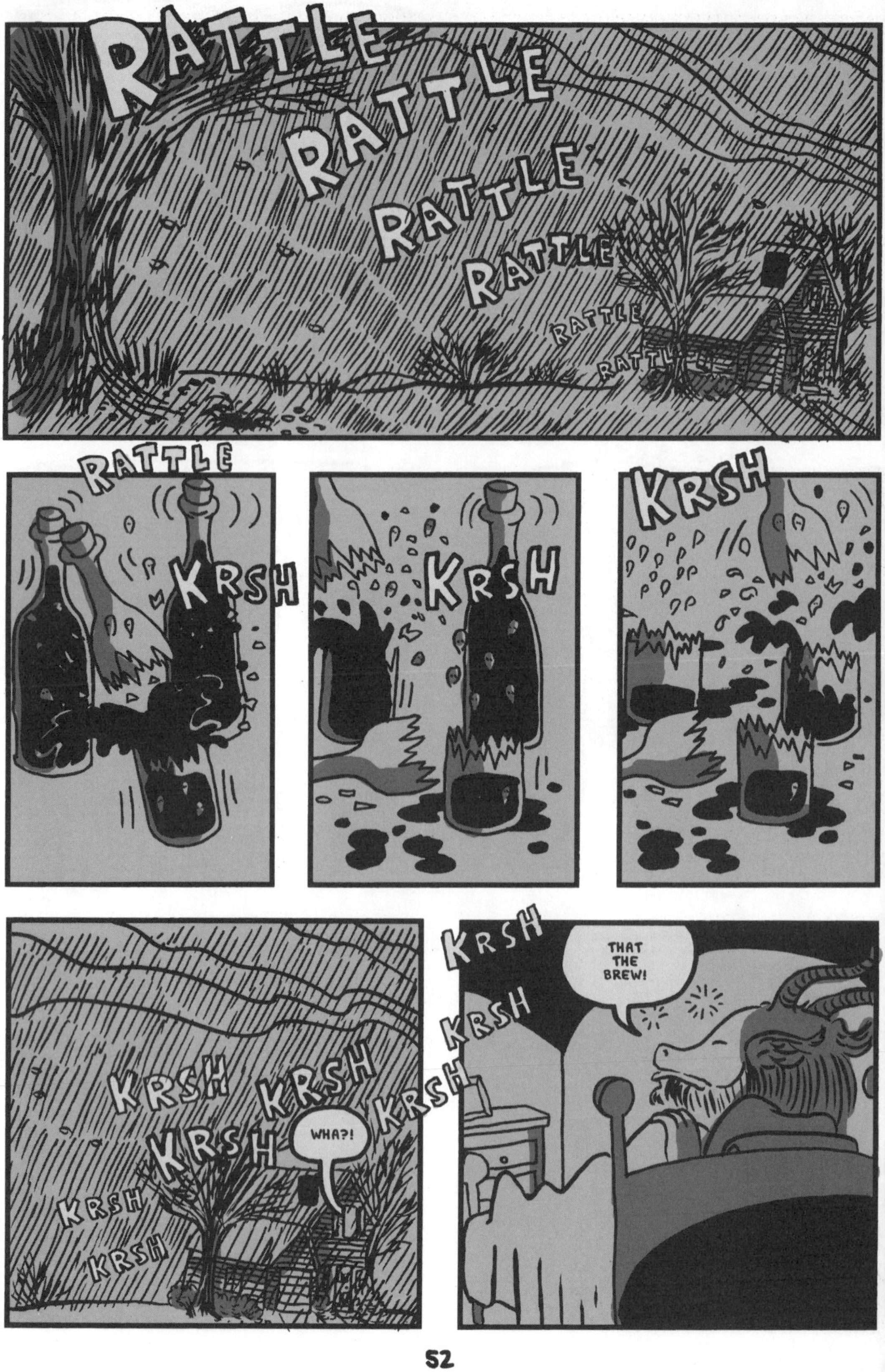
RATTLE
RATTLE
RATTLE
RATTLE
RATTLE
RATTLE
RATTL
RATTLE
KRSH
KRSH
KRSH
KRSH
KRSH
KRSH
KRSH
WHA?!
KRSH
KRSH
KRSH
KRSH
KRSH
KRSH
THAT THE BREW!

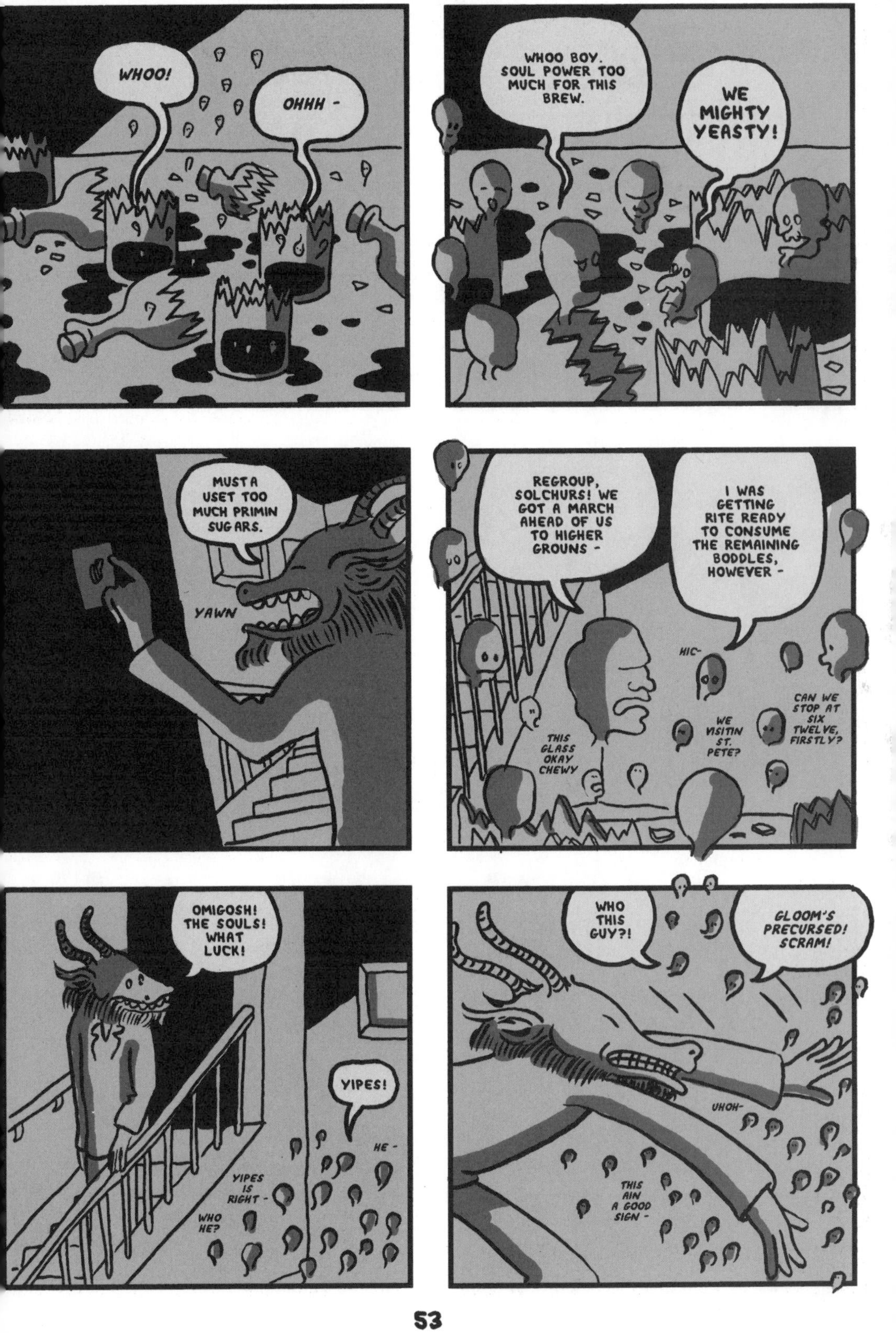
WHOO!
OHHH -
WHOO BOY. SOUL POWER TOO MUCH FOR THIS BREW.
WE MIGHTY YEASTY!
MUSTA USET TOO MUCH PRIMIN SUGARS.
YAWN
REGROUP, SOLCHURS! WE GOT A MARCH AHEAD OF US TO HIGHER GROUNS -
I WAS GETTING RITE READY TO CONSUME THE REMAINING BODDLES, HOWEVER -
HIC-
THIS GLASS OKAY CHEWY
WE VISITIN ST. PETE?
CAN WE STOP AT SIX TWELVE, FIRSTLY?
OMIGOSH! THE SOULS! WHAT LUCK!
YIPES!
HE -
YIPES IS RIGHT -
WHO HE?
WHO THIS GUY?!
GLOOM'S PRECURSED! SCRAM!
UHOH-
THIS AIN A GOOD SIGN -

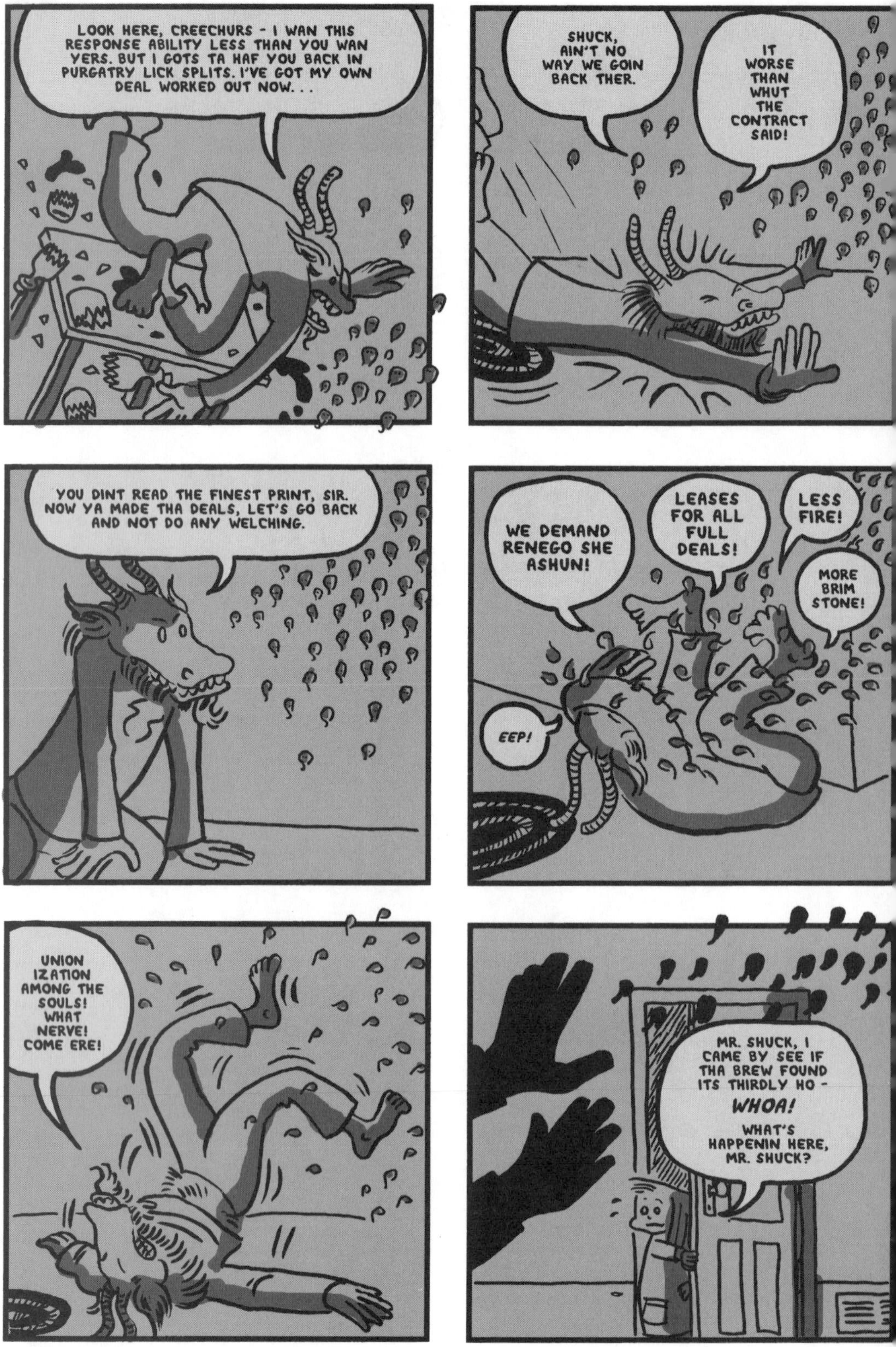
LOOK HERE, CREECHURS - I WAN THIS RESPONSE ABILITY LESS THAN YOU WAN YERS. BUT I GOTS TA HAF YOU BACK IN PURGATRY LICK SPLITS. I'VE GOT MY OWN DEAL WORKED OUT NOW. . .
SHUCK, AIN'T NO WAY WE GOIN BACK THER.
IT WORSE THAN WHUT THE CONTRACT SAID!
YOU DINT READ THE FINEST PRINT, SIR. NOW YA MADE THA DEALS, LET'S GO BACK AND NOT DO ANY WELCHING.
WE DEMAND RENEGO SHE ASHUN!
LEASES FOR ALL FULL DEALS!
LESS FIRE!
MORE BRIM STONE!
EEP!
UNION IZATION AMONG THE SOULS! WHAT NERVE! COME ERE!
MR. SHUCK, I CAME BY SEE IF THA BREW FOUND ITS THIRDLY HO -
WHOA!
WHAT'S HAPPENIN HERE, MR. SHUCK?

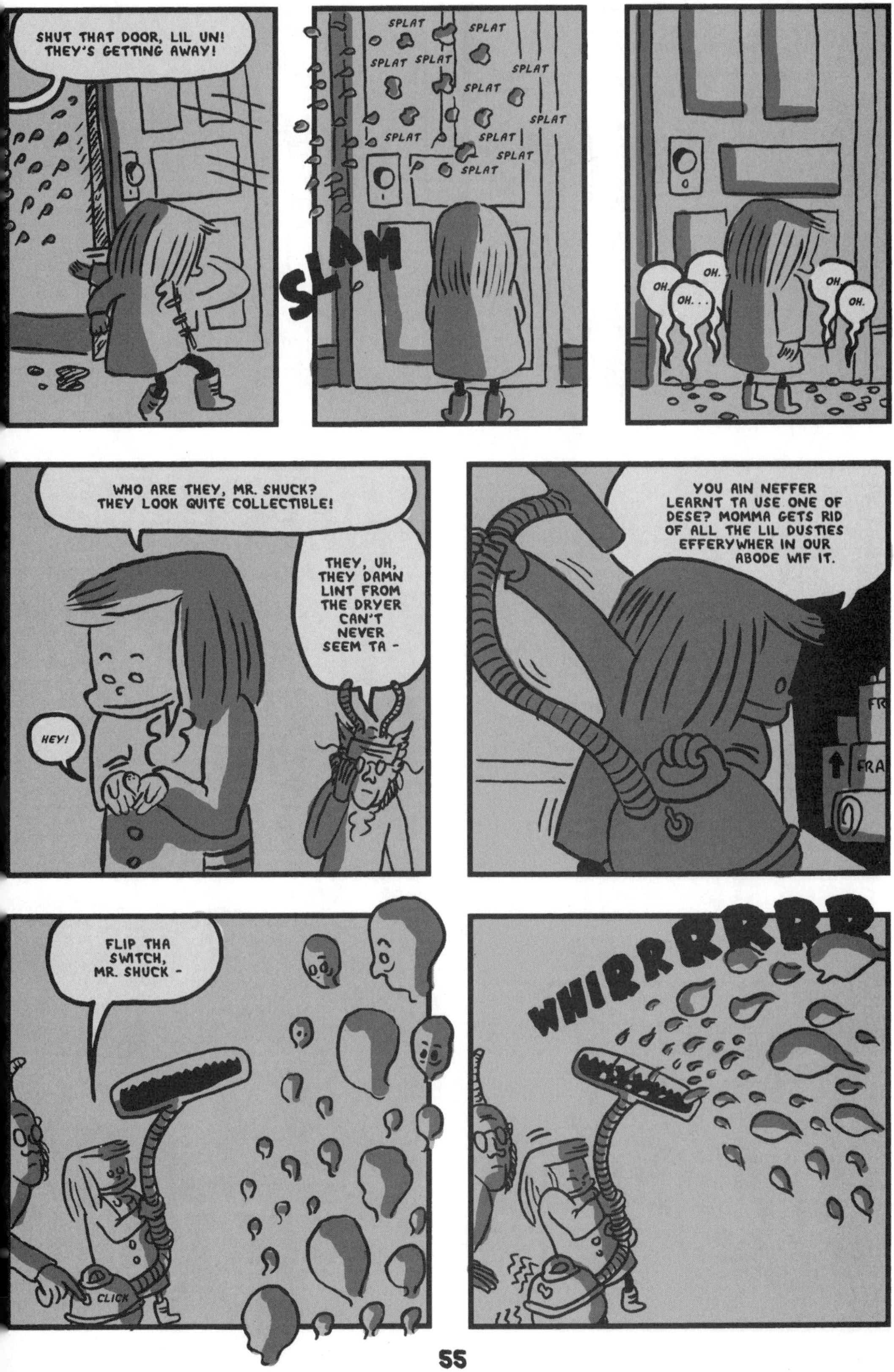

SHUT THAT DOOR, LIL UN! THEY'S GETTING AWAY!
SPLAT
SPLAT
SPLAT SPLAT
SPLAT
SPLAT
SPLAT
SPLAT
SPLAT
SPLAT
SPLAT
SLAM
OH.
OH.
OH...
OH.
OH.
WHO ARE THEY, MR. SHUCK? THEY LOOK QUITE COLLECTIBLE!
THEY, UH, THEY DAMN LINT FROM THE DRYER CAN'T NEVER SEEM TA -
HEY!
YOU AIN NEFFER LEARNT TA USE ONE OF DESE? MOMMA GETS RID OF ALL THE LIL DUSTIES EFFERYWHER IN OUR ABODE WIF IT.
FLIP THA SWITCH, MR. SHUCK -
CLICK
WHIRRRRRRR

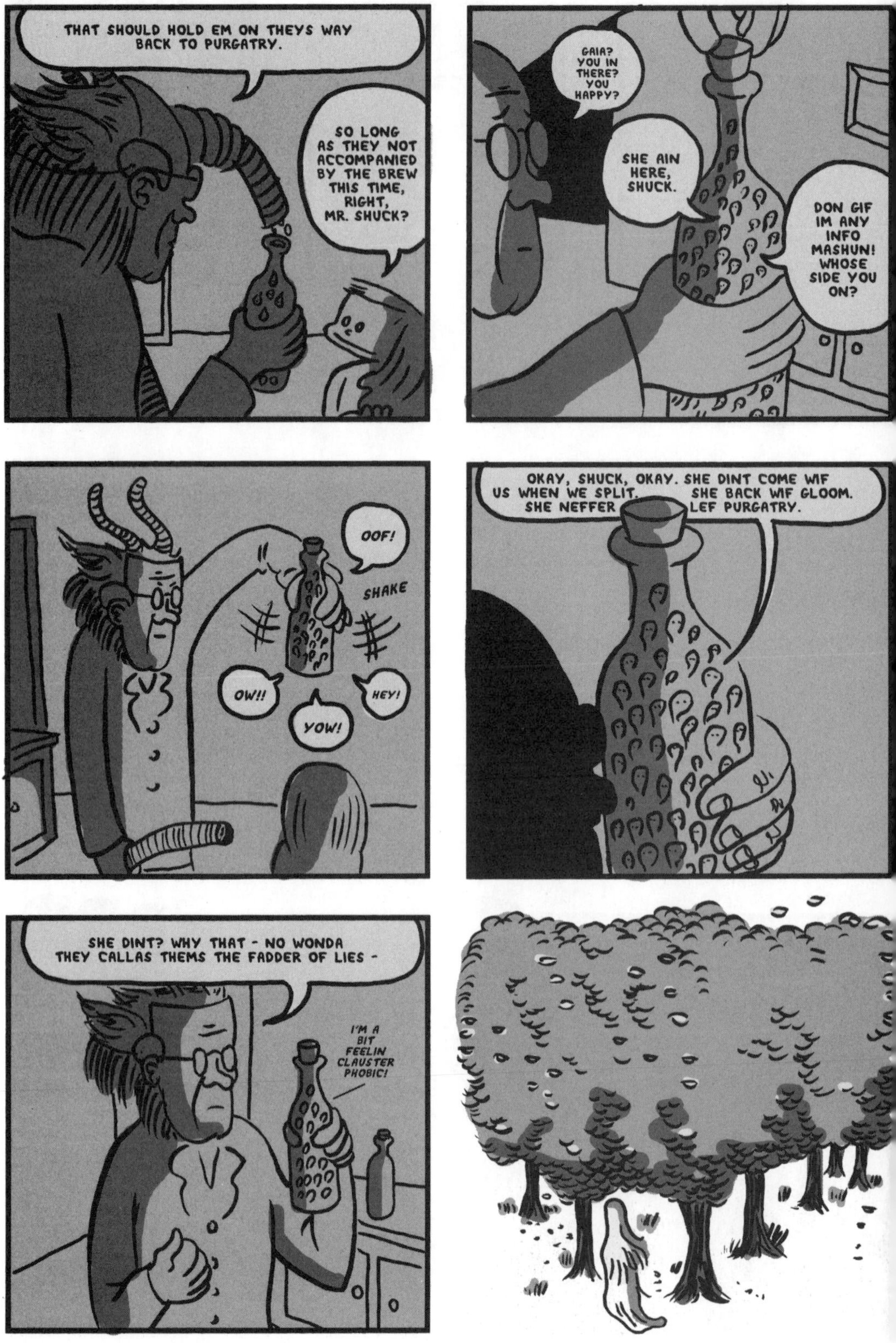
THAT SHOULD HOLD EM ON THEYS WAY BACK TO PURGATRY.
SO LONG AS THEY NOT ACCOMPANIED BY THE BREW THIS TIME, RIGHT, MR. SHUCK?
GAIA? YOU IN THERE? YOU HAPPY?
SHE AIN HERE, SHUCK.
DON GIF IM ANY INFO MASHUN! WHOSE SIDE YOU ON?
OOF!
SHAKE
OW!!
YOW!
HEY!
OKAY, SHUCK, OKAY. SHE DINT COME WIF US WHEN WE SPLIT. SHE NEFFER LEF PURGATRY. SHE BACK WIF GLOOM.
SHE DINT? WHY THAT - NO WONDA THEY CALLAS THEMS THE FADDER OF LIES -
I'M A BIT FEELIN CLAUSTER PHOBIC!

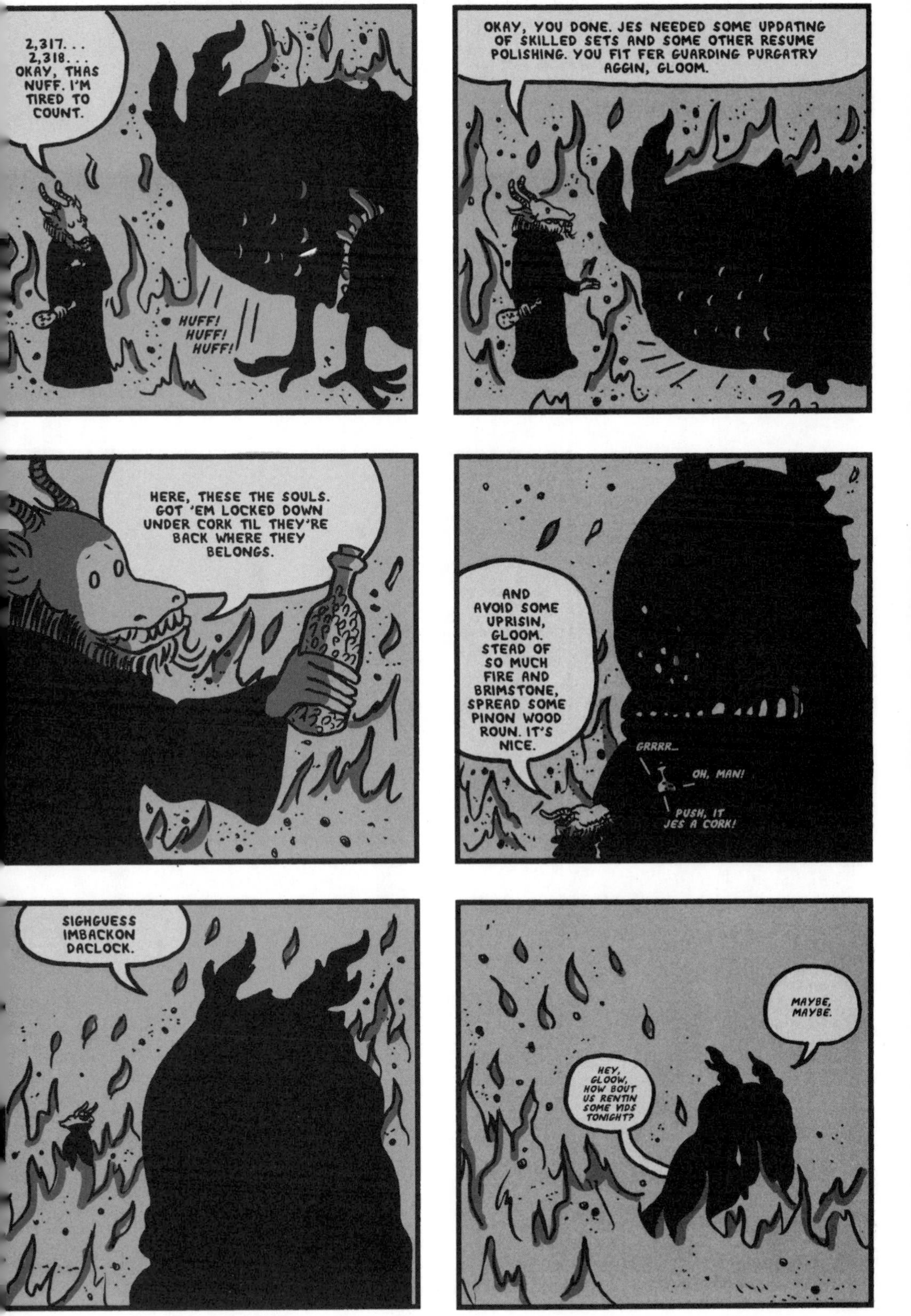
2,317. . . 2,318. . . OKAY, THAS NUFF. I'M TIRED TO COUNT.
HUFF! HUFF! HUFF!
OKAY, YOU DONE. JES NEEDED SOME UPDATING OF SKILLED SETS AND SOME OTHER RESUME POLISHING. YOU FIT FER GUARDING PURGATRY AGGIN, GLOOM.
HERE, THESE THE SOULS. GOT 'EM LOCKED DOWN UNDER CORK TIL THEY'RE BACK WHERE THEY BELONGS.
AND AVOID SOME UPRISIN, GLOOM. STEAD OF SO MUCH FIRE AND BRIMSTONE, SPREAD SOME PINON WOOD ROUN. IT'S NICE.
GRRRR...
OH, MAN!
PUSH, IT JES A CORK!
SIGHGUESS IMBACKON DACLOCK.
HEY, GLOOW, HOW BOUT US RENTIN SOME VIDS TONIGHT?
MAYBE, MAYBE.

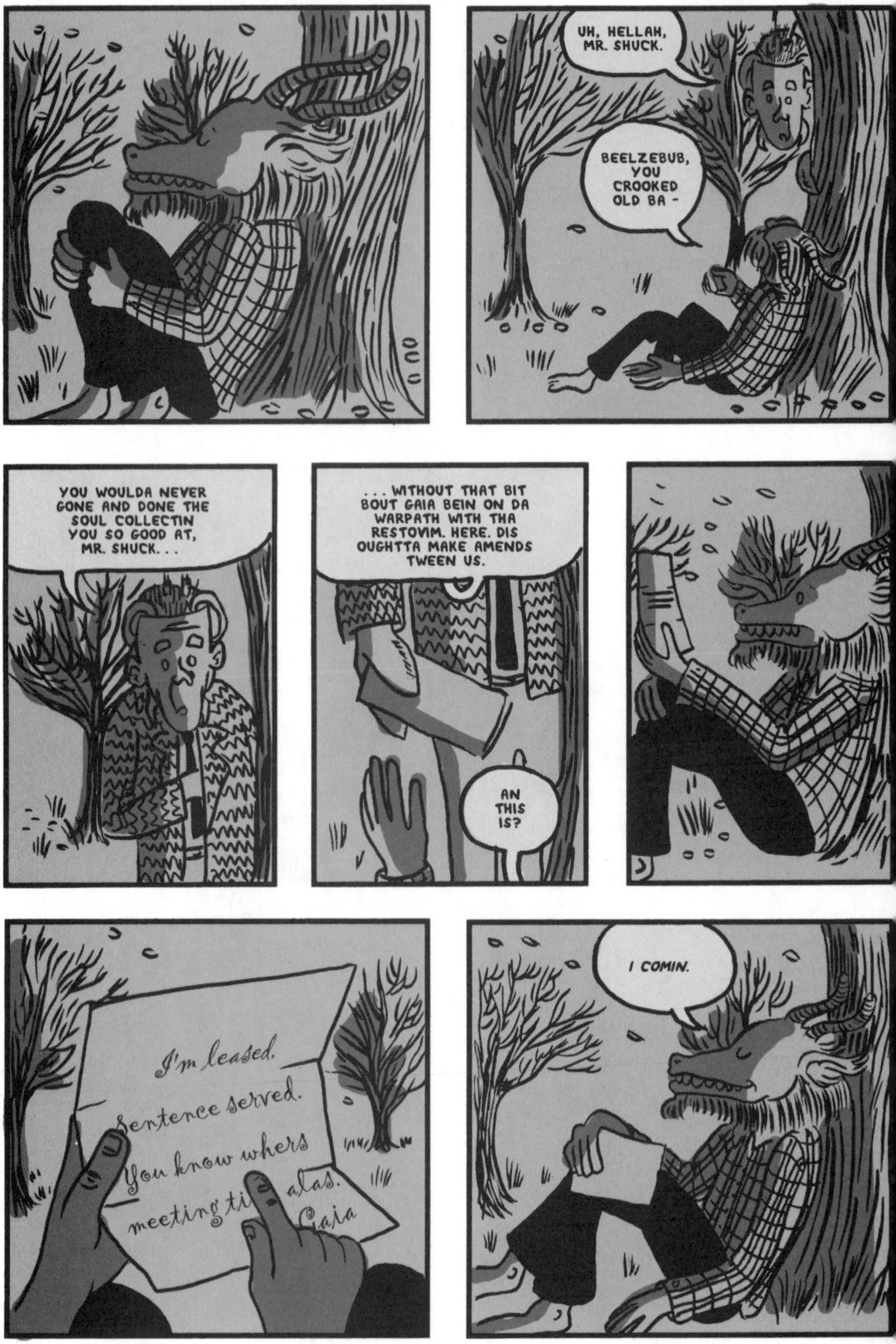
UH, HELLAH, MR. SHUCK.
BEELZEBUB, YOU CROOKED OLD BA -
YOU WOULDA NEVER GONE AND DONE THE SOUL COLLECTIN YOU SO GOOD AT, MR. SHUCK...
...WITHOUT THAT BIT BOUT GAIA BEIN ON DA WARPATH WITH THA RESTOVIM. HERE. DIS OUGHTTA MAKE AMENDS TWEEN US.
AN THIS IS?
I'm leased, sentence served. You know whers meeting ti alas. Gaia
I COMIN.

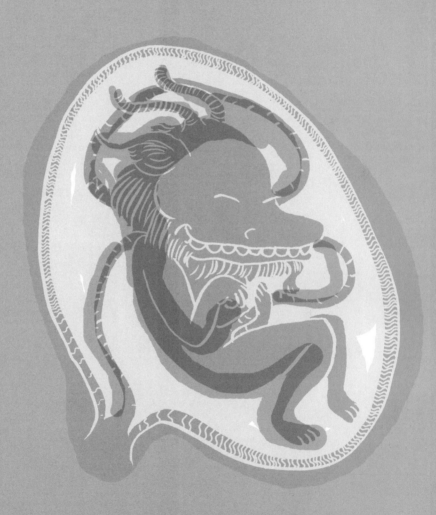

BIRTH OF THE SULFURSTAR

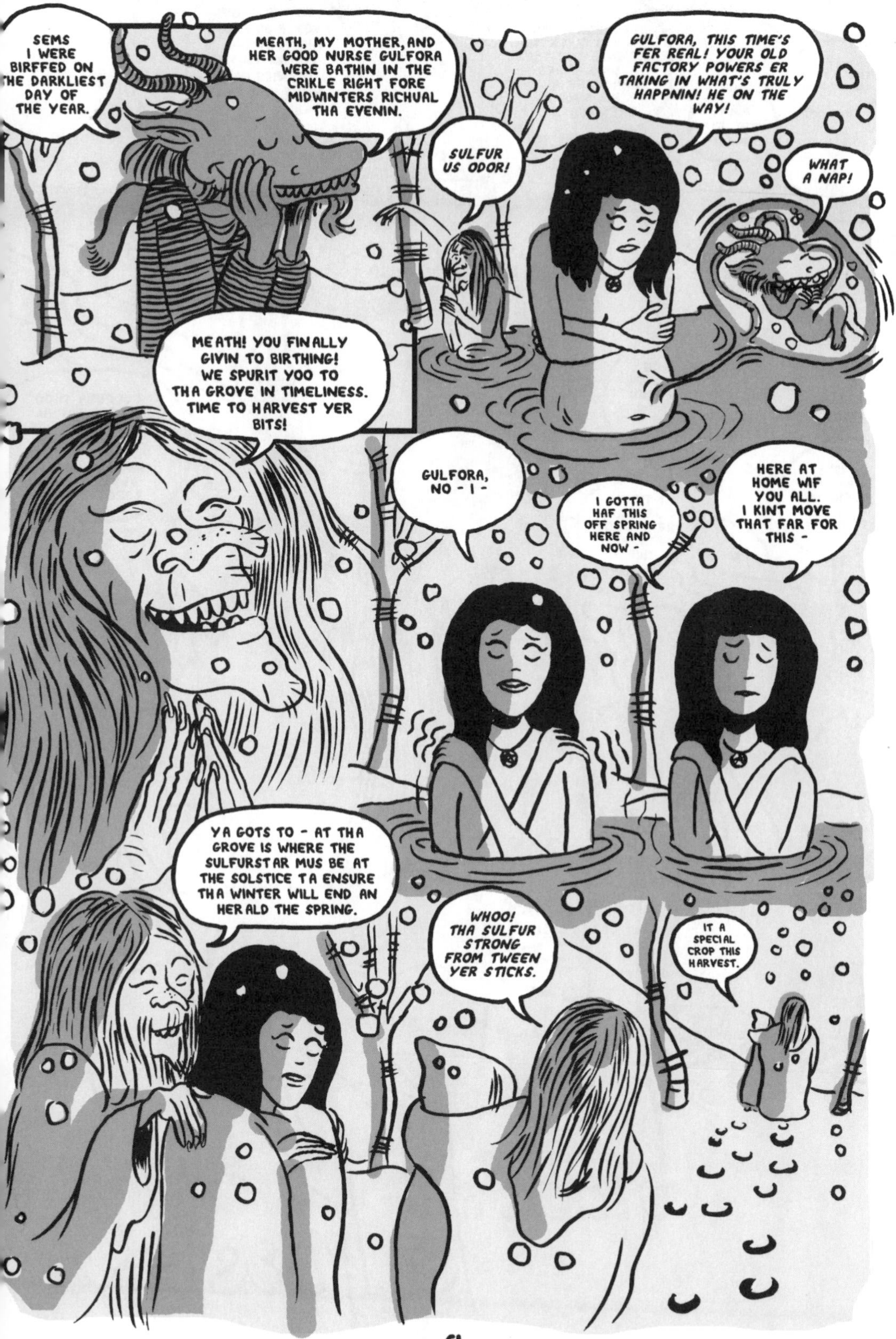
SEMS I WERE BIRFFED ON THE DARKLIEST DAY OF THE YEAR.
MEATH, MY MOTHER, AND HER GOOD NURSE GULFORA WERE BATHIN IN THE CRIKLE RIGHT FORE MIDWINTERS RICHUAL THA EVENIN.
SULFUR US ODOR!
GULFORA, THIS TIME'S FER REAL! YOUR OLD FACTORY POWERS ER TAKING IN WHAT'S TRULY HAPPNIN! HE ON THE WAY!
WHAT A NAP!
MEATH! YOU FINALLY GIVIN TO BIRTHING! WE SPURIT YOO TO THA GROVE IN TIMELINESS. TIME TO HARVEST YER BITS!
GULFORA, NO - I -
I GOTTA HAF THIS OFF SPRING HERE AND NOW -
HERE AT HOME WIF YOU ALL. I KINT MOVE THAT FAR FOR THIS -
YA GOTS TO - AT THA GROVE IS WHERE THE SULFURSTAR MUS BE AT THE SOLSTICE TA ENSURE THA WINTER WILL END AN HERALD THE SPRING.
WHOO! THA SULFUR STRONG FROM TWEEN YER STICKS.
IT A SPECIAL CROP THIS HARVEST.

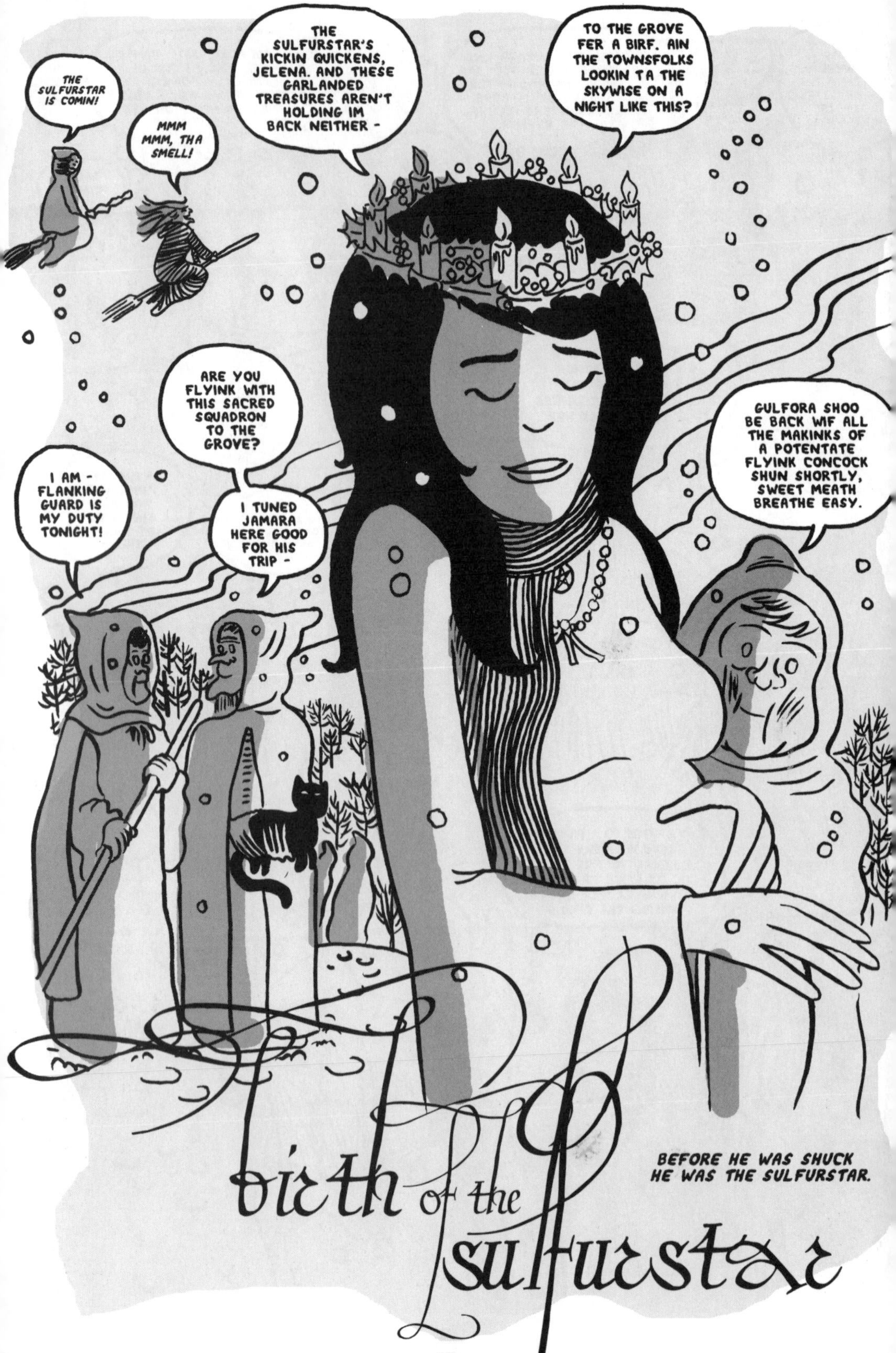
THE SULFURSTAR IS COMIN!
MMM MMM, THA SMELL!
THE SULFURSTAR'S KICKIN QUICKENS, JELENA. AND THESE GARLANDED TREASURES AREN'T HOLDING IM BACK NEITHER -
TO THE GROVE FER A BIRF. AIN THE TOWNSFOLKS LOOKIN TA THE SKYWISE ON A NIGHT LIKE THIS?
ARE YOU FLYINK WITH THIS SACRED SQUADRON TO THE GROVE?
I AM - FLANKING GUARD IS MY DUTY TONIGHT!
I TUNED JAMARA HERE GOOD FOR HIS TRIP -
GULFORA SHOO BE BACK WIF ALL THE MAKINKS OF A POTENTATE FLYINK CONCOCK SHUN SHORTLY, SWEET MEATH BREATHE EASY.
birth of the sulfurstar
BEFORE HE WAS SHUCK HE WAS THE SULFURSTAR.

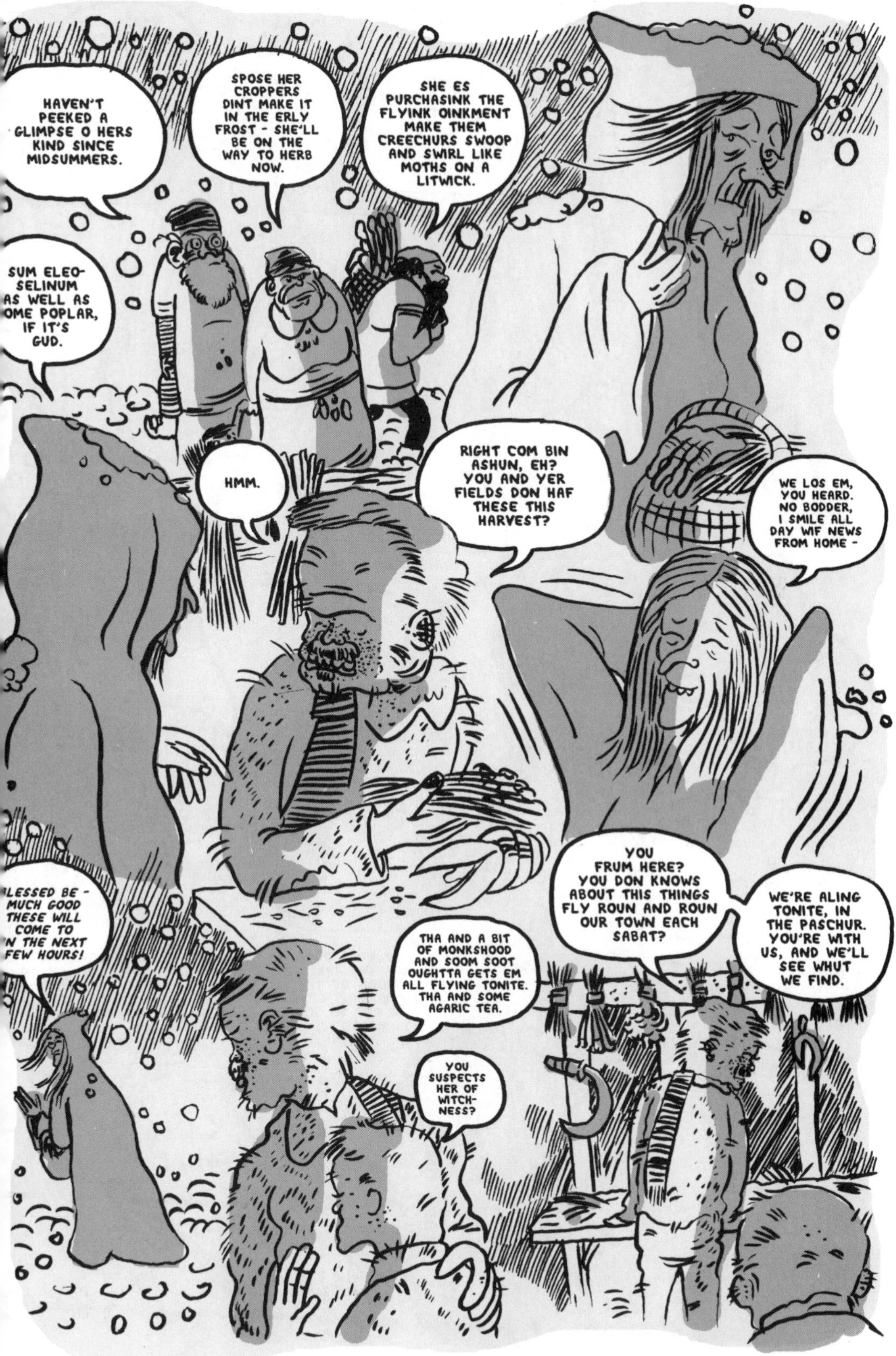

HAVEN'T PEEKED A GLIMPSE O HERS KIND SINCE MIDSUMMERS.
SPOSE HER CROPPERS DINT MAKE IT IN THE ERLY FROST - SHE'LL BE ON THE WAY TO HERB NOW.
SHE ES PURCHASINK THE FLYINK OINKMENT MAKE THEM CREECHURS SWOOP AND SWIRL LIKE MOTHS ON A LITWICK.
SUM ELEO-SELINUM AS WELL AS OME POPLAR, IF IT'S GUD.
HMM.
RIGHT COM BIN ASHUN, EH? YOU AND YER FIELDS DON HAF THESE THIS HARVEST?
WE LOS EM, YOU HEARD. NO BODDER, I SMILE ALL DAY WIF NEWS FROM HOME -
LESSED BE - MUCH GOOD THESE WILL COME TO N THE NEXT FEW HOURS!
THA AND A BIT OF MONKSHOOD AND SOOM SOOT OUGHTTA GETS EM ALL FLYING TONITE. THA AND SOME AGARIC TEA.
YOU FRUM HERE? YOU DON KNOWS ABOUT THIS THINGS FLY ROUN AND ROUN OUR TOWN EACH SABAT?
WE'RE ALING TONITE, IN THE PASCHUR. YOU'RE WITH US, AND WE'LL SEE WHUT WE FIND.
YOU SUSPECTS HER OF WITCH-NESS?

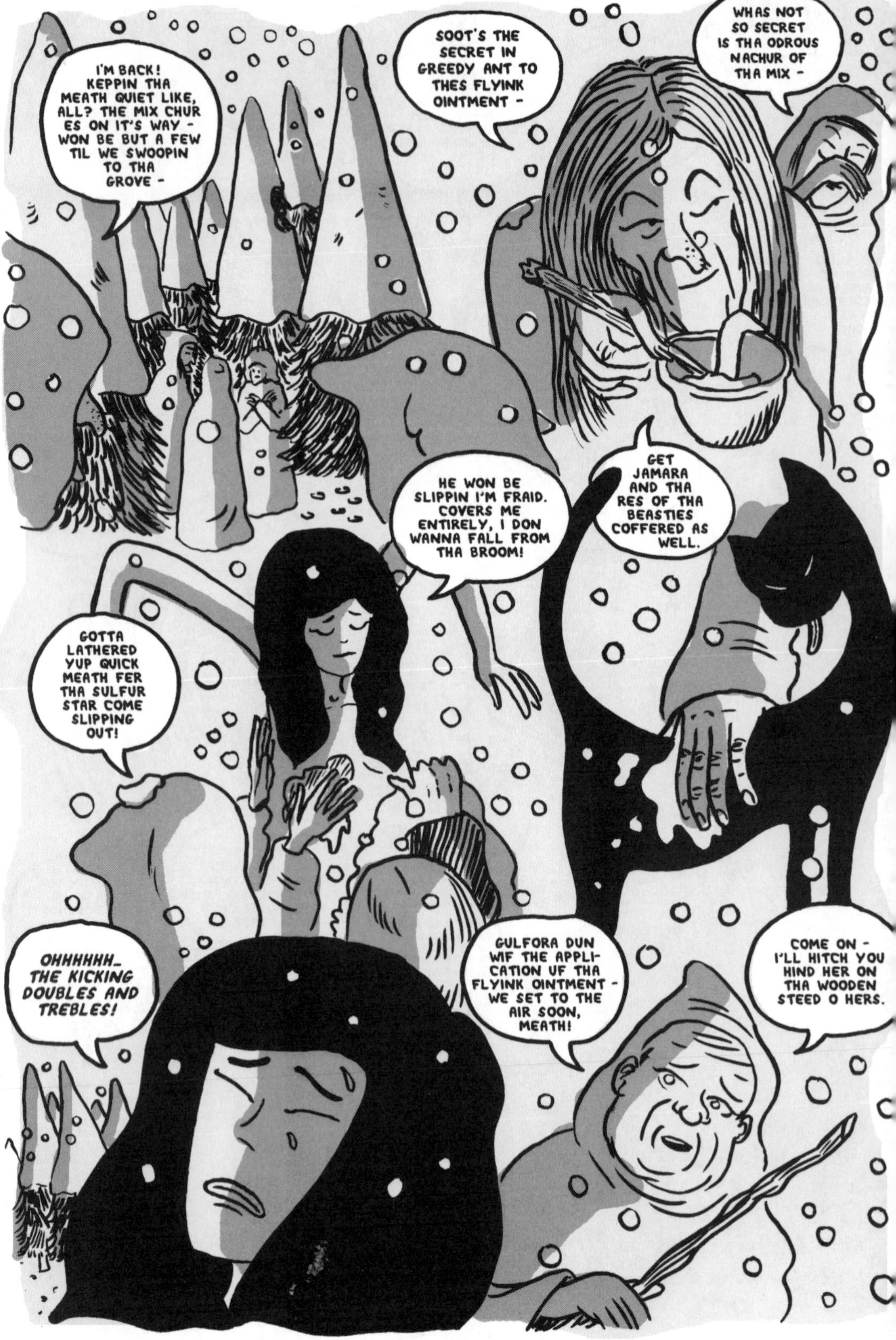
I'M BACK! KEPPIN THA MEATH QUIET LIKE, ALL? THE MIX CHURES ON IT'S WAY - WON BE BUT A FEW TIL WE SWOOPIN TO THA GROVE -
SOOT'S THE SECRET IN GREEDY ANT TO THES FLYINK OINTMENT -
WHAS NOT SO SECRET IS THA ODROUS NACHUR OF THA MIX -
HE WON BE SLIPPIN I'M FRAID. COVERS ME ENTIRELY, I DON WANNA FALL FROM THA BROOM!
GET JAMARA AND THA RES OF THA BEASTIES COFFERED AS WELL.
GOTTA LATHERED YUP QUICK MEATH FER THA SULFUR STAR COME SLIPPING OUT!
OHHHHHH_ THE KICKING DOUBLES AND TREBLES!
GULFORA DUN WIF THE APPLICATION UF THA FLYINK OINTMENT - WE SET TO THE AIR SOON, MEATH!
COME ON - I'LL HITCH YOU HIND HER ON THA WOODEN STEED O HERS.

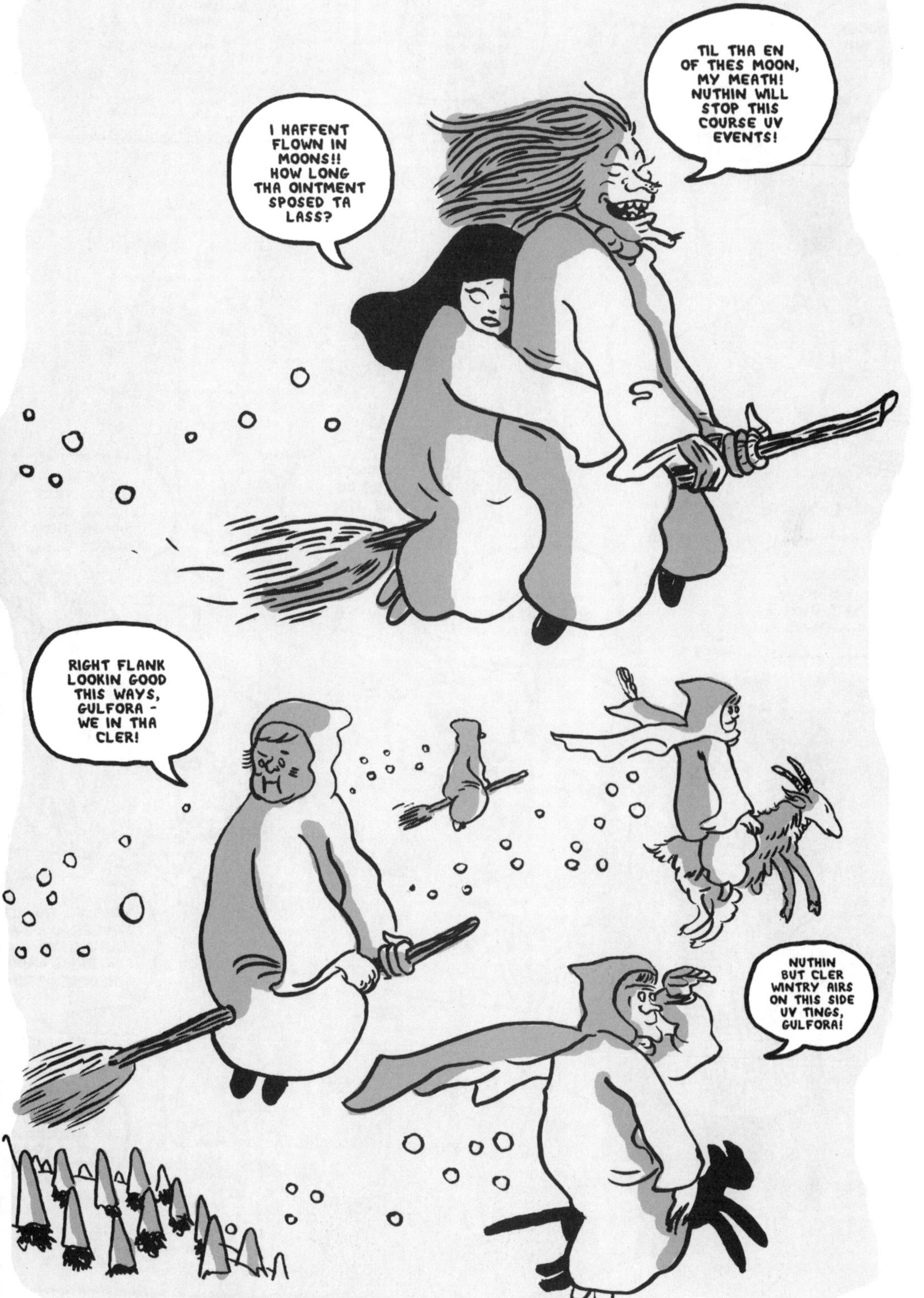
I HAFFENT FLOWN IN MOONS!! HOW LONG THA OINTMENT SPOSED TA LASS?
TIL THA EN OF THES MOON, MY MEATH! NUTHIN WILL STOP THIS COURSE UV EVENTS!
RIGHT FLANK LOOKIN GOOD THIS WAYS, GULFORA - WE IN THA CLER!
NUTHIN BUT CLER WINTRY AIRS ON THIS SIDE UV TINGS, GULFORA!

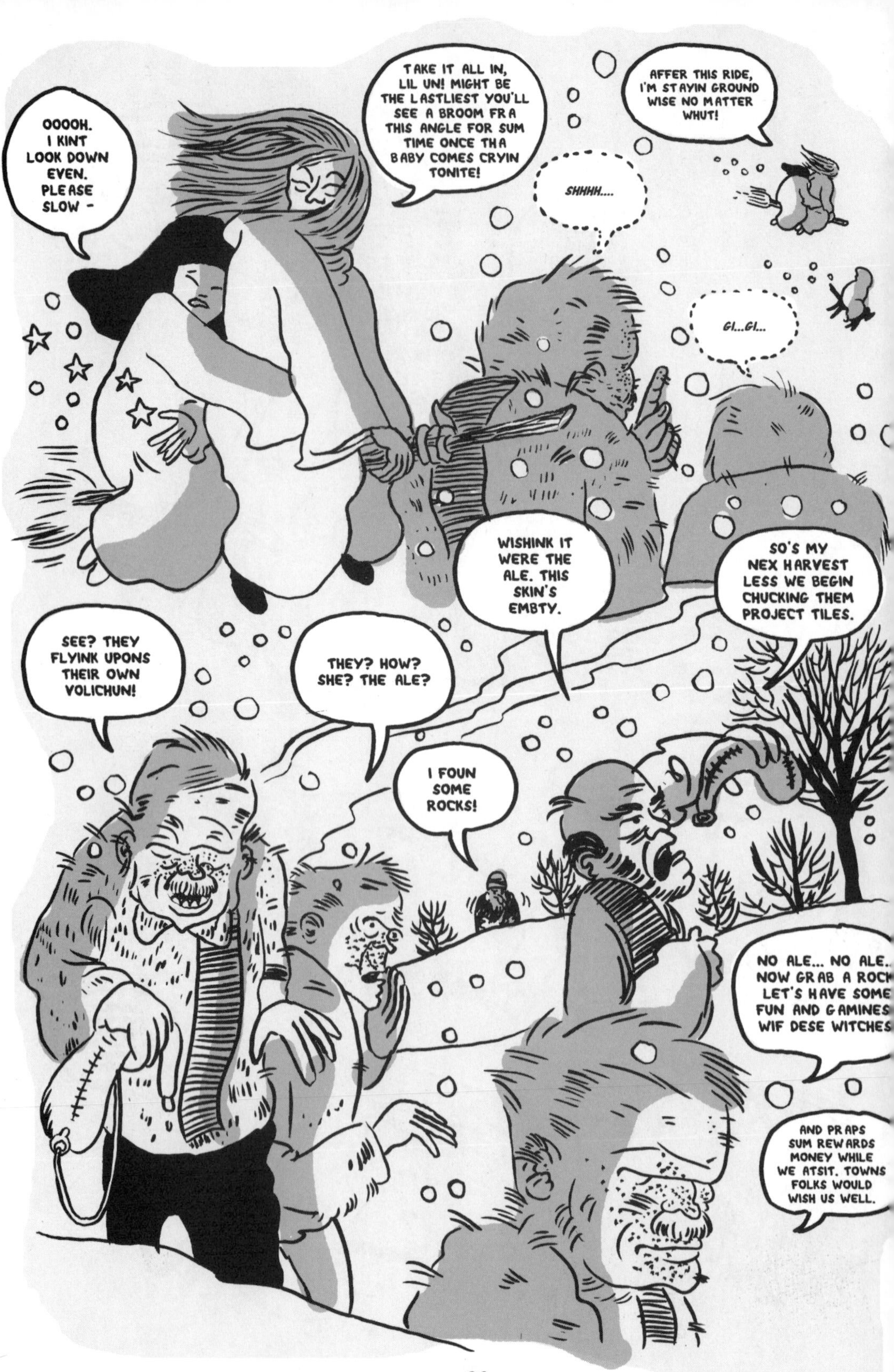
OOOOH. I KINT LOOK DOWN EVEN. PLEASE SLOW -
TAKE IT ALL IN, LIL UN! MIGHT BE THE LASTLIEST YOU'LL SEE A BROOM FRA THIS ANGLE FOR SUM TIME ONCE THA BABY COMES CRYIN TONITE!
SHHHH....
AFFER THIS RIDE, I'M STAYIN GROUND WISE NO MATTER WHUT!
GI...GI...
WISHINK IT WERE THE ALE. THIS SKIN'S EMBTY.
SO'S MY NEX HARVEST LESS WE BEGIN CHUCKING THEM PROJECT TILES.
SEE? THEY FLYINK UPONS THEIR OWN VOLICHUN!
THEY? HOW? SHE? THE ALE?
I FOUN SOME ROCKS!
NO ALE... NO ALE.. NOW GRAB A ROCK LET'S HAVE SOME FUN AND GAMINES WIF DESE WITCHES
AND PRAPS SUM REWARDS MONEY WHILE WE ATSIT. TOWNS FOLKS WOULD WISH US WELL.

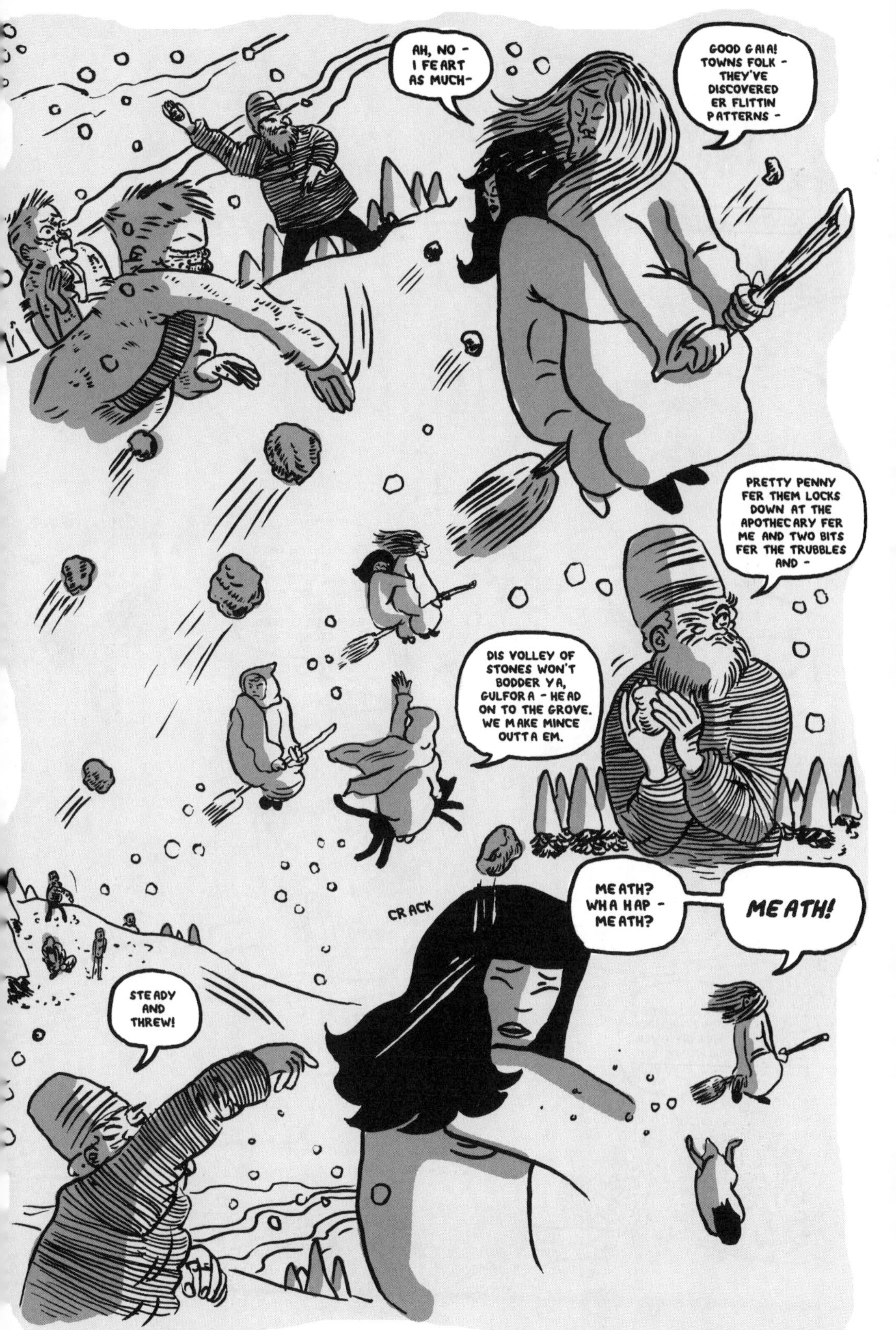
AH, NO - I FEART AS MUCH-
GOOD GAIA! TOWNS FOLK - THEY'VE DISCOVERED ER FLITTIN PATTERNS -
PRETTY PENNY FER THEM LOCKS DOWN AT THE APOTHECARY FER ME AND TWO BITS FER THE TRUBBLES AND -
DIS VOLLEY OF STONES WON'T BODDER YA, GULFORA - HEAD ON TO THE GROVE. WE MAKE MINCE OUTTA EM.
CRACK
MEATH? WHA HAP - MEATH?
MEATH!
STEADY AND THREW!

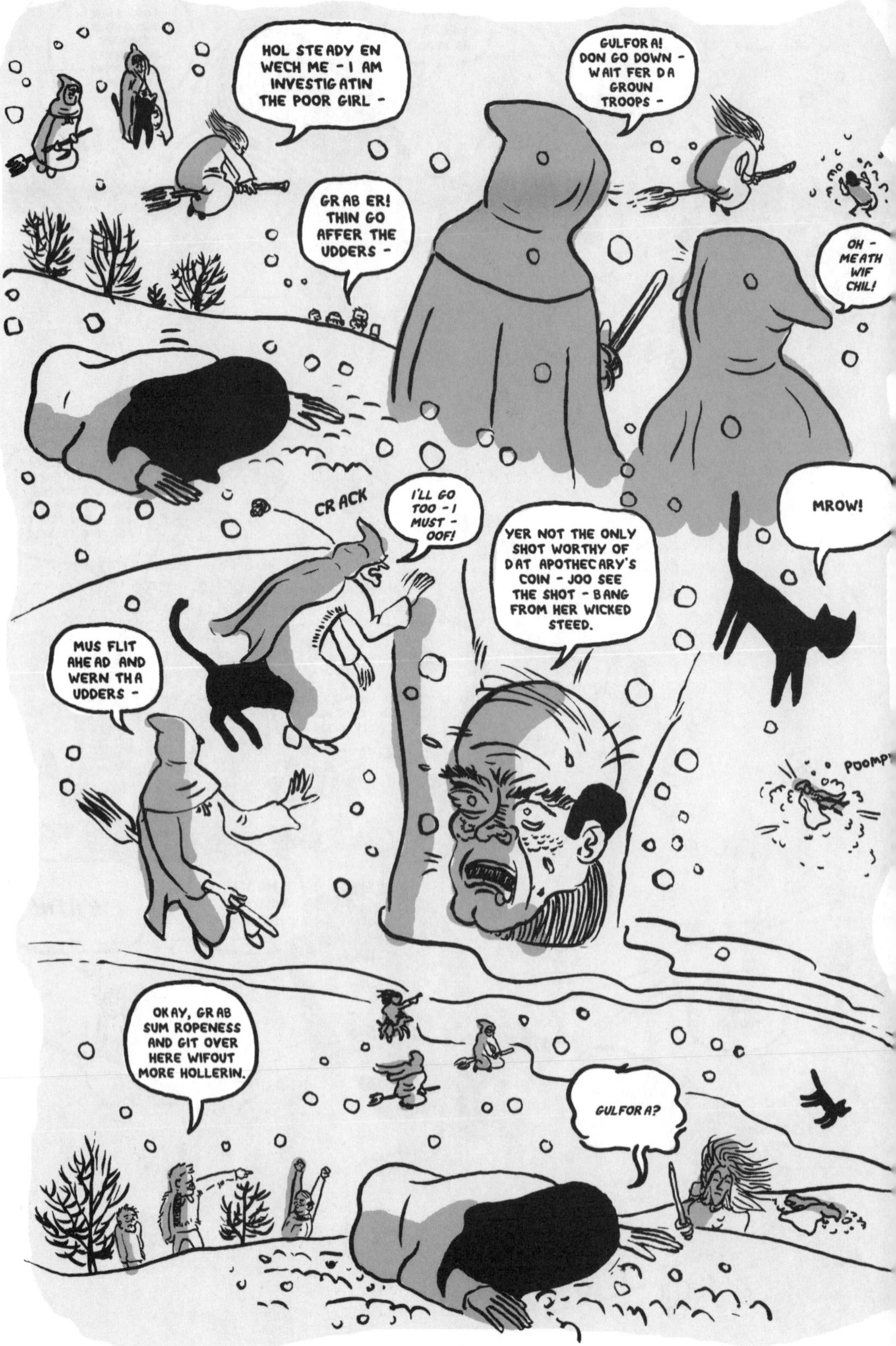
HOL STEADY EN WECH ME - I AM INVESTIGATIN THE POOR GIRL -
GRAB ER! THIN GO AFFER THE UDDERS -
GULFORA! DON GO DOWN - WAIT FER DA GROUN TROOPS -
OH - MEATH WIF CHIL!
CRACK
I'LL GO TOO - I MUST - OOF!
YER NOT THE ONLY SHOT WORTHY OF DAT APOTHECARY'S COIN - JOO SEE THE SHOT - BANG FROM HER WICKED STEED.
MROW!
MUS FLIT AHEAD AND WERN THA UDDERS -
POOMP
OKAY, GRAB SUM ROPENESS AND GIT OVER HERE WIFOUT MORE HOLLERIN.
GULFORA?

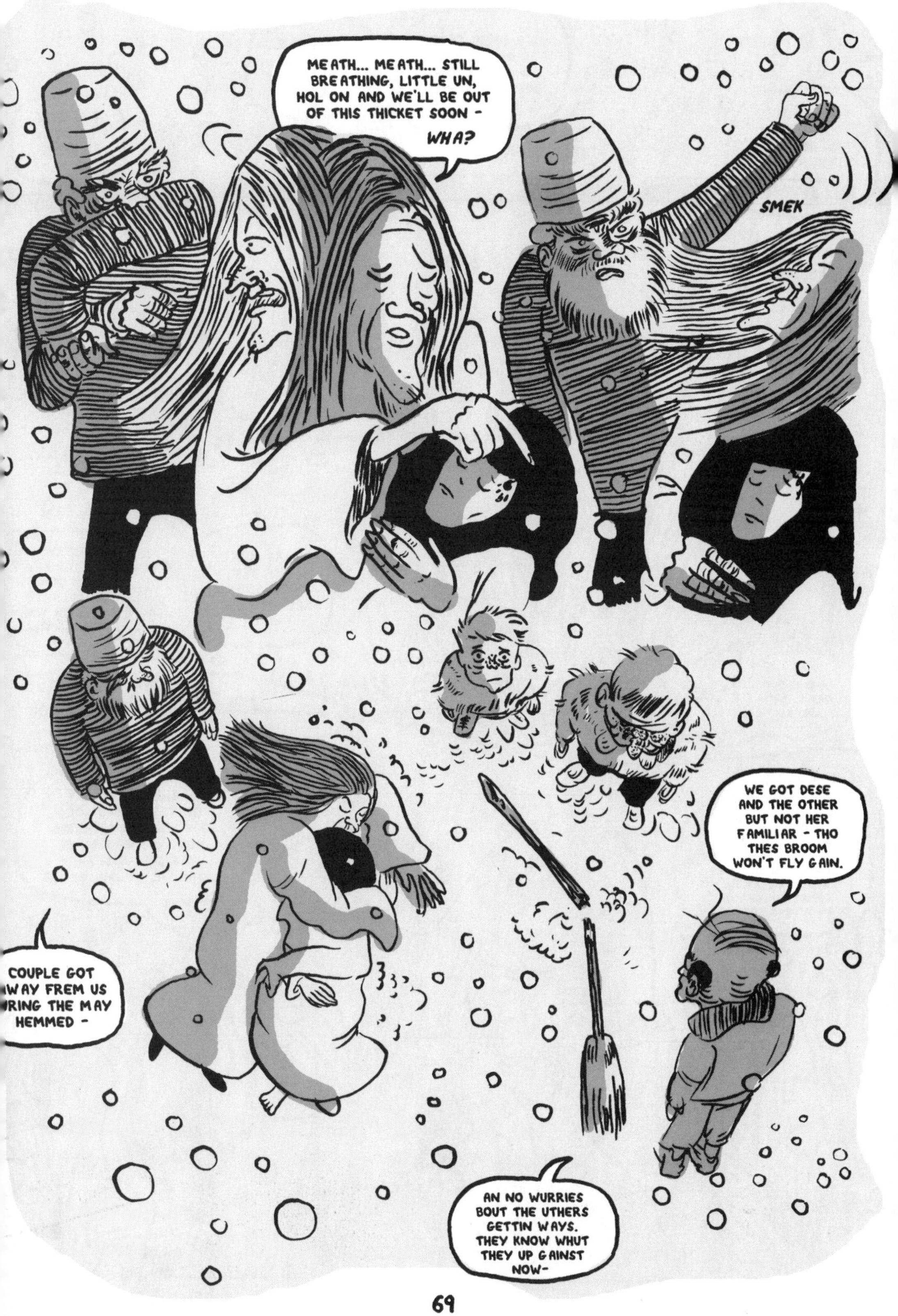
MEATH... MEATH... STILL BREATHING, LITTLE UN, HOL ON AND WE'LL BE OUT OF THIS THICKET SOON - WHA?
SMEK
WE GOT DESE AND THE OTHER BUT NOT HER FAMILIAR - THO THES BROOM WON'T FLY GAIN.
COUPLE GOT WAY FREM US RING THE MAY HEMMED -
AN NO WURRIES BOUT THE UTHERS GETTIN WAYS. THEY KNOW WHUT THEY UP GAINST NOW-

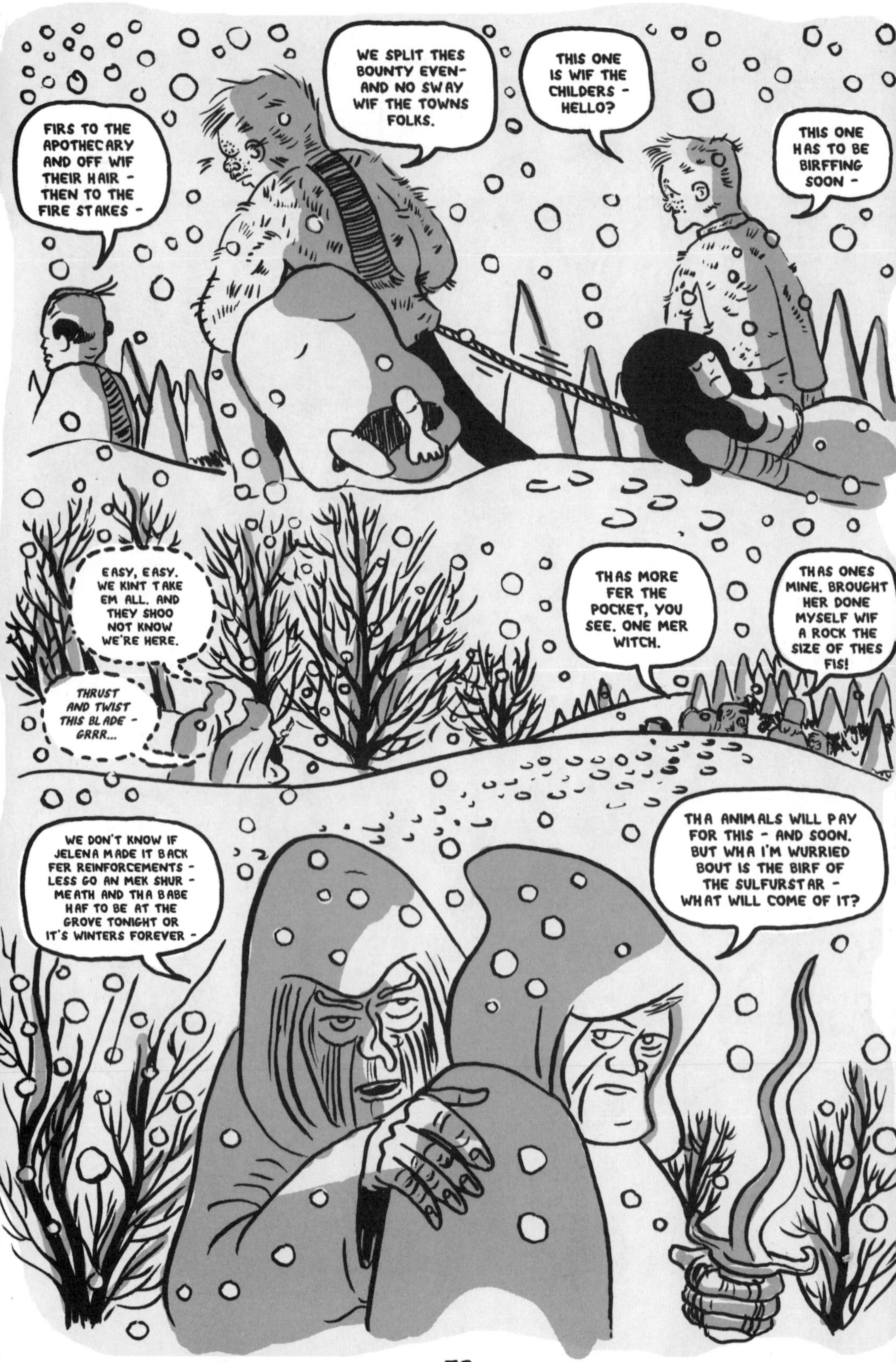
FIRS TO THE APOTHECARY AND OFF WIF THEIR HAIR - THEN TO THE FIRE STAKES -
WE SPLIT THES BOUNTY EVEN- AND NO SWAY WIF THE TOWNS FOLKS.
THIS ONE IS WIF THE CHILDERS - HELLO?
THIS ONE HAS TO BE BIRFFING SOON -
EASY, EASY. WE KINT TAKE EM ALL. AND THEY SHOO NOT KNOW WE'RE HERE.
THRUST AND TWIST THIS BLADE - GRRR...
THAS MORE FER THE POCKET, YOU SEE. ONE MER WITCH.
THAS ONES MINE. BROUGHT HER DONE MYSELF WIF A ROCK THE SIZE OF THES FIS!
WE DON'T KNOW IF JELENA MADE IT BACK FER REINFORCEMENTS - LESS GO AN MEK SHUR - MEATH AND THA BABE HAF TO BE AT THE GROVE TONIGHT OR IT'S WINTERS FOREVER -
THA ANIMALS WILL PAY FOR THIS - AND SOON. BUT WHA I'M WURRIED BOUT IS THE BIRF OF THE SULFURSTAR - WHAT WILL COME OF IT?

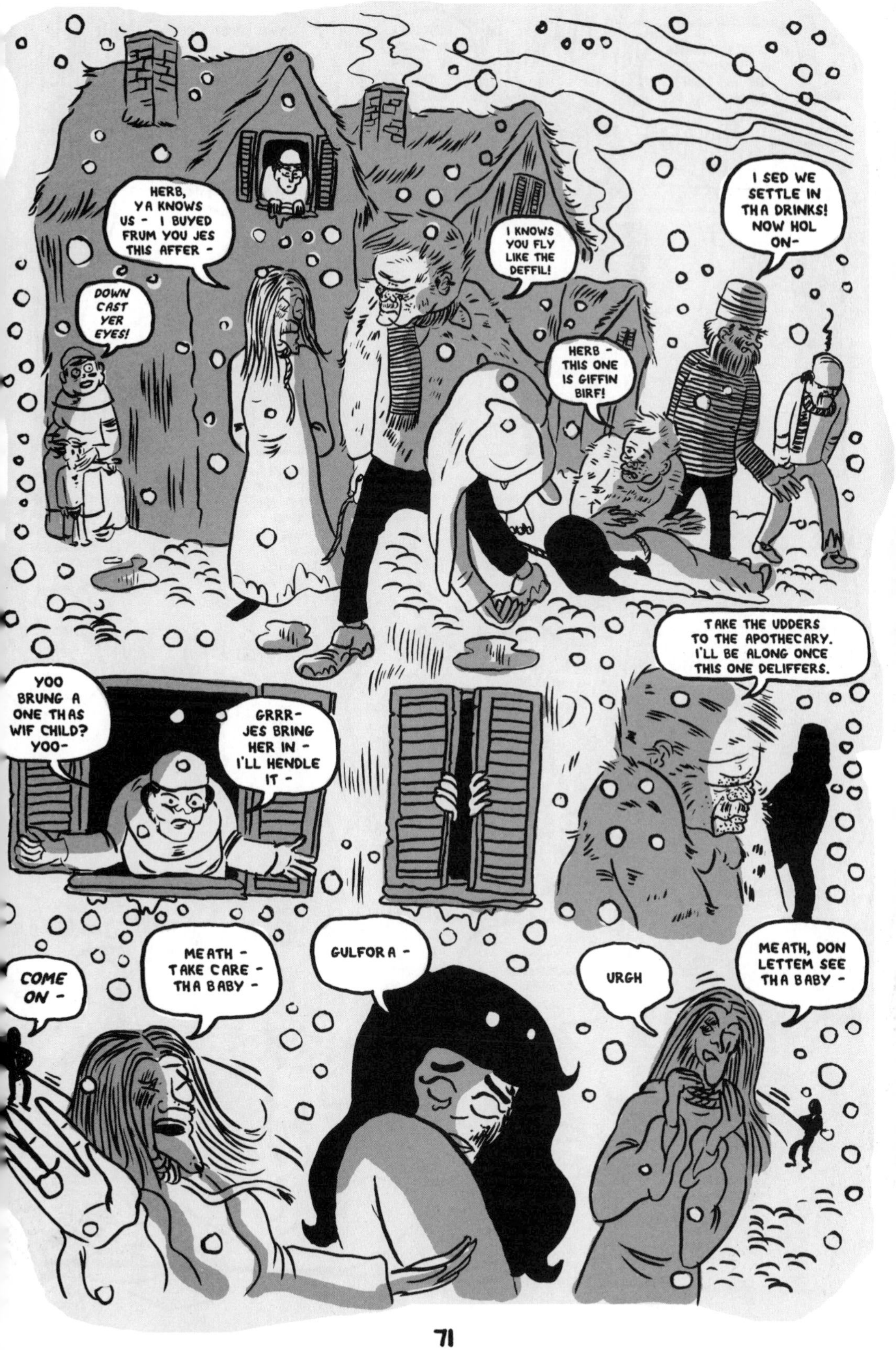
HERB, YA KNOWS US - I BUYED FRUM YOU JES THIS AFFER -
DOWN CAST YER EYES!
I KNOWS YOU FLY LIKE THE DEFFIL!
I SED WE SETTLE IN THA DRINKS! NOW HOL ON-
HERB - THIS ONE IS GIFFIN BIRF!
TAKE THE UDDERS TO THE APOTHECARY. I'LL BE ALONG ONCE THIS ONE DELIFFERS.
YOO BRUNG A ONE THAS WIF CHILD? YOO-
GRRR- JES BRING HER IN - I'LL HENDLE IT -
COME ON -
MEATH - TAKE CARE - THA BABY -
GULFORA -
URGH
MEATH, DON LETTEM SEE THA BABY -

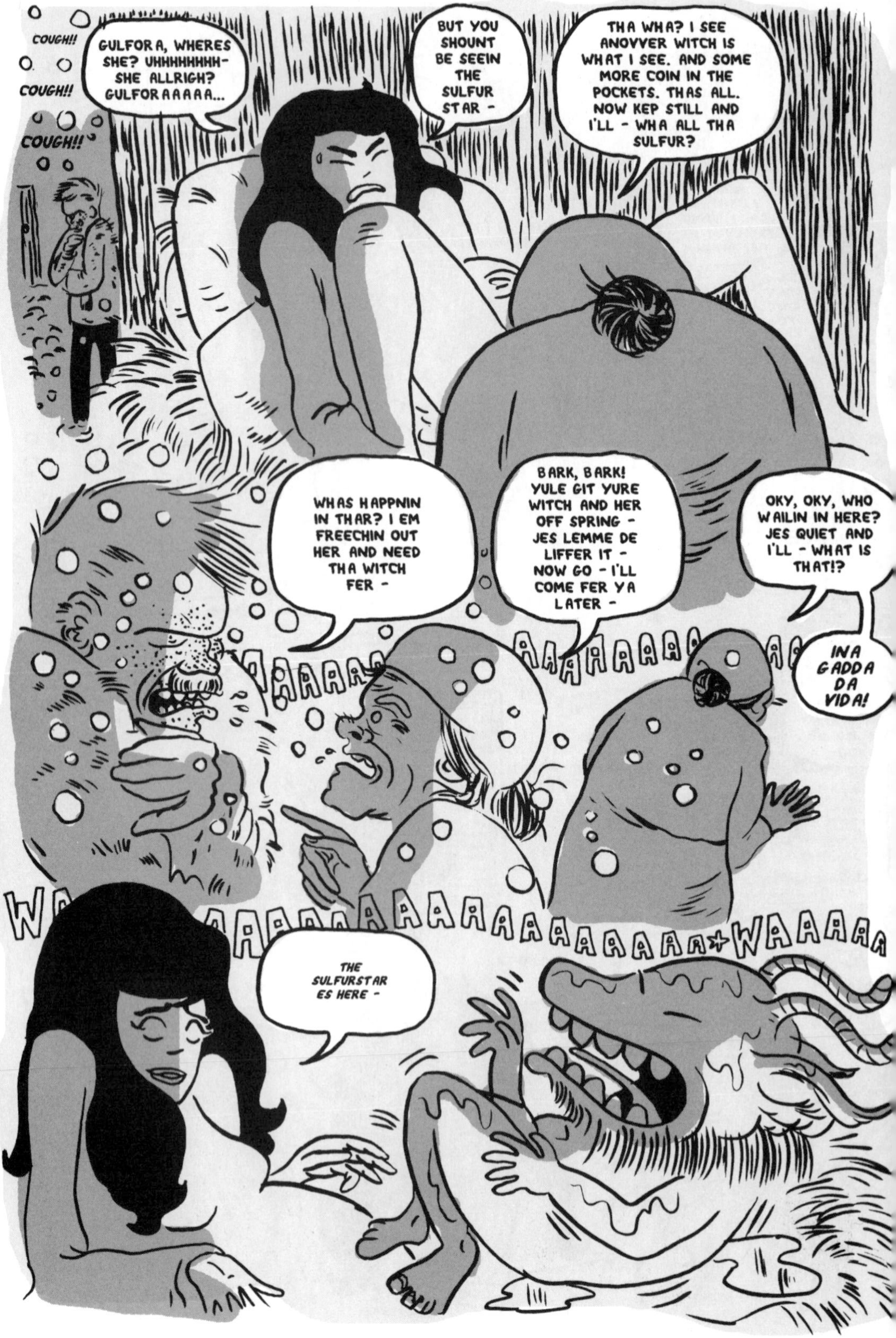
COUGH!!
COUGH!!
COUGH!!
GULFORA, WHERES SHE? UHHHHHHHH- SHE ALLRIGH? GULFORAAAAA...
BUT YOU SHOUNT BE SEEIN THE SULFUR STAR -
THA WHA? I SEE ANOVVER WITCH IS WHAT I SEE. AND SOME MORE COIN IN THE POCKETS. THAS ALL. NOW KEP STILL AND I'LL - WHA ALL THA SULFUR?
WHAS HAPPNIN IN THAR? I EM FREECHIN OUT HER AND NEED THA WITCH FER -
BARK, BARK! YULE GIT YURE WITCH AND HER OFF SPRING - JES LEMME DE LIFFER IT - NOW GO - I'LL COME FER YA LATER -
OKY, OKY, WHO WAILIN IN HERE? JES QUIET AND I'LL - WHAT IS THAT!?
INA GADDA DA VIDA!
WAAAAAAAAAAAAAAAAAAAAAAA
THE SULFURSTAR ES HERE -

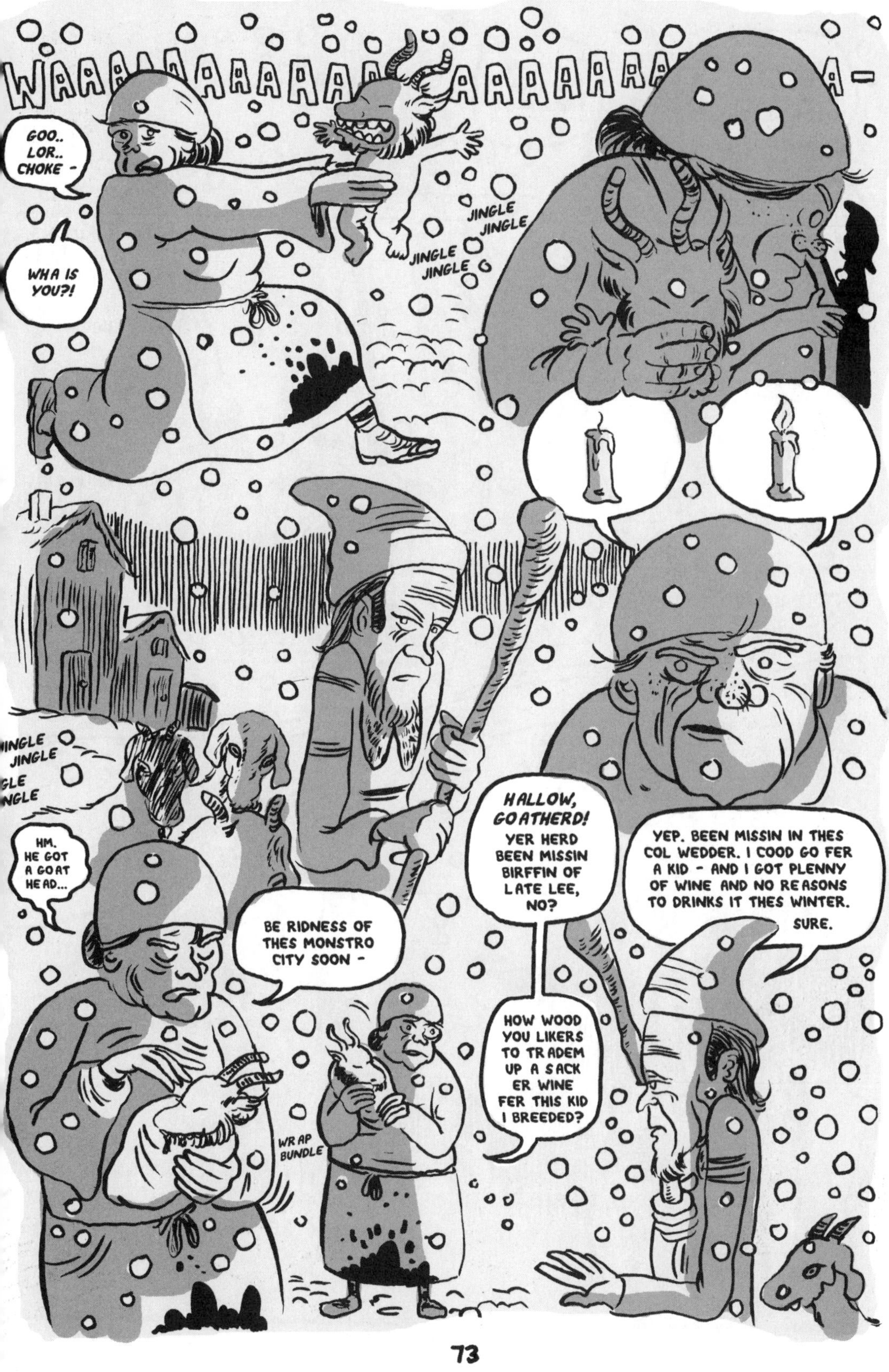

WAAAAAAAAAAAAAAAAAAAAAAAA-
GOO.. LOR.. CHOKE -
WHA IS YOU?!
JINGLE JINGLE
JINGLE JINGLE
JINGLE JINGLE
HM. HE GOT A GOAT HEAD...
BE RIDNESS OF THES MONSTRO CITY SOON -
HALLOW, GOATHERD!
YER HERD BEEN MISSIN BIRFFIN OF LATE LEE, NO?
HOW WOOD YOU LIKERS TO TRADEM UP A SACK ER WINE FER THIS KID I BREEDED?
YEP. BEEN MISSIN IN THES COL WEDDER. I COOD GO FER A KID - AND I GOT PLENNY OF WINE AND NO REASONS TO DRINKS IT THES WINTER.
SURE.
WRAP BUNDLE

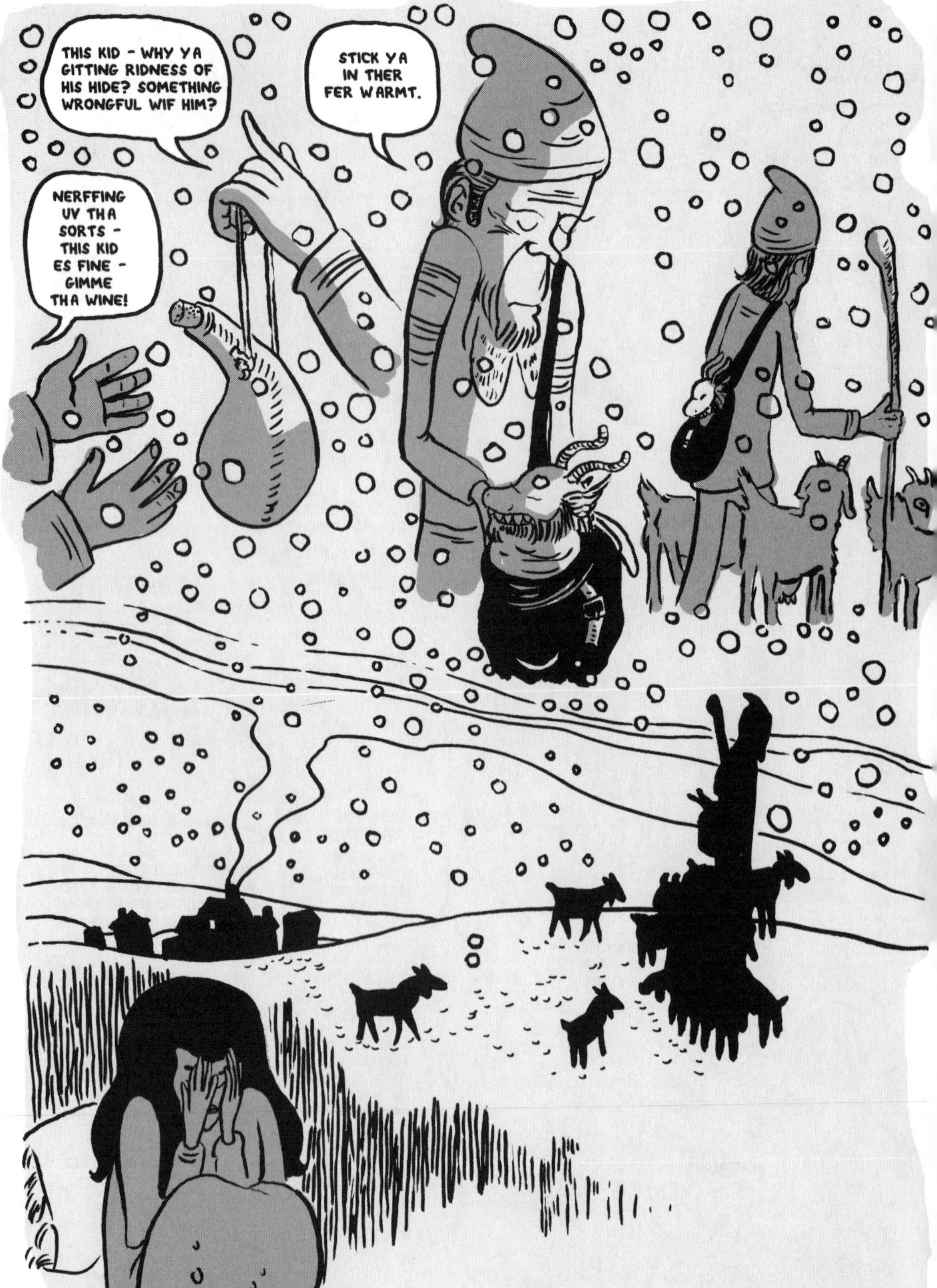
THIS KID - WHY YA GITTING RIDNESS OF HIS HIDE? SOMETHING WRONGFUL WIF HIM?
STICK YA IN THER FER WARMT.
NERFFING UV THA SORTS - THIS KID ES FINE - GIMME THA WINE!

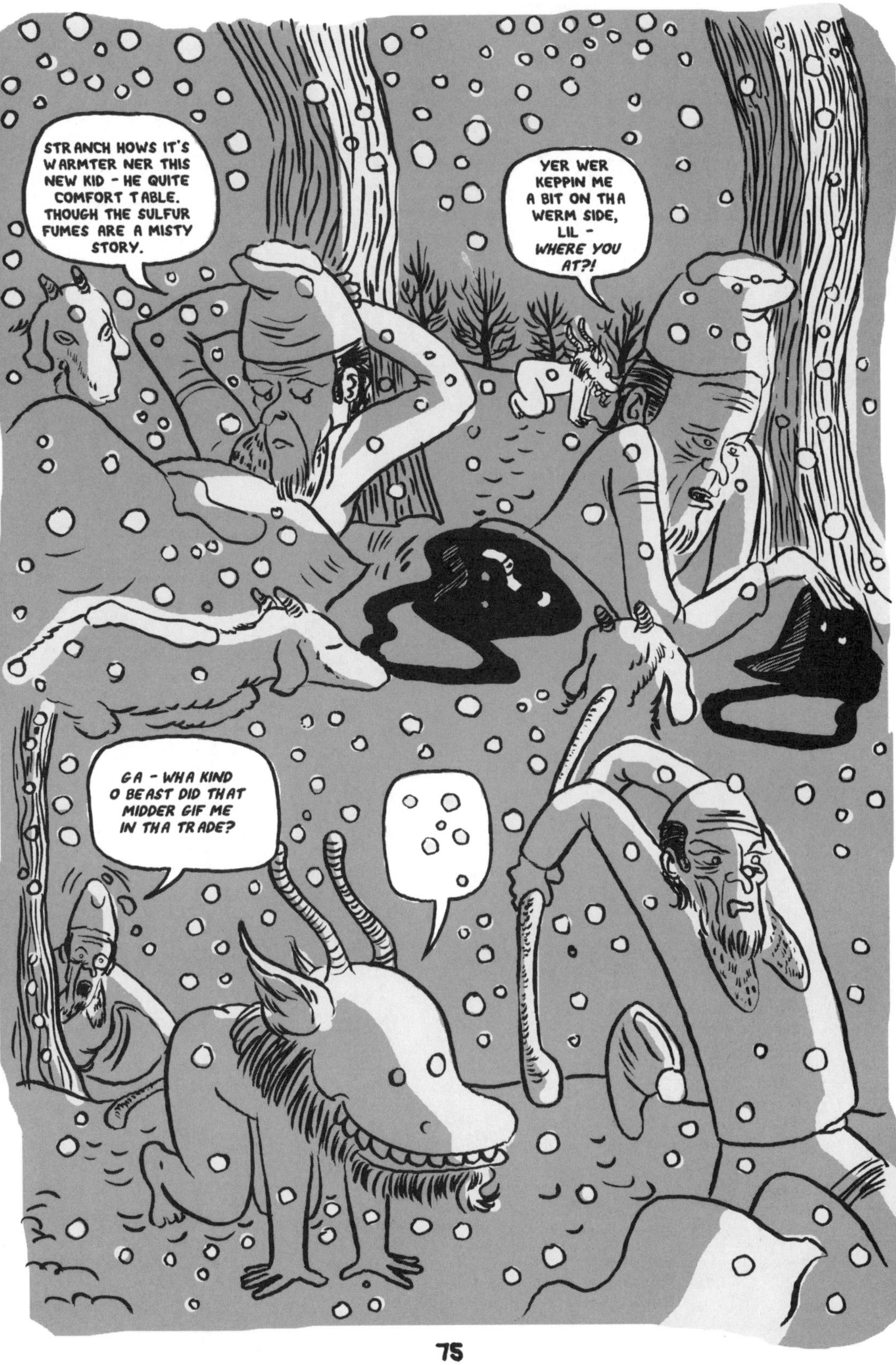
STRANCH HOWS IT'S WARMTER NER THIS NEW KID - HE QUITE COMFORT TABLE. THOUGH THE SULFUR FUMES ARE A MISTY STORY.
YER WER KEPPIN ME A BIT ON THA WERM SIDE, LIL - *WHERE YOU AT?!*
GA - WHA KIND O BEAST DID THAT MIDDER GIF ME IN THA TRADE?

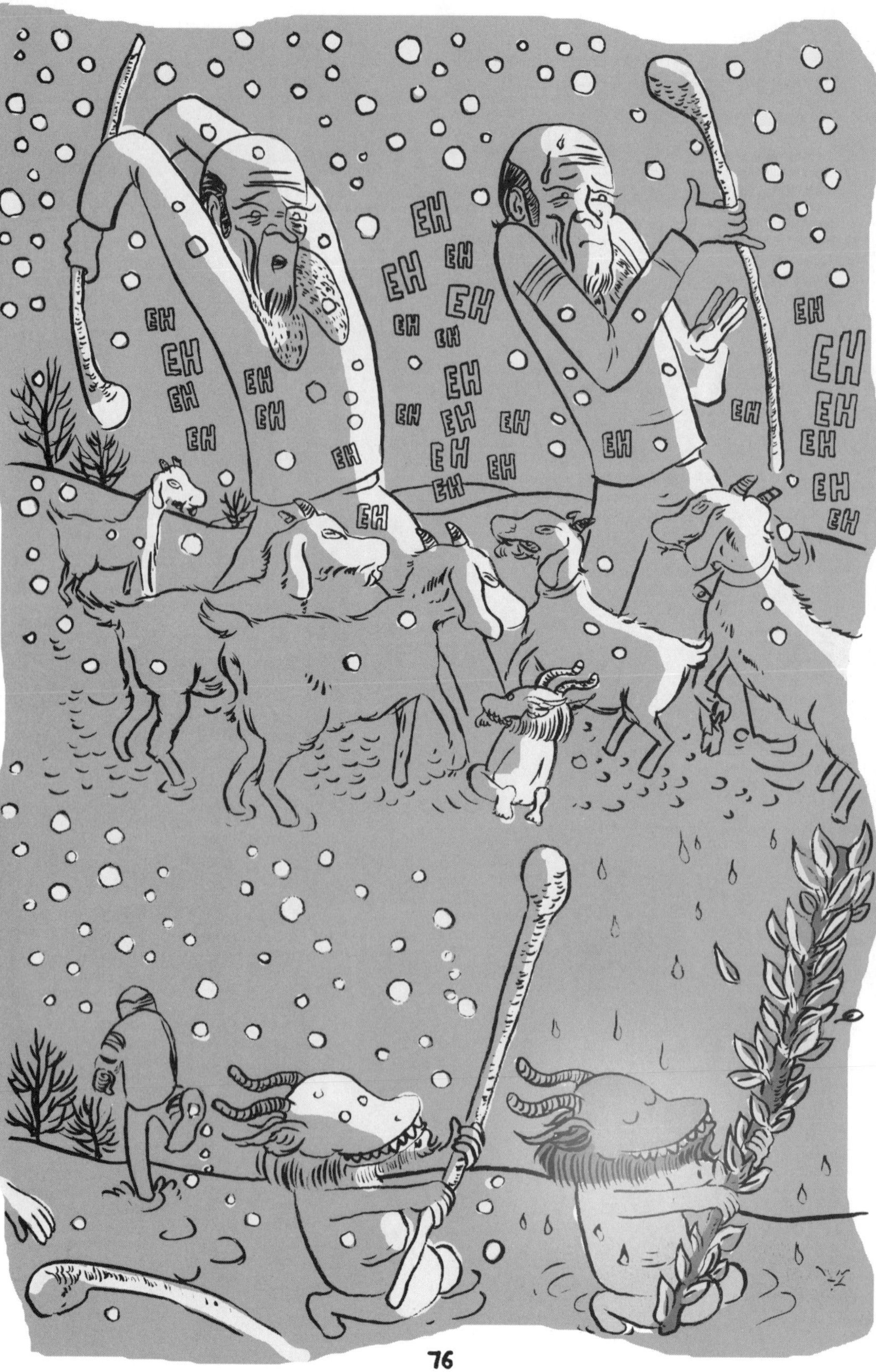
EH EH EH EH EH EH EH EH EH EH EH EH EH EH EH EH EH EH EH EH EH EH EH EH EH EH EH

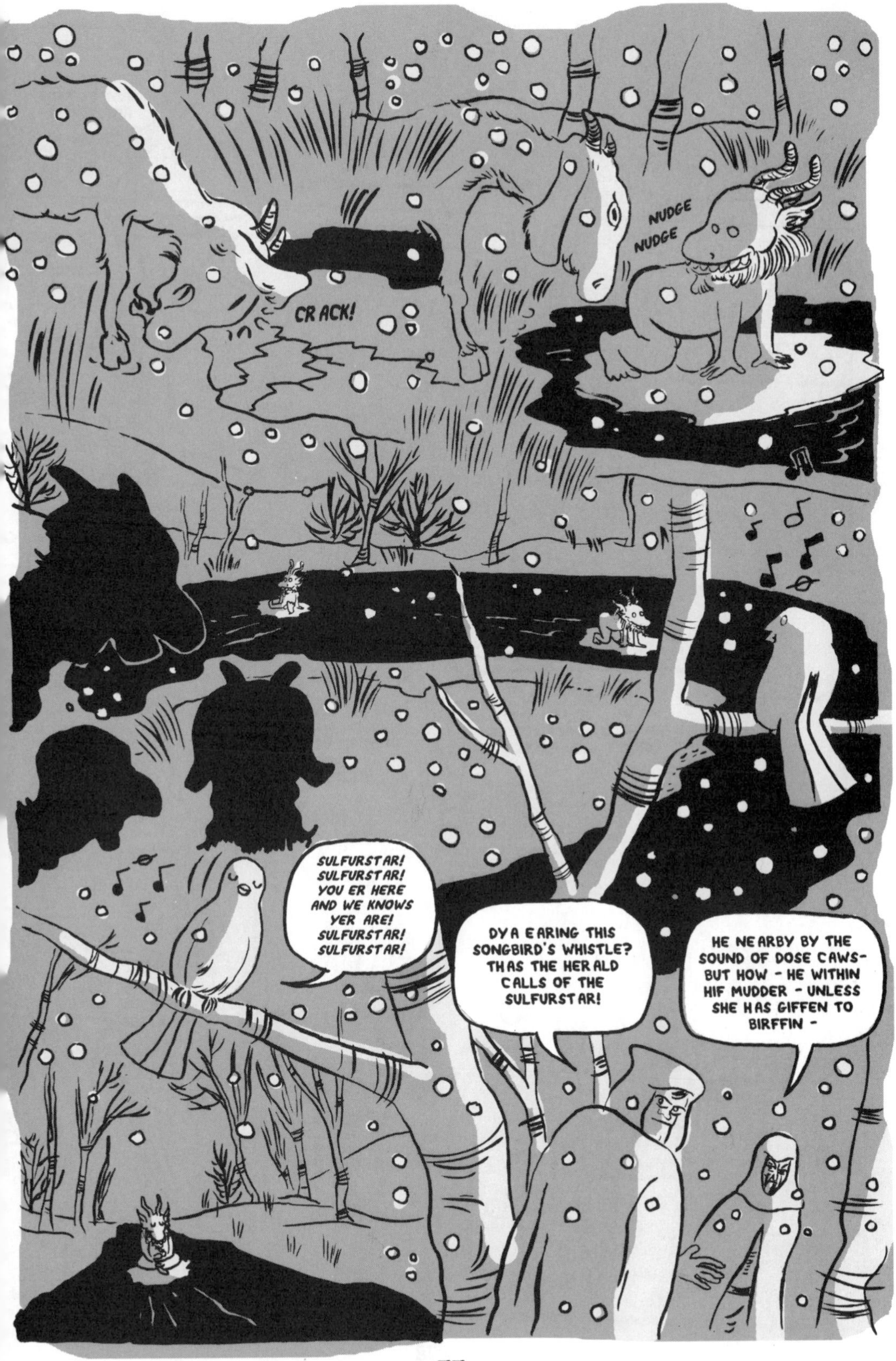
CRACK!
NUDGE
NUDGE
SULFURSTAR! SULFURSTAR! YOU ER HERE AND WE KNOWS YER ARE! SULFURSTAR! SULFURSTAR!
DYA EARING THIS SONGBIRD'S WHISTLE? THAS THE HERALD CALLS OF THE SULFURSTAR!
HE NEARBY BY THE SOUND OF DOSE CAWS- BUT HOW - HE WITHIN HIF MUDDER - UNLESS SHE HAS GIFFEN TO BIRFFIN -

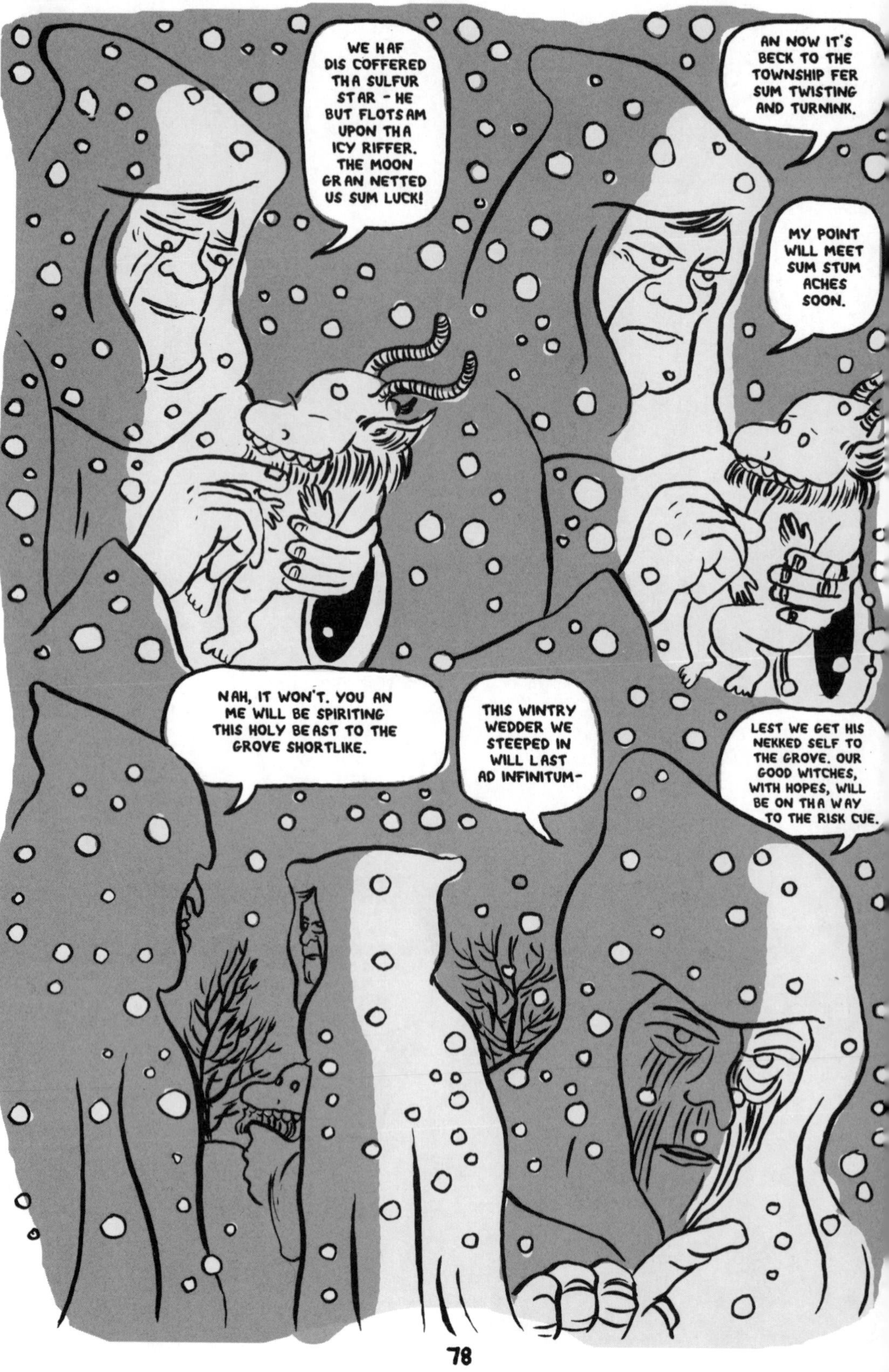
WE HAF DIS COFFERED THA SULFUR STAR - HE BUT FLOTSAM UPON THA ICY RIFFER. THE MOON GRAN NETTED US SUM LUCK!
AN NOW IT'S BECK TO THE TOWNSHIP FER SUM TWISTING AND TURNINK.
MY POINT WILL MEET SUM STUM ACHES SOON.
NAH, IT WON'T. YOU AN ME WILL BE SPIRITING THIS HOLY BEAST TO THE GROVE SHORTLIKE.
THIS WINTRY WEDDER WE STEEPED IN WILL LAST AD INFINITUM-
LEST WE GET HIS NEKKED SELF TO THE GROVE. OUR GOOD WITCHES, WITH HOPES, WILL BE ON THA WAY TO THE RISK CUE.

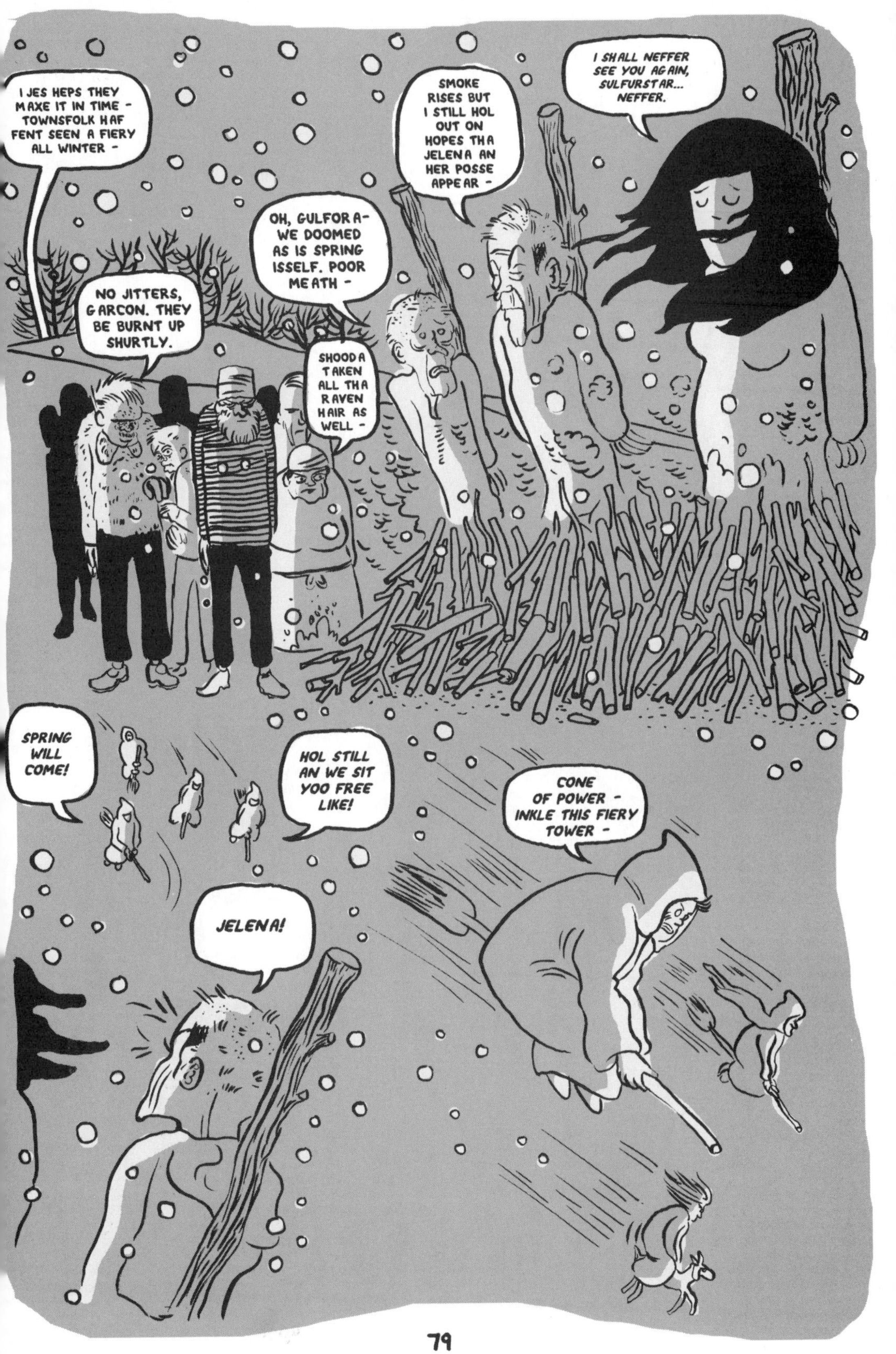
I JES HEPS THEY MAXE IT IN TIME - TOWNSFOLK HAF FENT SEEN A FIERY ALL WINTER -
SMOKE RISES BUT I STILL HOL OUT ON HOPES THA JELENA AN HER POSSE APPEAR -
I SHALL NEFFER SEE YOU AGAIN, SULFURSTAR... NEFFER.
OH, GULFORA- WE DOOMED AS IS SPRING ISSELF. POOR MEATH -
NO JITTERS, GARCON. THEY BE BURNT UP SHURTLY.
SHOODA TAKEN ALL THA RAVEN HAIR AS WELL -
SPRING WILL COME!
HOL STILL AN WE SIT YOO FREE LIKE!
CONE OF POWER - INKLE THIS FIERY TOWER -
JELENA!

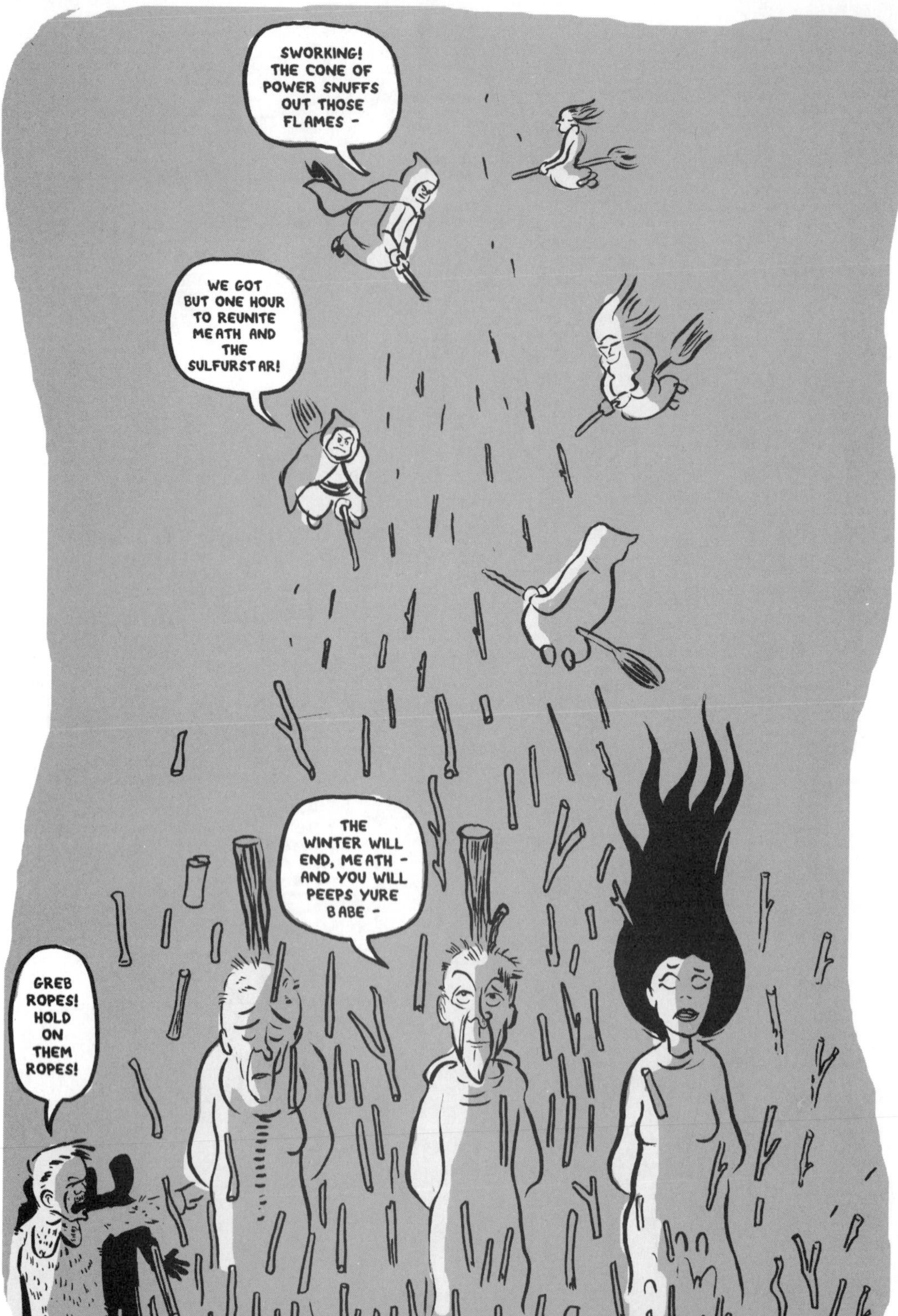
SWORKING! THE CONE OF POWER SNUFFS OUT THOSE FLAMES -
WE GOT BUT ONE HOUR TO REUNITE MEATH AND THE SULFURSTAR!
THE WINTER WILL END, MEATH - AND YOU WILL PEEPS YURE BABE -
GREB ROPES! HOLD ON THEM ROPES!

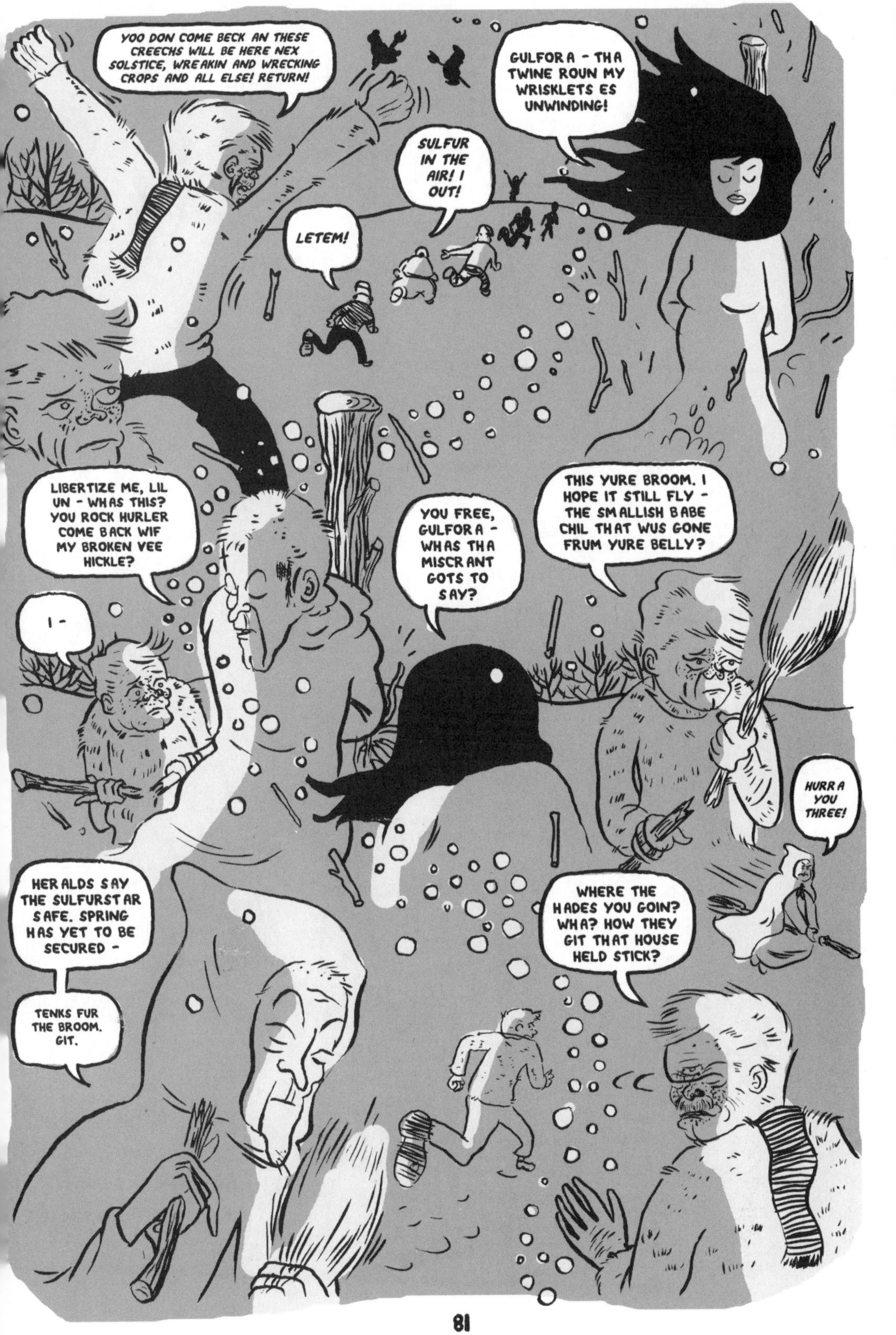
YOO DON COME BECK AN THESE CREECHS WILL BE HERE NEX SOLSTICE, WREAKIN AND WRECKING CROPS AND ALL ELSE! RETURN!
GULFORA - THA TWINE ROUN MY WRISKLETS ES UNWINDING!
SULFUR IN THE AIR! I OUT!
LETEM!
LIBERTIZE ME, LIL UN - WHAS THIS? YOU ROCK HURLER COME BACK WIF MY BROKEN VEE HICKLE?
YOU FREE, GULFORA - WHAS THA MISCRANT GOTS TO SAY?
THIS YURE BROOM. I HOPE IT STILL FLY - THE SMALLISH BABE CHIL THAT WUS GONE FRUM YURE BELLY?
I -
HURRA YOU THREE!
HERALDS SAY THE SULFURSTAR SAFE. SPRING HAS YET TO BE SECURED -
TENKS FUR THE BROOM. GIT.
WHERE THE HADES YOU GOIN? WHA? HOW THEY GIT THAT HOUSE HELD STICK?

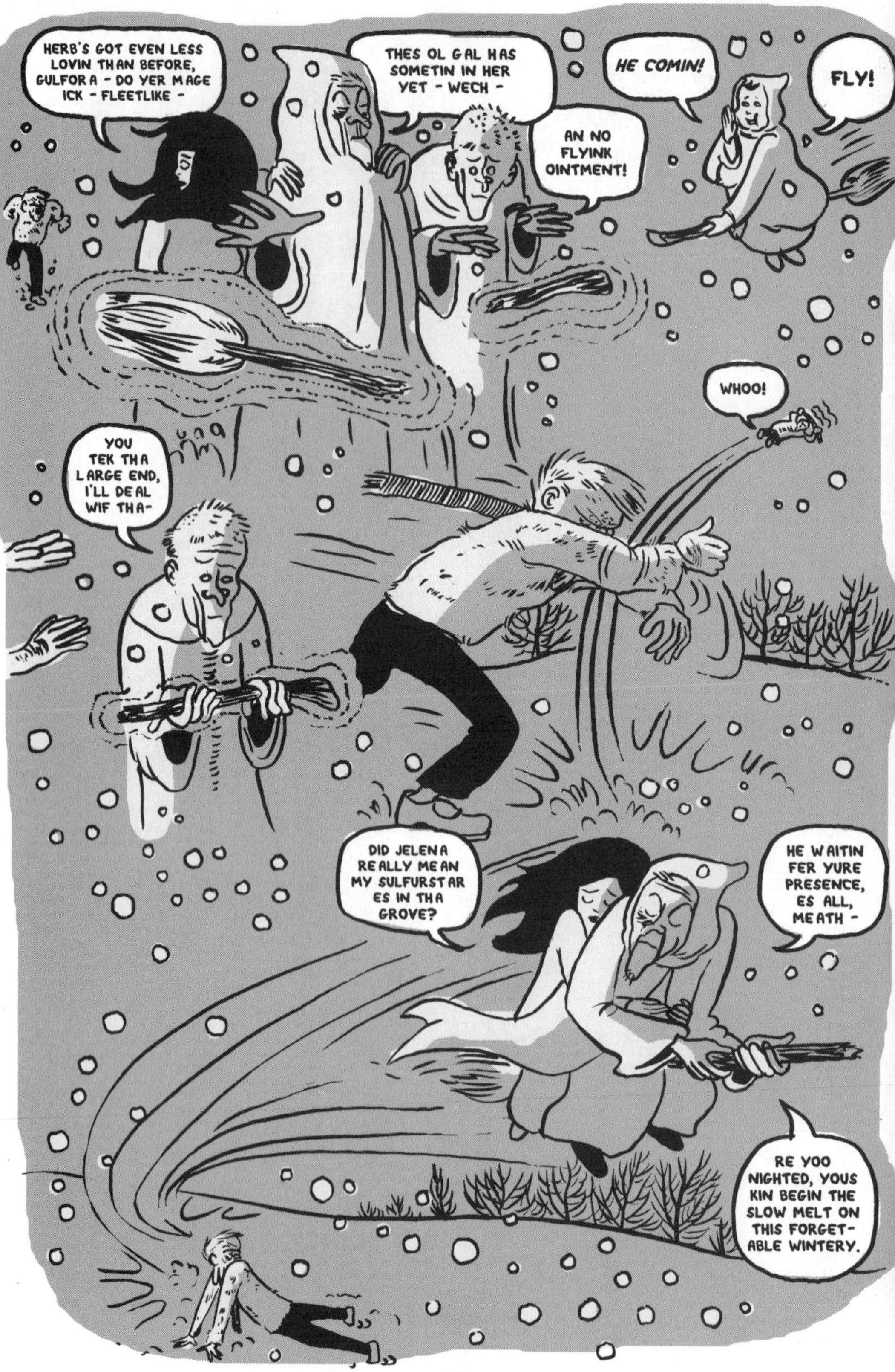
HERB'S GOT EVEN LESS LOVIN THAN BEFORE, GULFORA - DO YER MAGE ICK - FLEETLIKE -
THES OL GAL HAS SOMETIN IN HER YET - WECH -
AN NO FLYINK OINTMENT!
HE COMIN!
FLY!
WHOO!
YOU TEK THA LARGE END, I'LL DEAL WIF THA-
DID JELENA REALLY MEAN MY SULFURSTARES IN THA GROVE?
HE WAITIN FER YURE PRESENCE, ES ALL, MEATH -
RE YOO NIGHTED, YOUS KIN BEGIN THE SLOW MELT ON THIS FORGET-ABLE WINTERY.

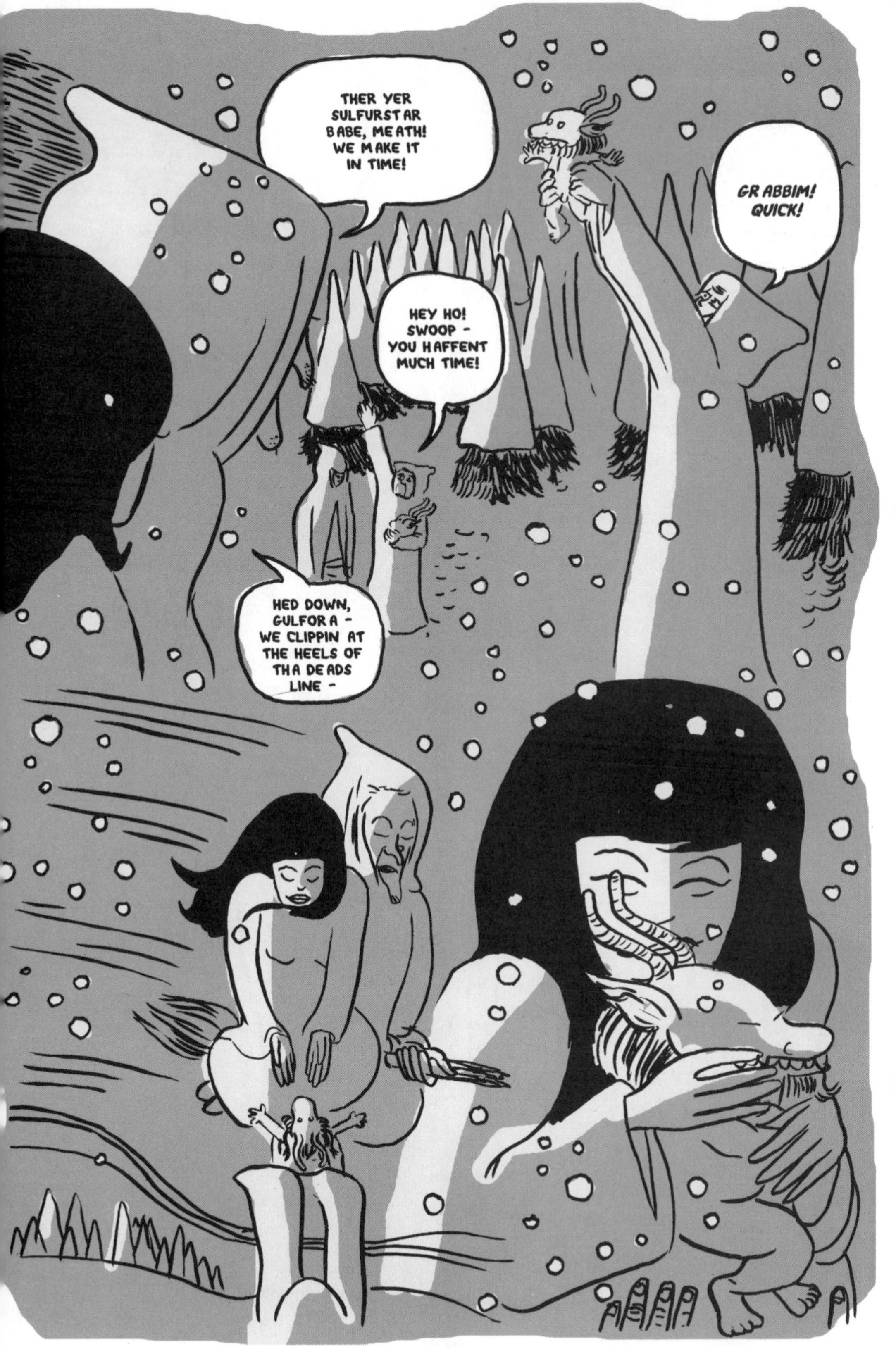
THER YER SULFURSTAR BABE, MEATH! WE MAKE IT IN TIME!
GRABBIM! QUICK!
HEY HO! SWOOP - YOU HAFFENT MUCH TIME!
HED DOWN, GULFORA - WE CLIPPIN AT THE HEELS OF THA DEADS LINE -

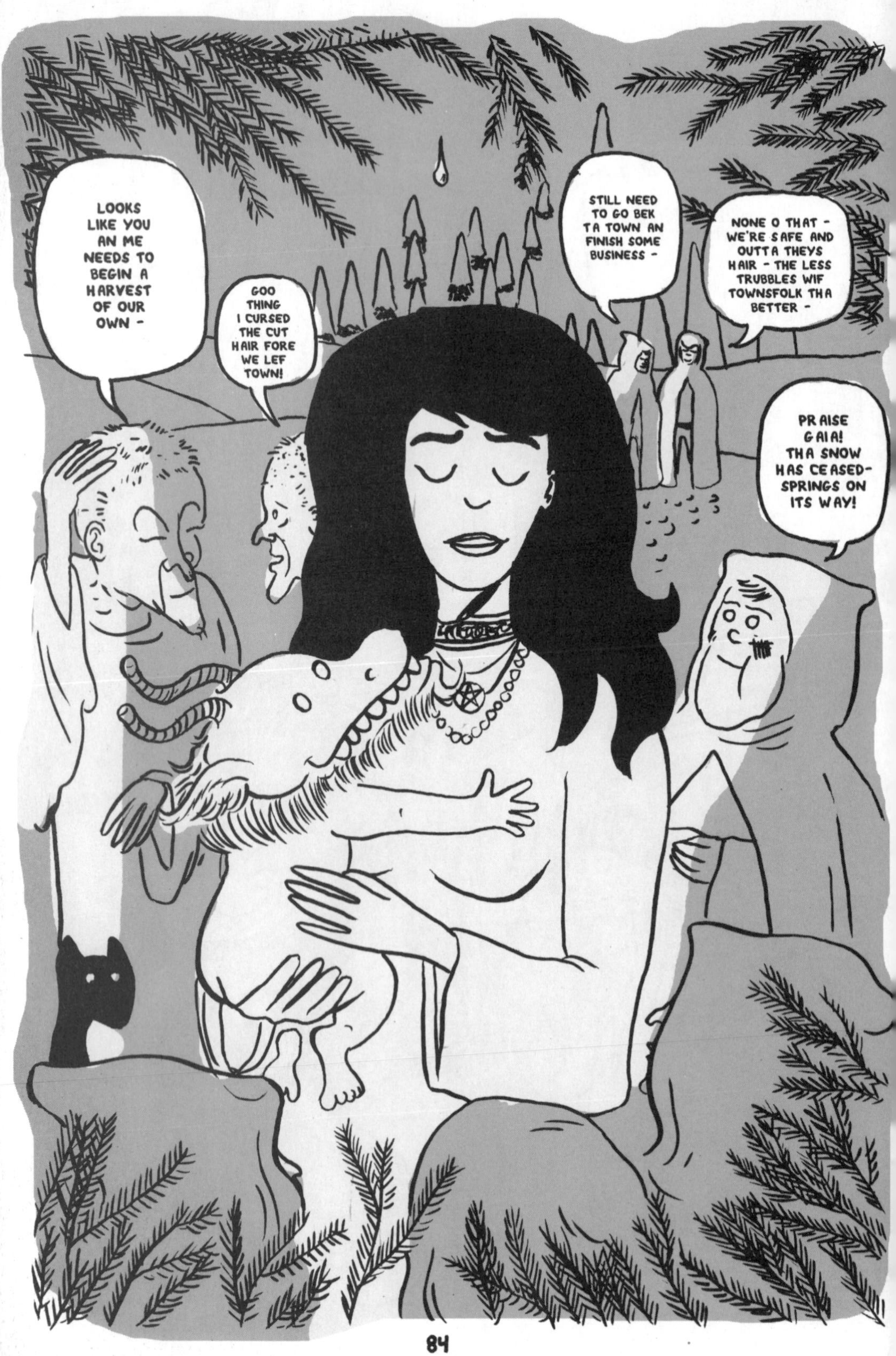
LOOKS LIKE YOU AN ME NEEDS TO BEGIN A HARVEST OF OUR OWN -
GOO THING I CURSED THE CUT HAIR FORE WE LEF TOWN!
STILL NEED TO GO BEK TA TOWN AN FINISH SOME BUSINESS -
NONE O THAT - WE'RE SAFE AND OUTTA THEYS HAIR - THE LESS TRUBBLES WIF TOWNSFOLK THA BETTER -
PRAISE GAIA! THA SNOW HAS CEASED- SPRINGS ON ITS WAY!

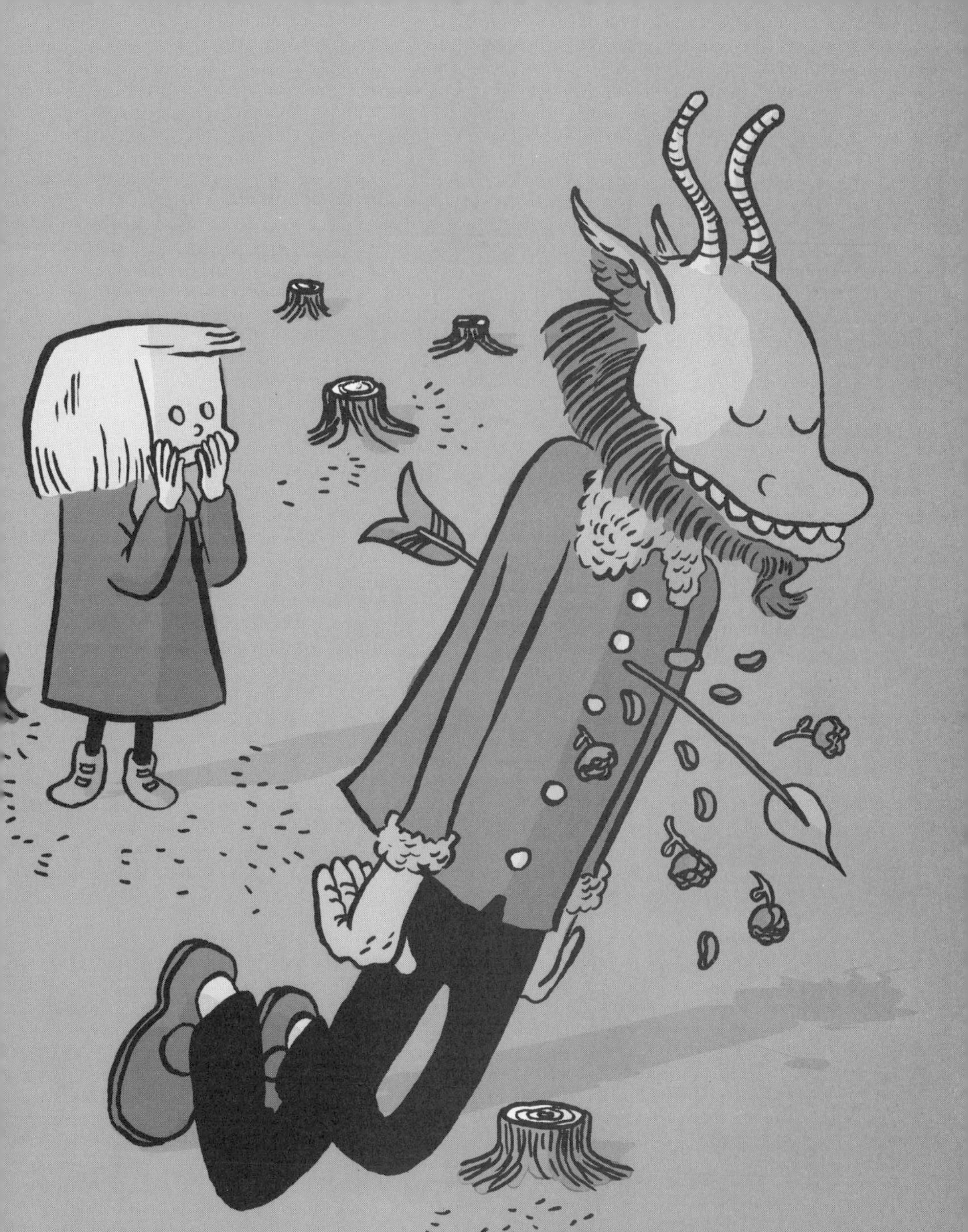

FIR FREE FEVER

THERE ALLUS SEMS TO BE THA SLUMPY FEELINK IN THA AIR AFFER HOLY DAYS ETCH YER, HUH, JAMARA?

WHY ETCH OF EM HAF TO END AD ALL IS FURDER FROM ME THAN WHYS WE CON COCT THE TREACHEROUS OCCASIONS WITH THEMS FREE LICKING DEITIES IN THA FIRS PLACE.

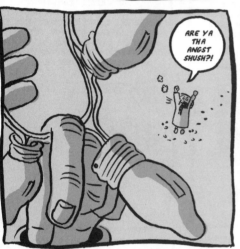

ARE YA THA ANGST SHUSH?!

WHYNCHA LEAF EM UP PERM LIKE? NO WORSEN FER WEAR AN WE CON TINUE TO LIF IN PEACEFUL GLOWS OF LITWICKS –

LEAVIN UP EFFERY WHICH STRINGLY BLINKER AND EMBELLISHED ORNAMENTALS WILL KEPS ETCH OF US IN THE SPURIT THA MUCH LONG-ERISH THROUGH THES GLOOMY MONKS, NO?

I SAY YEAH. LESS DUST EM OFF AND KEP AT IT YER ROUN.

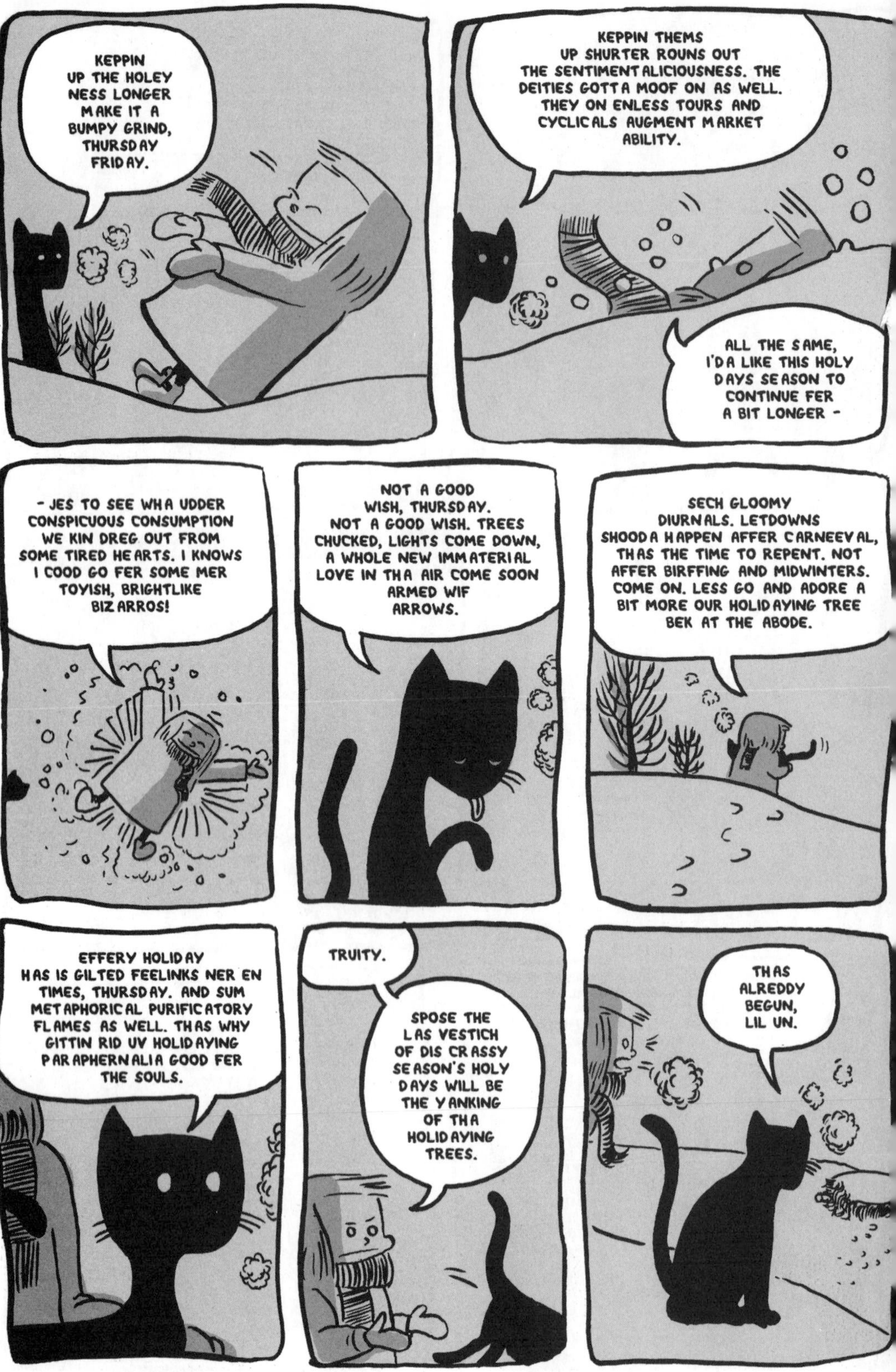
KEPPIN UP THE HOLEY NESS LONGER MAKE IT A BUMPY GRIND, THURSDAY FRIDAY.
KEPPIN THEMS UP SHURTER ROUNS OUT THE SENTIMENTALICIOUSNESS. THE DEITIES GOTTA MOOF ON AS WELL. THEY ON ENLESS TOURS AND CYCLICALS AUGMENT MARKET ABILITY.
ALL THE SAME, I'DA LIKE THIS HOLY DAYS SEASON TO CONTINUE FER A BIT LONGER -
- JES TO SEE WHA UDDER CONSPICUOUS CONSUMPTION WE KIN DREG OUT FROM SOME TIRED HEARTS. I KNOWS I COOD GO FER SOME MER TOYISH, BRIGHTLIKE BIZARROS!
NOT A GOOD WISH, THURSDAY. NOT A GOOD WISH. TREES CHUCKED, LIGHTS COME DOWN, A WHOLE NEW IMMATERIAL LOVE IN THA AIR COME SOON ARMED WIF ARROWS.
SECH GLOOMY DIURNALS. LETDOWNS SHOODA HAPPEN AFFER CARNEEVAL, THAS THE TIME TO REPENT. NOT AFFER BIRFFING AND MIDWINTERS. COME ON. LESS GO AND ADORE A BIT MORE OUR HOLIDAYING TREE BEK AT THE ABODE.
EFFERY HOLIDAY HAS IS GILTED FEELINKS NER EN TIMES, THURSDAY. AND SUM METAPHORICAL PURIFICATORY FLAMES AS WELL. THAS WHY GITTIN RID UV HOLIDAYING PARAPHERNALIA GOOD FER THE SOULS.
TRUITY.
SPOSE THE LAS VESTICH OF DIS CRASSY SEASON'S HOLY DAYS WILL BE THE YANKING OF THA HOLIDAYING TREES.
THAS ALREDDY BEGUN, LIL UN.

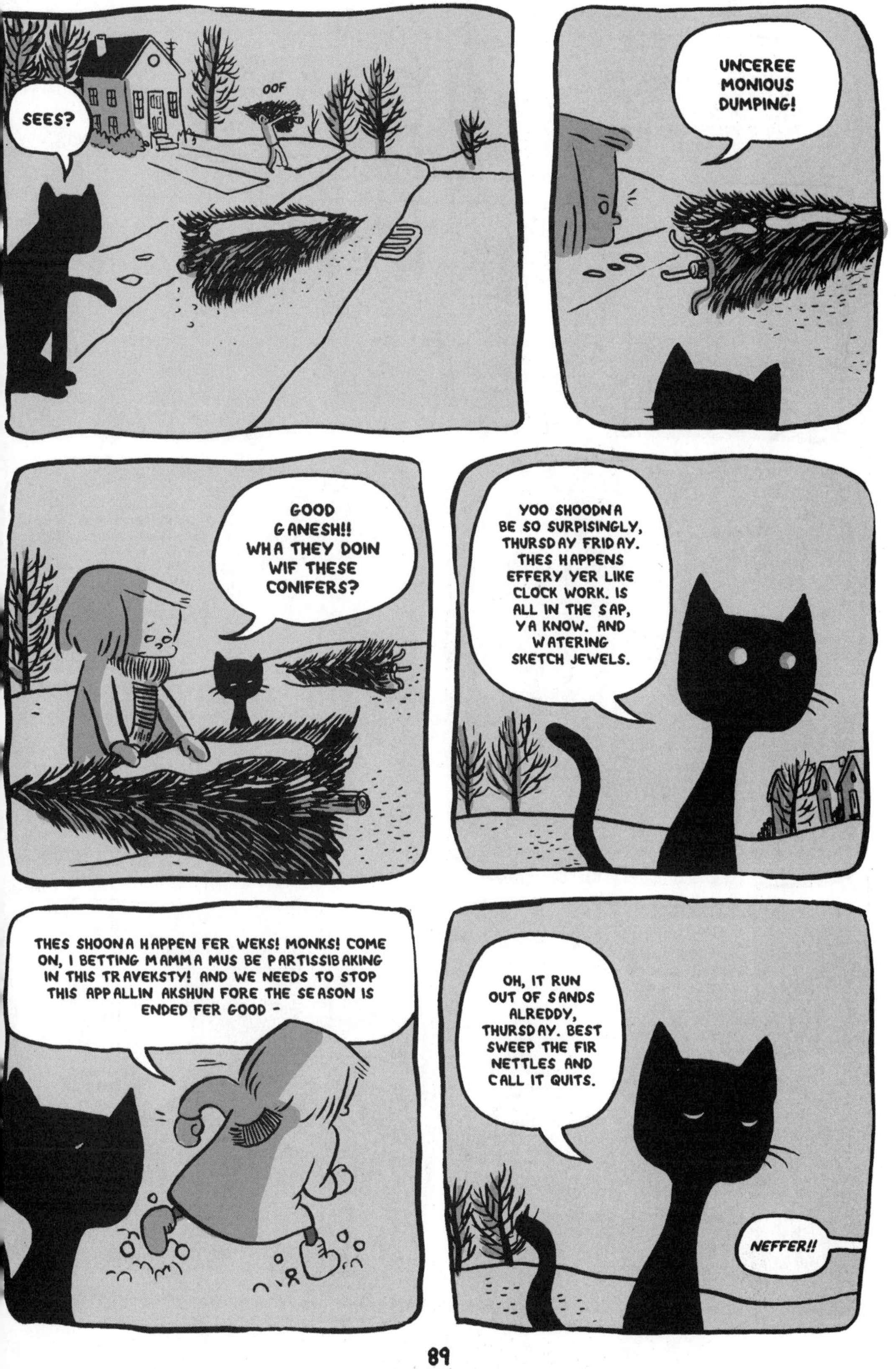
SEES?
OOF
UNCEREE MONIOUS DUMPING!
GOOD GANESH!! WHA THEY DOIN WIF THESE CONIFERS?
YOO SHOODNA BE SO SURPISINGLY, THURSDAY FRIDAY. THES HAPPENS EFFERY YER LIKE CLOCK WORK. IS ALL IN THE SAP, YA KNOW. AND WATERING SKETCH JEWELS.
THES SHOONA HAPPEN FER WEKS! MONKS! COME ON, I BETTING MAMMA MUS BE PARTISSIBAKING IN THIS TRAVEKSTY! AND WE NEEDS TO STOP THIS APPALLIN AKSHUN FORE THE SEASON IS ENDED FER GOOD -
OH, IT RUN OUT OF SANDS ALREDDY, THURSDAY. BEST SWEEP THE FIR NETTLES AND CALL IT QUITS.
NEFFER!!

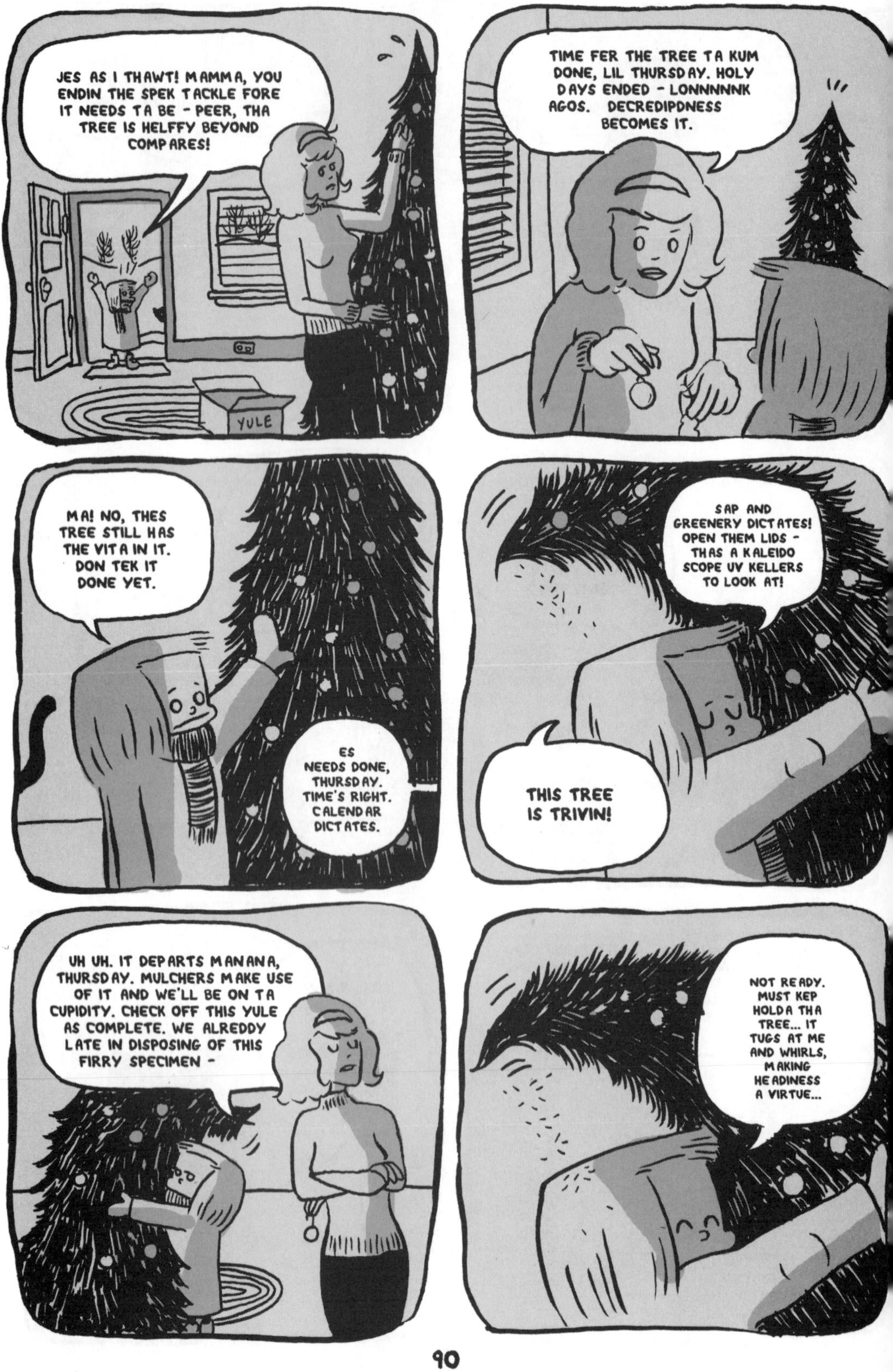
JES AS I THAWT! MAMMA, YOU ENDIN THE SPEK TACKLE FORE IT NEEDS TA BE - PEER, THA TREE IS HELFFY BEYOND COMPARES!
YULE
TIME FER THE TREE TA KUM DONE, LIL THURSDAY. HOLY DAYS ENDED - LONNNNNK AGOS. DECREDIPDNESS BECOMES IT.
MA! NO, THES TREE STILL HAS THE VITA IN IT. DON TEK IT DONE YET.
ES NEEDS DONE, THURSDAY. TIME'S RIGHT. CALENDAR DICTATES.
SAP AND GREENERY DICTATES! OPEN THEM LIDS - THAS A KALEIDO SCOPE UV KELLERS TO LOOK AT!
THIS TREE IS TRIVIN!
UH UH. IT DEPARTS MANANA, THURSDAY. MULCHERS MAKE USE OF IT AND WE'LL BE ON TA CUPIDITY. CHECK OFF THIS YULE AS COMPLETE. WE ALREDDY LATE IN DISPOSING OF THIS FIRRY SPECIMEN -
NOT READY. MUST KEP HOLDA THA TREE... IT TUGS AT ME AND WHIRLS, MAKING HEADINESS A VIRTUE...

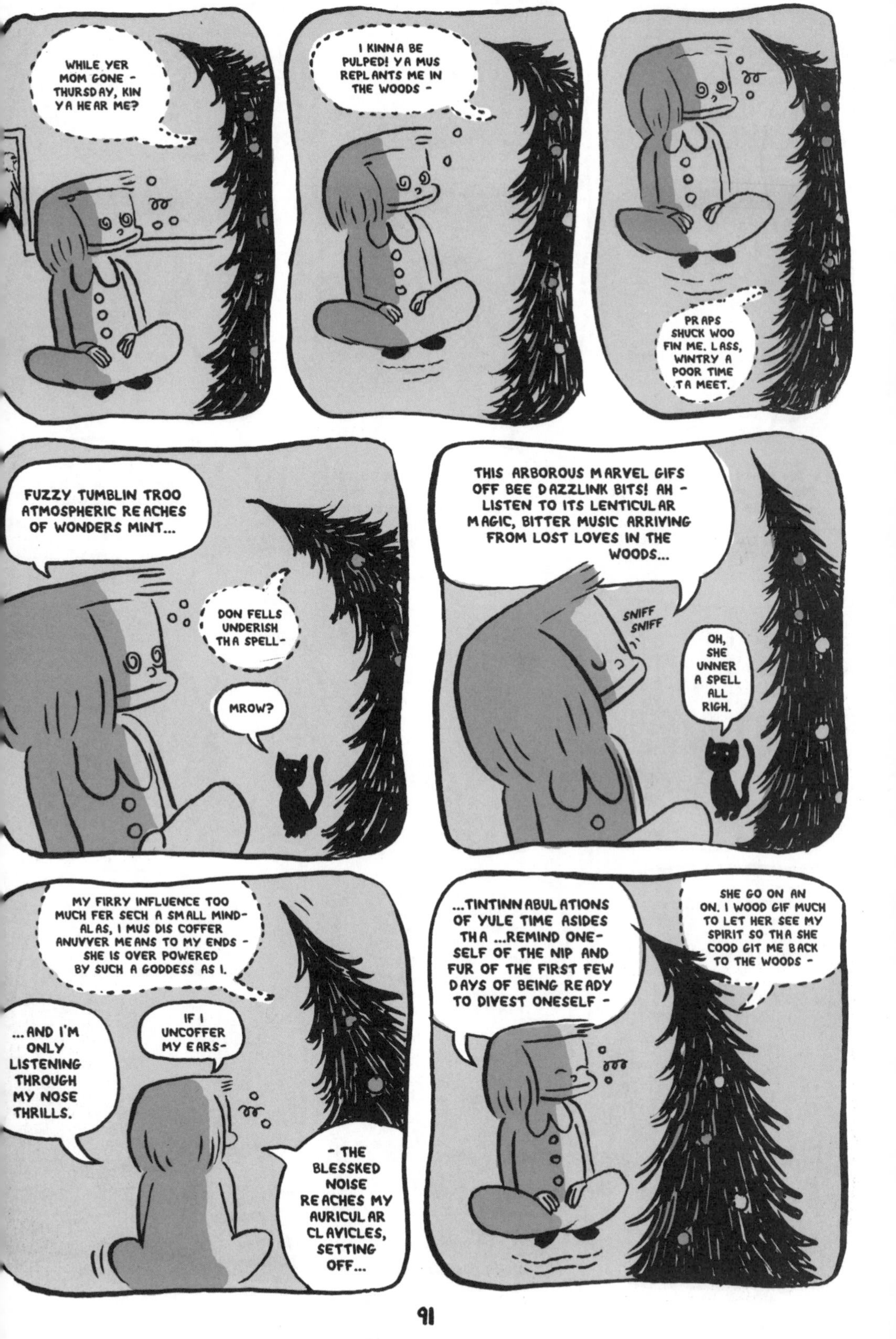
WHILE YER MOM GONE - THURSDAY, KIN YA HEAR ME?
I KINNA BE PULPED! YA MUS REPLANTS ME IN THE WOODS -
PRAPS SHUCK WOO FIN ME. LASS, WINTRY A POOR TIME TA MEET.
FUZZY TUMBLIN TROO ATMOSPHERIC REACHES OF WONDERS MINT...
DON FELLS UNDERISH THA SPELL-
MROW?
THIS ARBOROUS MARVEL GIFS OFF BEE DAZZLINK BITS! AH - LISTEN TO ITS LENTICULAR MAGIC, BITTER MUSIC ARRIVING FROM LOST LOVES IN THE WOODS...
SNIFF SNIFF
OH, SHE UNNER A SPELL ALL RIGH.
MY FIRRY INFLUENCE TOO MUCH FER SECH A SMALL MIND- ALAS, I MUS DIS COFFER ANUVVER MEANS TO MY ENDS - SHE IS OVER POWERED BY SUCH A GODDESS AS I.
...AND I'M ONLY LISTENING THROUGH MY NOSE THRILLS.
IF I UNCOFFER MY EARS-
- THE BLESSKED NOISE REACHES MY AURICULAR CLAVICLES, SETTING OFF...
...TINTINNABULATIONS OF YULE TIME ASIDES THA ...REMIND ONE- SELF OF THE NIP AND FUR OF THE FIRST FEW DAYS OF BEING READY TO DIVEST ONESELF -
SHE GO ON AN ON. I WOOD GIF MUCH TO LET HER SEE MY SPIRIT SO THA SHE COOD GIT ME BACK TO THE WOODS -

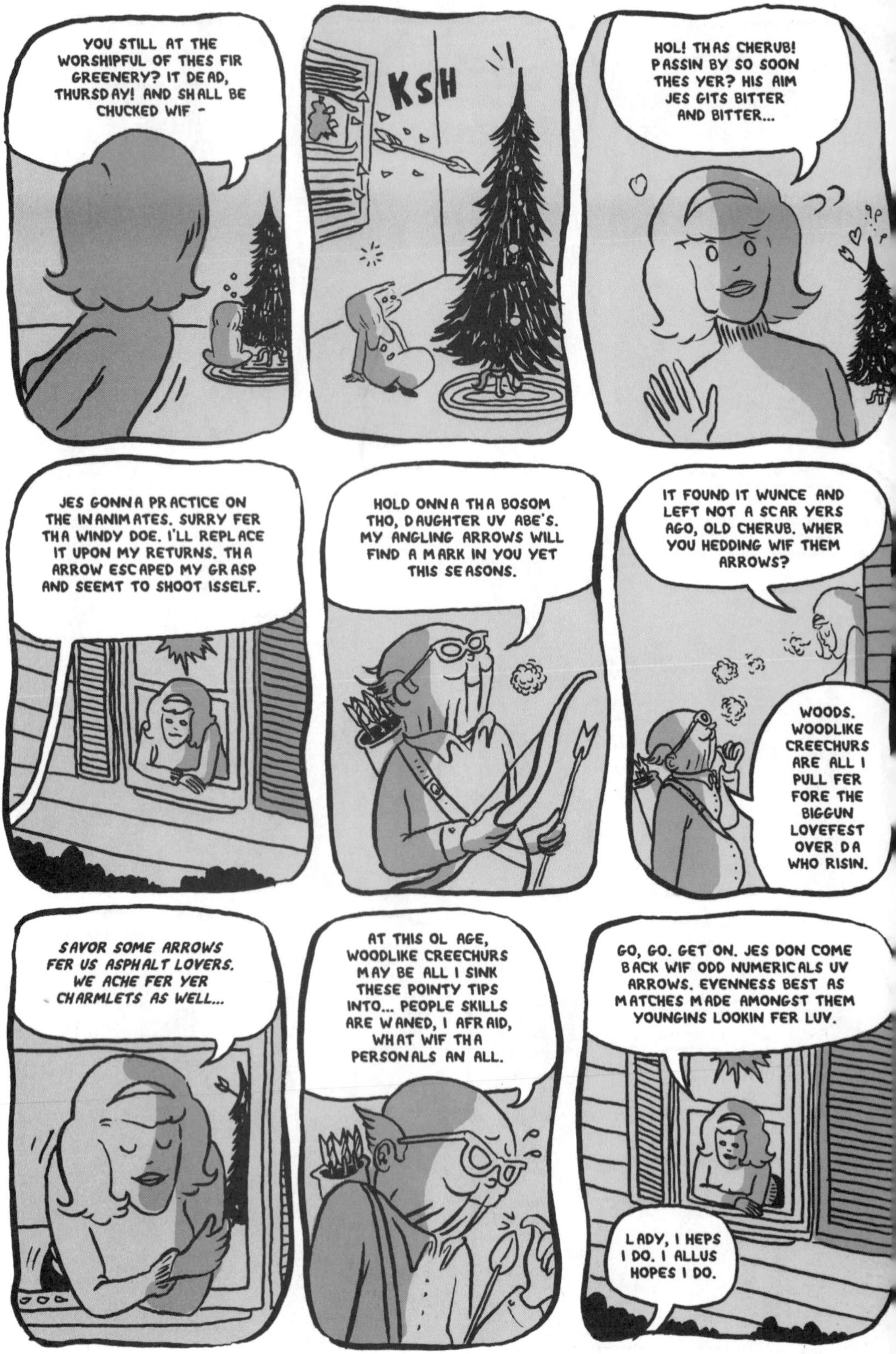
YOU STILL AT THE WORSHIPFUL OF THES FIR GREENERY? IT DEAD, THURSDAY! AND SHALL BE CHUCKED WIF -
KSH
HOL! THAS CHERUB! PASSIN BY SO SOON THES YER? HIS AIM JES GITS BITTER AND BITTER...
JES GONNA PRACTICE ON THE INANIMATES. SURRY FER THA WINDY DOE. I'LL REPLACE IT UPON MY RETURNS. THA ARROW ESCAPED MY GRASP AND SEEMT TO SHOOT ISSELF.
HOLD ONNA THA BOSOM THO, DAUGHTER UV ABE'S. MY ANGLING ARROWS WILL FIND A MARK IN YOU YET THIS SEASONS.
IT FOUND IT WUNCE AND LEFT NOT A SCAR YERS AGO, OLD CHERUB. WHER YOU HEDDING WIF THEM ARROWS?
WOODS. WOODLIKE CREECHURS ARE ALL I PULL FER FORE THE BIGGUN LOVEFEST OVER DA WHO RISIN.
SAVOR SOME ARROWS FER US ASPHALT LOVERS. WE ACHE FER YER CHARMLETS AS WELL...
AT THIS OL AGE, WOODLIKE CREECHURS MAY BE ALL I SINK THESE POINTY TIPS INTO... PEOPLE SKILLS ARE WANED, I AFRAID, WHAT WIF THA PERSONALS AN ALL.
GO, GO. GET ON. JES DON COME BACK WIF ODD NUMERICALS UV ARROWS. EVENNESS BEST AS MATCHES MADE AMONGST THEM YOUNGINS LOOKIN FER LUV.
LADY, I HEPS I DO. I ALLUS HOPES I DO.

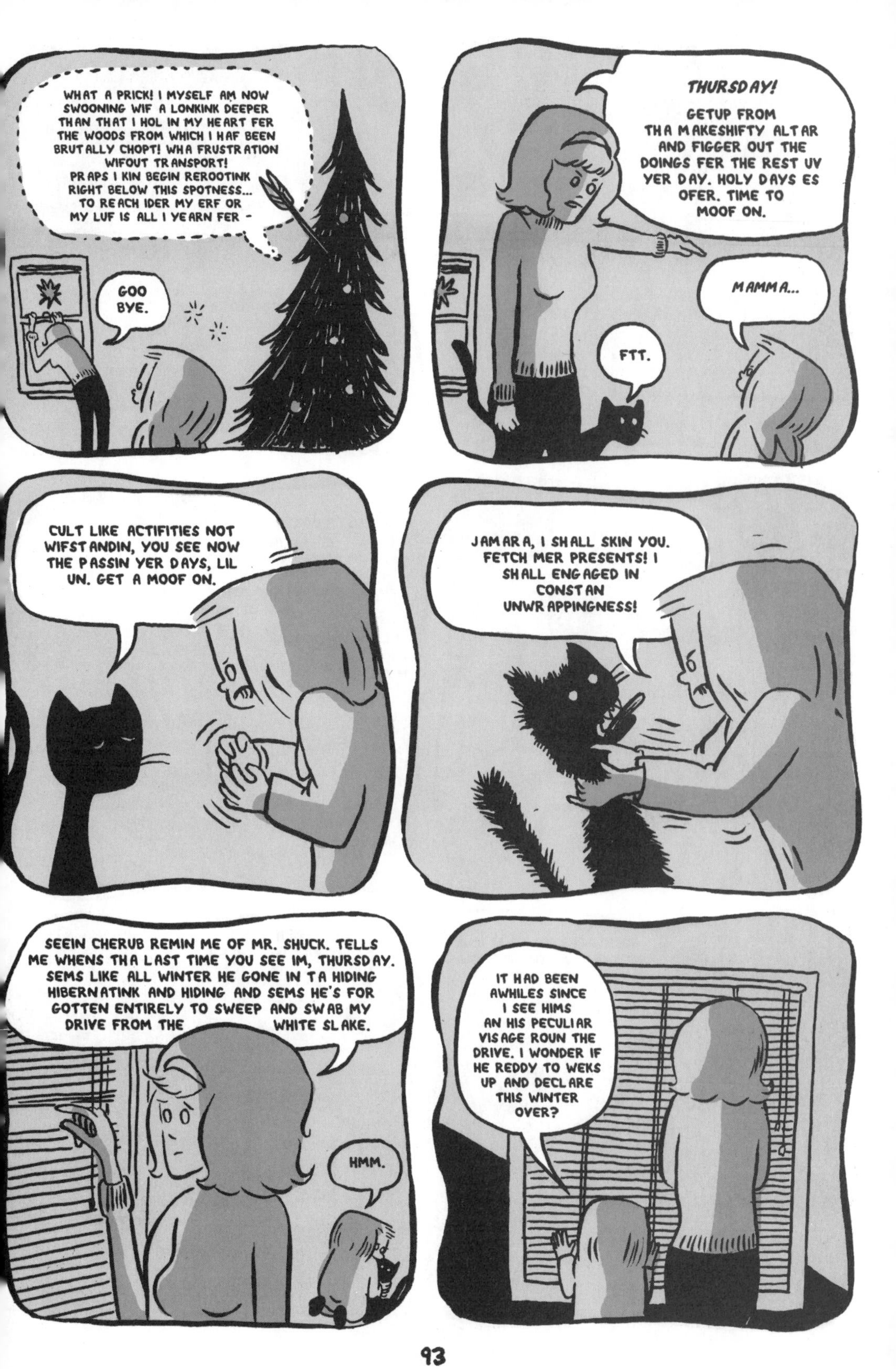
WHAT A PRICK! I MYSELF AM NOW SWOONING WIF A LONKINK DEEPER THAN THAT I HOL IN MY HEART FER THE WOODS FROM WHICH I HAF BEEN BRUTALLY CHOPT! WHA FRUSTRATION WIFOUT TRANSPORT! PRAPS I KIN BEGIN REROOTINK RIGHT BELOW THIS SPOTNESS... TO REACH IDER MY ERF OR MY LUF IS ALL I YEARN FER -
GOO BYE.
THURSDAY!
GETUP FROM THA MAKESHIFTY ALTAR AND FIGGER OUT THE DOINGS FER THE REST UV YER DAY. HOLY DAYS ES OFER. TIME TO MOOF ON.
MAMMA...
FTT.
CULT LIKE ACTIFITIES NOT WIFSTANDIN, YOU SEE NOW THE PASSIN YER DAYS, LIL UN. GET A MOOF ON.
JAMARA, I SHALL SKIN YOU. FETCH MER PRESENTS! I SHALL ENGAGED IN CONSTAN UNWRAPPINGNESS!
SEEIN CHERUB REMIN ME OF MR. SHUCK. TELLS ME WHENS THA LAST TIME YOU SEE IM, THURSDAY. SEMS LIKE ALL WINTER HE GONE IN TA HIDING HIBERNATINK AND HIDING AND SEMS HE'S FOR GOTTEN ENTIRELY TO SWEEP AND SWAB MY DRIVE FROM THE WHITE SLAKE.
HMM.
IT HAD BEEN AWHILES SINCE I SEE HIMS AN HIS PECULIAR VISAGE ROUN THE DRIVE. I WONDER IF HE REDDY TO WEKS UP AND DECLARE THIS WINTER OVER?

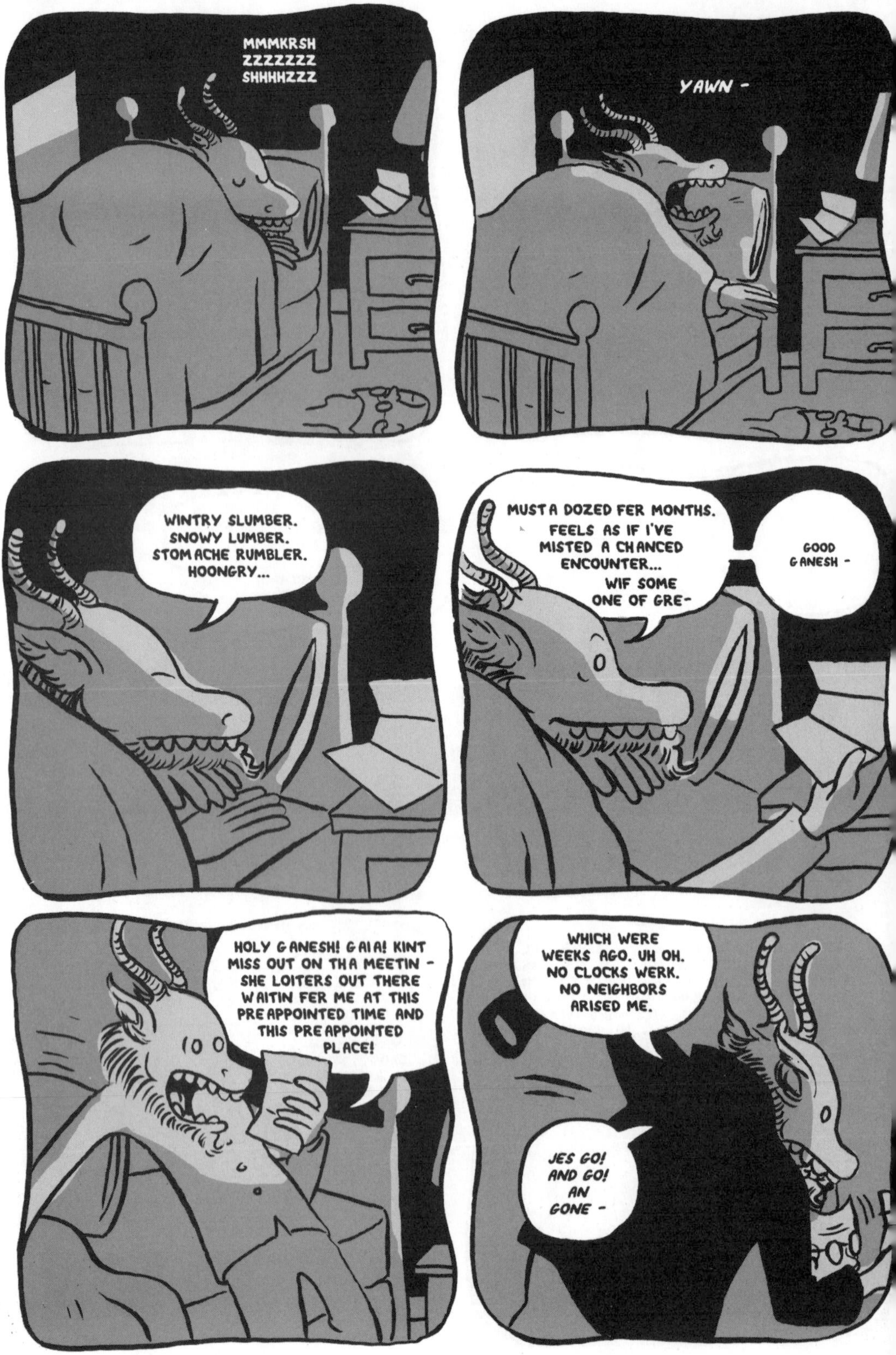
MMMKRSH ZZZZZZZ SHHHHZZZ
YAWN -
WINTRY SLUMBER. SNOWY LUMBER. STOMACHE RUMBLER. HOONGRY...
MUSTA DOZED FER MONTHS. FEELS AS IF I'VE MISTED A CHANCED ENCOUNTER... WIF SOME ONE OF GRE-
GOOD GANESH -
HOLY GANESH! GAIA! KINT MISS OUT ON THA MEETIN - SHE LOITERS OUT THERE WAITIN FER ME AT THIS PREAPPOINTED TIME AND THIS PREAPPOINTED PLACE!
WHICH WERE WEEKS AGO. UH OH. NO CLOCKS WERK. NO NEIGHBORS ARISED ME.
JES GO! AND GO! AN GONE -

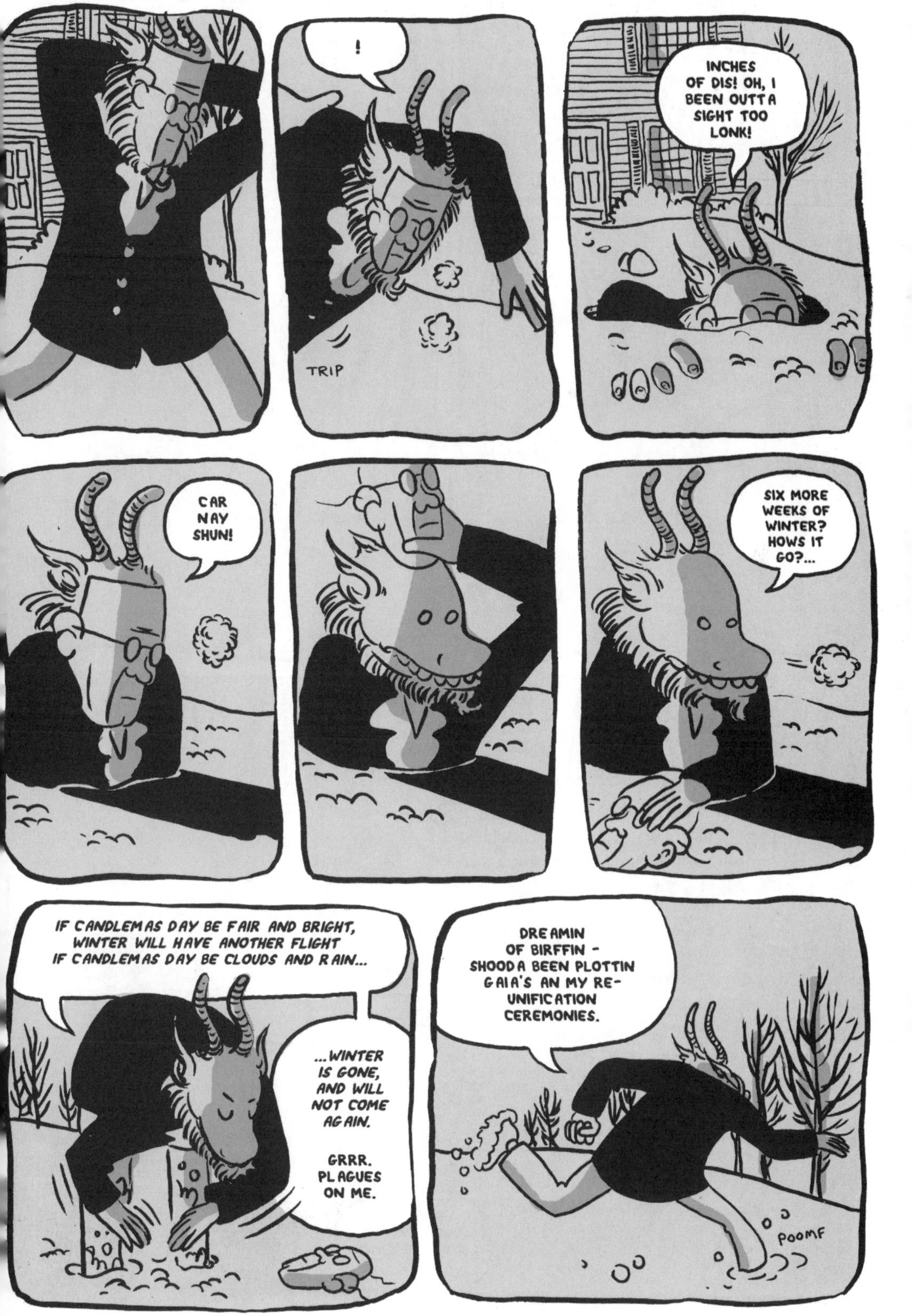
!
TRIP
INCHES OF DIS! OH, I BEEN OUTTA SIGHT TOO LONK!
CAR NAY SHUN!
SIX MORE WEEKS OF WINTER? HOWS IT GO?...
IF CANDLEMAS DAY BE FAIR AND BRIGHT, WINTER WILL HAVE ANOTHER FLIGHT IF CANDLEMAS DAY BE CLOUDS AND RAIN...
...WINTER IS GONE, AND WILL NOT COME AGAIN.
GRRR. PLAGUES ON ME.
DREAMIN OF BIRFFIN - SHOODA BEEN PLOTTIN GAIA'S AN MY RE-UNIFICATION CEREMONIES.
POOMF

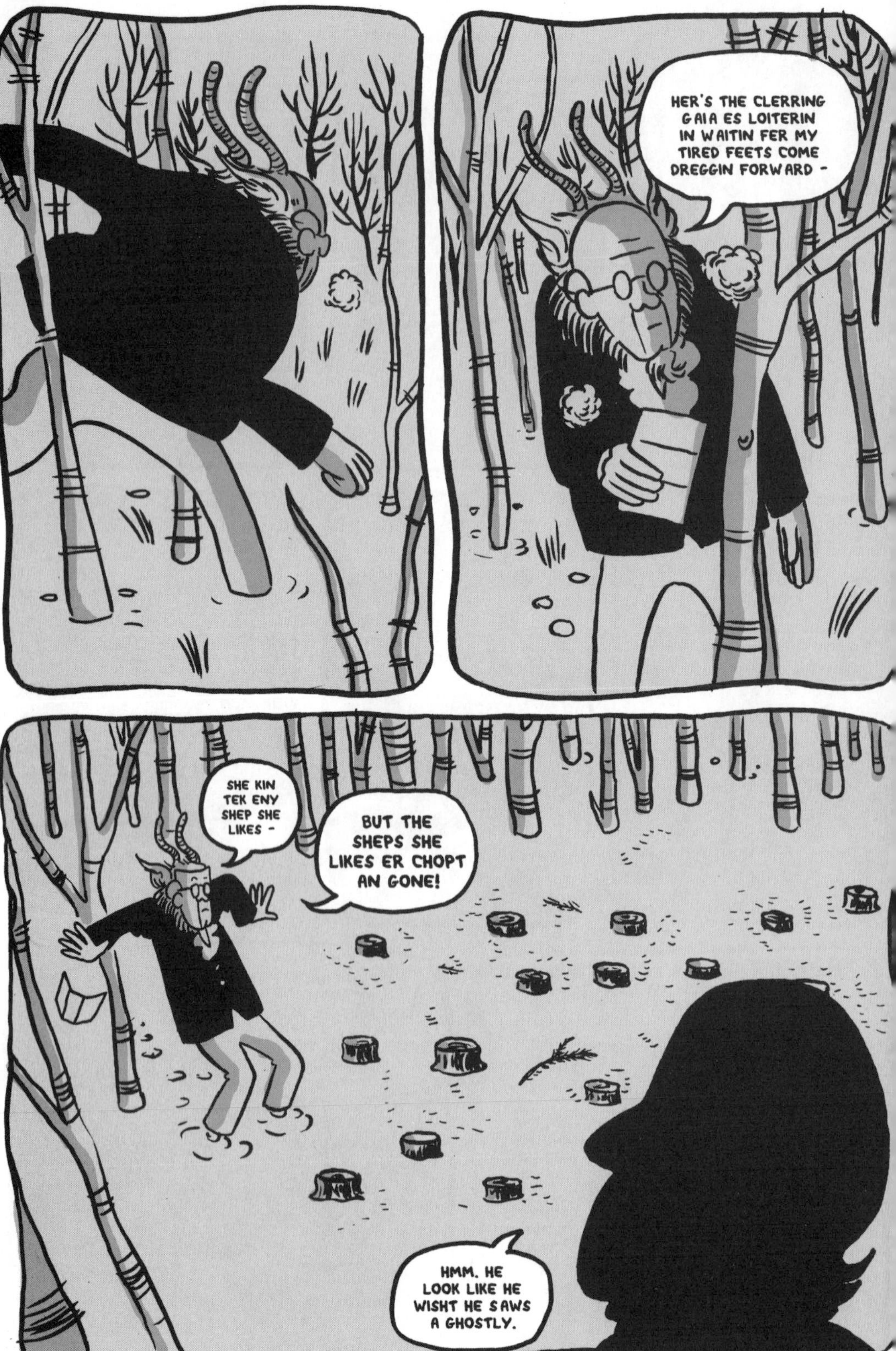
HER'S THE CLERRING GAIA ES LOITERIN IN WAITIN FER MY TIRED FEETS COME DREGGIN FORWARD -
SHE KIN TEK ENY SHEP SHE LIKES -
BUT THE SHEPS SHE LIKES ER CHOPT AN GONE!
HMM. HE LOOK LIKE HE WISHT HE SAWS A GHOSTLY.

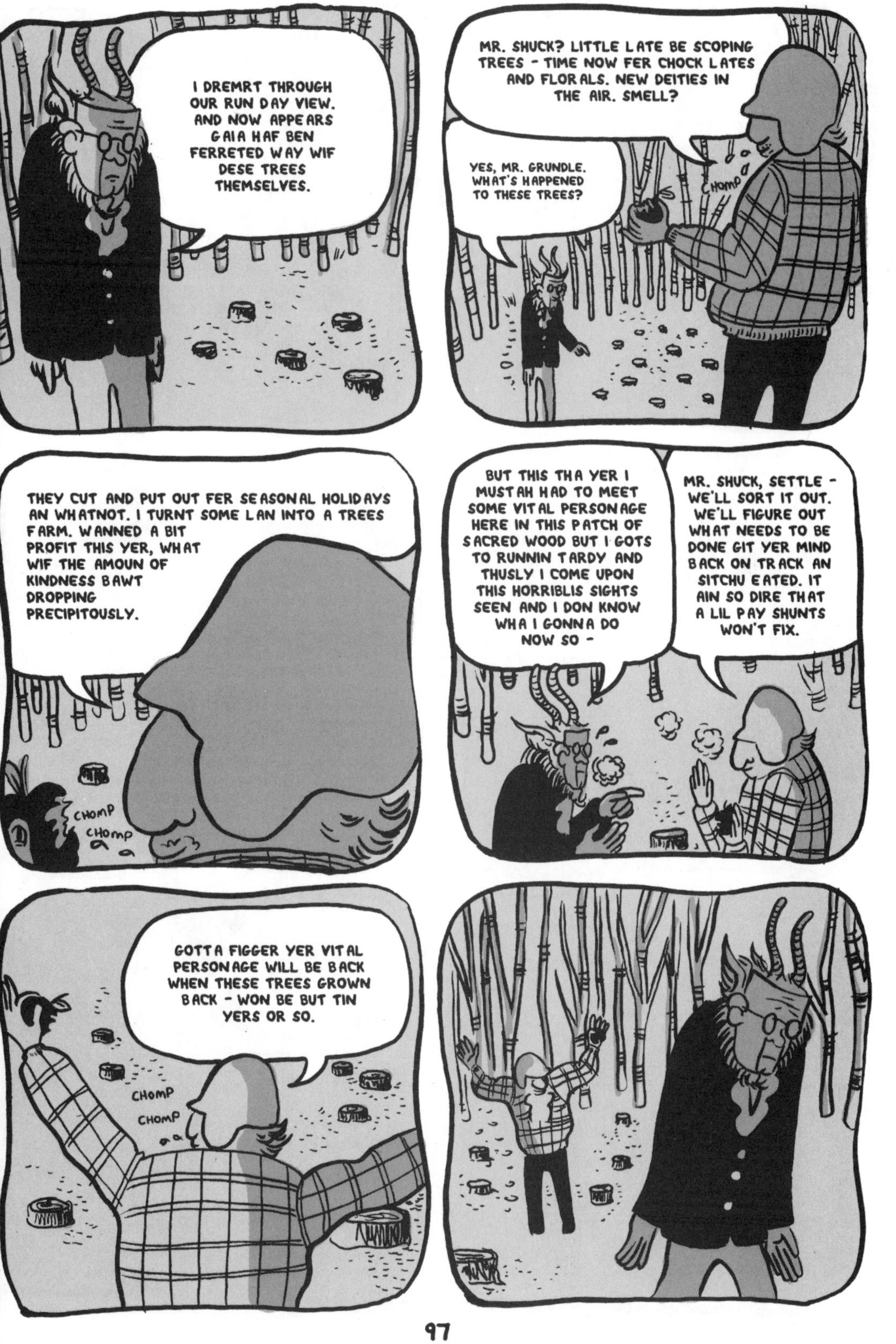
I DREMRT THROUGH OUR RUN DAY VIEW. AND NOW APPEARS GAIA HAF BEN FERRETED WAY WIF DESE TREES THEMSELVES.
MR. SHUCK? LITTLE LATE BE SCOPING TREES - TIME NOW FER CHOCK LATES AND FLORALS. NEW DEITIES IN THE AIR. SMELL?
YES, MR. GRUNDLE. WHAT'S HAPPENED TO THESE TREES?
CHOMP
THEY CUT AND PUT OUT FER SEASONAL HOLIDAYS AN WHATNOT. I TURNT SOME LAN INTO A TREES FARM. WANNED A BIT PROFIT THIS YER, WHAT WIF THE AMOUN OF KINDNESS BAWT DROPPING PRECIPITOUSLY.
CHOMP
CHOMP
BUT THIS THA YER I MUSTAH HAD TO MEET SOME VITAL PERSONAGE HERE IN THIS PATCH OF SACRED WOOD BUT I GOTS TO RUNNIN TARDY AND THUSLY I COME UPON THIS HORRIBLIS SIGHTS SEEN AND I DON KNOW WHA I GONNA DO NOW SO -
MR. SHUCK, SETTLE - WE'LL SORT IT OUT. WE'LL FIGURE OUT WHAT NEEDS TO BE DONE GIT YER MIND BACK ON TRACK AN SITCHU EATED. IT AIN SO DIRE THAT A LIL PAY SHUNTS WON'T FIX.
GOTTA FIGGER YER VITAL PERSONAGE WILL BE BACK WHEN THESE TREES GROWN BACK - WON BE BUT TIN YERS OR SO.
CHOMP
CHOMP

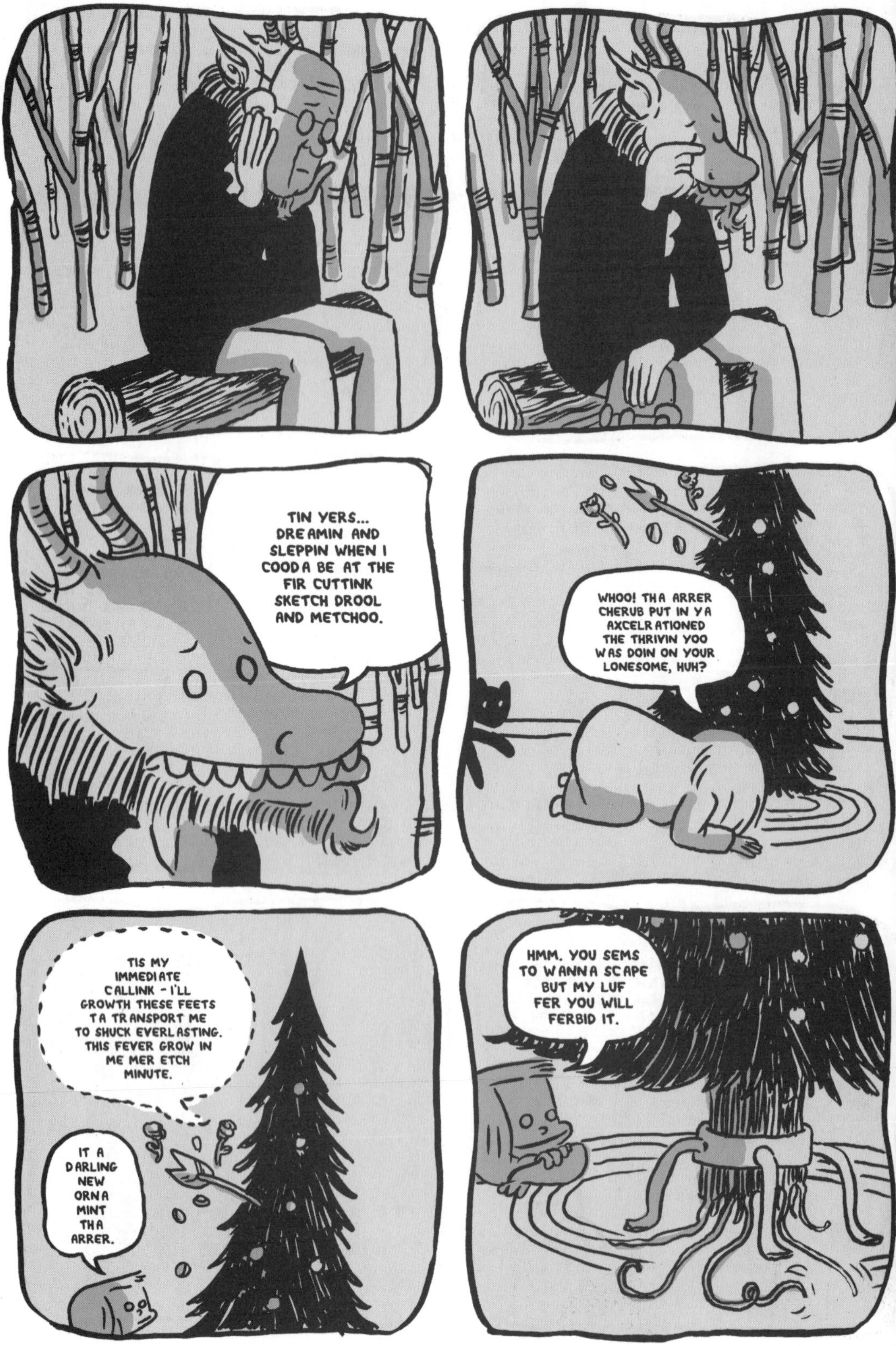
TIN YERS... DREAMIN AND SLEPPIN WHEN I COODA BE AT THE FIR CUTTINK SKETCH DROOL AND METCHOO.
WHOO! THA ARRER CHERUB PUT IN YA AXCELRATIONED THE THRIVIN YOO WAS DOIN ON YOUR LONESOME, HUH?
TIS MY IMMEDIATE CALLINK - I'LL GROWTH THESE FEETS TA TRANSPORT ME TO SHUCK EVERLASTING. THIS FEVER GROW IN ME MER ETCH MINUTE.
IT A DARLING NEW ORNA MINT THA ARRER.
HMM. YOU SEMS TO WANNA SCAPE BUT MY LUF FER YOU WILL FERBID IT.

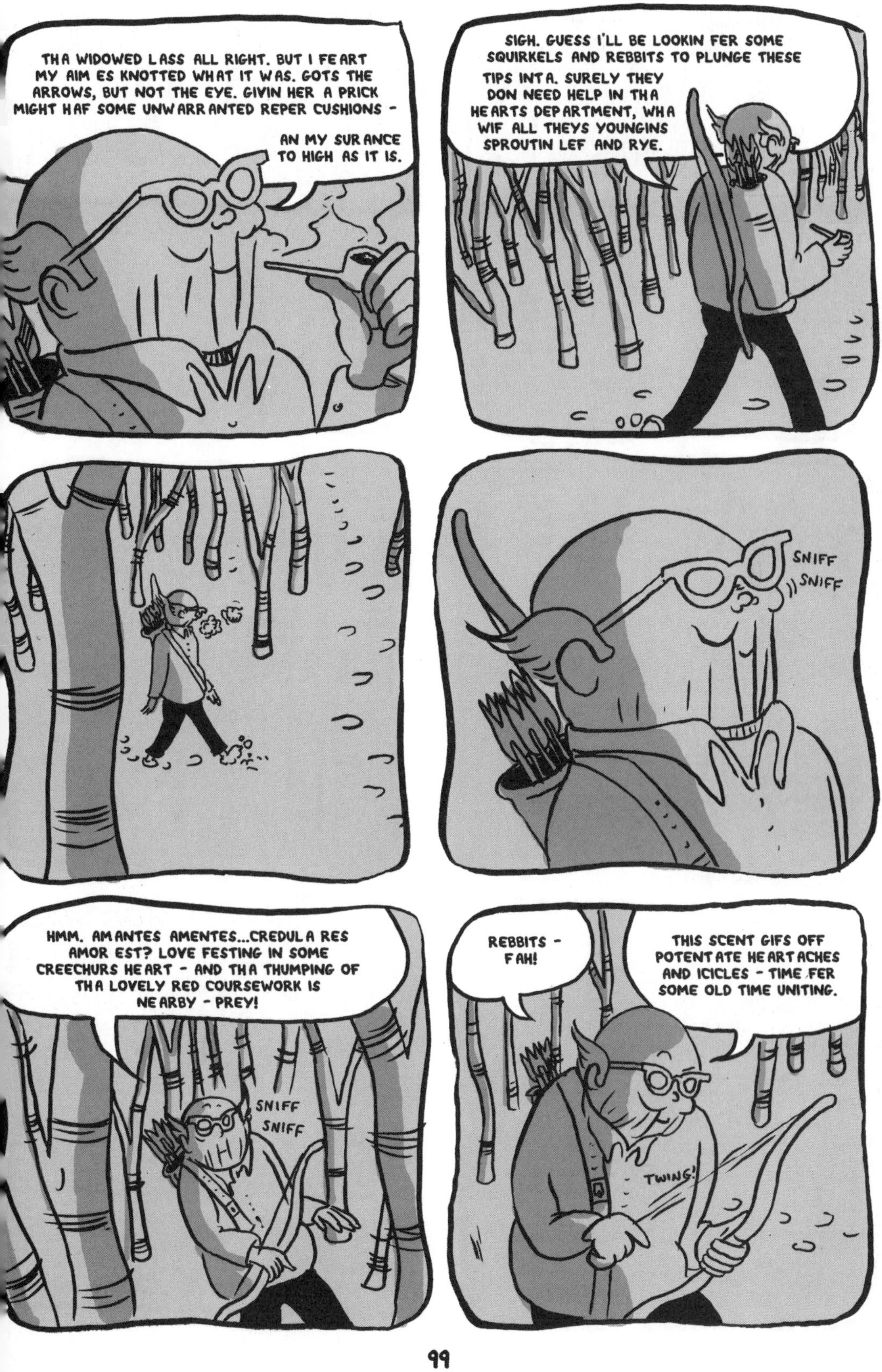
THA WIDOWED LASS ALL RIGHT. BUT I FEART MY AIM ES KNOTTED WHAT IT WAS. GOTS THE ARROWS, BUT NOT THE EYE. GIVIN HER A PRICK MIGHT HAF SOME UNWARRANTED REPER CUSHIONS -
AN MY SURANCE TO HIGH AS IT IS.
SIGH. GUESS I'LL BE LOOKIN FER SOME SQUIRKELS AND REBBITS TO PLUNGE THESE TIPS INTA. SURELY THEY DON NEED HELP IN THA HEARTS DEPARTMENT, WHA WIF ALL THEYS YOUNGINS SPROUTIN LEF AND RYE.
SNIFF
SNIFF
HMM. AMANTES AMENTES...CREDULA RES AMOR EST? LOVE FESTING IN SOME CREECHURS HEART - AND THA THUMPING OF THA LOVELY RED COURSEWORK IS NEARBY - PREY!
SNIFF
SNIFF
REBBITS - FAH!
THIS SCENT GIFS OFF POTENTATE HEARTACHES AND ICICLES - TIME FER SOME OLD TIME UNITING.
TWING!

GOBBLE! EES JES A HORNT CREECH!

HMM. HOPINK FER SOME PEOPLING BUT THA HORNS SIGNIFY GRET PREY NONETHELESS — AN GRETTER PAYOFF IF HIT! PULSE, YOU ARROW. FIN YER MARK.

JES A NIP AN TUCK —

OOOH. KINT WET TO GIT TO MAH DAY!

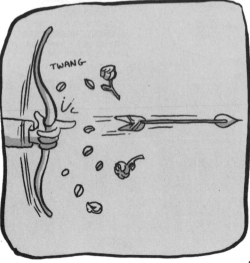

TWANG

WHACK

100

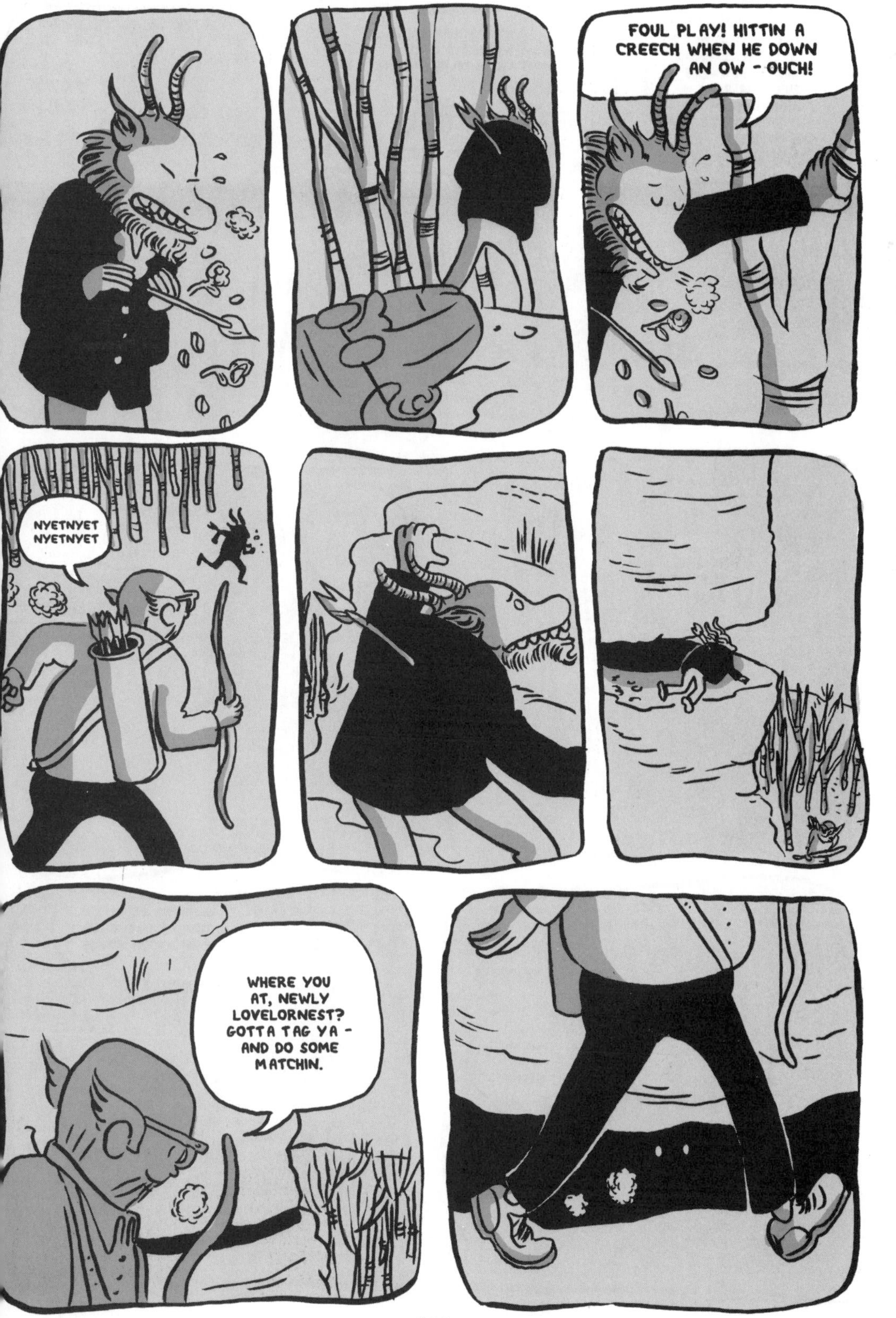
FOUL PLAY! HITTIN A CREECH WHEN HE DOWN AN OW - OUCH!
NYETNYET NYETNYET
WHERE YOU AT, NEWLY LOVELORNEST? GOTTA TAG YA - AND DO SOME MATCHIN.

HOW LONG I BEEN LYING HER? DIZZINESS AND WRETCHEDNESS FILLS ME TO THE BRIM. ONE MORE SIP UV THIS FEELINK IN MY HEART AND I SHALL VANISH.

JES TA HAF MY GAIA. SALL I WISHT. AND NOW I WISHT IT MER THAN PRAPS I CAN BEAR.

OUCH! THIS ARRER HARMFUL!

GITTIN RID OF IT SHALL BE MY GOAL —

SHHHHUUUUUCCCCKKKKKK...

THA GAIA'S VOCALS —

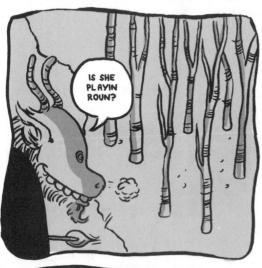

IS SHE PLAYIN ROUN?

PRAPS JES CHANGED SHEP?

HERES I AM! I LUNGE AT YER VOCATIONAL WITH DISASTROUS RESULTS!

SHHHHUUUUCK...I AM ENCASED SPURICHUALLY IN A CHOPT TREE...AND ACHE FER YOU AS WELL...

OH, I ACHE ALL RIGHT?

I SPURICHUALLY CHOPPED TO BITS, GAIA AS WELL! CHOPPED! TATTERED!! WHERE YOU? WHERE? WHICH ARBOR YOU IN?

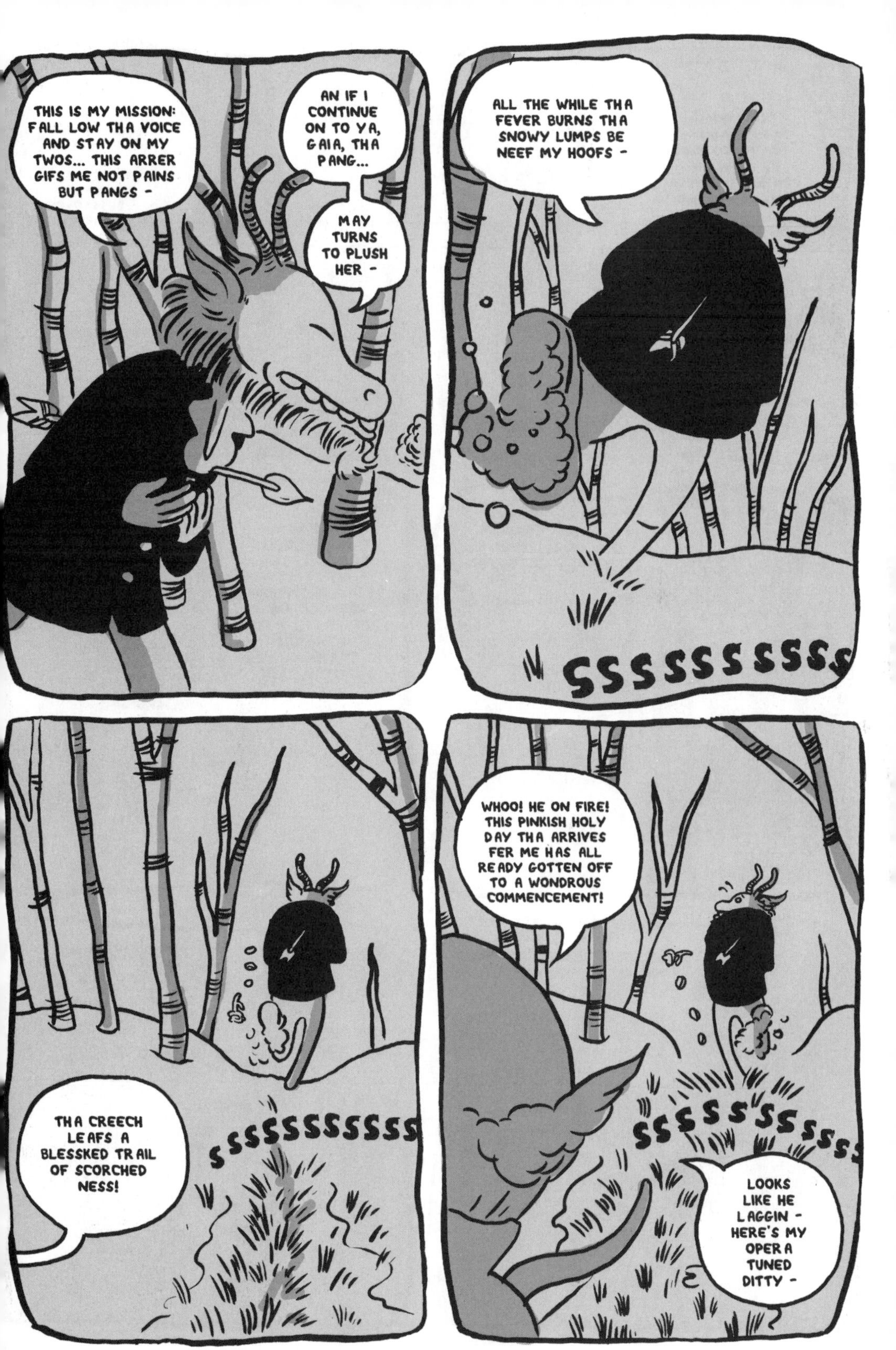
THIS IS MY MISSION: FALL LOW THA VOICE AND STAY ON MY TWOS... THIS ARRER GIFS ME NOT PAINS BUT PANGS -
AN IF I CONTINUE ON TO YA, GAIA, THA PANG...
MAY TURNS TO PLUSH HER -
ALL THE WHILE THA FEVER BURNS THA SNOWY LUMPS BE NEEF MY HOOFS -
SSSSSSSSSSS
SSSSSSSSSSSS
THA CREECH LEAFS A BLESSKED TRAIL OF SCORCHED NESS!
WHOO! HE ON FIRE! THIS PINKISH HOLY DAY THA ARRIVES FER ME HAS ALL READY GOTTEN OFF TO A WONDROUS COMMENCEMENT!
SSSSSSSSSS
LOOKS LIKE HE LAGGIN - HERE'S MY OPERA TUNED DITTY -

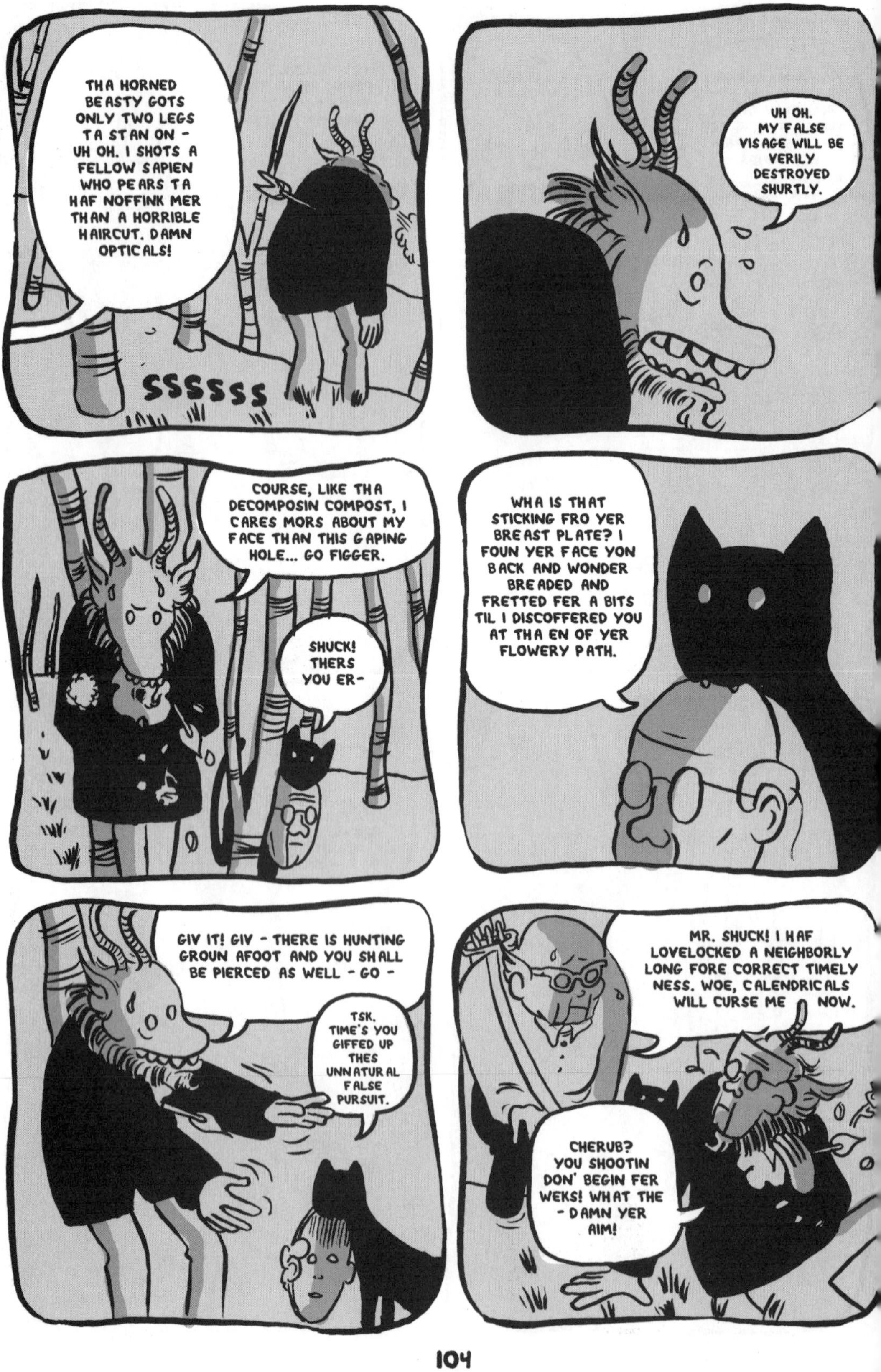
THA HORNED BEASTY GOTS ONLY TWO LEGS TA STAN ON - UH OH. I SHOTS A FELLOW SAPIEN WHO PEARS TA HAF NOFFINK MER THAN A HORRIBLE HAIRCUT. DAMN OPTICALS!
SSSSSS
UH OH. MY FALSE VISAGE WILL BE VERILY DESTROYED SHURTLY.
COURSE, LIKE THA DECOMPOSIN COMPOST, I CARES MORS ABOUT MY FACE THAN THIS GAPING HOLE... GO FIGGER.
SHUCK! THERS YOU ER-
WHA IS THAT STICKING FRO YER BREAST PLATE? I FOUN YER FACE YON BACK AND WONDER BREADED AND FRETTED FER A BITS TIL I DISCOFFERED YOU AT THA EN OF YER FLOWERY PATH.
GIV IT! GIV - THERE IS HUNTING GROUN AFOOT AND YOU SHALL BE PIERCED AS WELL - GO -
TSK. TIME'S YOU GIFFED UP THES UNNATURAL FALSE PURSUIT.
MR. SHUCK! I HAF LOVELOCKED A NEIGHBORLY LONG FORE CORRECT TIMELY NESS. WOE, CALENDRICALS WILL CURSE ME NOW.
CHERUB? YOU SHOOTIN DON' BEGIN FER WEKS! WHAT THE - DAMN YER AIM!

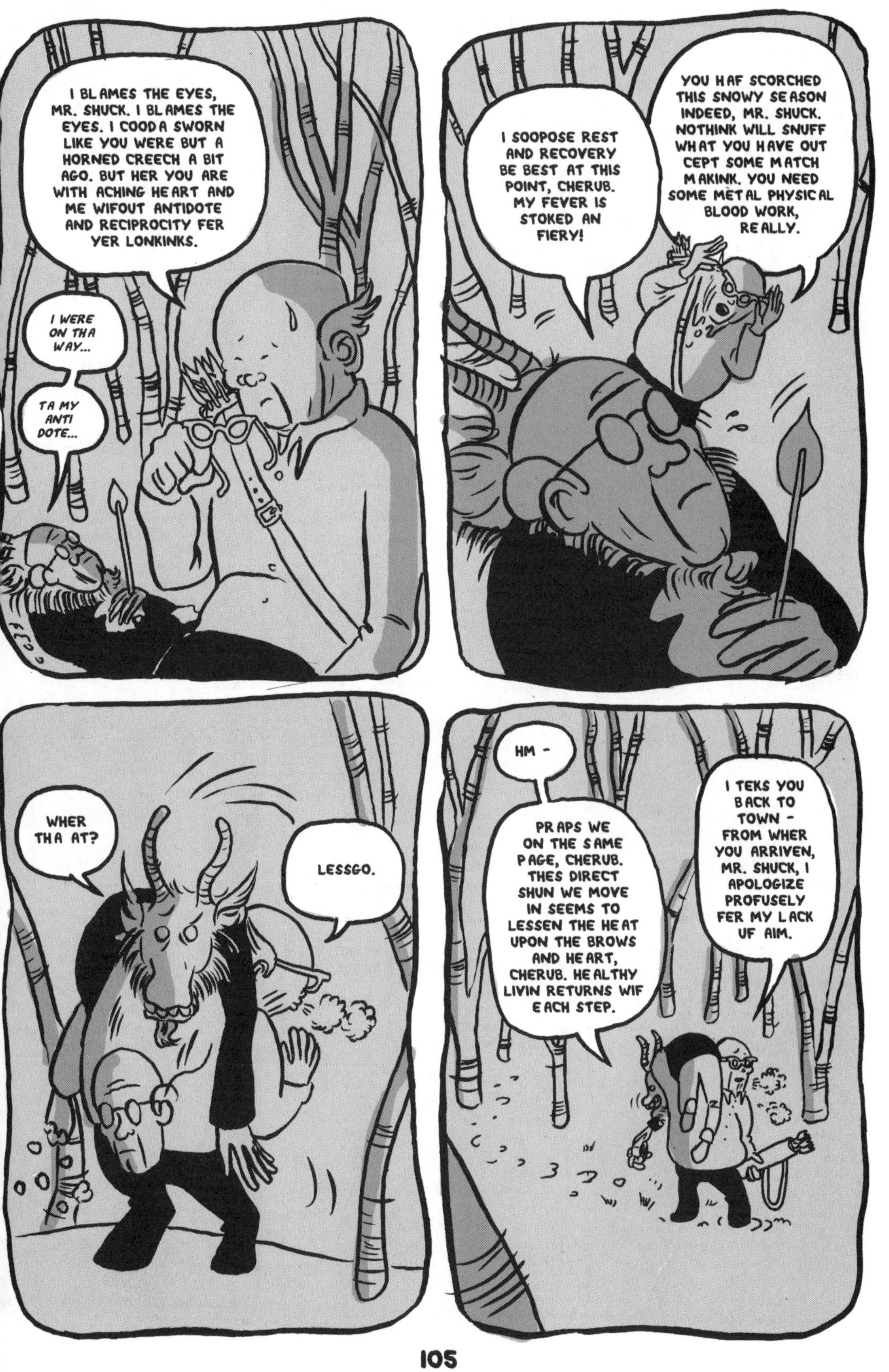
I BLAMES THE EYES, MR. SHUCK. I BLAMES THE EYES. I COODA SWORN LIKE YOU WERE BUT A HORNED CREECH A BIT AGO. BUT HER YOU ARE WITH ACHING HEART AND ME WIFOUT ANTIDOTE AND RECIPROCITY FER YER LONKINKS.
I WERE ON THA WAY...
TA MY ANTI DOTE...
I SOOPOSE REST AND RECOVERY BE BEST AT THIS POINT, CHERUB. MY FEVER IS STOKED AN FIERY!
YOU HAF SCORCHED THIS SNOWY SEASON INDEED, MR. SHUCK. NOTHINK WILL SNUFF WHAT YOU HAVE OUT CEPT SOME MATCH MAKINK. YOU NEED SOME METAL PHYSICAL BLOOD WORK, REALLY.
WHER THA AT?
LESSGO.
HM -
PRAPS WE ON THE SAME PAGE, CHERUB. THES DIRECT SHUN WE MOVE IN SEEMS TO LESSEN THE HEAT UPON THE BROWS AND HEART, CHERUB. HEALTHY LIVIN RETURNS WIF EACH STEP.
I TEKS YOU BACK TO TOWN - FROM WHER YOU ARRIVEN, MR. SHUCK, I APOLOGIZE PROFUSELY FER MY LACK UF AIM.

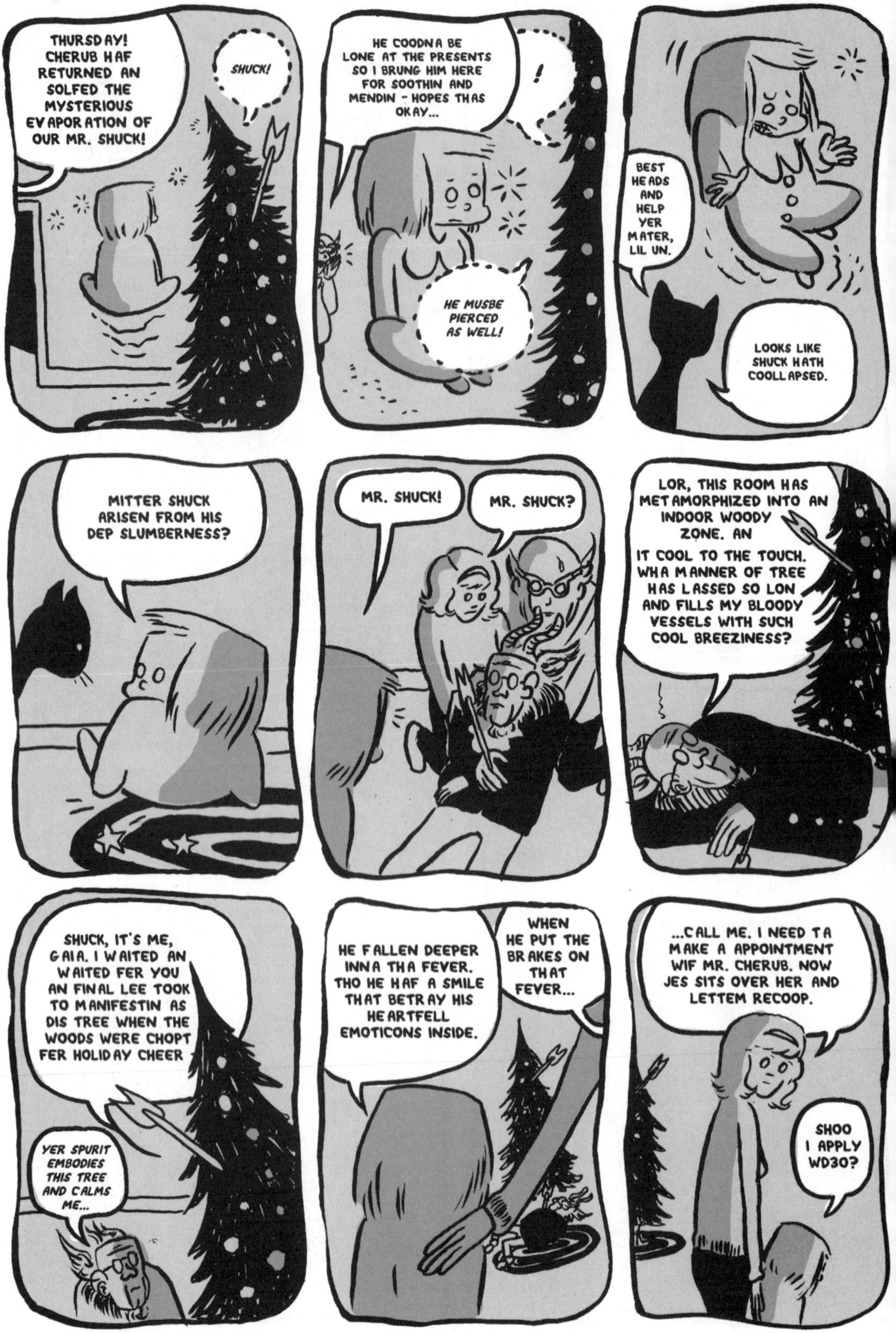
THURSDAY! CHERUB HAF RETURNED AN SOLFED THE MYSTERIOUS EVAPORATION OF OUR MR. SHUCK!
SHUCK!
HE COODNA BE LONE AT THE PRESENTS SO I BRUNG HIM HERE FOR SOOTHIN AND MENDIN - HOPES THAS OKAY...
!
HE MUSBE PIERCED AS WELL!
BEST HEADS AND HELP YER MATER, LIL UN.
LOOKS LIKE SHUCK HATH COOLLAPSED.
MITTER SHUCK ARISEN FROM HIS DEP SLUMBERNESS?
MR. SHUCK!
MR. SHUCK?
LOR, THIS ROOM HAS METAMORPHIZED INTO AN INDOOR WOODY ZONE. AN
IT COOL TO THE TOUCH. WHA MANNER OF TREE HAS LASSED SO LON AND FILLS MY BLOODY VESSELS WITH SUCH COOL BREEZINESS?
SHUCK, IT'S ME, GAIA. I WAITED AN WAITED FER YOU AN FINAL LEE TOOK TO MANIFESTIN AS DIS TREE WHEN THE WOODS WERE CHOPT FER HOLIDAY CHEER
YER SPURIT EMBODIES THIS TREE AND CALMS ME...
HE FALLEN DEEPER INNA THA FEVER. THO HE HAF A SMILE THAT BETRAY HIS HEARTFELL EMOTICONS INSIDE.
WHEN HE PUT THE BRAKES ON THAT FEVER...
...CALL ME. I NEED TA MAKE A APPOINTMENT WIF MR. CHERUB. NOW JES SITS OVER HER AND LETTEM RECOOP.
SHOO I APPLY WD30?

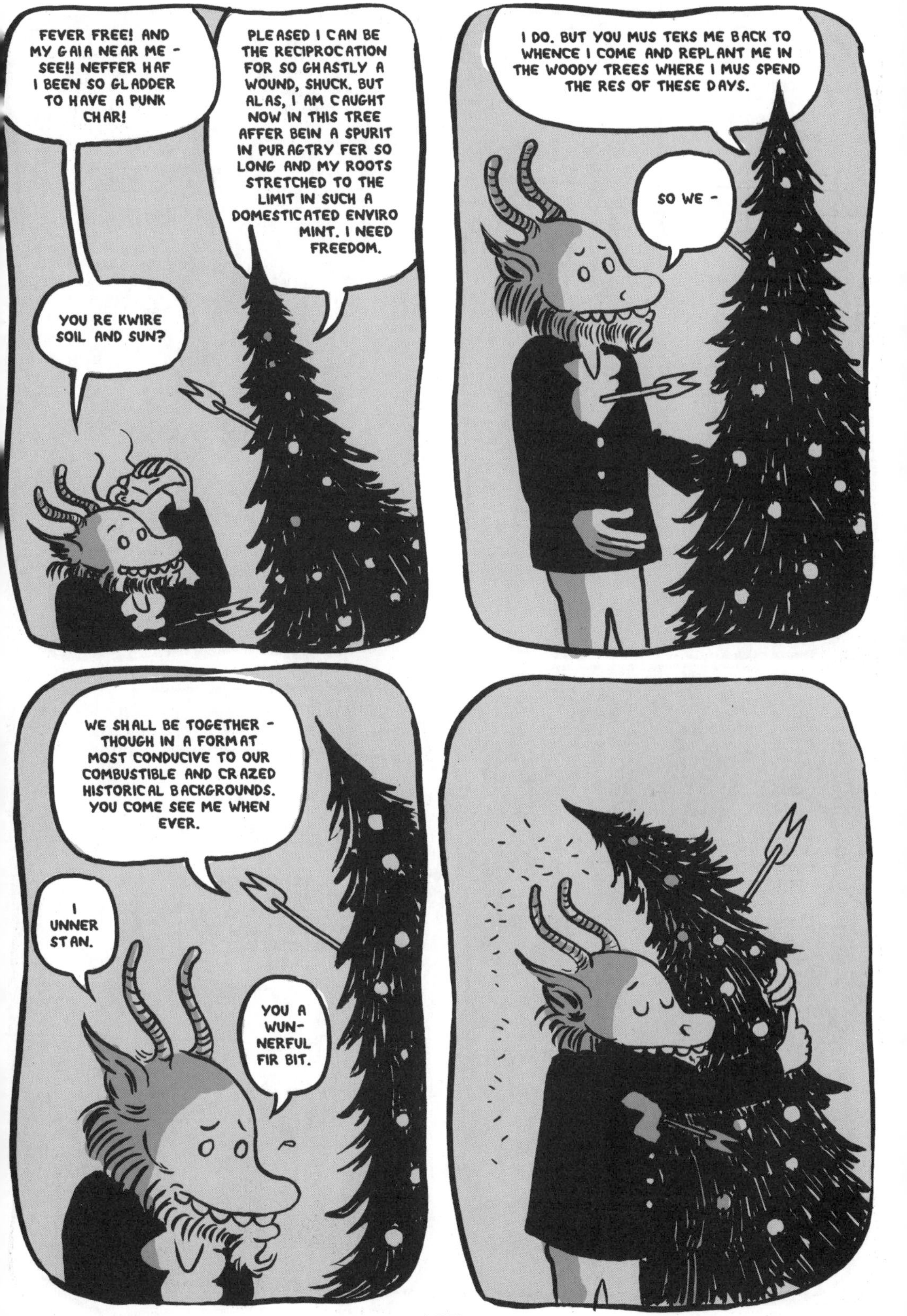
FEVER FREE! AND MY GAIA NEAR ME - SEE!! NEFFER HAF I BEEN SO GLADDER TO HAVE A PUNK CHAR!
PLEASED I CAN BE THE RECIPROCATION FOR SO GHASTLY A WOUND, SHUCK. BUT ALAS, I AM CAUGHT NOW IN THIS TREE AFFER BEIN A SPURIT IN PURAGTRY FER SO LONG AND MY ROOTS STRETCHED TO THE LIMIT IN SUCH A DOMESTICATED ENVIRO MINT. I NEED FREEDOM.
YOU RE KWIRE SOIL AND SUN?
I DO. BUT YOU MUS TEKS ME BACK TO WHENCE I COME AND REPLANT ME IN THE WOODY TREES WHERE I MUS SPEND THE RES OF THESE DAYS.
SO WE -
WE SHALL BE TOGETHER - THOUGH IN A FORMAT MOST CONDUCIVE TO OUR COMBUSTIBLE AND CRAZED HISTORICAL BACKGROUNDS. YOU COME SEE ME WHEN EVER.
I UNNER STAN.
YOU A WUN-NERFUL FIR BIT.

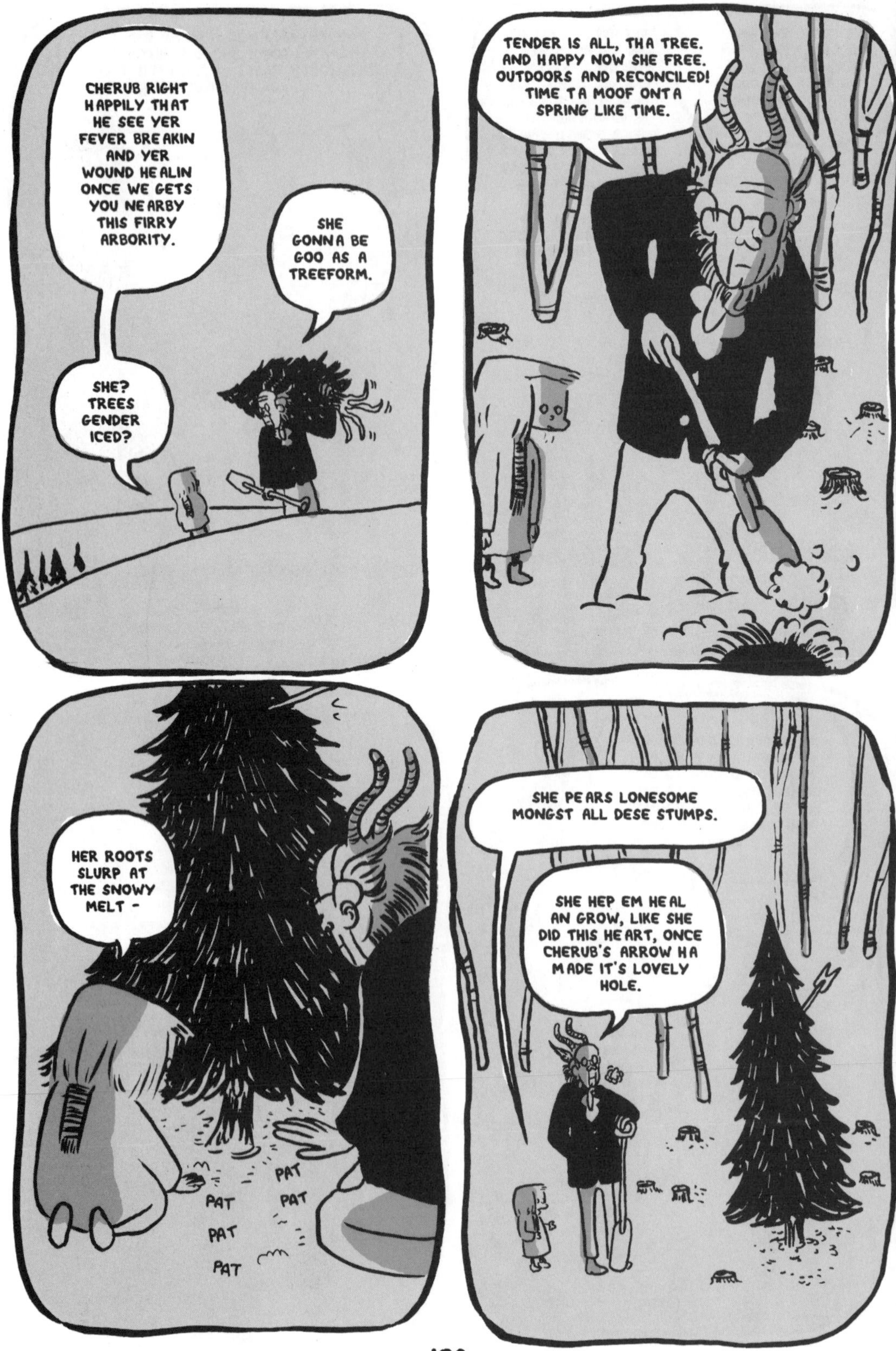
CHERUB RIGHT HAPPILY THAT HE SEE YER FEVER BREAKIN AND YER WOUND HEALIN ONCE WE GETS YOU NEARBY THIS FIRRY ARBORITY.
SHE GONNA BE GOO AS A TREEFORM.
SHE? TREES GENDER ICED?
TENDER IS ALL, THA TREE. AND HAPPY NOW SHE FREE. OUTDOORS AND RECONCILED! TIME TA MOOF ONTA SPRING LIKE TIME.
HER ROOTS SLURP AT THE SNOWY MELT -
PAT
PAT
PAT
PAT
PAT
PAT
SHE PEARS LONESOME MONGST ALL DESE STUMPS.
SHE HEP EM HEAL AN GROW, LIKE SHE DID THIS HEART, ONCE CHERUB'S ARROW HA MADE IT'S LOVELY HOLE.

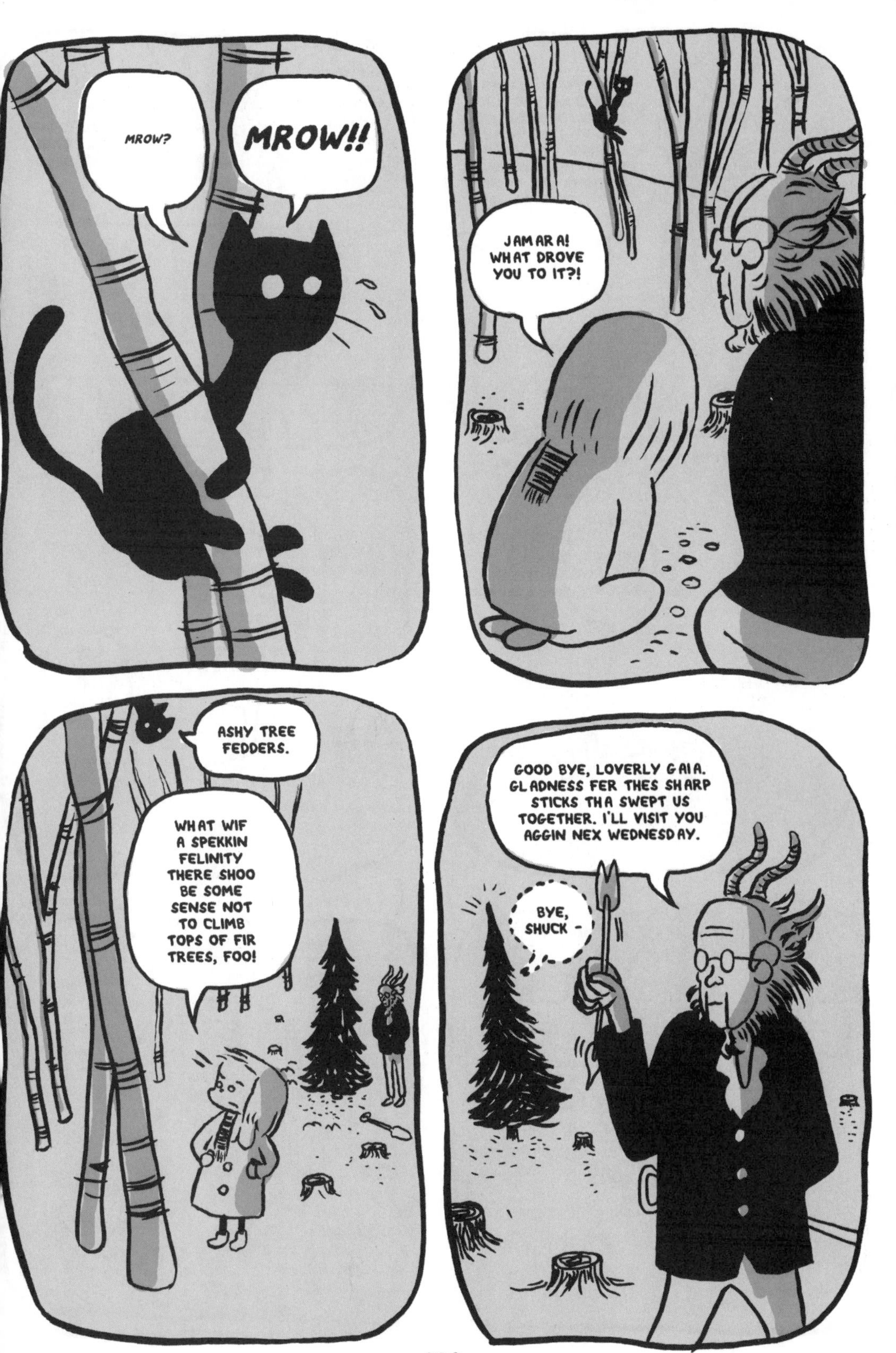
MROW?
MROW!!
JAMARA! WHAT DROVE YOU TO IT?!
ASHY TREE FEDDERS.
WHAT WIF A SPEKKIN FELINITY THERE SHOO BE SOME SENSE NOT TO CLIMB TOPS OF FIR TREES, FOO!
GOOD BYE, LOVERLY GAIA. GLADNESS FER THES SHARP STICKS THA SWEPT US TOGETHER. I'LL VISIT YOU AGGIN NEX WEDNESDAY.
BYE, SHUCK -

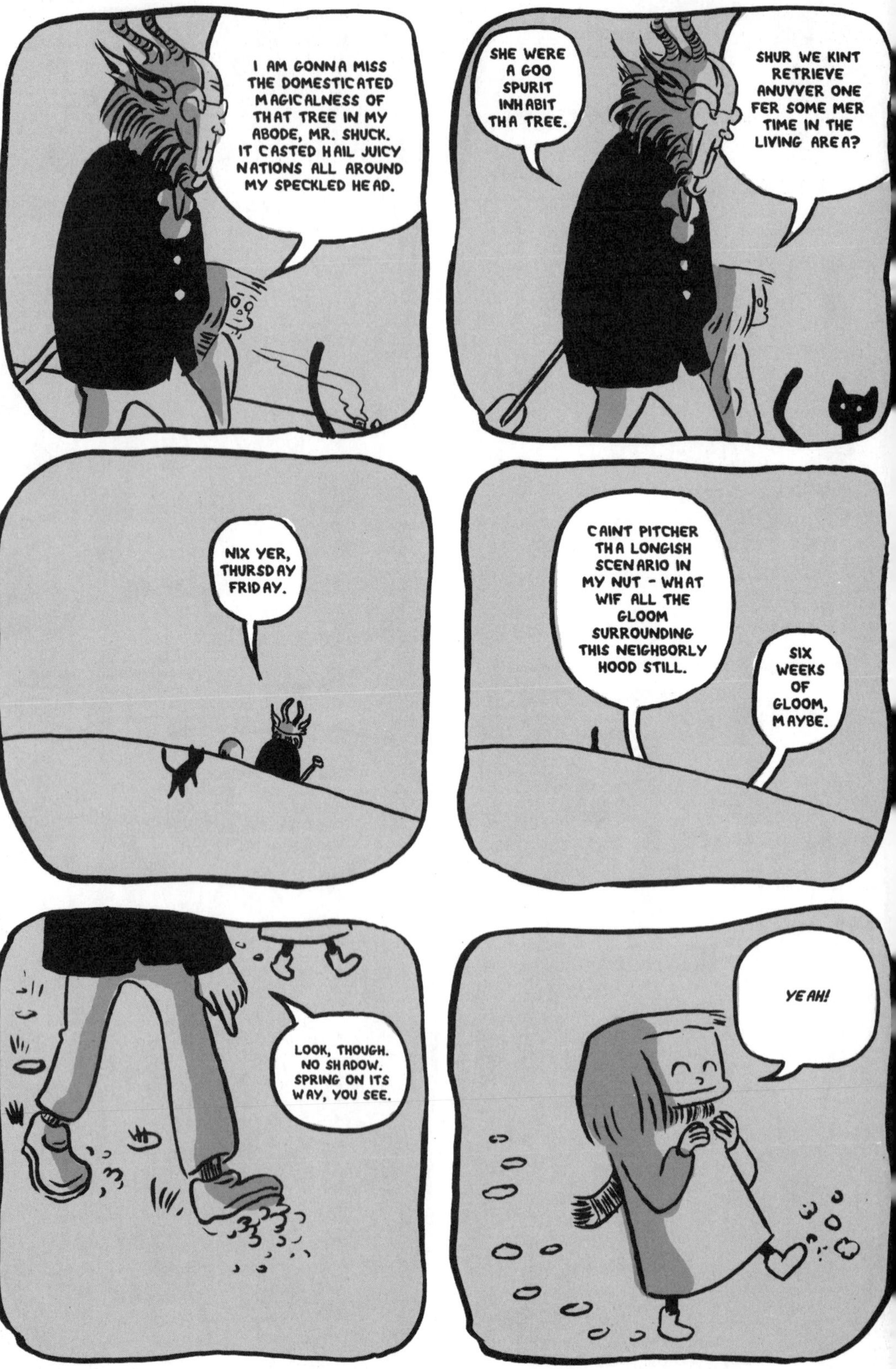
I AM GONNA MISS THE DOMESTICATED MAGICALNESS OF THAT TREE IN MY ABODE, MR. SHUCK. IT CASTED HAIL JUICY NATIONS ALL AROUND MY SPECKLED HEAD.
SHE WERE A GOO SPURIT INHABIT THA TREE.
SHUR WE KINT RETRIEVE ANUVVER ONE FER SOME MER TIME IN THE LIVING AREA?
NIX YER, THURSDAY FRIDAY.
CAINT PITCHER THA LONGISH SCENARIO IN MY NUT - WHAT WIF ALL THE GLOOM SURROUNDING THIS NEIGHBORLY HOOD STILL.
SIX WEEKS OF GLOOM, MAYBE.
LOOK, THOUGH. NO SHADOW. SPRING ON ITS WAY, YOU SEE.
YEAH!

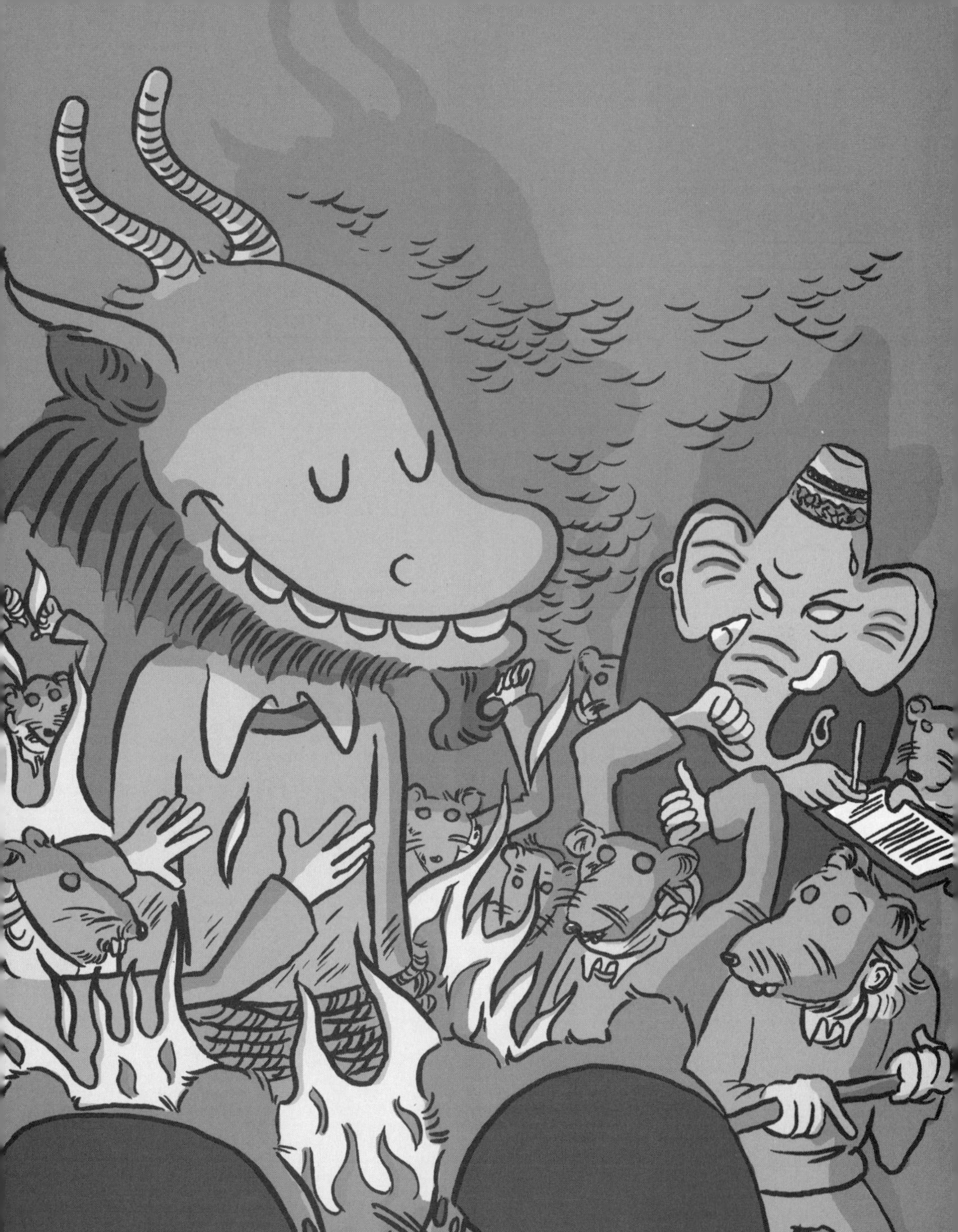

DEVILISH DHARMA

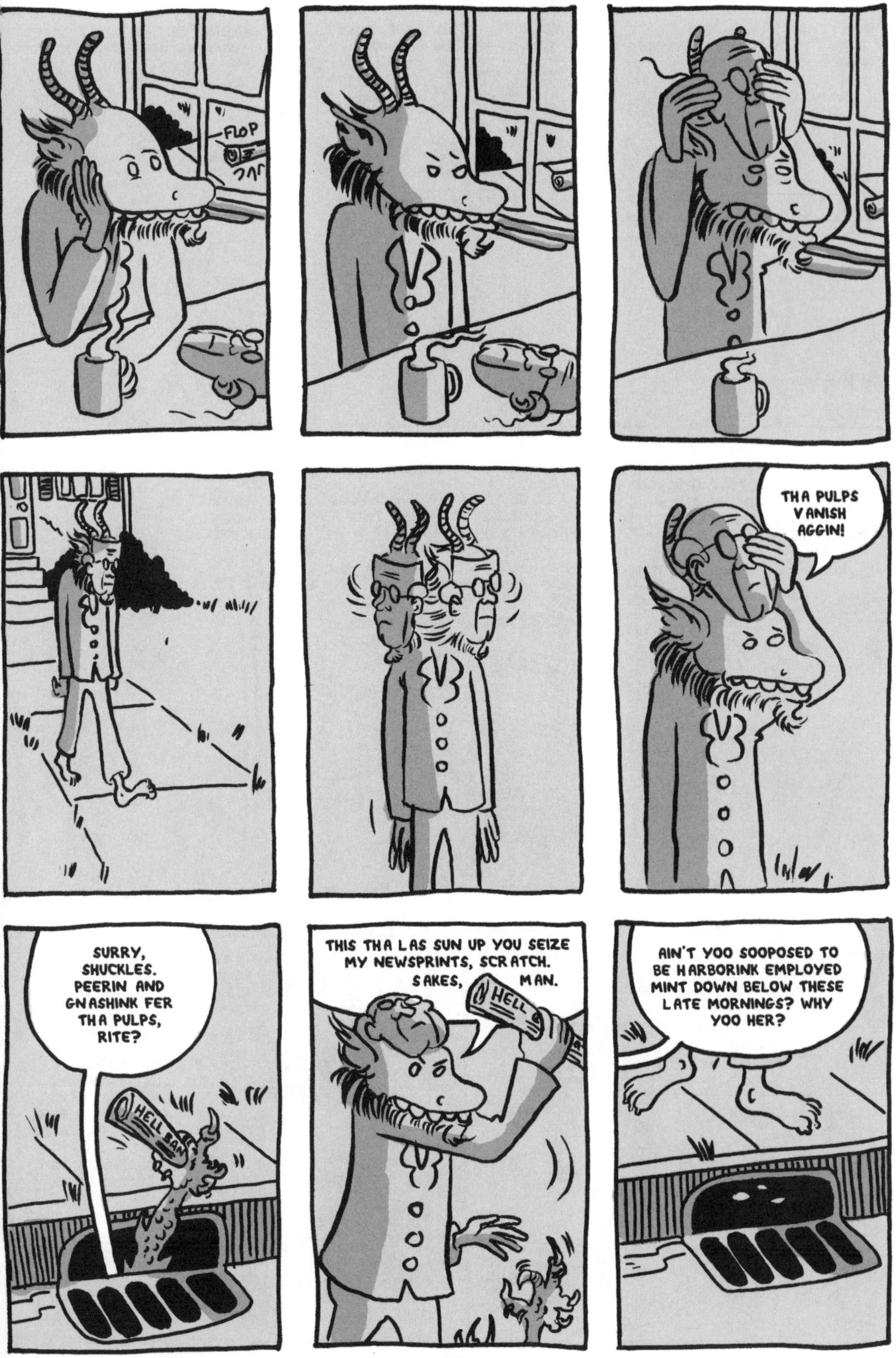
FLOP
THA PULPS VANISH AGGIN!
SURRY, SHUCKLES. PEERIN AND GNASHINK FER THA PULPS, RITE?
THIS THA LAS SUN UP YOU SEIZE MY NEWSPRINTS, SCRATCH. SAKES, MAN.
AIN'T YOO SOOPOSED TO BE HARBORINK EMPLOYED MINT DOWN BELOW THESE LATE MORNINGS? WHY YOO HER?

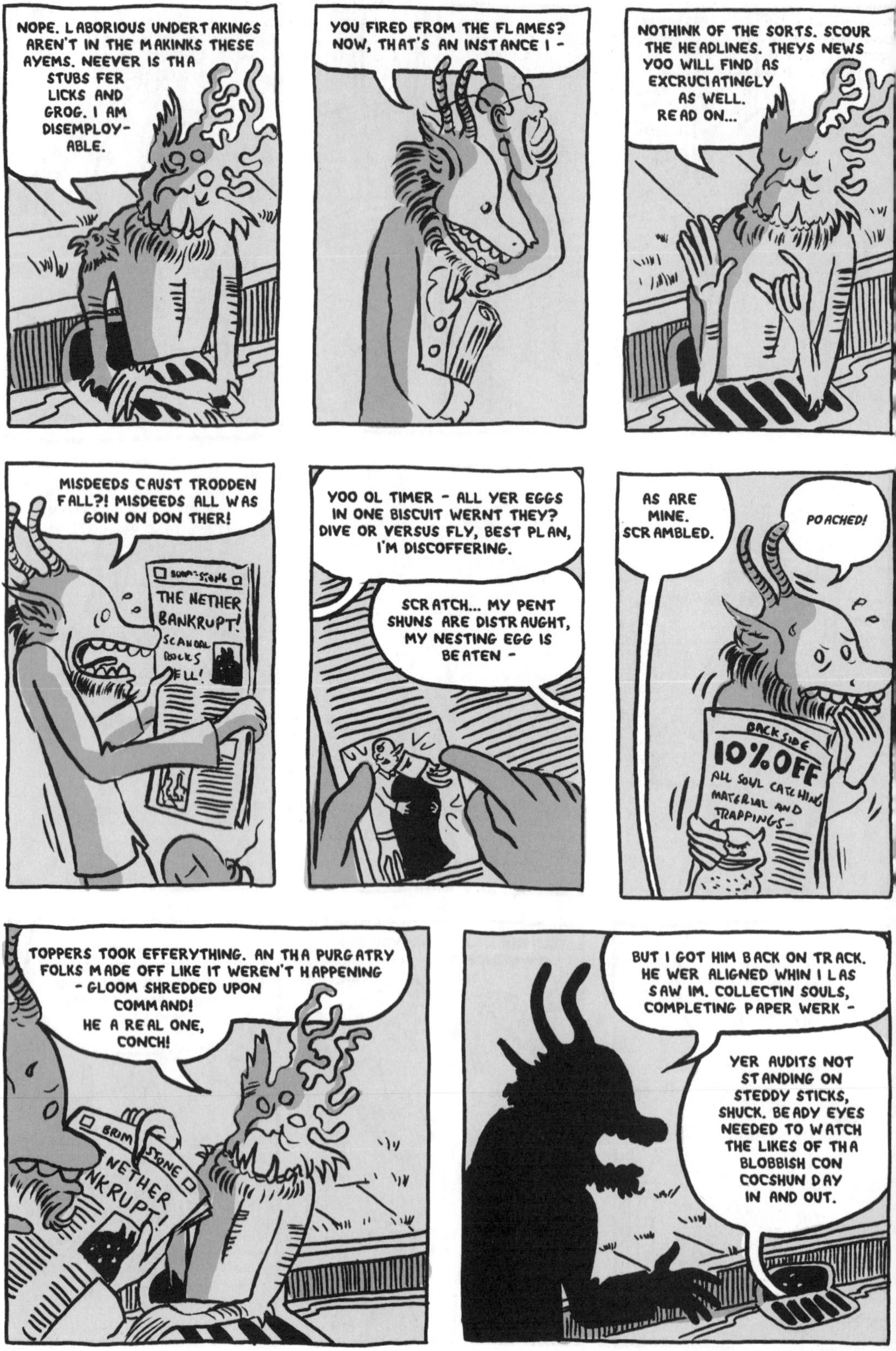

NOPE. LABORIOUS UNDERTAKINGS AREN'T IN THE MAKINKS THESE AYEMS. NEEVER IS THA STUBS FER LICKS AND GROG. I AM DISEMPLOY-ABLE.
YOU FIRED FROM THE FLAMES? NOW, THAT'S AN INSTANCE I -
NOTHINK OF THE SORTS. SCOUR THE HEADLINES. THEYS NEWS YOO WILL FIND AS EXCRUCIATINGLY AS WELL. READ ON...
MISDEEDS CAUST TRODDEN FALL?! MISDEEDS ALL WAS GOIN ON DON THER!
THE NETHER BANKRUPT!
SCANDAL ROCKS HELL!
YOO OL TIMER - ALL YER EGGS IN ONE BISCUIT WERNT THEY? DIVE OR VERSUS FLY, BEST PLAN, I'M DISCOFFERING.
SCRATCH... MY PENT SHUNS ARE DISTRAUGHT, MY NESTING EGG IS BEATEN -
AS ARE MINE. SCRAMBLED.
POACHED!
BACK SIDE
10% OFF
ALL SOUL CATCHING MATERIAL AND TRAPPINGS-
TOPPERS TOOK EFFERYTHING. AN THA PURGATRY FOLKS MADE OFF LIKE IT WEREN'T HAPPENING - GLOOM SHREDDED UPON COMMAND! HE A REAL ONE, CONCH!
BRIMSTONE
NETHER NKRUPT!
BUT I GOT HIM BACK ON TRACK. HE WER ALIGNED WHIN I LAS SAW IM. COLLECTIN SOULS, COMPLETING PAPER WERK -
YER AUDITS NOT STANDING ON STEDDY STICKS, SHUCK. BEADY EYES NEEDED TO WATCH THE LIKES OF THA BLOBBISH CON COCSHUN DAY IN AND OUT.

RESUME WORKINK. GOTTA GET BACK ON THA ASSEMBLY LINE. NEFFER AGGIN, I SED, WHAT JOB'S BEFUR ME? MY ONLY LONELY EXPERIENCES ARE WIF THAT WHICH HAS GONE EVEN DEEPER THAN WHERE IT WAS BEFORE. GONE!

IT GONE!

ALLOIT!

WHER WILL I PLY THE AWE FILLED TRADES THA FILL THIS DECRIPPLED PARCHED MINT? WHO WILL NEED THESE DUSTBIN SKILLS?

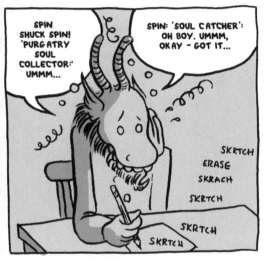

SPIN SHUCK SPIN! 'PURGATRY SOUL COLLECTOR:' UMMM...

SPIN: 'SOUL CATCHER': OH BOY. UMMM, OKAY - GOT IT...

SKRTCH
ERASE
SKRACH
SKRTCH
SKRTCH

'DEBT COLLECTING SPECIALIST' AN 'CONTRACT NEGOTIATIONS.'

YES, YES -

OKAY, OKAY RIGHT, WRITE! YES, OKAY. OKAY, I GOT IT NOW.

SKRTCH
SKRTCH
SKRTCH
SKRTCH
SKRTCH

'GREAT BEAST': NOW, THA WAS SOMEONE ELSERS -

NO, I DID HOLD THA POSITION FER A YER FER MR. CROWLEY WHEN HE -

GNAW
GNAW

SPIN, SPIN, SPIN: 'MANAGING DIRECTOR OF MERGERS AND ACQUISITIONS' HMMM.

OH, BOY. NAW BADDER...

NAW GOO, EEDER.

BOOKSHOP

COFFEE

GREY AGE BOOK AND CRYSTAL SHOP

OPEN

HELP WANTED

YOGA CLASSES

THIS RESUMED LIFE I CURRY IN THIS SATCHEL IS HEVVIER AND HEVVIER. I'LL UNLOAD IT CLOSEST TO HOME BASE. HER'E A POSSIBILIKITY: GREY AGE CRYSTALS AND BOOKS, PERHAPS.

OPEN

YOGA

RING RING

VISIT THE FOURTH WORLD

YOG CLASS

BET KITSCH UP: 'KEY TO THA TRUE AGE OF THEN.' HMM?

BAD CHECKS CURSED MGMT.

YOGI CLASSES

'BACK OFF I'M A GODDESS?'

CAN I HEP YOO?

I'D LIKE TO POUR MYSELF INTO THA JOB YOOV GOT PASTED OUT FRONT.

116

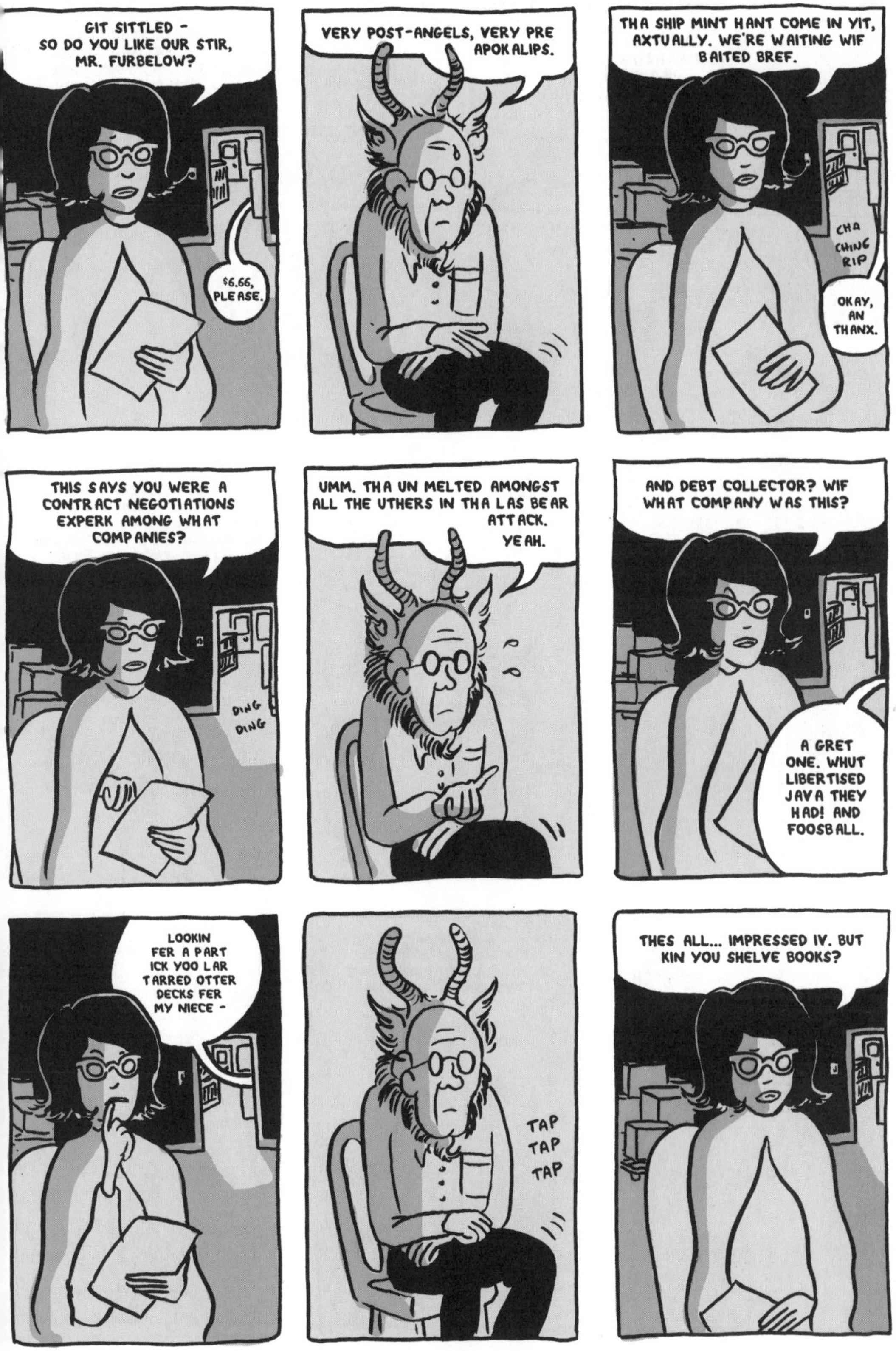

GIT SITTLED - SO DO YOU LIKE OUR STIR, MR. FURBELOW?
$6.66, PLEASE.
VERY POST-ANGELS, VERY PRE APOKALIPS.
THA SHIP MINT HANT COME IN YIT, AXTUALLY. WE'RE WAITING WIF BAITED BREF.
CHA CHING RIP
OKAY, AN THANX.
THIS SAYS YOU WERE A CONTRACT NEGOTIATIONS EXPERK AMONG WHAT COMPANIES?
DING DING
UMM. THA UN MELTED AMONGST ALL THE UTHERS IN THA LAS BEAR ATTACK.
YEAH.
AND DEBT COLLECTOR? WIF WHAT COMPANY WAS THIS?
A GRET ONE. WHUT LIBERTISED JAVA THEY HAD! AND FOOSBALL.
LOOKIN FER A PART ICK YOO LAR TARRED OTTER DECKS FER MY NIECE -
TAP TAP TAP
THES ALL... IMPRESSED IV. BUT KIN YOU SHELVE BOOKS?

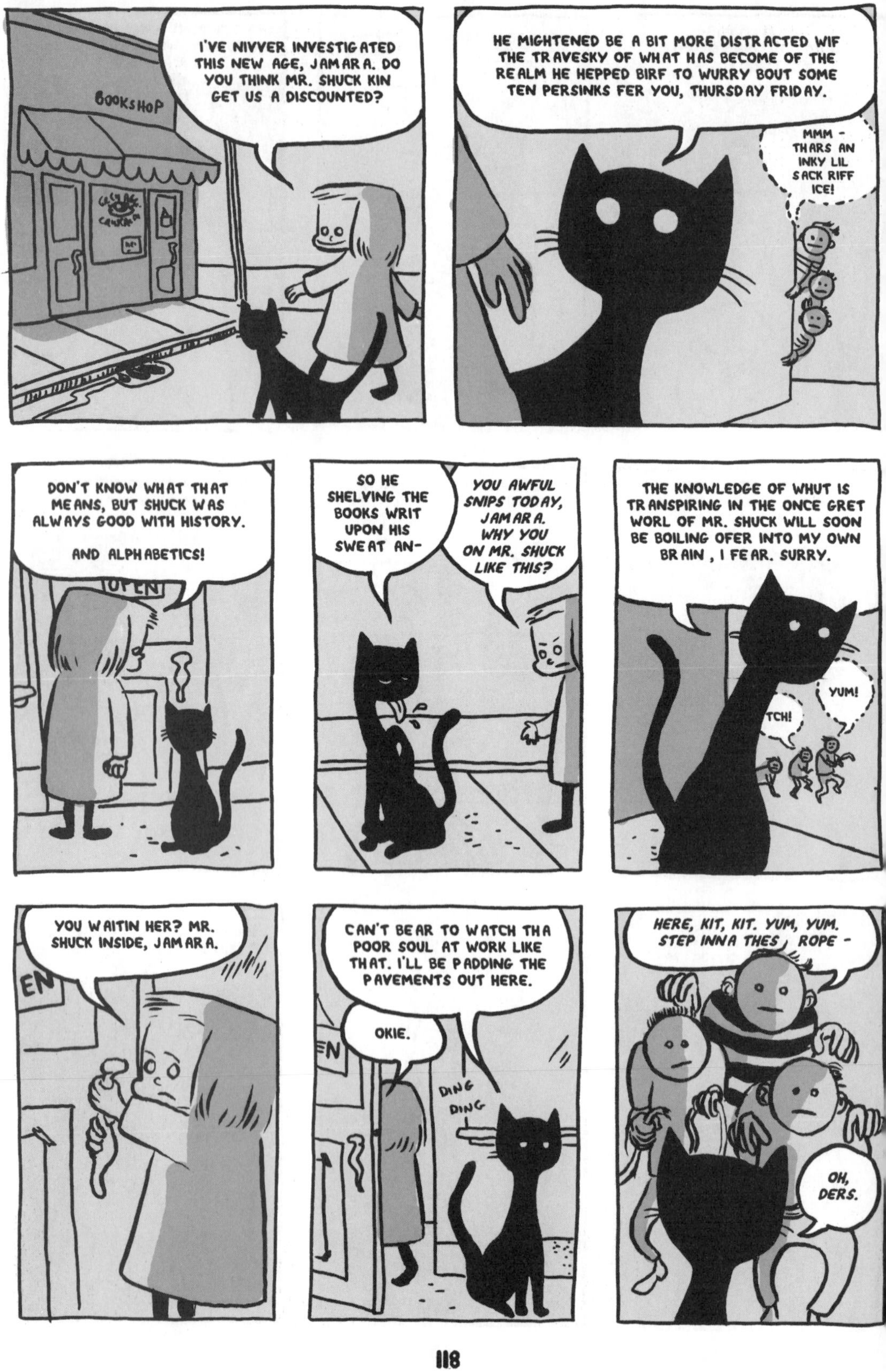
I'VE NIVVER INVESTIGATED THIS NEW AGE, JAMARA. DO YOU THINK MR. SHUCK KIN GET US A DISCOUNTED?
BOOKSHOP
HE MIGHTENED BE A BIT MORE DISTRACTED WIF THE TRAVESKY OF WHAT HAS BECOME OF THE REALM HE HEPPED BIRF TO WURRY BOUT SOME TEN PERSINKS FER YOU, THURSDAY FRIDAY.
MMM - THARS AN INKY LIL SACK RIFF ICE!
DON'T KNOW WHAT THAT MEANS, BUT SHUCK WAS ALWAYS GOOD WITH HISTORY.
AND ALPHABETICS!
OPEN
SO HE SHELVING THE BOOKS WRIT UPON HIS SWEAT AN-
YOU AWFUL SNIPS TODAY, JAMARA. WHY YOU ON MR. SHUCK LIKE THIS?
THE KNOWLEDGE OF WHUT IS TRANSPIRING IN THE ONCE GRET WORL OF MR. SHUCK WILL SOON BE BOILING OFER INTO MY OWN BRAIN, I FEAR. SURRY.
YUM!
TCH!
YOU WAITIN HER? MR. SHUCK INSIDE, JAMARA.
EN
CAN'T BEAR TO WATCH THA POOR SOUL AT WORK LIKE THAT. I'LL BE PADDING THE PAVEMENTS OUT HERE.
OKIE.
DING DING
HERE, KIT, KIT. YUM, YUM. STEP INNA THES ROPE -
OH, DERS.

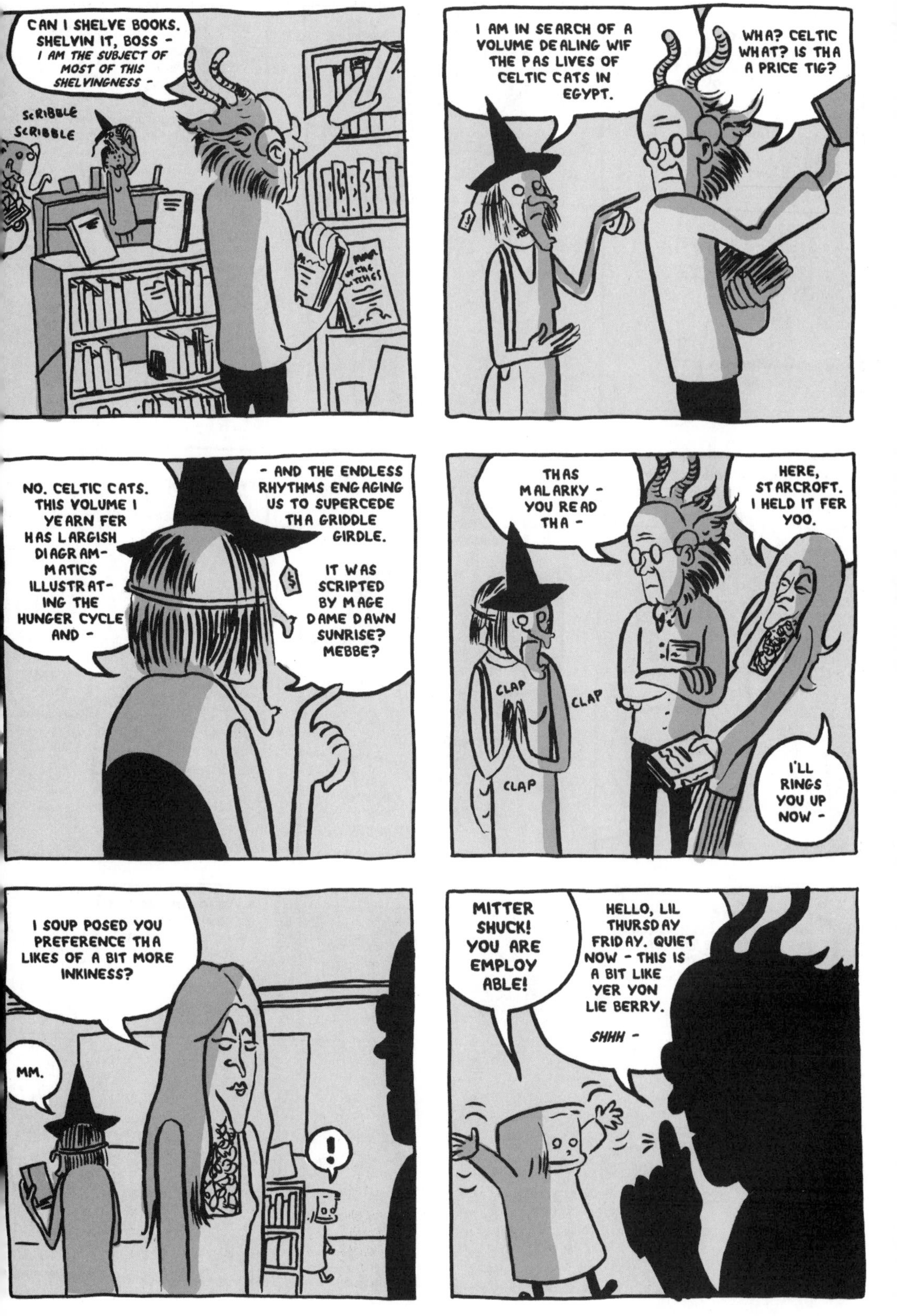
CAN I SHELVE BOOKS. SHELVIN IT, BOSS - I AM THE SUBJECT OF MOST OF THIS SHELVINGNESS -
SCRIBBLE SCRIBBLE
I AM IN SEARCH OF A VOLUME DEALING WIF THE PAS LIVES OF CELTIC CATS IN EGYPT.
WHA? CELTIC WHAT? IS THA A PRICE TIG?
NO. CELTIC CATS. THIS VOLUME I YEARN FER HAS LARGISH DIAGRAM-MATICS ILLUSTRAT-ING THE HUNGER CYCLE AND -
- AND THE ENDLESS RHYTHMS ENGAGING US TO SUPERCEDE THA GRIDDLE GIRDLE.
IT WAS SCRIPTED BY MAGE DAME DAWN SUNRISE? MEBBE?
THAS MALARKY - YOU READ THA -
HERE, STARCROFT. I HELD IT FER YOO.
CLAP CLAP CLAP
I'LL RINGS YOU UP NOW -
I SOUP POSED YOU PREFERENCE THA LIKES OF A BIT MORE INKINESS?
MM.
!
MITTER SHUCK! YOU ARE EMPLOY ABLE!
HELLO, LIL THURSDAY FRIDAY. QUIET NOW - THIS IS A BIT LIKE YER YON LIE BERRY.
SHHH -

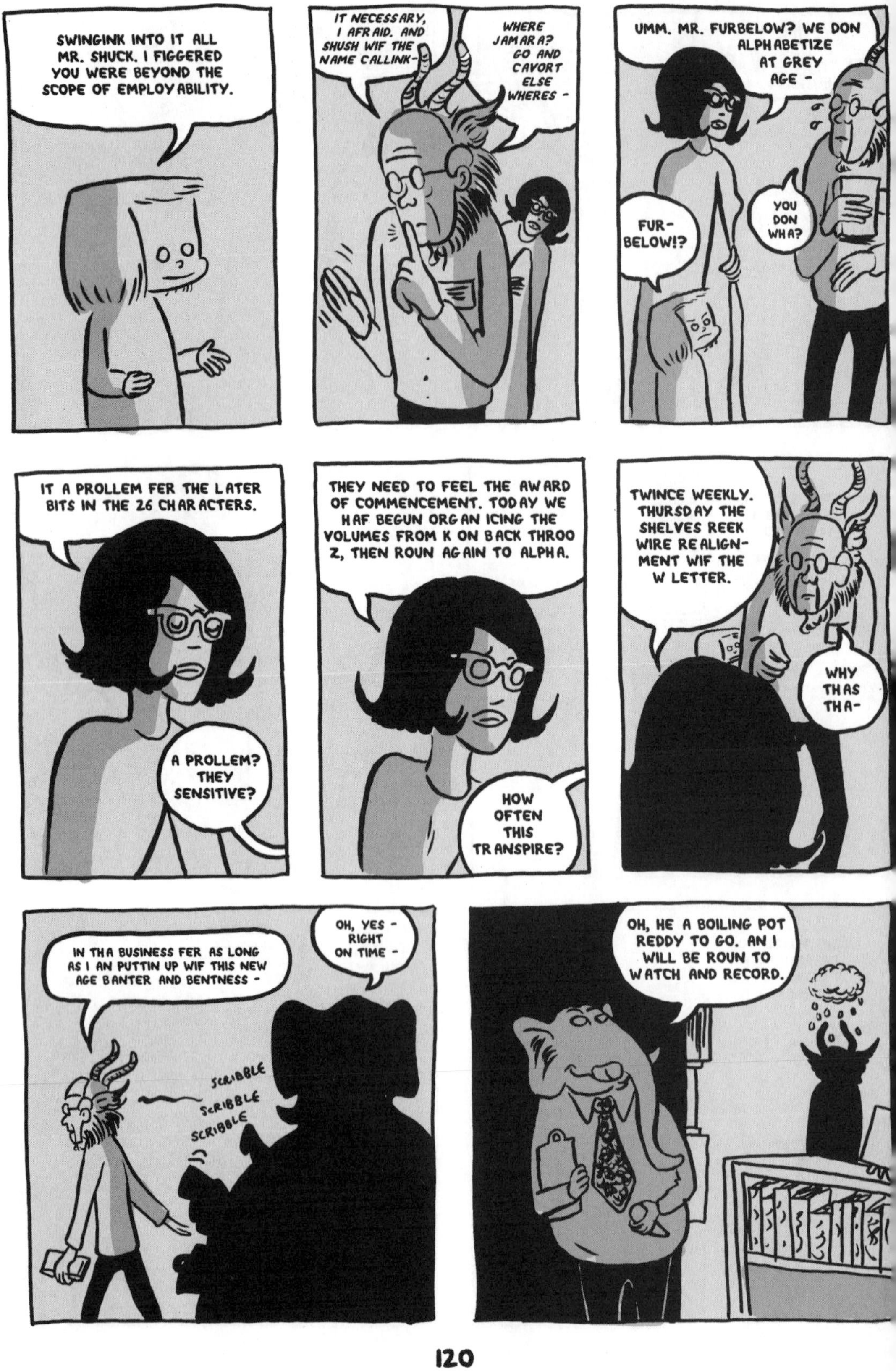
SWINGINK INTO IT ALL MR. SHUCK. I FIGGERED YOU WERE BEYOND THE SCOPE OF EMPLOYABILITY.
IT NECESSARY, I AFRAID. AND SHUSH WIF THE NAME CALLINK-
WHERE JAMARA? GO AND CAVORT ELSE WHERES -
UMM. MR. FURBELOW? WE DON ALPHABETIZE AT GREY AGE -
FUR-BELOW!?
YOU DON WHA?
IT A PROLLEM FER THE LATER BITS IN THE 26 CHARACTERS.
A PROLLEM? THEY SENSITIVE?
THEY NEED TO FEEL THE AWARD OF COMMENCEMENT. TODAY WE HAF BEGUN ORGAN ICING THE VOLUMES FROM K ON BACK THROO Z, THEN ROUN AGAIN TO ALPHA.
HOW OFTEN THIS TRANSPIRE?
TWINCE WEEKLY. THURSDAY THE SHELVES REEK WIRE REALIGN-MENT WIF THE W LETTER.
WHY THAS THA-
IN THA BUSINESS FER AS LONG AS I AN PUTTIN UP WIF THIS NEW AGE BANTER AND BENTNESS -
OH, YES - RIGHT ON TIME -
SCRIBBLE
SCRIBBLE
SCRIBBLE
OH, HE A BOILING POT REDDY TO GO. AN I WILL BE ROUN TO WATCH AND RECORD.

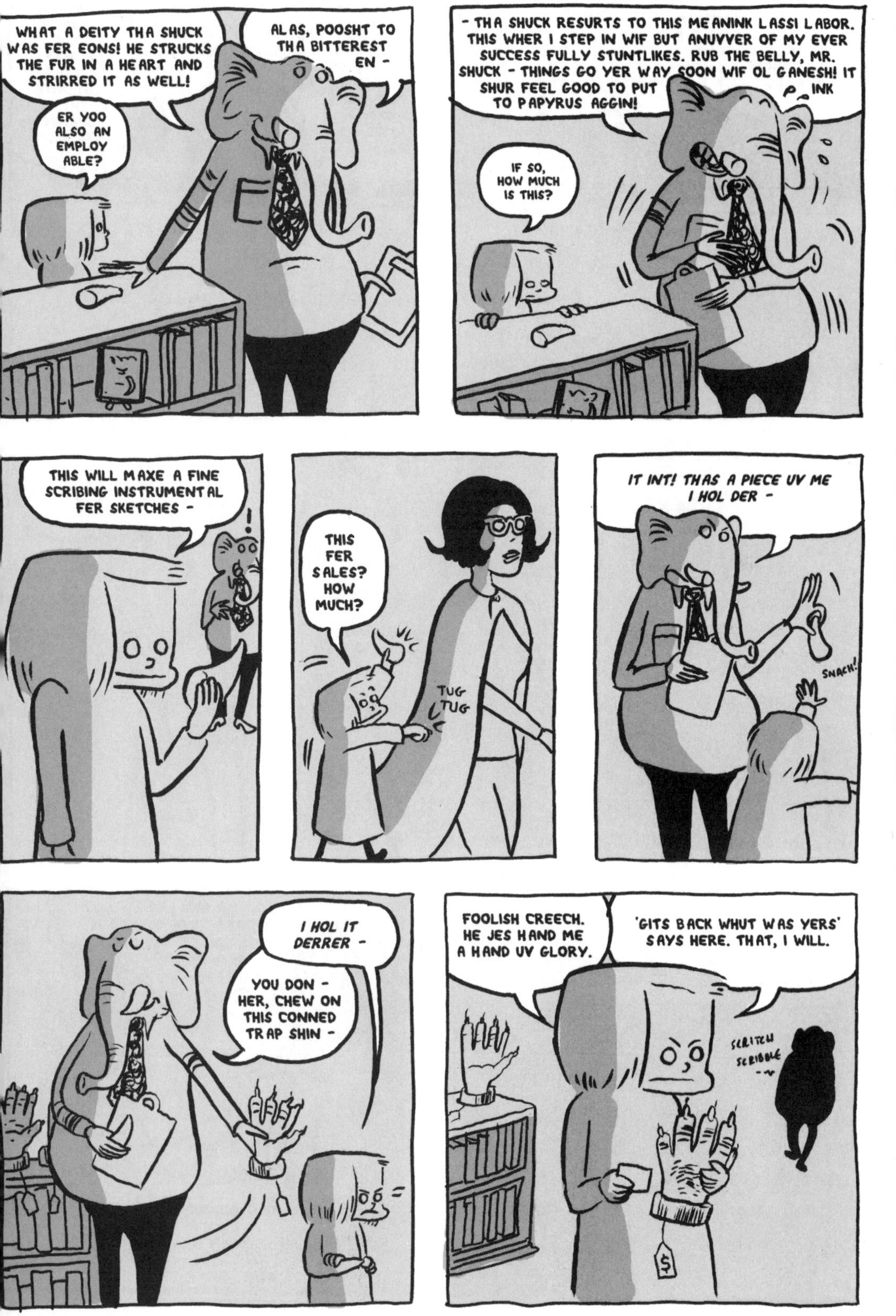
WHAT A DEITY THA SHUCK WAS FER EONS! HE STRUCKS THE FUR IN A HEART AND STRIRRED IT AS WELL!
ALAS, POOSHT TO THA BITTEREST EN -
ER YOO ALSO AN EMPLOY ABLE?
- THA SHUCK RESURTS TO THIS MEANINK LASSI LABOR. THIS WHER I STEP IN WIF BUT ANUVVER OF MY EVER SUCCESS FULLY STUNTLIKES. RUB THE BELLY, MR. SHUCK - THINGS GO YER WAY SOON WIF OL GANESH! IT SHUR FEEL GOOD TO PUT INK TO PAPYRUS AGGIN!
IF SO, HOW MUCH IS THIS?
THIS WILL MAXE A FINE SCRIBING INSTRUMENTAL FER SKETCHES -
THIS FER SALES? HOW MUCH?
TUG TUG
IT INT! THAS A PIECE UV ME I HOL DER -
SNACH!
I HOL IT DERRER -
YOU DON - HER, CHEW ON THIS CONNED TRAP SHIN -
FOOLISH CREECH. HE JES HAND ME A HAND UV GLORY.
'GITS BACK WHUT WAS YERS' SAYS HERE. THAT, I WILL.
SCRITCH SCRIBBLE

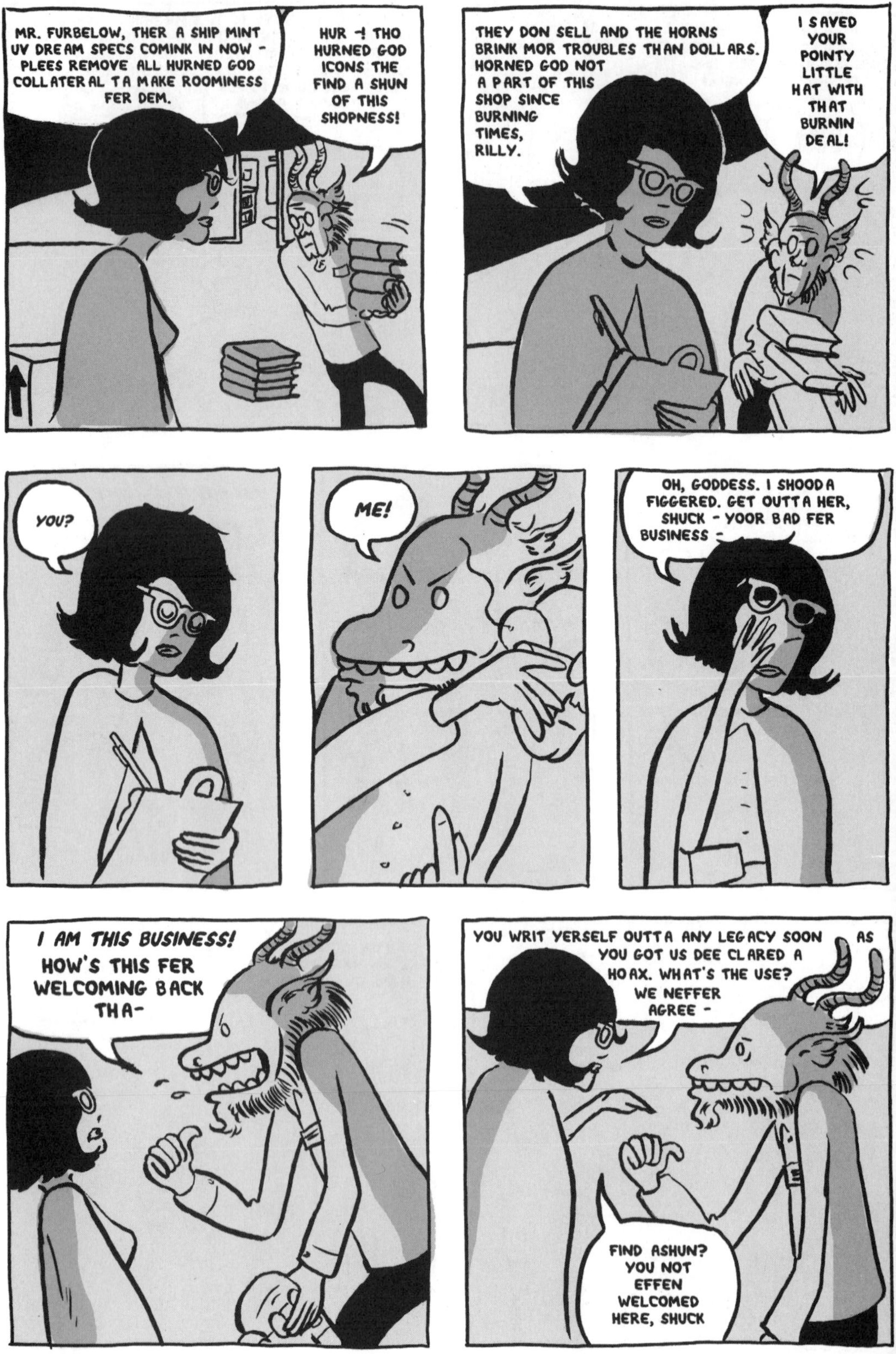
MR. FURBELOW, THER A SHIP MINT UV DREAM SPECS COMINK IN NOW - PLEES REMOVE ALL HURNED GOD COLLATERAL TA MAKE ROOMINESS FER DEM.
HUR -! THO HURNED GOD ICONS THE FIND A SHUN OF THIS SHOPNESS!
THEY DON SELL AND THE HORNS BRINK MOR TROUBLES THAN DOLLARS. HORNED GOD NOT A PART OF THIS SHOP SINCE BURNING TIMES, RILLY.
I SAVED YOUR POINTY LITTLE HAT WITH THAT BURNIN DEAL!
YOU?
ME!
OH, GODDESS. I SHOODA FIGGERED. GET OUTTA HER, SHUCK - YOOR BAD FER BUSINESS -
I AM THIS BUSINESS! HOW'S THIS FER WELCOMING BACK THA-
YOU WRIT YERSELF OUTTA ANY LEGACY SOON AS YOU GOT US DEE CLARED A HOAX. WHAT'S THE USE? WE NEFFER AGREE -
FIND ASHUN? YOU NOT EFFEN WELCOMED HERE, SHUCK

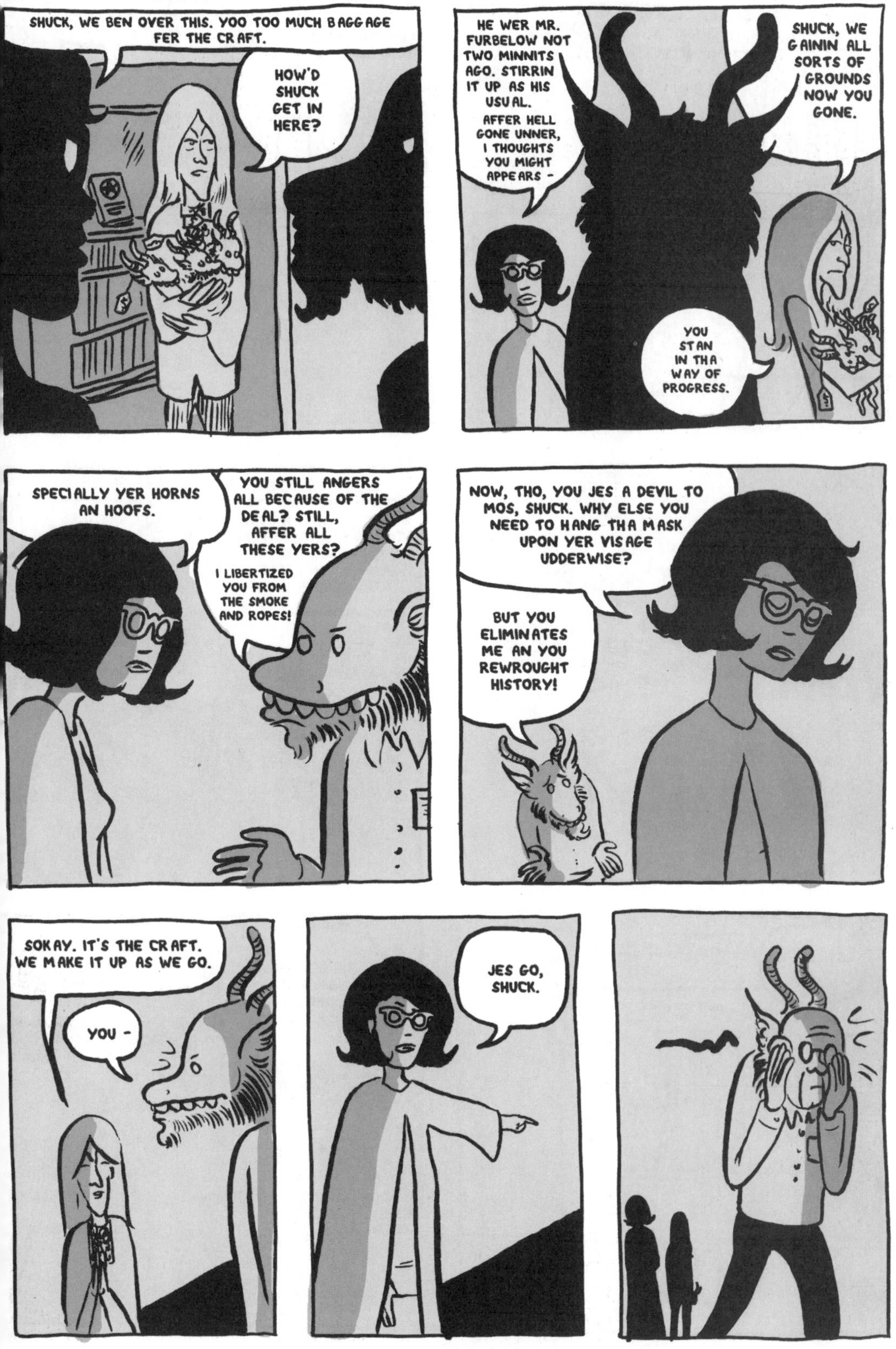
SHUCK, WE BEN OVER THIS. YOO TOO MUCH BAGGAGE FER THE CRAFT.
HOW'D SHUCK GET IN HERE?
HE WER MR. FURBELOW NOT TWO MINNITS AGO. STIRRIN IT UP AS HIS USUAL.
AFFER HELL GONE UNNER, I THOUGHTS YOU MIGHT APPEARS -
SHUCK, WE GAININ ALL SORTS OF GROUNDS NOW YOU GONE.
YOU STAN IN THA WAY OF PROGRESS.
SPECIALLY YER HORNS AN HOOFS.
YOU STILL ANGERS ALL BECAUSE OF THE DEAL? STILL, AFFER ALL THESE YERS?
I LIBERTIZED YOU FROM THE SMOKE AND ROPES!
NOW, THO, YOU JES A DEVIL TO MOS, SHUCK. WHY ELSE YOU NEED TO HANG THA MASK UPON YER VISAGE UDDERWISE?
BUT YOU ELIMINATES ME AN YOU REWROUGHT HISTORY!
SOKAY. IT'S THE CRAFT. WE MAKE IT UP AS WE GO.
YOU -
JES GO, SHUCK.

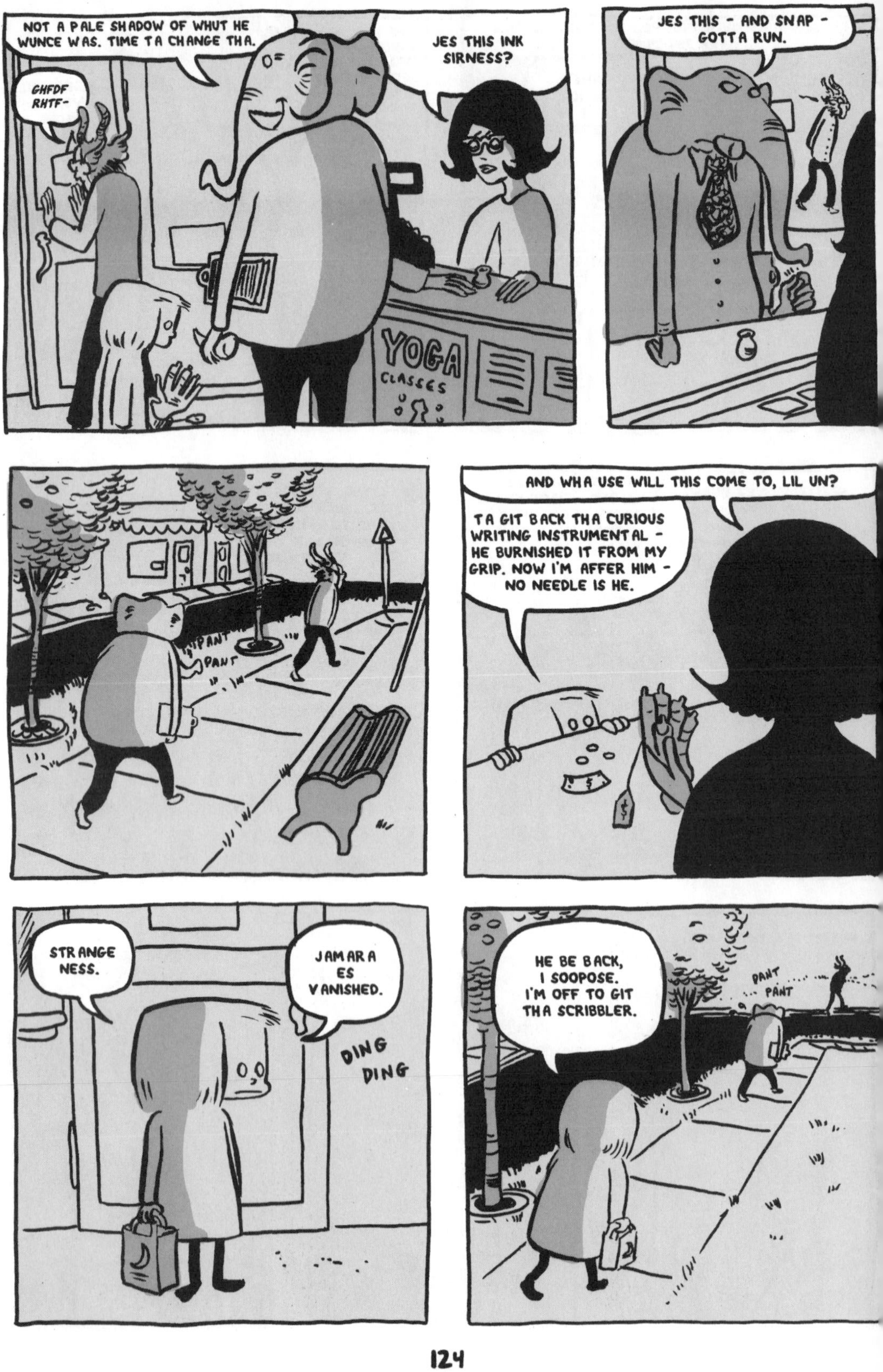
NOT A PALE SHADOW OF WHUT HE WUNCE WAS. TIME TA CHANGE THA.
GHFDF RHTF-
JES THIS INK SIRNESS?
YOGA CLASSES
JES THIS - AND SNAP - GOTTA RUN.
PANT PANT
AND WHA USE WILL THIS COME TO, LIL UN?
TA GIT BACK THA CURIOUS WRITING INSTRUMENTAL - HE BURNISHED IT FROM MY GRIP. NOW I'M AFFER HIM - NO NEEDLE IS HE.
STRANGE NESS.
JAMARA ES VANISHED.
DING DING
HE BE BACK, I SOOPOSE. I'M OFF TO GIT THA SCRIBBLER.
PANT PANT

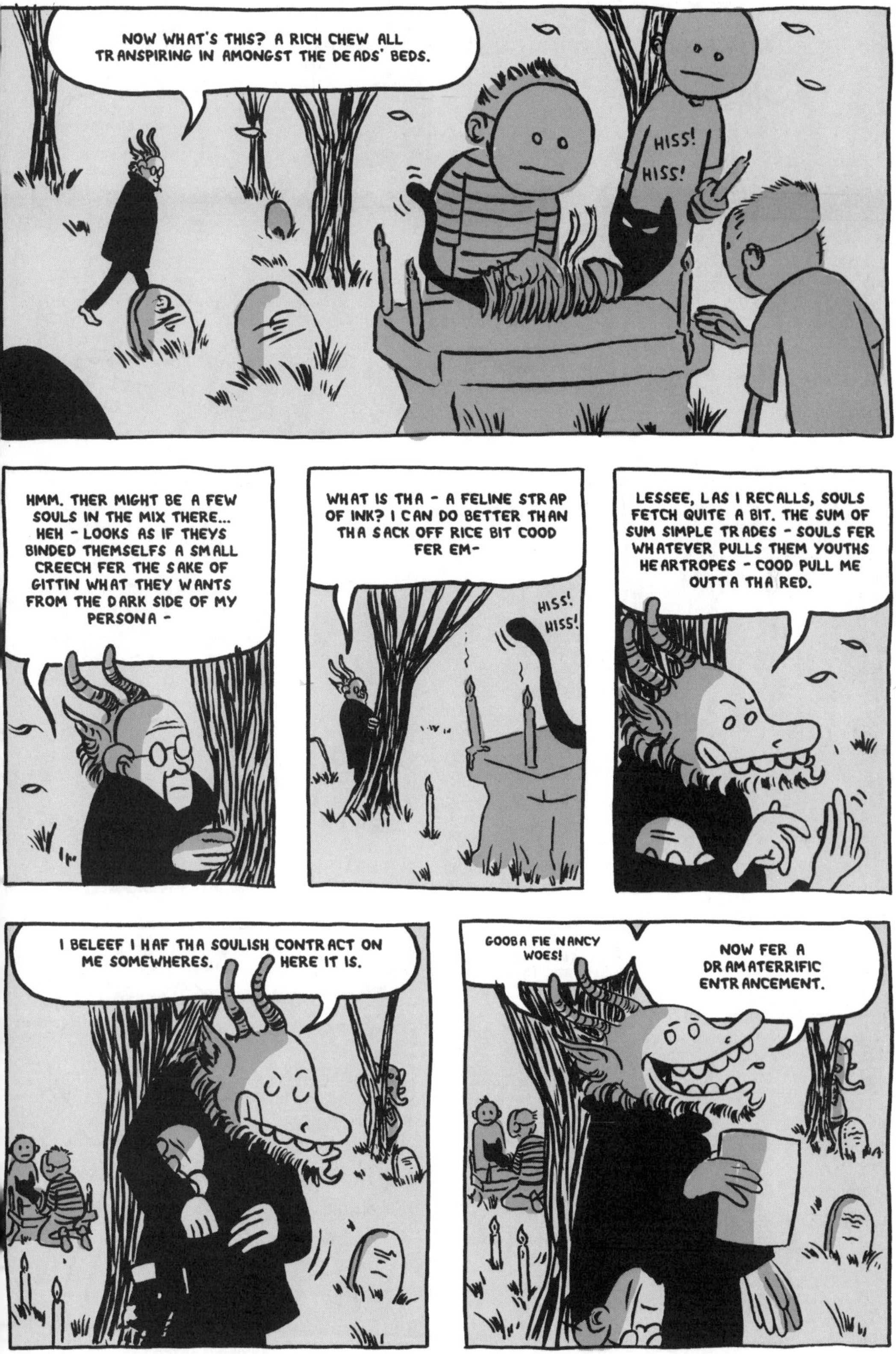
NOW WHAT'S THIS? A RICH CHEW ALL TRANSPIRING IN AMONGST THE DEADS' BEDS.
HISS! HISS!
HMM. THER MIGHT BE A FEW SOULS IN THE MIX THERE... HEH - LOOKS AS IF THEYS BINDED THEMSELFS A SMALL CREECH FER THE SAKE OF GITTIN WHAT THEY WANTS FROM THE DARK SIDE OF MY PERSONA -
WHAT IS THA - A FELINE STRAP OF INK? I CAN DO BETTER THAN THA SACK OFF RICE BIT COOD FER EM-
HISS! HISS!
LESSEE, LAS I RECALLS, SOULS FETCH QUITE A BIT. THE SUM OF SUM SIMPLE TRADES - SOULS FER WHATEVER PULLS THEM YOUTHS HEARTROPES - COOD PULL ME OUTTA THA RED.
I BELEEF I HAF THA SOULISH CONTRACT ON ME SOMEWHERES.
HERE IT IS.
GOOBA FIE NANCY WOES!
NOW FER A DRAMATERRIFIC ENTRANCEMENT.

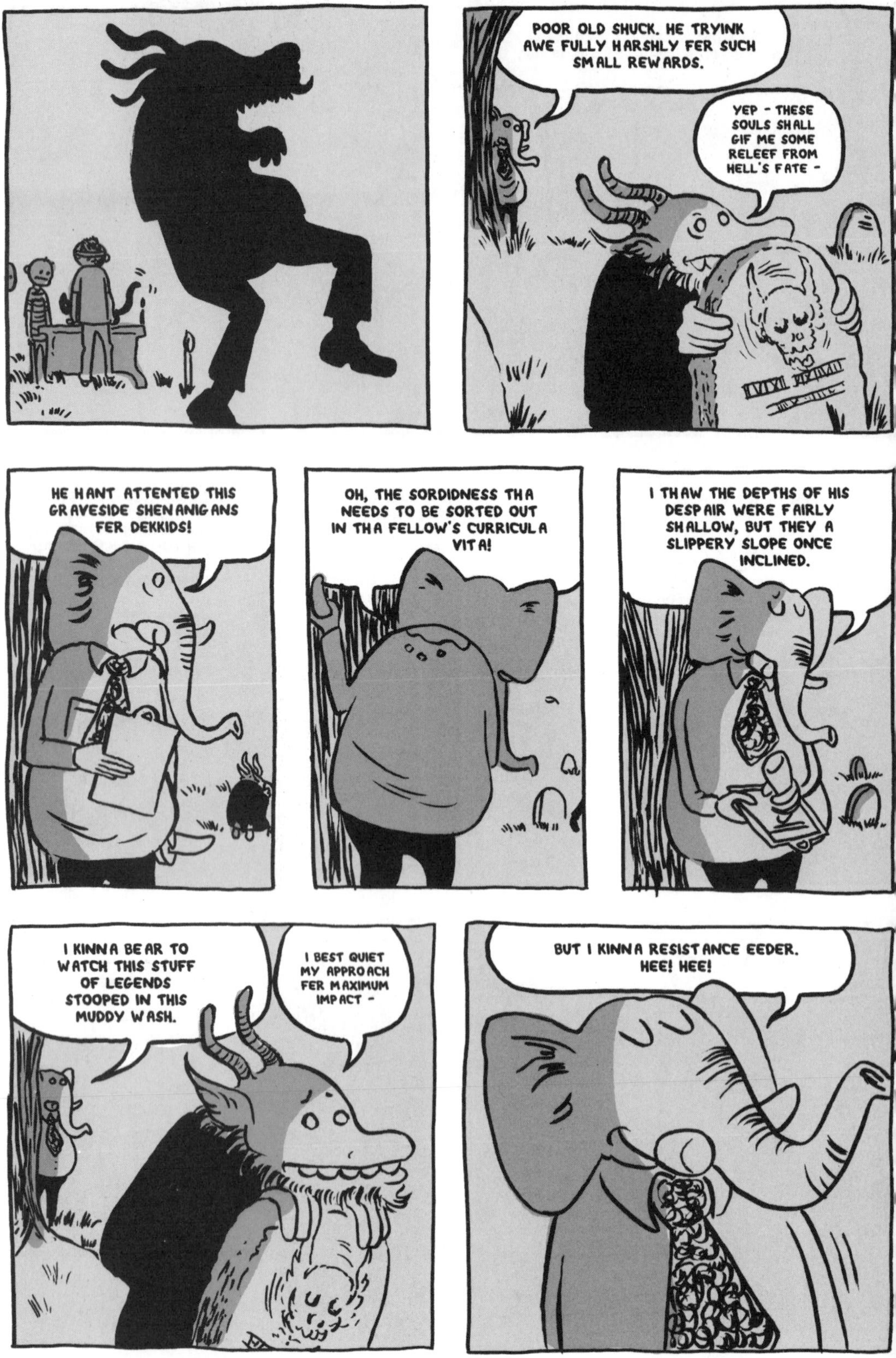

POOR OLD SHUCK. HE TRYINK AWE FULLY HARSHLY FER SUCH SMALL REWARDS.
YEP - THESE SOULS SHALL GIF ME SOME RELEEF FROM HELL'S FATE -
HE HANT ATTENTED THIS GRAVESIDE SHENANIGANS FER DEKKIDS!
OH, THE SORDIDNESS THA NEEDS TO BE SORTED OUT IN THA FELLOW'S CURRICULA VITA!
I THAW THE DEPTHS OF HIS DESPAIR WERE FAIRLY SHALLOW, BUT THEY A SLIPPERY SLOPE ONCE INCLINED.
I KINNA BEAR TO WATCH THIS STUFF OF LEGENDS STOOPED IN THIS MUDDY WASH.
I BEST QUIET MY APPROACH FER MAXIMUM IMPACT -
BUT I KINNA RESISTANCE EEDER. HEE! HEE!

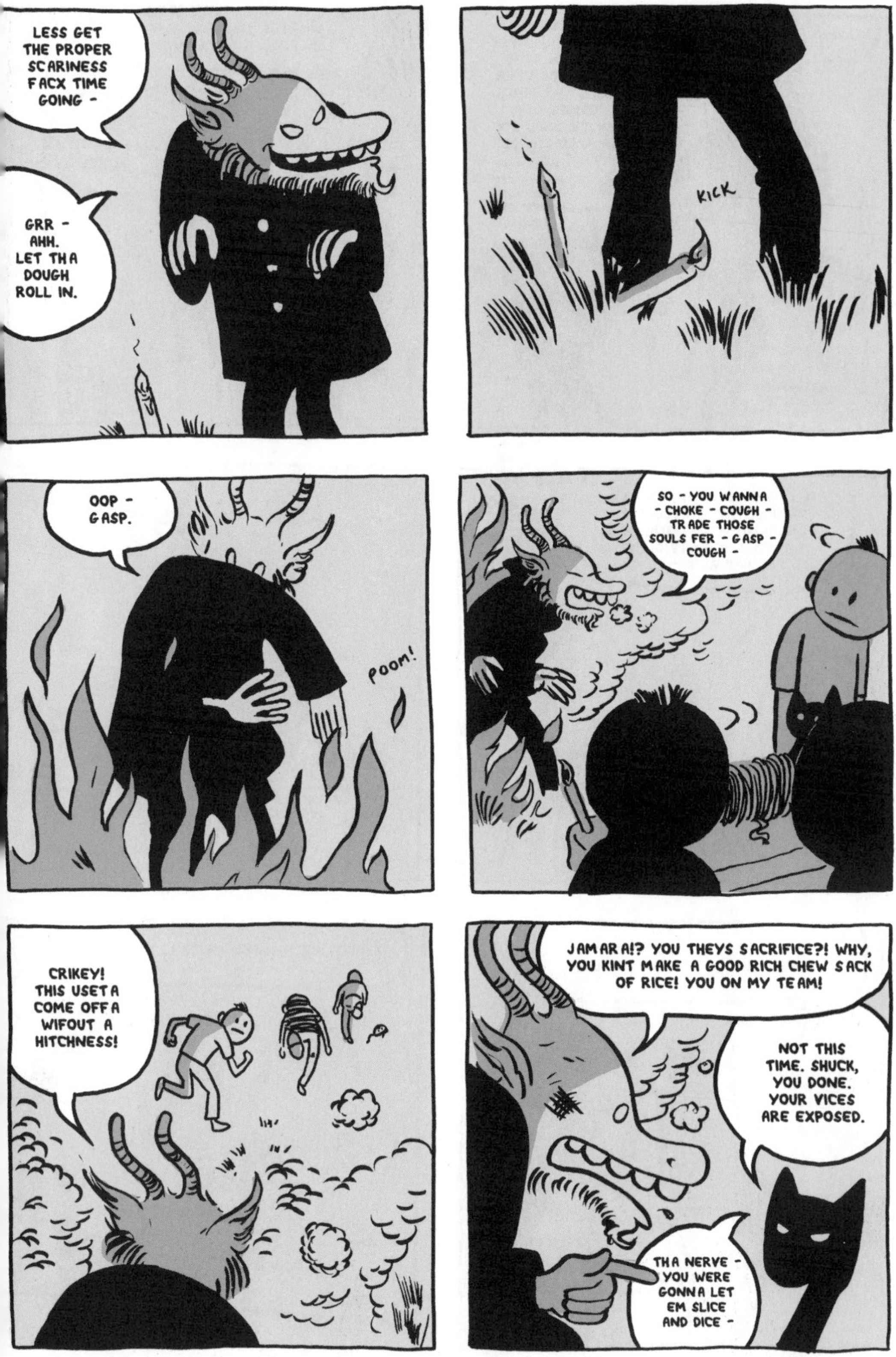
LESS GET THE PROPER SCARINESS FACX TIME GOING -
GRR - AHH. LET THA DOUGH ROLL IN.
KICK
OOP - GASP.
POOM!
SO - YOU WANNA - CHOKE - COUGH - TRADE THOSE SOULS FER - GASP - COUGH -
CRIKEY! THIS USETA COME OFFA WIFOUT A HITCHNESS!
JAMARA!? YOU THEYS SACRIFICE?! WHY, YOU KINT MAKE A GOOD RICH CHEW SACK OF RICE! YOU ON MY TEAM!
NOT THIS TIME. SHUCK, YOU DONE. YOUR VICES ARE EXPOSED.
THA NERVE - YOU WERE GONNA LET EM SLICE AND DICE -

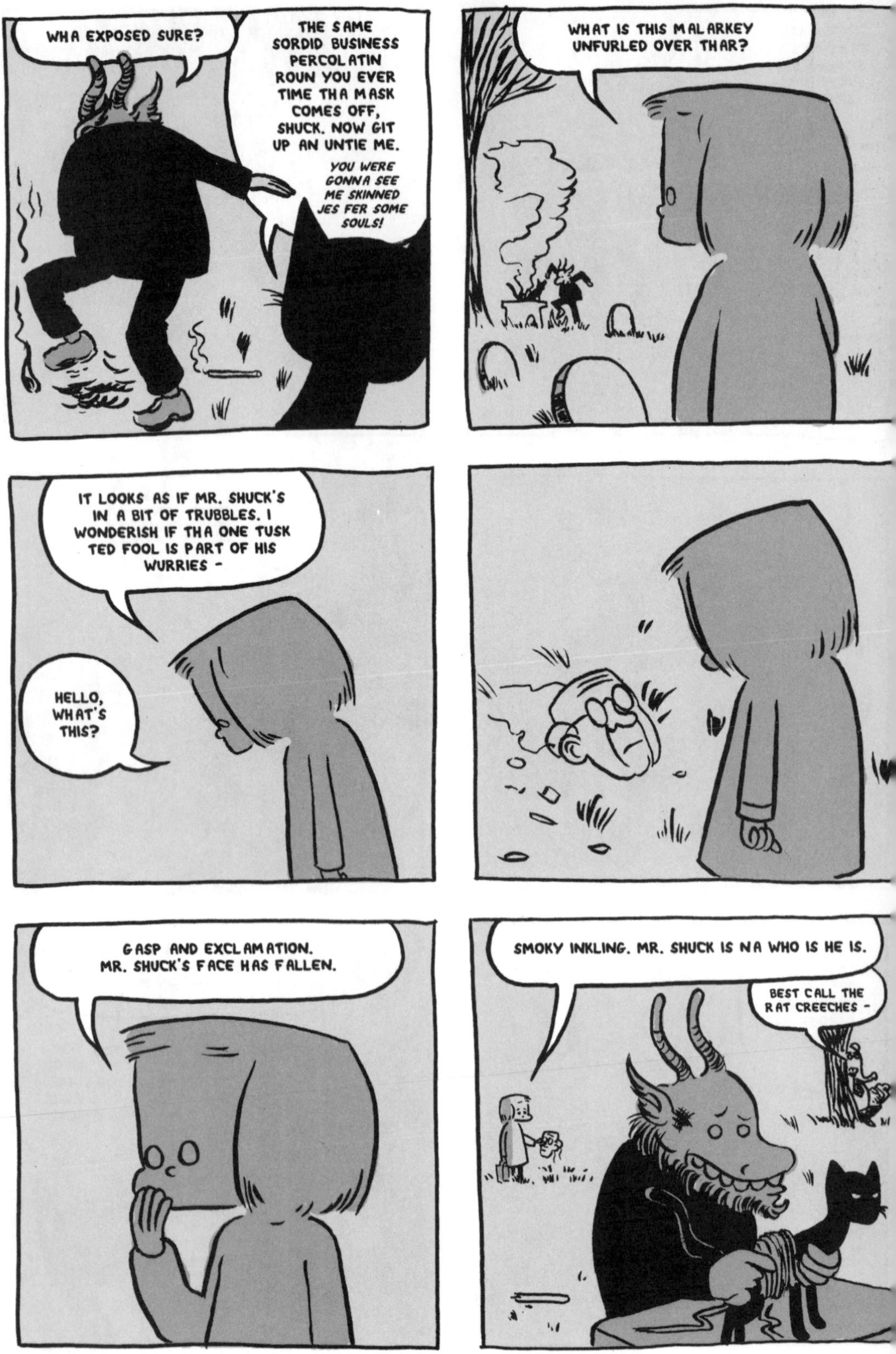
WHA EXPOSED SURE?
THE SAME SORDID BUSINESS PERCOLATIN ROUN YOU EVER TIME THA MASK COMES OFF, SHUCK. NOW GIT UP AN UNTIE ME.
YOU WERE GONNA SEE ME SKINNED JES FER SOME SOULS!
WHAT IS THIS MALARKEY UNFURLED OVER THAR?
IT LOOKS AS IF MR. SHUCK'S IN A BIT OF TRUBBLES. I WONDERISH IF THA ONE TUSK TED FOOL IS PART OF HIS WURRIES -
HELLO, WHAT'S THIS?
GASP AND EXCLAMATION. MR. SHUCK'S FACE HAS FALLEN.
SMOKY INKLING. MR. SHUCK IS NA WHO IS HE IS.
BEST CALL THE RAT CREECHES -

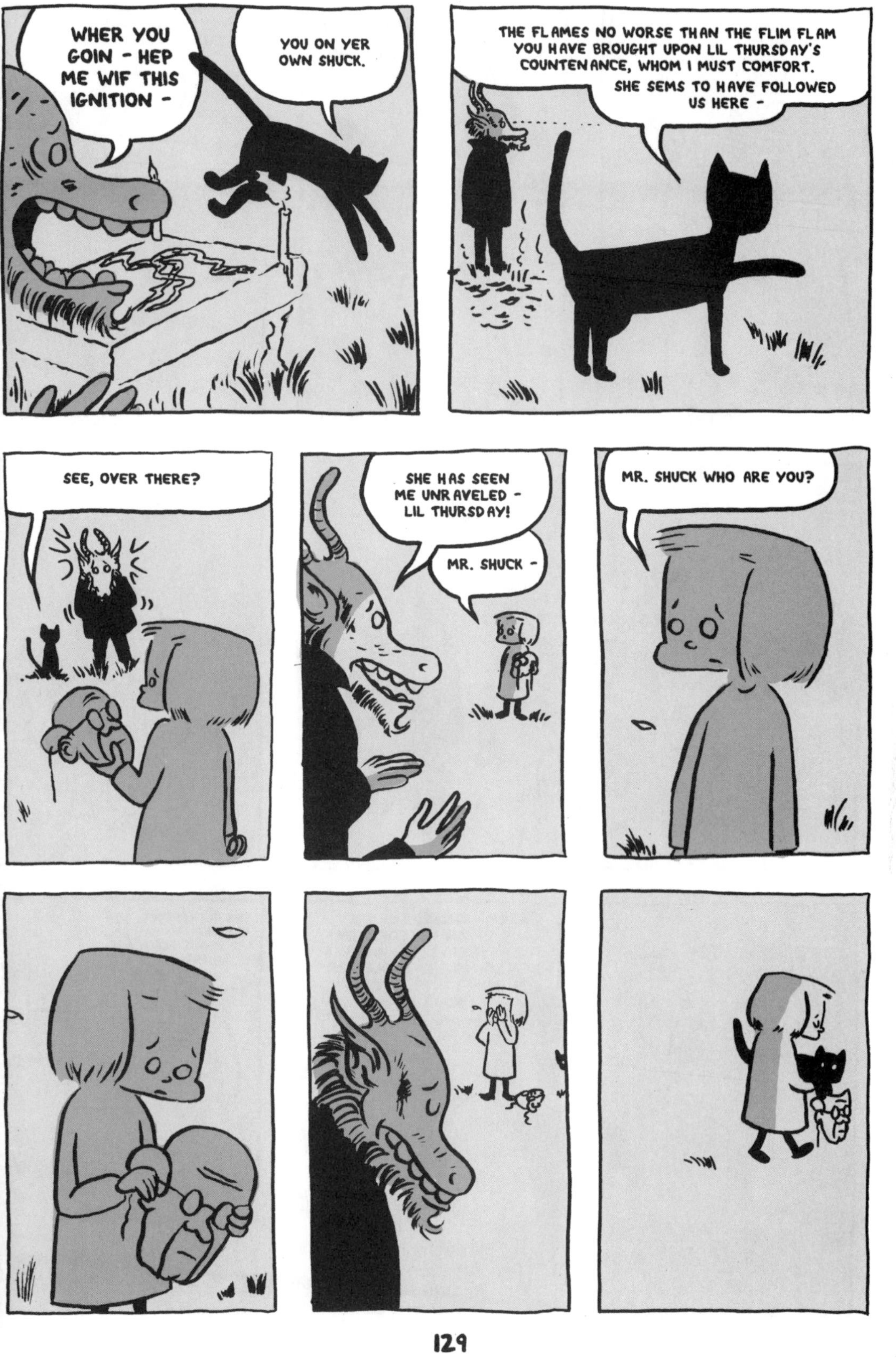
WHER YOU GOIN - HEP ME WIF THIS IGNITION -
YOU ON YER OWN SHUCK.
THE FLAMES NO WORSE THAN THE FLIM FLAM YOU HAVE BROUGHT UPON LIL THURSDAY'S COUNTENANCE, WHOM I MUST COMFORT.
SHE SEMS TO HAVE FOLLOWED US HERE -
SEE, OVER THERE?
SHE HAS SEEN ME UNRAVELED - LIL THURSDAY!
MR. SHUCK -
MR. SHUCK WHO ARE YOU?

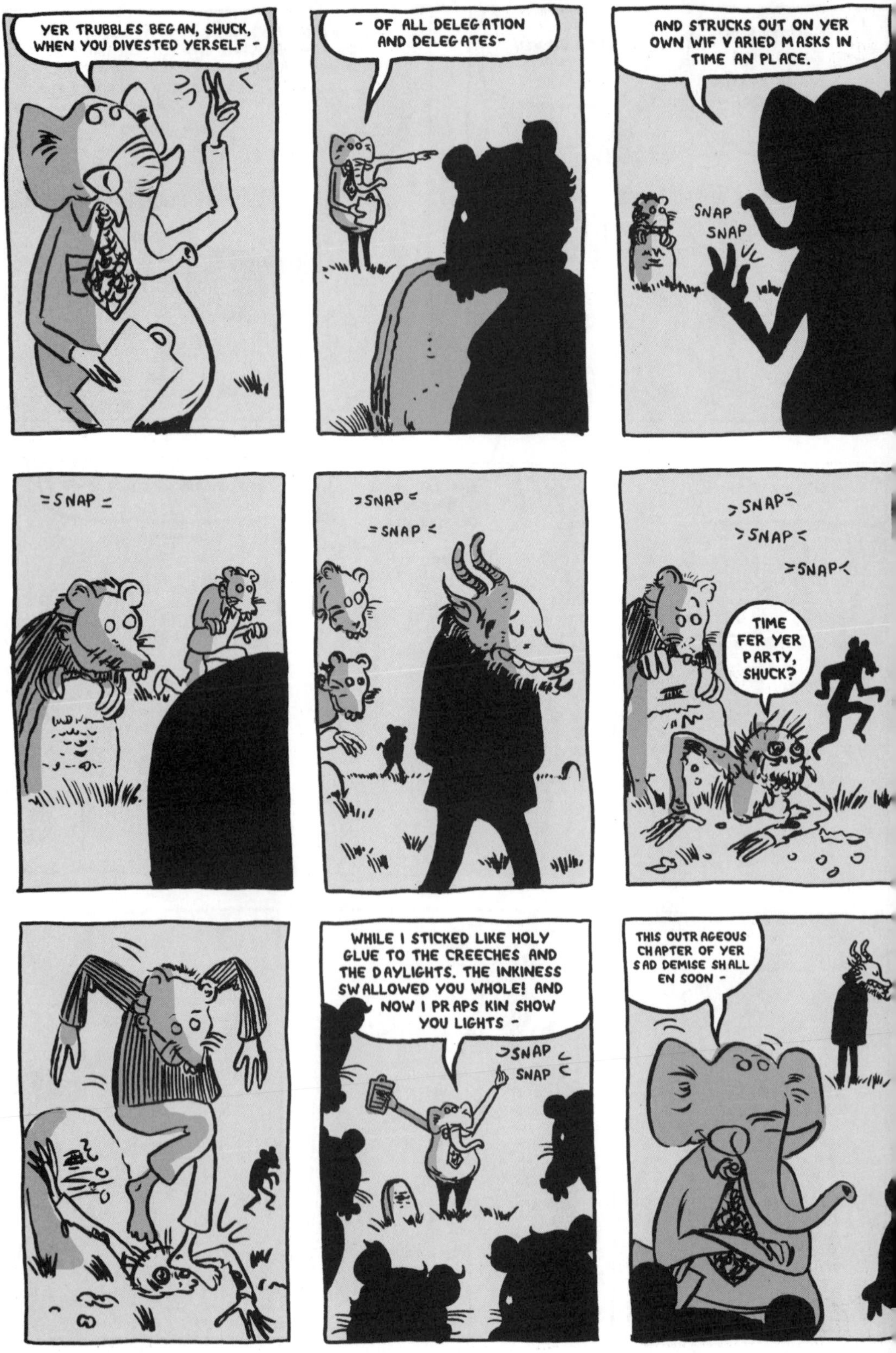
YER TRUBBLES BEGAN, SHUCK, WHEN YOU DIVESTED YERSELF -
- OF ALL DELEGATION AND DELEGATES-
AND STRUCKS OUT ON YER OWN WIF VARIED MASKS IN TIME AN PLACE.
SNAP
SNAP
SNAP
SNAP
SNAP
SNAP
SNAP
SNAP
TIME FER YER PARTY, SHUCK?
WHILE I STICKED LIKE HOLY GLUE TO THE CREECHES AND THE DAYLIGHTS. THE INKINESS SWALLOWED YOU WHOLE! AND NOW I PRAPS KIN SHOW YOU LIGHTS -
SNAP
SNAP
THIS OUTRAGEOUS CHAPTER OF YER SAD DEMISE SHALL EN SOON -

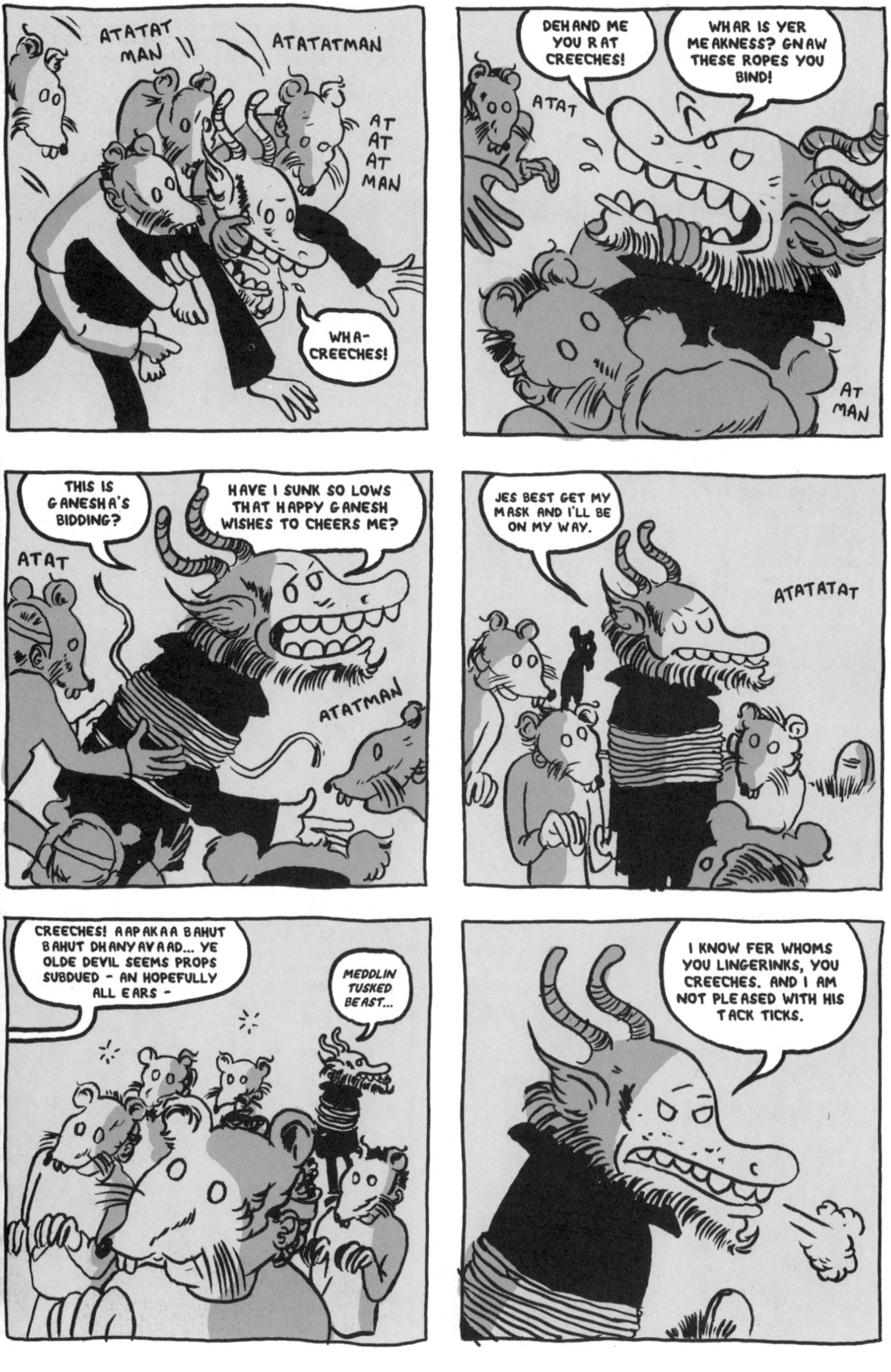
ATATAT MAN
ATATATMAN
AT AT AT MAN
WHA-CREECHES!
DEHAND ME YOU RAT CREECHES!
WHAR IS YER MEAKNESS? GNAW THESE ROPES YOU BIND!
ATAT
AT MAN
THIS IS GANESHA'S BIDDING?
HAVE I SUNK SO LOWS THAT HAPPY GANESH WISHES TO CHEERS ME?
ATAT
ATATMAN
JES BEST GET MY MASK AND I'LL BE ON MY WAY.
ATATATAT
CREECHES! AAPAKAA BAHUT BAHUT DHANYAVAAD... YE OLDE DEVIL SEEMS PROPS SUBDUED - AN HOPEFULLY ALL EARS -
MEDDLIN TUSKED BEAST...
I KNOW FER WHOMS YOU LINGERINKS, YOU CREECHES. AND I AM NOT PLEASED WITH HIS TACK TICKS.

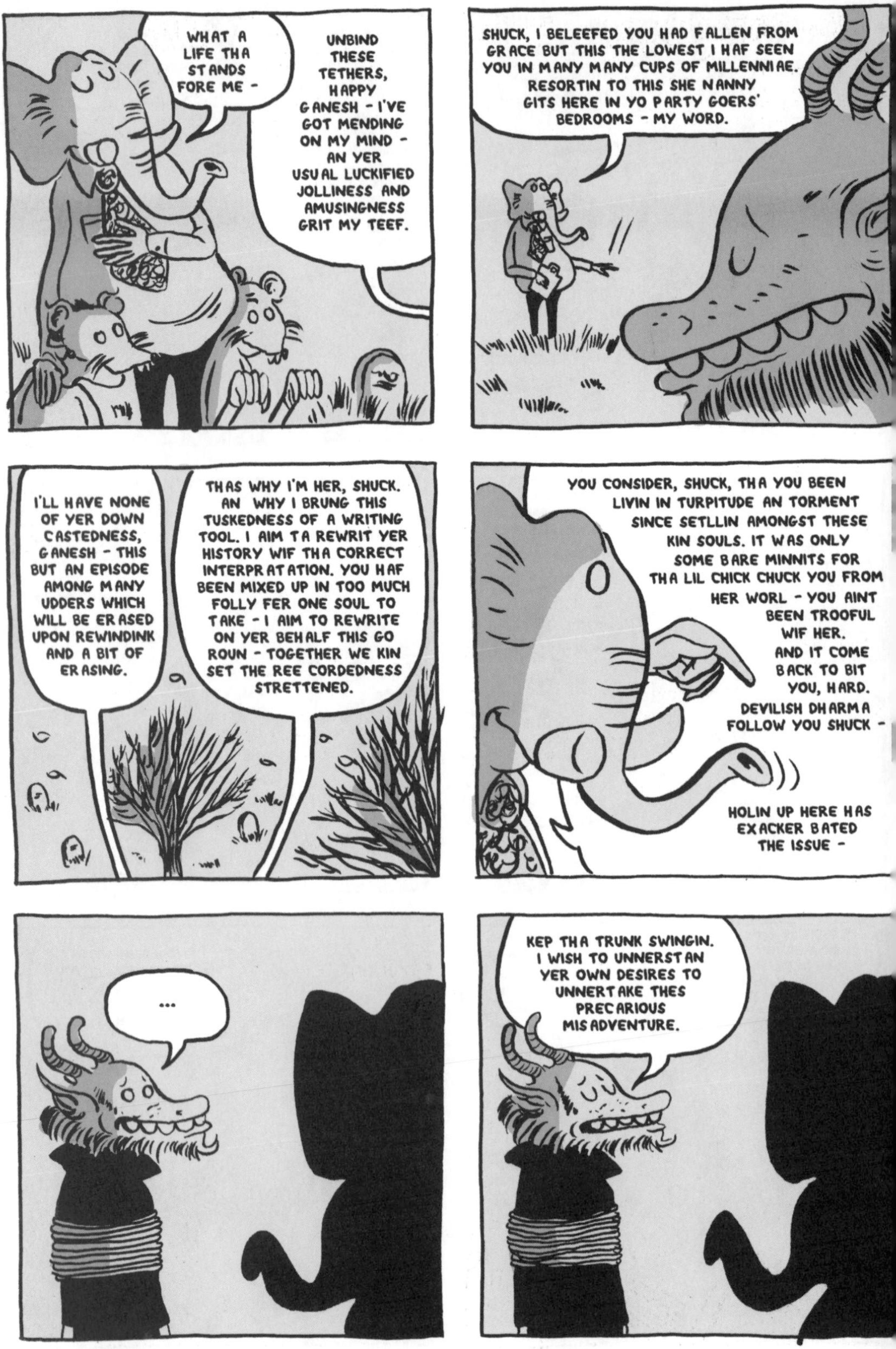
WHAT A LIFE THA STANDS FORE ME -
UNBIND THESE TETHERS, HAPPY GANESH - I'VE GOT MENDING ON MY MIND - AN YER USUAL LUCKIFIED JOLLINESS AND AMUSINGNESS GRIT MY TEEF.
SHUCK, I BELEEFED YOU HAD FALLEN FROM GRACE BUT THIS THE LOWEST I HAF SEEN YOU IN MANY MANY CUPS OF MILLENNIAE. RESORTIN TO THIS SHE NANNY GITS HERE IN YO PARTY GOERS' BEDROOMS - MY WORD.
I'LL HAVE NONE OF YER DOWN CASTEDNESS, GANESH - THIS BUT AN EPISODE AMONG MANY UDDERS WHICH WILL BE ERASED UPON REWINDINK AND A BIT OF ERASING.
THAS WHY I'M HER, SHUCK. AN WHY I BRUNG THIS TUSKEDNESS OF A WRITING TOOL. I AIM TA REWRIT YER HISTORY WIF THA CORRECT INTERPRATATION. YOU HAF BEEN MIXED UP IN TOO MUCH FOLLY FER ONE SOUL TO TAKE - I AIM TO REWRITE ON YER BEHALF THIS GO ROUN - TOGETHER WE KIN SET THE REE CORDEDNESS STRETTENED.
YOU CONSIDER, SHUCK, THA YOU BEEN LIVIN IN TURPITUDE AN TORMENT SINCE SETLLIN AMONGST THESE KIN SOULS. IT WAS ONLY SOME BARE MINNITS FOR THA LIL CHICK CHUCK YOU FROM HER WORL - YOU AINT BEEN TROOFUL WIF HER.
AND IT COME BACK TO BIT YOU, HARD.
DEVILISH DHARMA FOLLOW YOU SHUCK -
HOLIN UP HERE HAS EXACKER BATED THE ISSUE -
...
KEP THA TRUNK SWINGIN. I WISH TO UNNERSTAN YER OWN DESIRES TO UNNERTAKE THES PRECARIOUS MISADVENTURE.

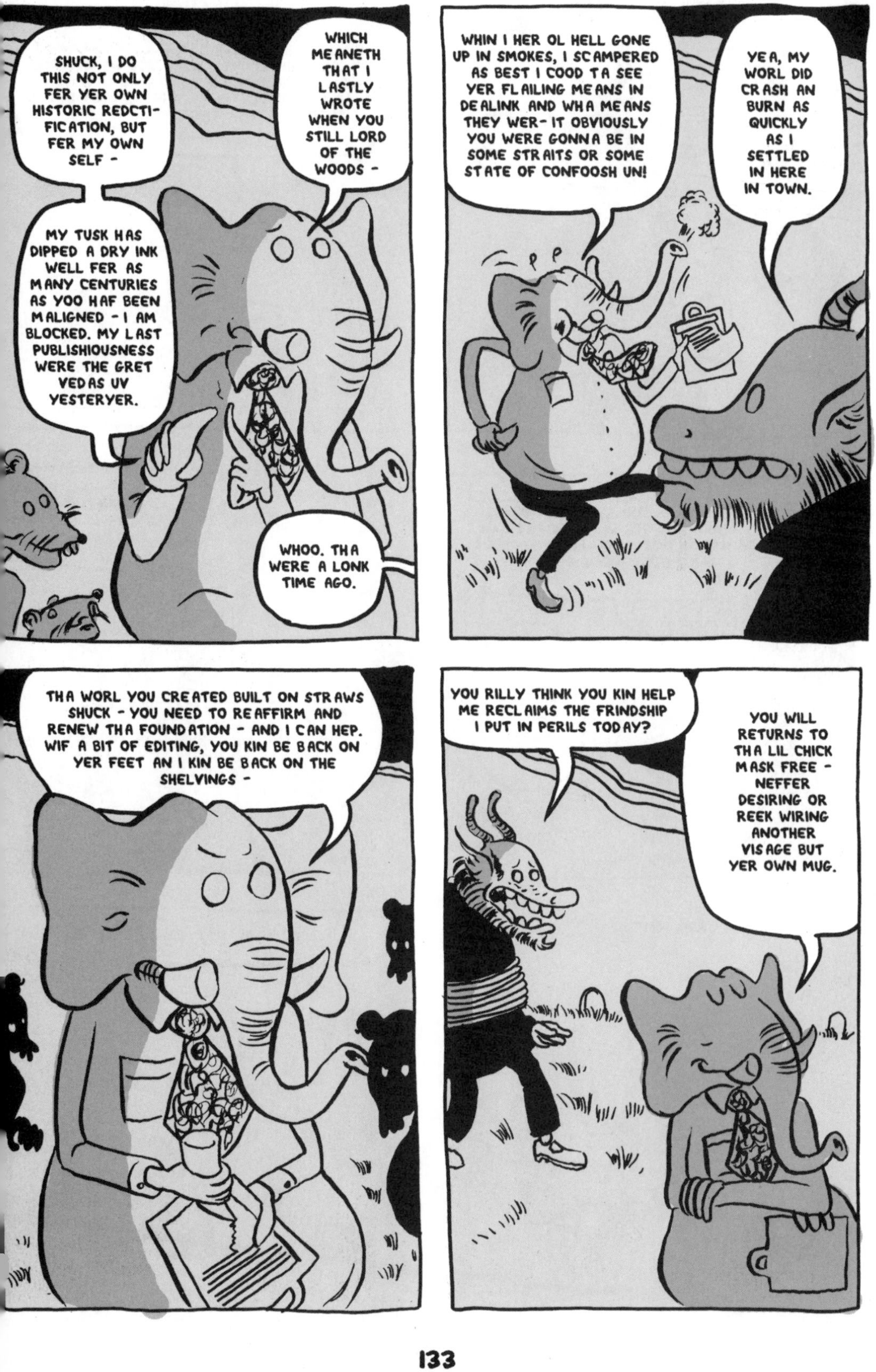
SHUCK, I DO THIS NOT ONLY FER YER OWN HISTORIC REDCTI-FICATION, BUT FER MY OWN SELF -
WHICH MEANETH THAT I LASTLY WROTE WHEN YOU STILL LORD OF THE WOODS -
MY TUSK HAS DIPPED A DRY INK WELL FER AS MANY CENTURIES AS YOO HAF BEEN MALIGNED - I AM BLOCKED. MY LAST PUBLISHIOUSNESS WERE THE GRET VEDAS UV YESTERYER.
WHOO. THA WERE A LONK TIME AGO.
WHIN I HER OL HELL GONE UP IN SMOKES, I SCAMPERED AS BEST I COOD TA SEE YER FLAILING MEANS IN DEALINK AND WHA MEANS THEY WER- IT OBVIOUSLY YOU WERE GONNA BE IN SOME STRAITS OR SOME STATE OF CONFOOSH UN!
YEA, MY WORL DID CRASH AN BURN AS QUICKLY AS I SETTLED IN HERE IN TOWN.
THA WORL YOU CREATED BUILT ON STRAWS SHUCK - YOU NEED TO REAFFIRM AND RENEW THA FOUNDATION - AND I CAN HEP. WIF A BIT OF EDITING, YOU KIN BE BACK ON YER FEET AN I KIN BE BACK ON THE SHELVINGS -
YOU RILLY THINK YOU KIN HELP ME RECLAIMS THE FRINDSHIP I PUT IN PERILS TODAY?
YOU WILL RETURNS TO THA LIL CHICK MASK FREE - NEFFER DESIRING OR REEK WIRING ANOTHER VISAGE BUT YER OWN MUG.

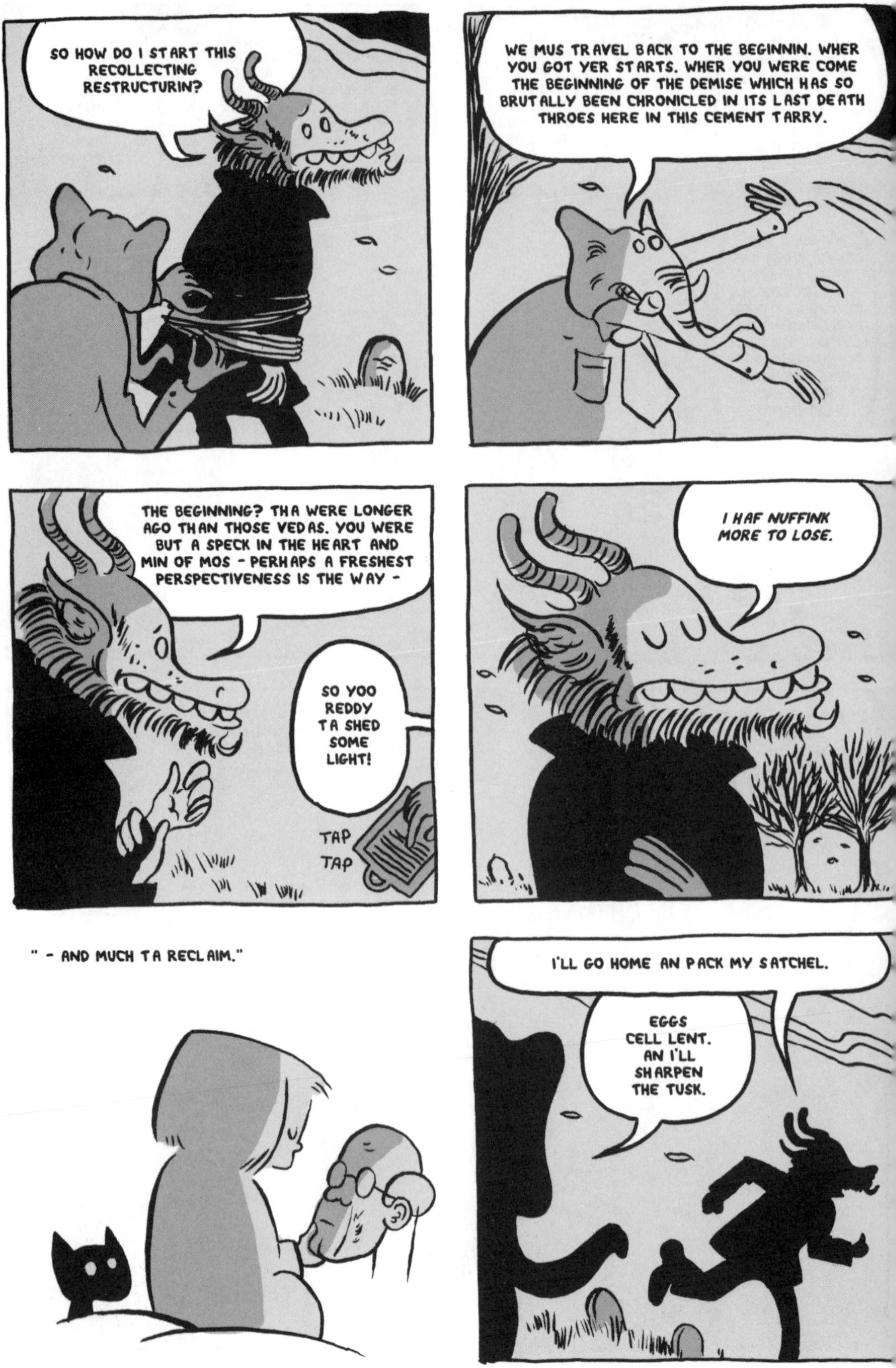
SO HOW DO I START THIS RECOLLECTING RESTRUCTURIN?
WE MUS TRAVEL BACK TO THE BEGINNIN. WHER YOU GOT YER STARTS. WHER YOU WERE COME THE BEGINNING OF THE DEMISE WHICH HAS SO BRUTALLY BEEN CHRONICLED IN ITS LAST DEATH THROES HERE IN THIS CEMENT TARRY.
THE BEGINNING? THA WERE LONGER AGO THAN THOSE VEDAS. YOU WERE BUT A SPECK IN THE HEART AND MIN OF MOS - PERHAPS A FRESHEST PERSPECTIVENESS IS THE WAY -
SO YOO REDDY TA SHED SOME LIGHT!
TAP
TAP
I HAF NUFFINK MORE TO LOSE.
" - AND MUCH TA RECLAIM."
I'LL GO HOME AN PACK MY SATCHEL.
EGGS CELL LENT. AN I'LL SHARPEN THE TUSK.

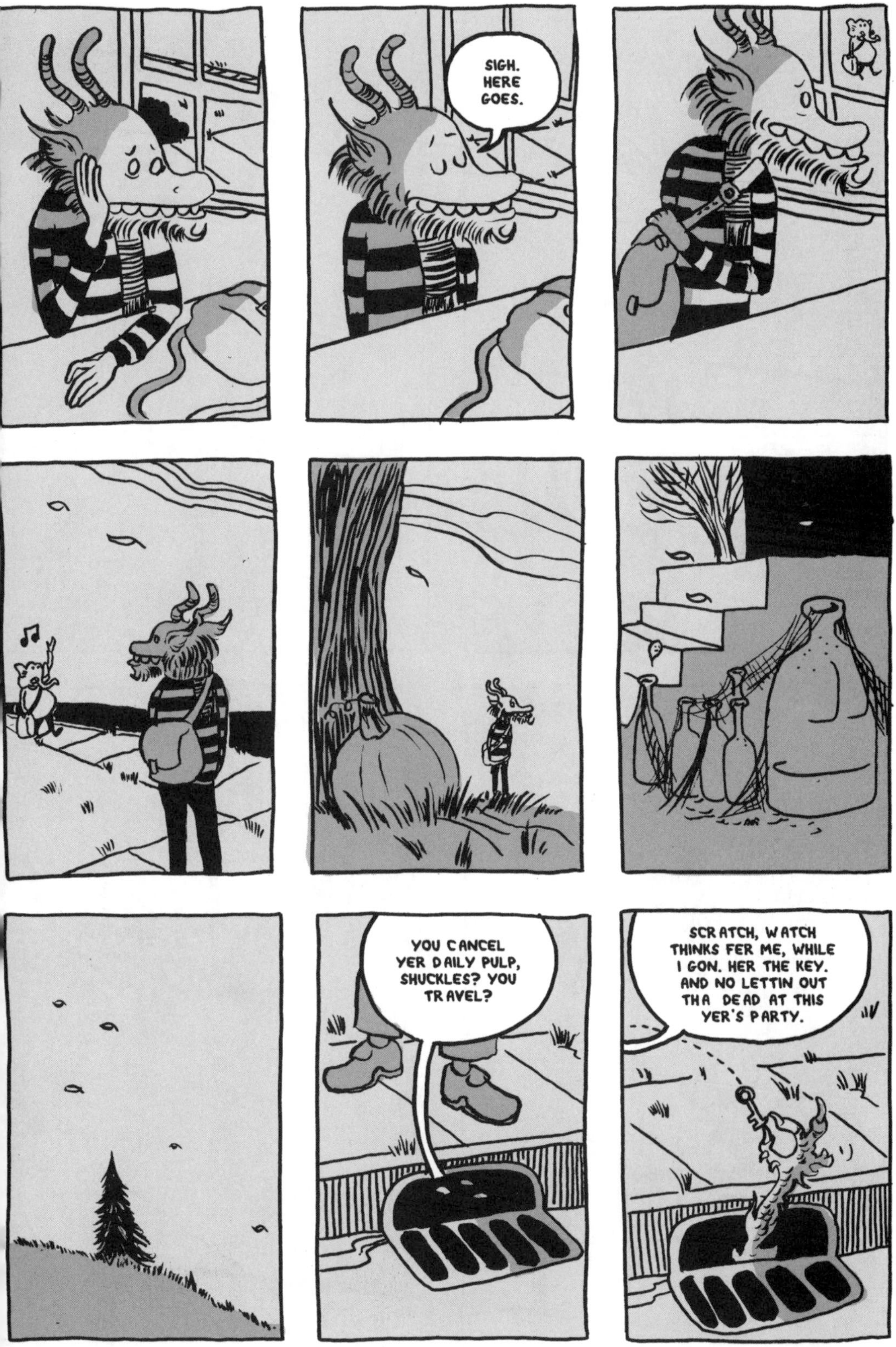
SIGH. HERE GOES.
YOU CANCEL YER DAILY PULP, SHUCKLES? YOU TRAVEL?
SCRATCH, WATCH THINKS FER ME, WHILE I GON. HER THE KEY. AND NO LETTIN OUT THA DEAD AT THIS YER'S PARTY.

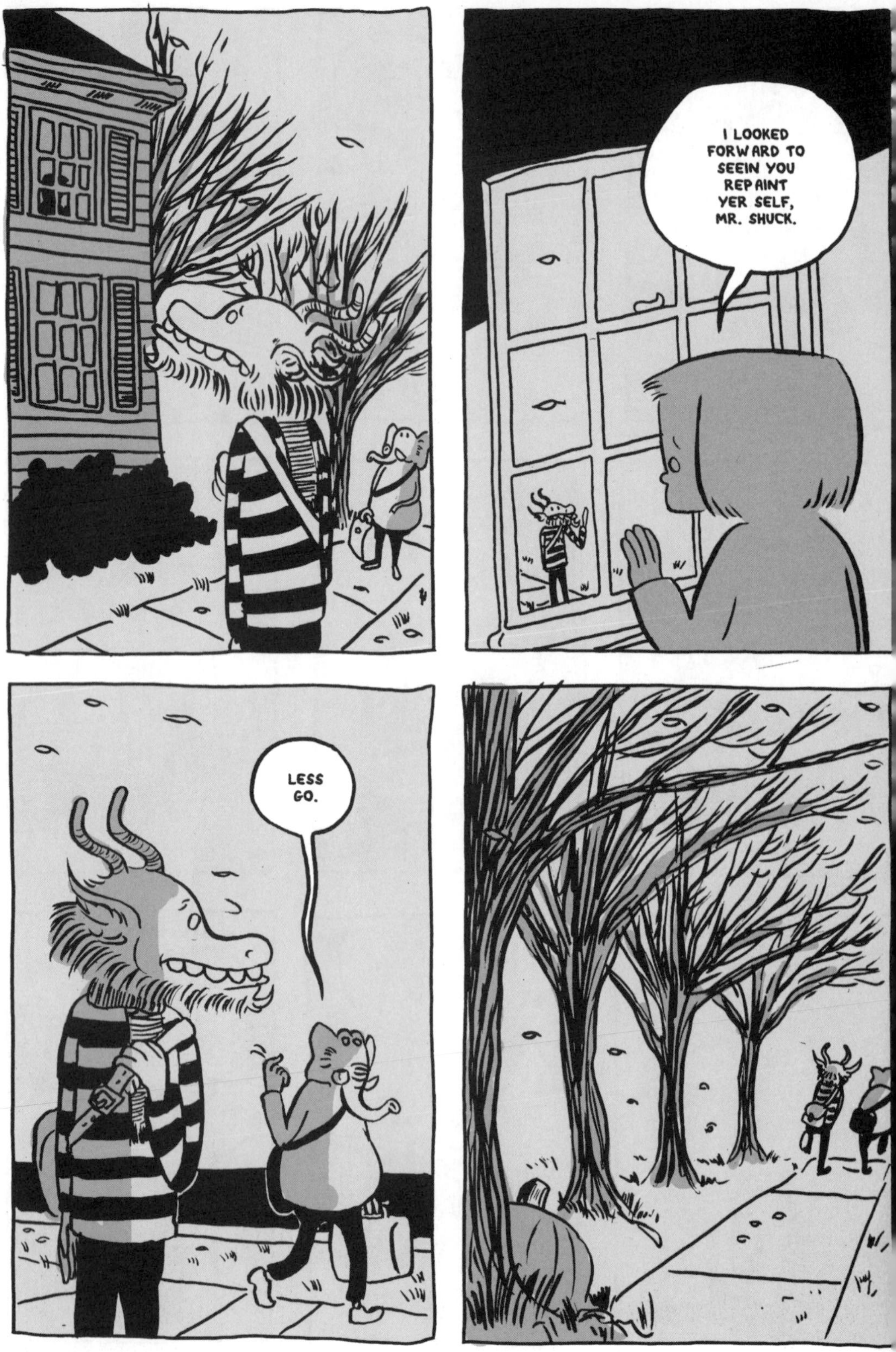
I LOOKED FORWARD TO SEEIN YOU REPAINT YER SELF, MR. SHUCK.
LESS GO.

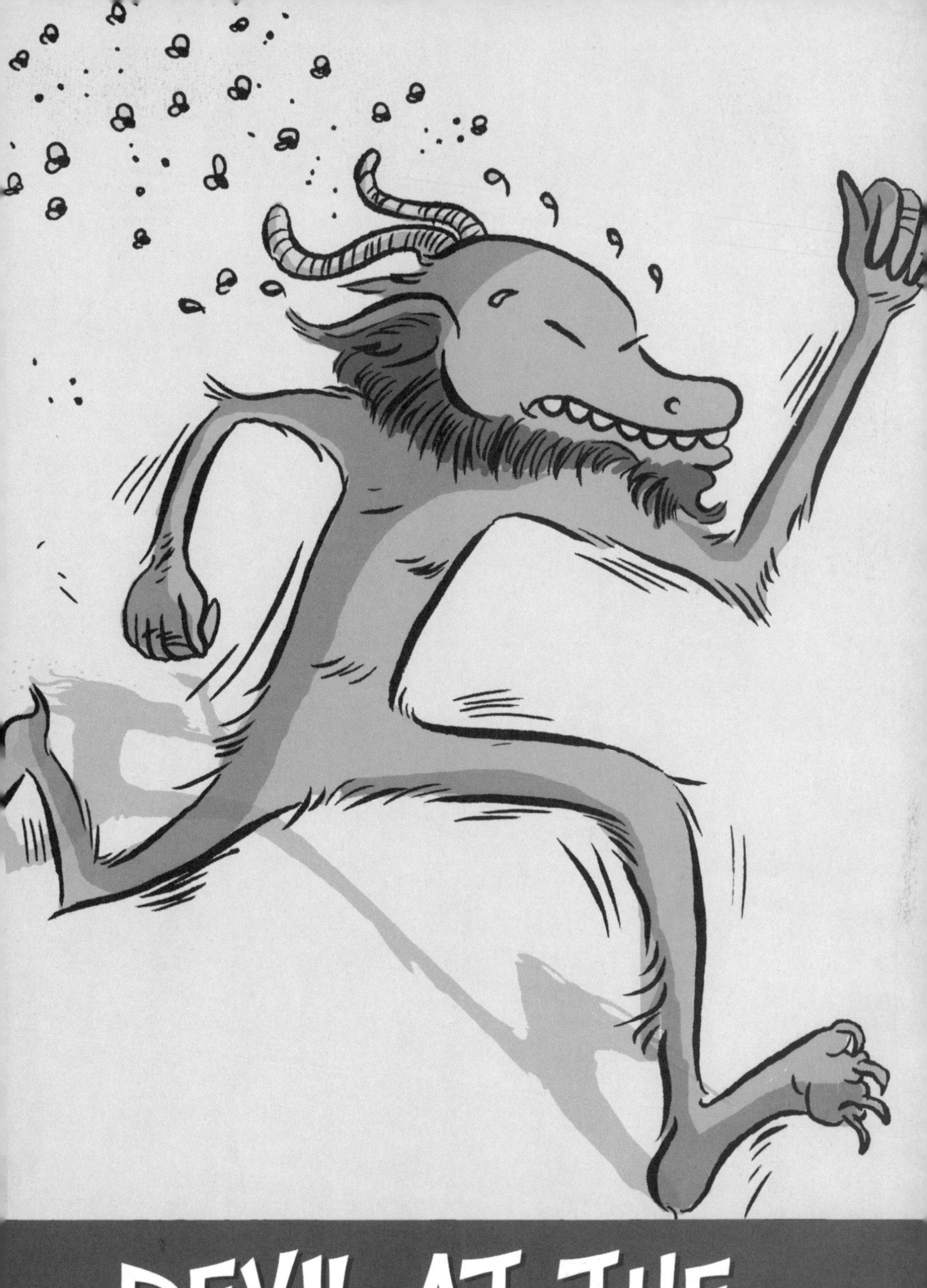

DEVIL AT THE CROSSROADS

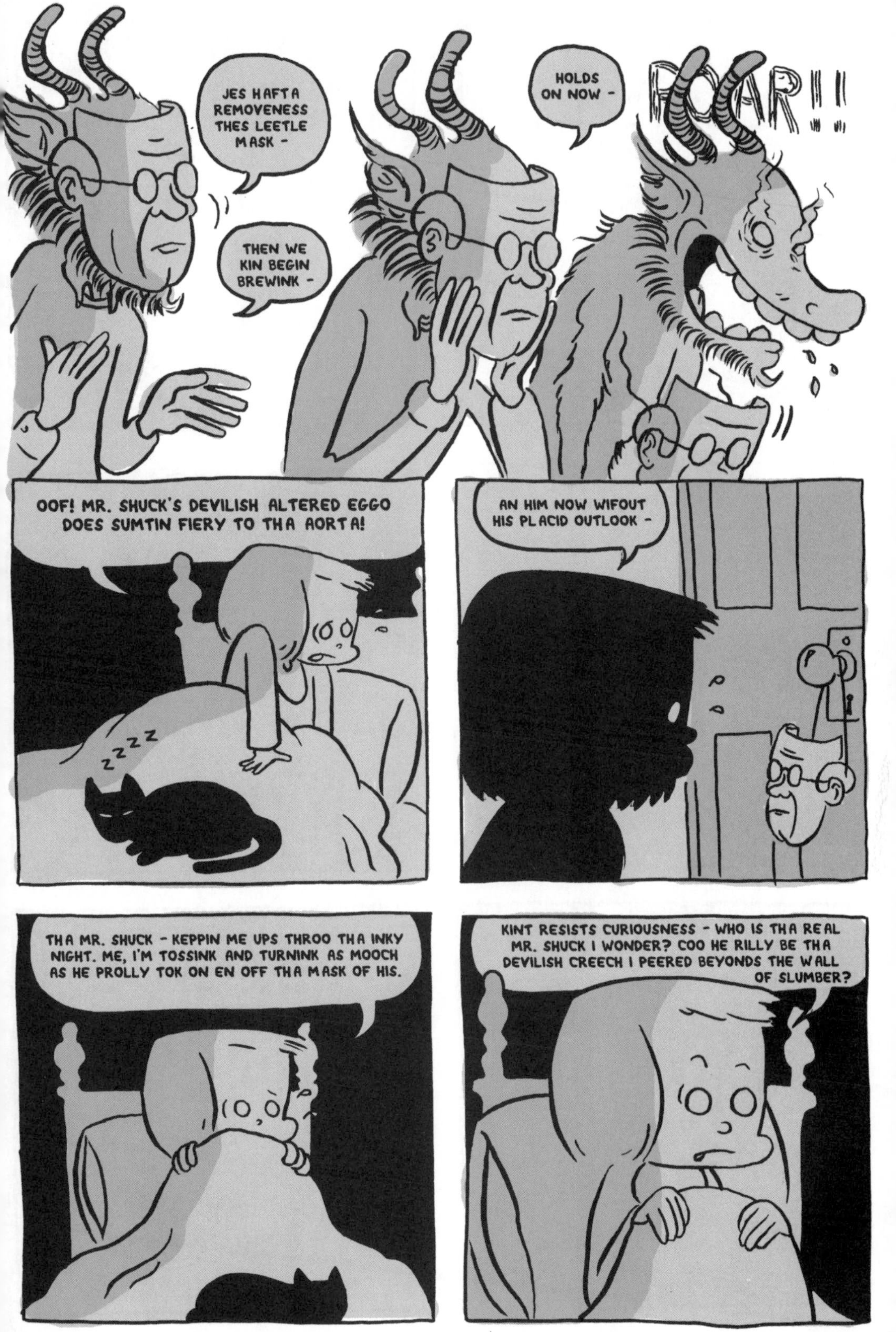
JES HAFTA REMOVENESS THES LEETLE MASK -
THEN WE KIN BEGIN BREWINK -
HOLDS ON NOW -
ROAR!!
OOF! MR. SHUCK'S DEVILISH ALTERED EGGO DOES SUMTIN FIERY TO THA AORTA!
ZZZZ
AN HIM NOW WIFOUT HIS PLACID OUTLOOK -
THA MR. SHUCK - KEPPIN ME UPS THROO THA INKY NIGHT. ME, I'M TOSSINK AND TURNINK AS MOOCH AS HE PROLLY TOK ON EN OFF THA MASK OF HIS.
KINT RESISTS CURIOUSNESS - WHO IS THA REAL MR. SHUCK I WONDER? COO HE RILLY BE THA DEVILISH CREECH I PEERED BEYONDS THE WALL OF SLUMBER?

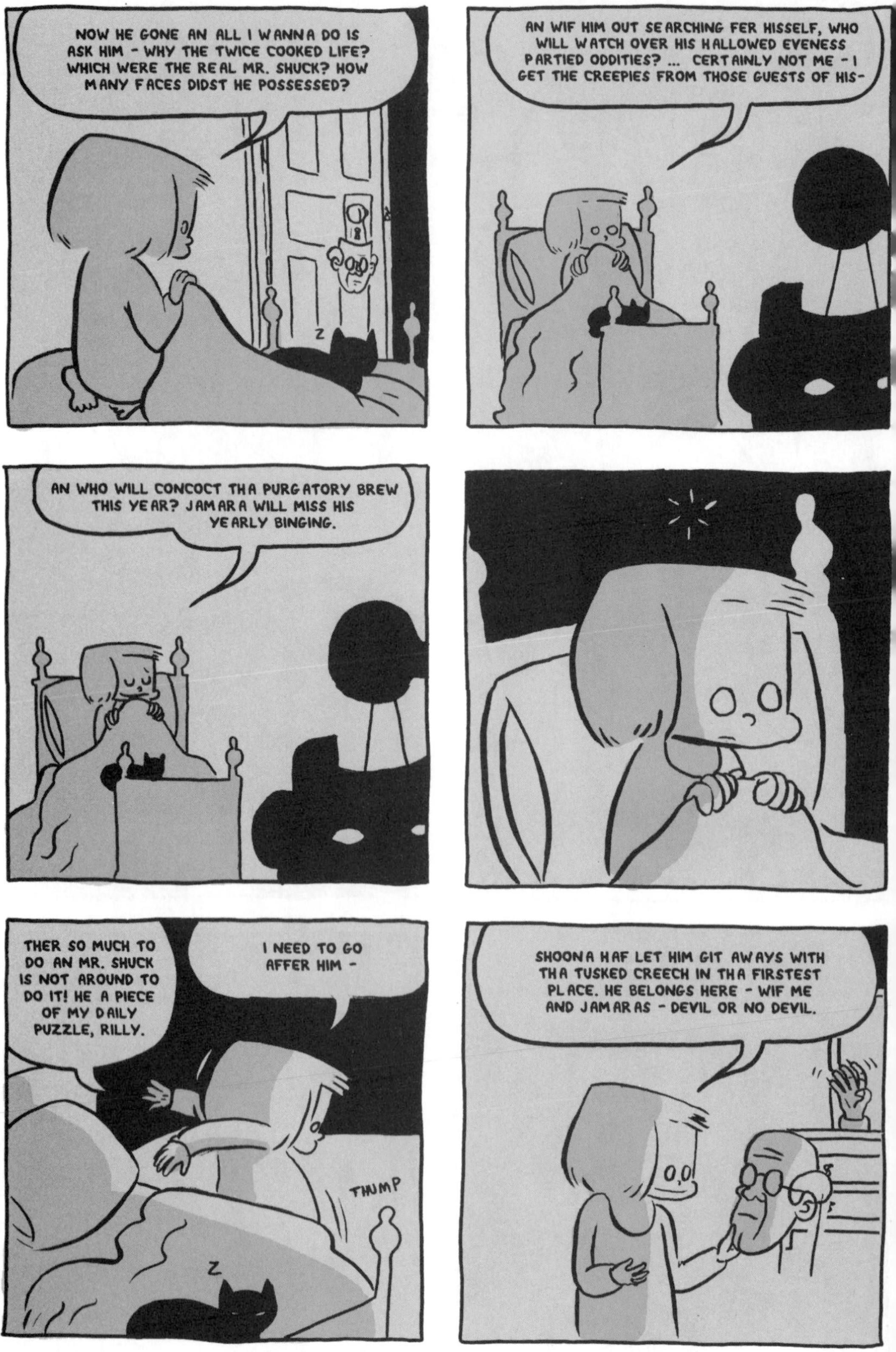
NOW HE GONE AN ALL I WANNA DO IS ASK HIM - WHY THE TWICE COOKED LIFE? WHICH WERE THE REAL MR. SHUCK? HOW MANY FACES DIDST HE POSSESSED?
Z
AN WIF HIM OUT SEARCHING FER HISSELF, WHO WILL WATCH OVER HIS HALLOWED EVENESS PARTIED ODDITIES? ... CERTAINLY NOT ME - I GET THE CREEPIES FROM THOSE GUESTS OF HIS-
AN WHO WILL CONCOCT THA PURGATORY BREW THIS YEAR? JAMARA WILL MISS HIS YEARLY BINGING.
THER SO MUCH TO DO AN MR. SHUCK IS NOT AROUND TO DO IT! HE A PIECE OF MY DAILY PUZZLE, RILLY.
I NEED TO GO AFFER HIM -
THUMP
Z
SHOONA HAF LET HIM GIT AWAYS WITH THA TUSKED CREECH IN THA FIRSTEST PLACE. HE BELONGS HERE - WIF ME AND JAMARAS - DEVIL OR NO DEVIL.

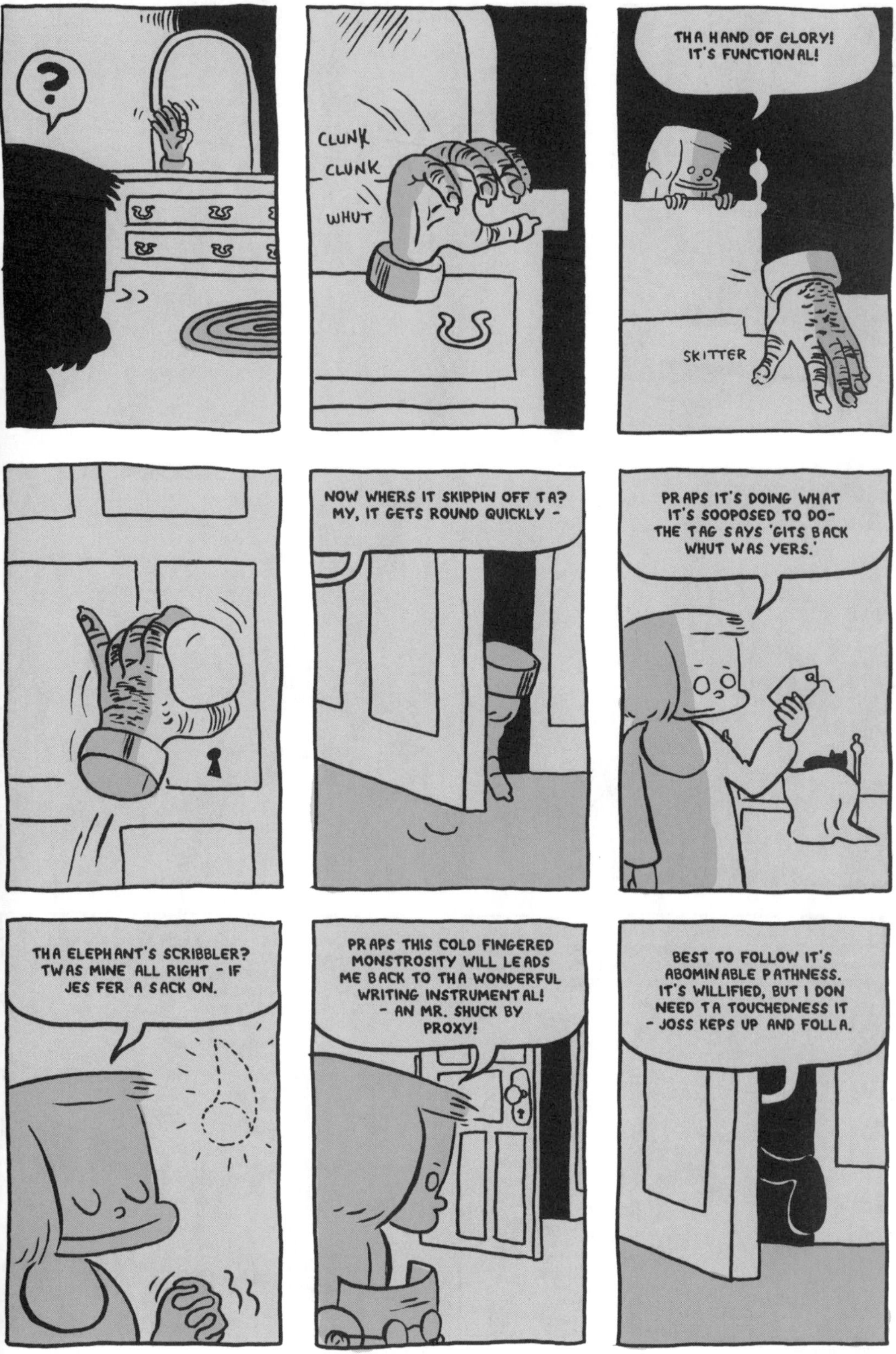
?
CLUNK
CLUNK
WHUT
THA HAND OF GLORY! IT'S FUNCTIONAL!
SKITTER
NOW WHERS IT SKIPPIN OFF TA? MY, IT GETS ROUND QUICKLY -
PRAPS IT'S DOING WHAT IT'S SOOPOSED TO DO- THE TAG SAYS 'GITS BACK WHUT WAS YERS.'
THA ELEPHANT'S SCRIBBLER? TWAS MINE ALL RIGHT - IF JES FER A SACK ON.
PRAPS THIS COLD FINGERED MONSTROSITY WILL LEADS ME BACK TO THA WONDERFUL WRITING INSTRUMENTAL! - AN MR. SHUCK BY PROXY!
BEST TO FOLLOW IT'S ABOMINABLE PATHNESS. IT'S WILLIFIED, BUT I DON NEED TA TOUCHEDNESS IT - JOSS KEPS UP AND FOLLA.

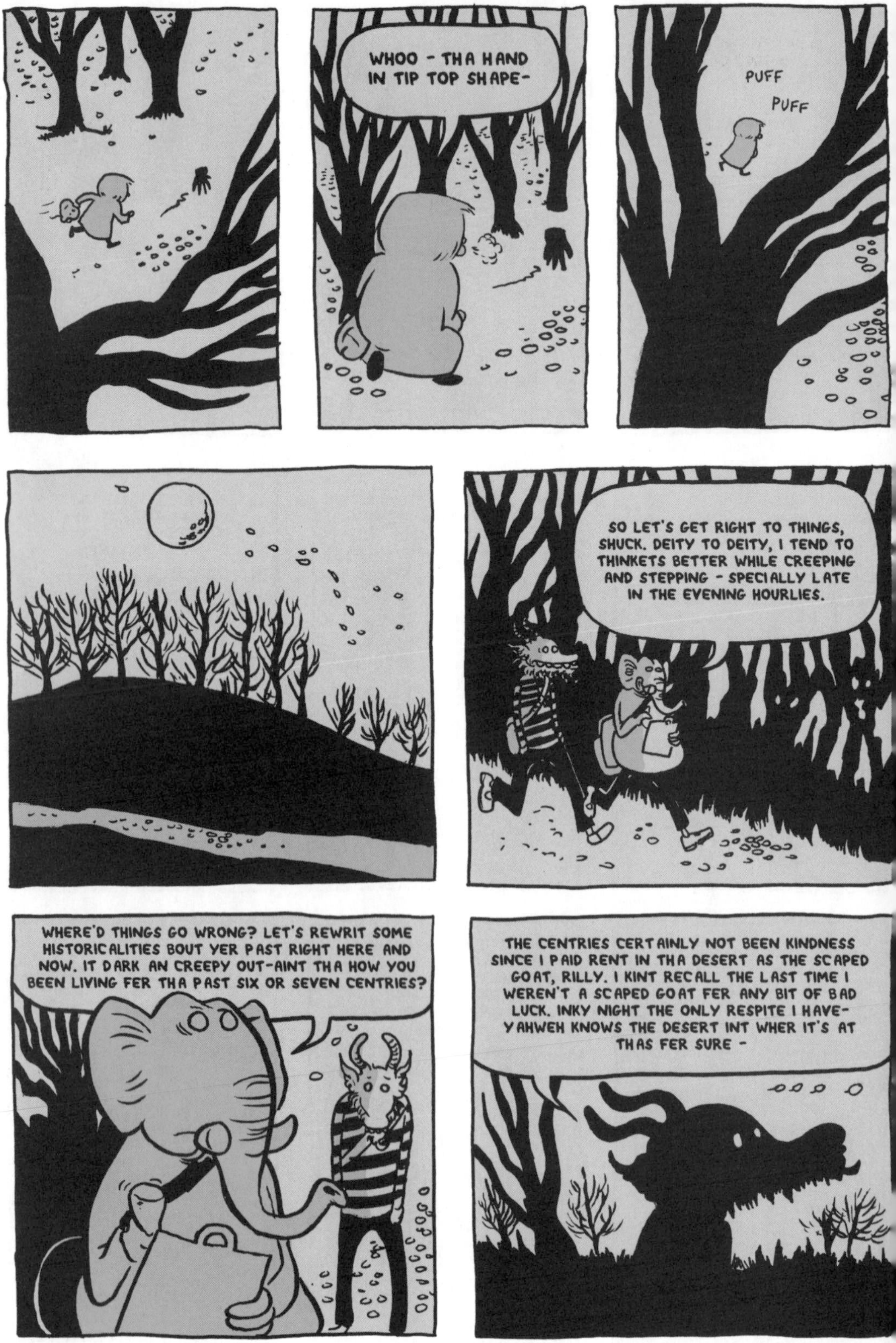
WHOO - THA HAND
IN TIP TOP SHAPE-
PUFF
PUFF
SO LET'S GET RIGHT TO THINGS, SHUCK. DEITY TO DEITY, I TEND TO THINKETS BETTER WHILE CREEPING AND STEPPING - SPECIALLY LATE IN THE EVENING HOURLIES.
WHERE'D THINGS GO WRONG? LET'S REWRIT SOME HISTORICALITIES BOUT YER PAST RIGHT HERE AND NOW. IT DARK AN CREEPY OUT-AINT THA HOW YOU BEEN LIVING FER THA PAST SIX OR SEVEN CENTRIES?
THE CENTRIES CERTAINLY NOT BEEN KINDNESS SINCE I PAID RENT IN THA DESERT AS THE SCAPED GOAT, RILLY. I KINT RECALL THE LAST TIME I WEREN'T A SCAPED GOAT FER ANY BIT OF BAD LUCK. INKY NIGHT THE ONLY RESPITE I HAVE- YAHWEH KNOWS THE DESERT INT WHER IT'S AT THAS FER SURE -

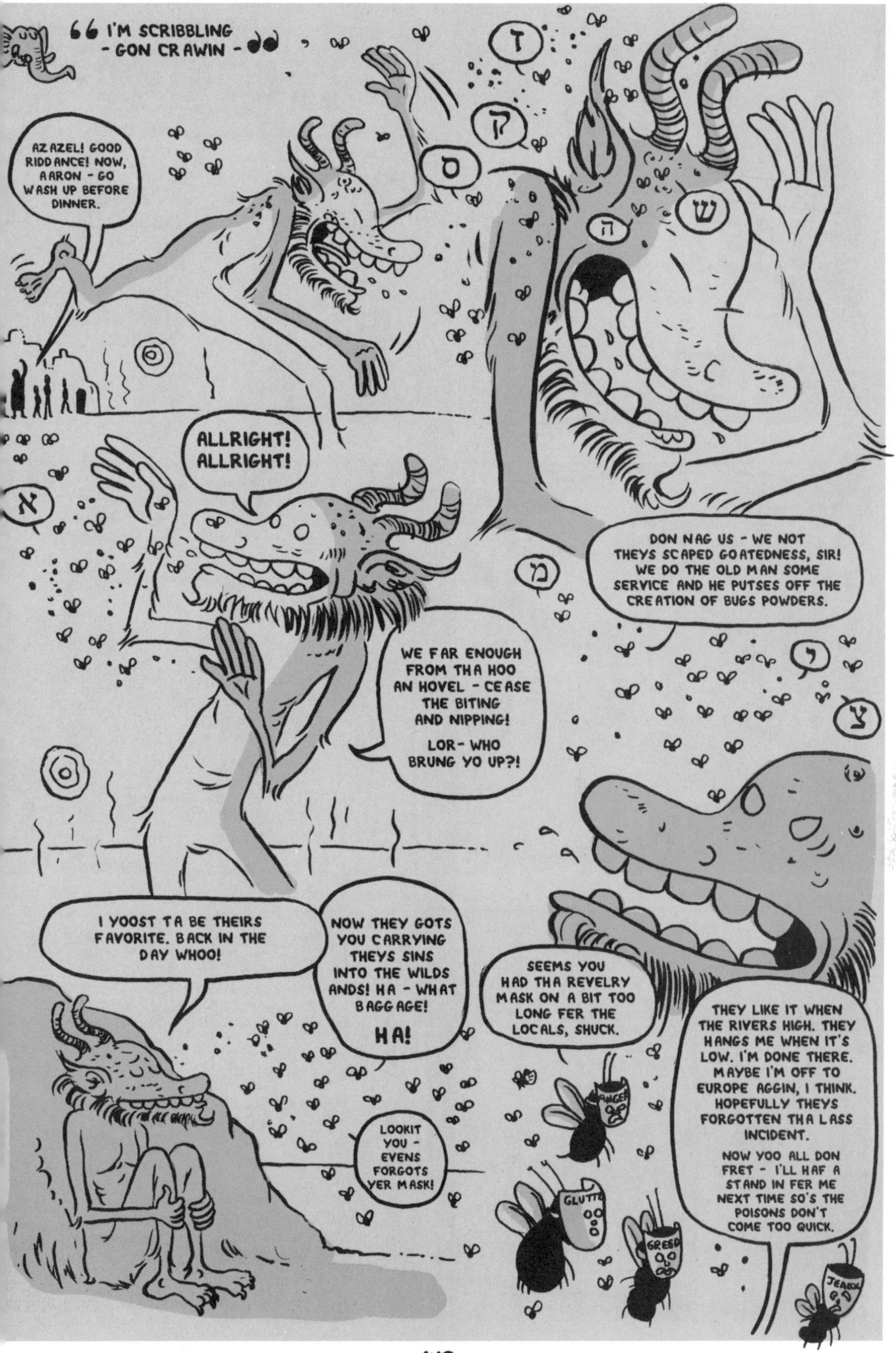
"I'M SCRIBBLING - GON CRAWIN -"
ד
ק
ס
ש
ה
AZAZEL! GOOD RIDDANCE! NOW, AARON - GO WASH UP BEFORE DINNER.
ALLRIGHT! ALLRIGHT!
א
DON NAG US - WE NOT THEYS SCAPED GOATEDNESS, SIR! WE DO THE OLD MAN SOME SERVICE AND HE PUTSES OFF THE CREATION OF BUGS POWDERS.
WE FAR ENOUGH FROM THA HOO AN HOVEL - CEASE THE BITING AND NIPPING!
LOR- WHO BRUNG YO UP?!
I YOOST TA BE THEIRS FAVORITE. BACK IN THE DAY WHOO!
NOW THEY GOTS YOU CARRYING THEYS SINS INTO THE WILDS ANDS! HA - WHAT BAGGAGE!
HA!
SEEMS YOU HAD THA REVELRY MASK ON A BIT TOO LONG FER THE LOCALS, SHUCK.
THEY LIKE IT WHEN THE RIVERS HIGH. THEY HANGS ME WHEN IT'S LOW. I'M DONE THERE. MAYBE I'M OFF TO EUROPE AGGIN, I THINK. HOPEFULLY THEYS FORGOTTEN THA LASS INCIDENT.
NOW YOO ALL DON FRET - I'LL HAF A STAND IN FER ME NEXT TIME SO'S THE POISONS DON'T COME TOO QUICK.
LOOKIT YOU - EVENS FORGOTS YER MASK!
GREED

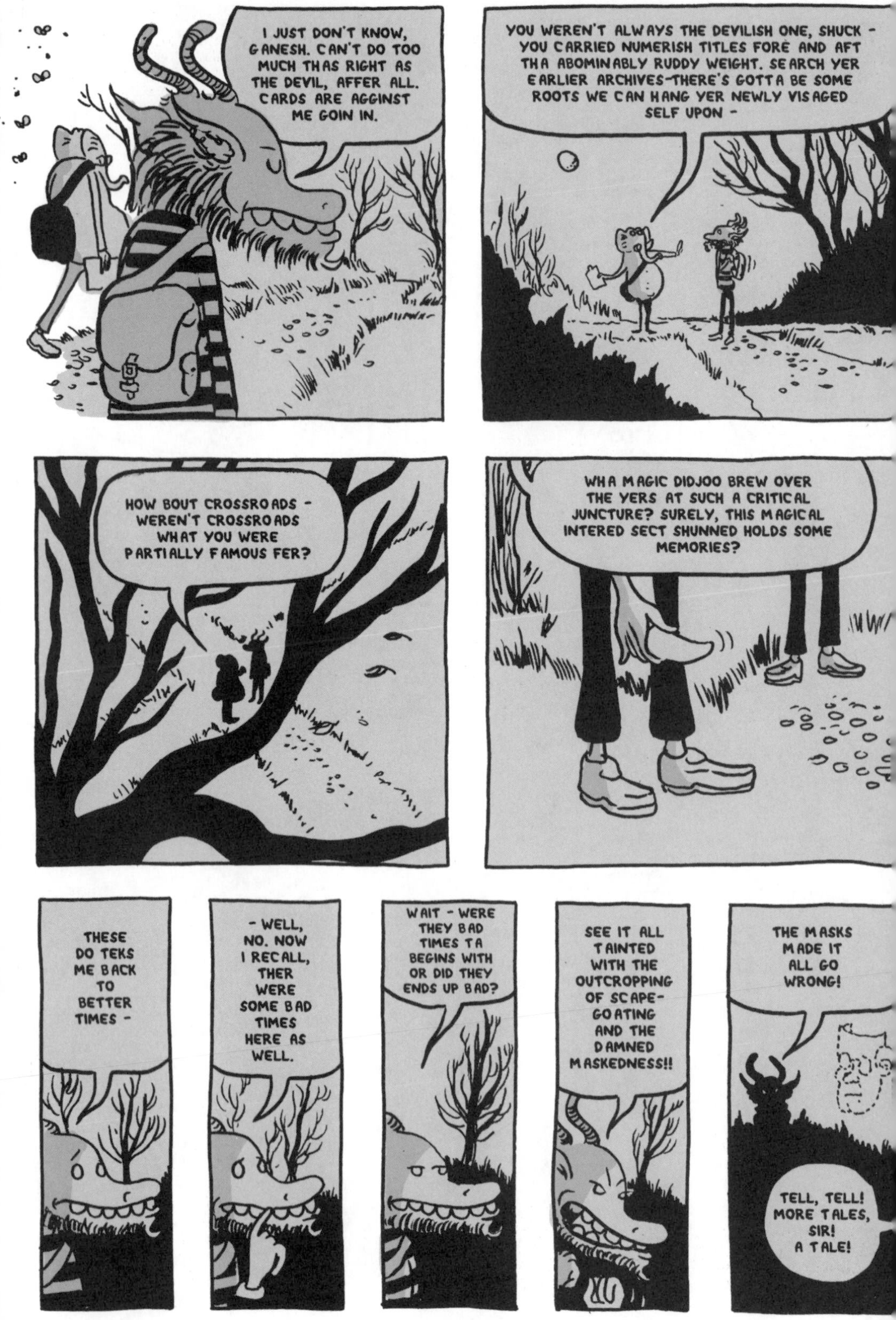
I JUST DON'T KNOW, GANESH. CAN'T DO TOO MUCH THAS RIGHT AS THE DEVIL, AFFER ALL. CARDS ARE AGGINST ME GOIN IN.
YOU WEREN'T ALWAYS THE DEVILISH ONE, SHUCK - YOU CARRIED NUMERISH TITLES FORE AND AFT THA ABOMINABLY RUDDY WEIGHT. SEARCH YER EARLIER ARCHIVES-THERE'S GOTTA BE SOME ROOTS WE CAN HANG YER NEWLY VISAGED SELF UPON -
HOW BOUT CROSSROADS - WEREN'T CROSSROADS WHAT YOU WERE PARTIALLY FAMOUS FER?
WHA MAGIC DIDJOO BREW OVER THE YERS AT SUCH A CRITICAL JUNCTURE? SURELY, THIS MAGICAL INTERED SECT SHUNNED HOLDS SOME MEMORIES?
THESE DO TEKS ME BACK TO BETTER TIMES -
- WELL, NO. NOW I RECALL, THER WERE SOME BAD TIMES HERE AS WELL.
WAIT - WERE THEY BAD TIMES TA BEGINS WITH OR DID THEY ENDS UP BAD?
SEE IT ALL TAINTED WITH THE OUTCROPPING OF SCAPE-GOATING AND THE DAMNED MASKEDNESS!!
THE MASKS MADE IT ALL GO WRONG!
TELL, TELL! MORE TALES, SIR! A TALE!

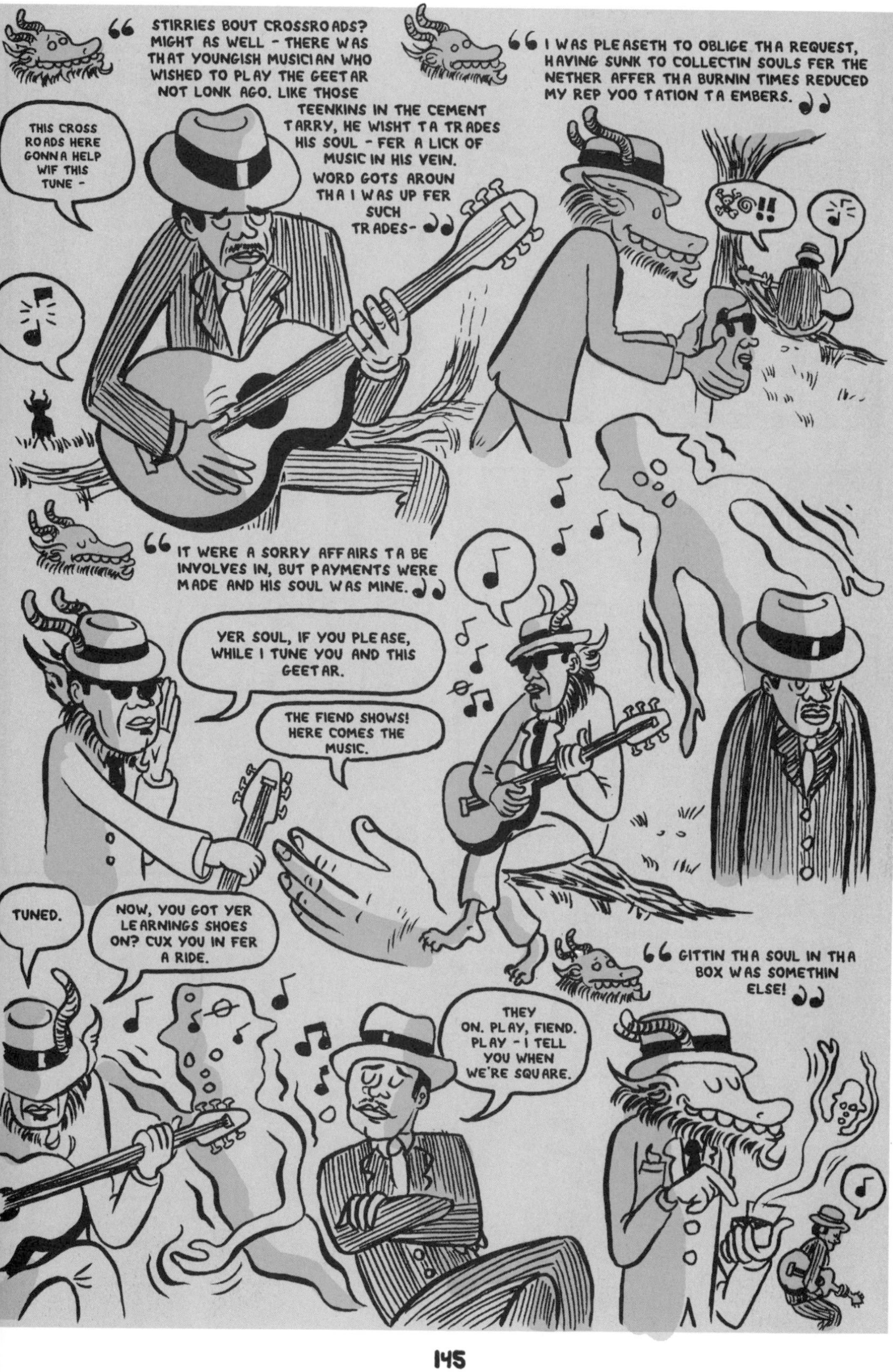

"STIRRIES BOUT CROSSROADS? MIGHT AS WELL - THERE WAS THAT YOUNGISH MUSICIAN WHO WISHED TO PLAY THE GEETAR NOT LONK AGO. LIKE THOSE TEENKINS IN THE CEMENT TARRY, HE WISHT TA TRADES HIS SOUL - FER A LICK OF MUSIC IN HIS VEIN. WORD GOTS AROUN THA I WAS UP FER SUCH TRADES-"
THIS CROSS ROADS HERE GONNA HELP WIF THIS TUNE -
"I WAS PLEASETH TO OBLIGE THA REQUEST, HAVING SUNK TO COLLECTIN SOULS FER THE NETHER AFFER THA BURNIN TIMES REDUCED MY REP YOO TATION TA EMBERS."
"IT WERE A SORRY AFFAIRS TA BE INVOLVES IN, BUT PAYMENTS WERE MADE AND HIS SOUL WAS MINE."
YER SOUL, IF YOU PLEASE, WHILE I TUNE YOU AND THIS GEETAR.
THE FIEND SHOWS! HERE COMES THE MUSIC.
TUNED.
NOW, YOU GOT YER LEARNINGS SHOES ON? CUX YOU IN FER A RIDE.
"GITTIN THA SOUL IN THA BOX WAS SOMETHIN ELSE!"
THEY ON. PLAY, FIEND. PLAY - I TELL YOU WHEN WE'RE SQUARE.

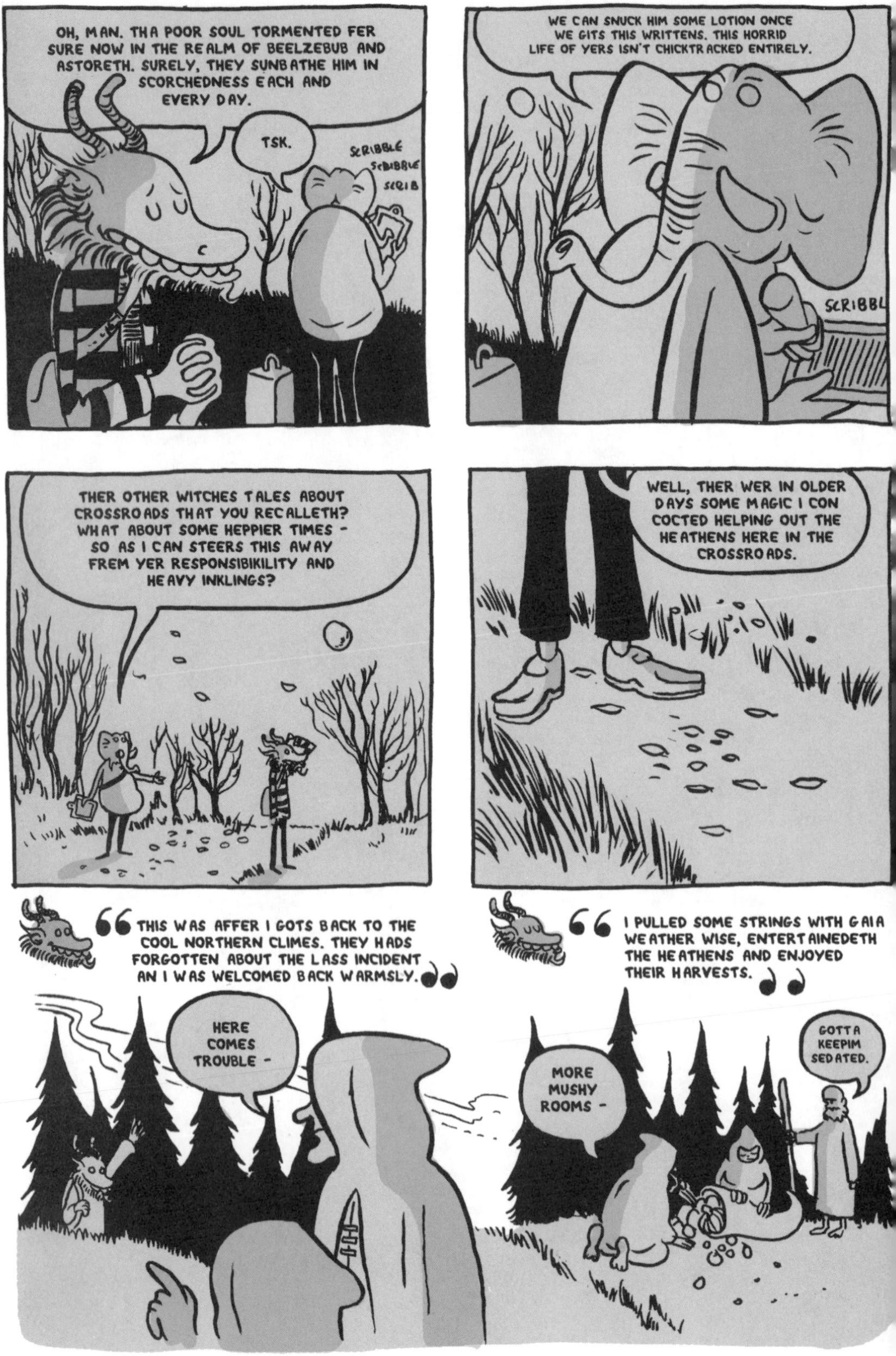
OH, MAN. THA POOR SOUL TORMENTED FER SURE NOW IN THE REALM OF BEELZEBUB AND ASTORETH. SURELY, THEY SUNBATHE HIM IN SCORCHEDNESS EACH AND EVERY DAY.
TSK.
SCRIBBLE SCRIBBLE SCRIB
WE CAN SNUCK HIM SOME LOTION ONCE WE GITS THIS WRITTENS. THIS HORRID LIFE OF YERS ISN'T CHICKTRACKED ENTIRELY.
SCRIBBL
THER OTHER WITCHES TALES ABOUT CROSSROADS THAT YOU RECALLETH? WHAT ABOUT SOME HEPPIER TIMES - SO AS I CAN STEERS THIS AWAY FREM YER RESPONSIBIKILITY AND HEAVY INKLINGS?
WELL, THER WER IN OLDER DAYS SOME MAGIC I CON COCTED HELPING OUT THE HEATHENS HERE IN THE CROSSROADS.
THIS WAS AFFER I GOTS BACK TO THE COOL NORTHERN CLIMES. THEY HADS FORGOTTEN ABOUT THE LASS INCIDENT AN I WAS WELCOMED BACK WARMSLY.
HERE COMES TROUBLE -
I PULLED SOME STRINGS WITH GAIA WEATHER WISE, ENTERTAINEDETH THE HEATHENS AND ENJOYED THEIR HARVESTS.
MORE MUSHY ROOMS -
GOTTA KEEPIM SEDATED.

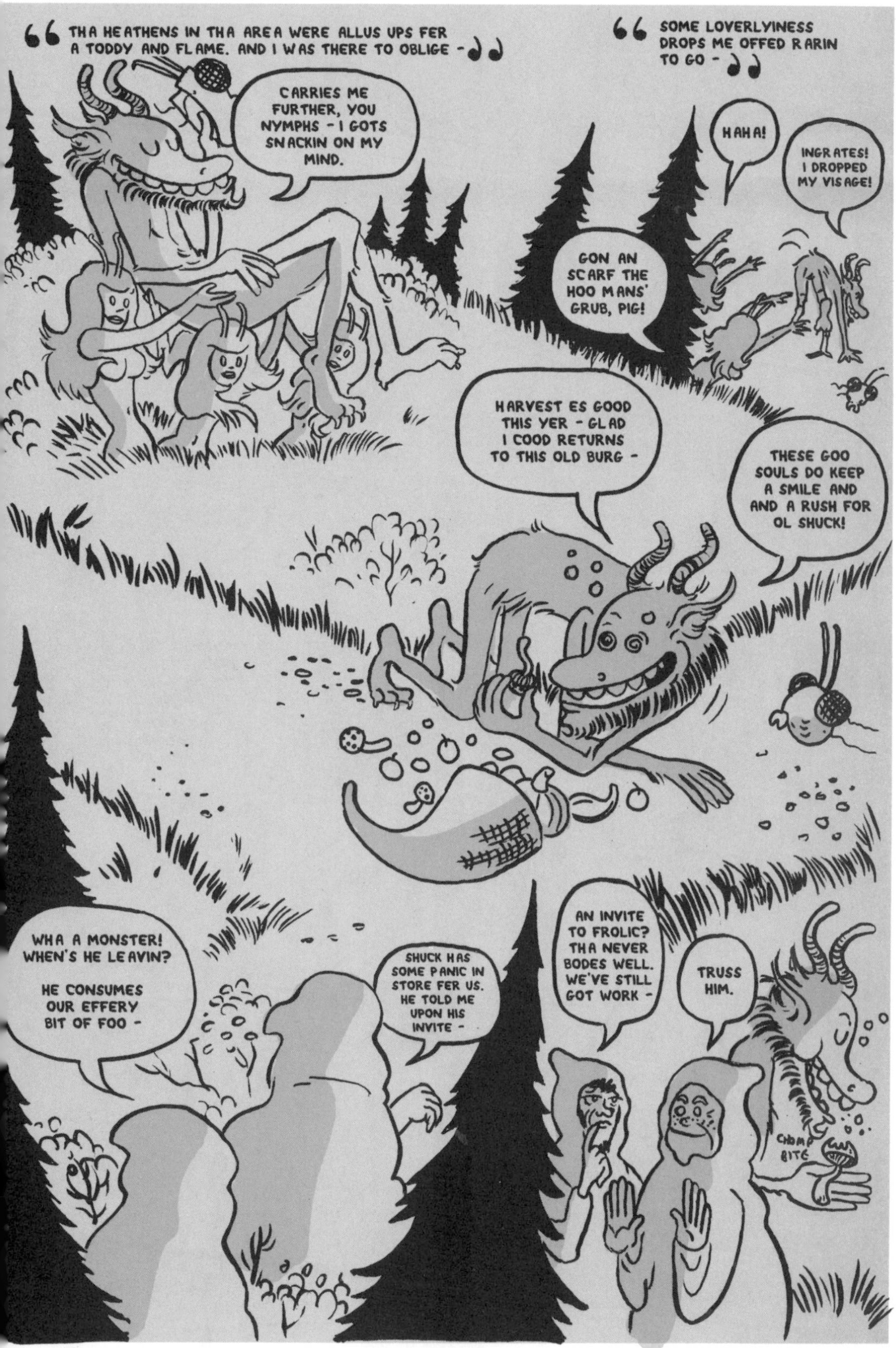
"THA HEATHENS IN THA AREA WERE ALLUS UPS FER A TODDY AND FLAME. AND I WAS THERE TO OBLIGE -"
CARRIES ME FURTHER, YOU NYMPHS - I GOTS SNACKIN ON MY MIND.
"SOME LOVERLYINESS DROPS ME OFFED RARIN TO GO -"
HAHA!
INGRATES! I DROPPED MY VISAGE!
GON AN SCARF THE HOO MANS' GRUB, PIG!
HARVEST ES GOOD THIS YER - GLAD I COOD RETURNS TO THIS OLD BURG -
THESE GOO SOULS DO KEEP A SMILE AND AND A RUSH FOR OL SHUCK!
WHA A MONSTER! WHEN'S HE LEAVIN?
HE CONSUMES OUR EFFERY BIT OF FOO -
SHUCK HAS SOME PANIC IN STORE FER US. HE TOLD ME UPON HIS INVITE -
AN INVITE TO FROLIC? THA NEVER BODES WELL. WE'VE STILL GOT WORK -
TRUSS HIM.
CHOMP BITE

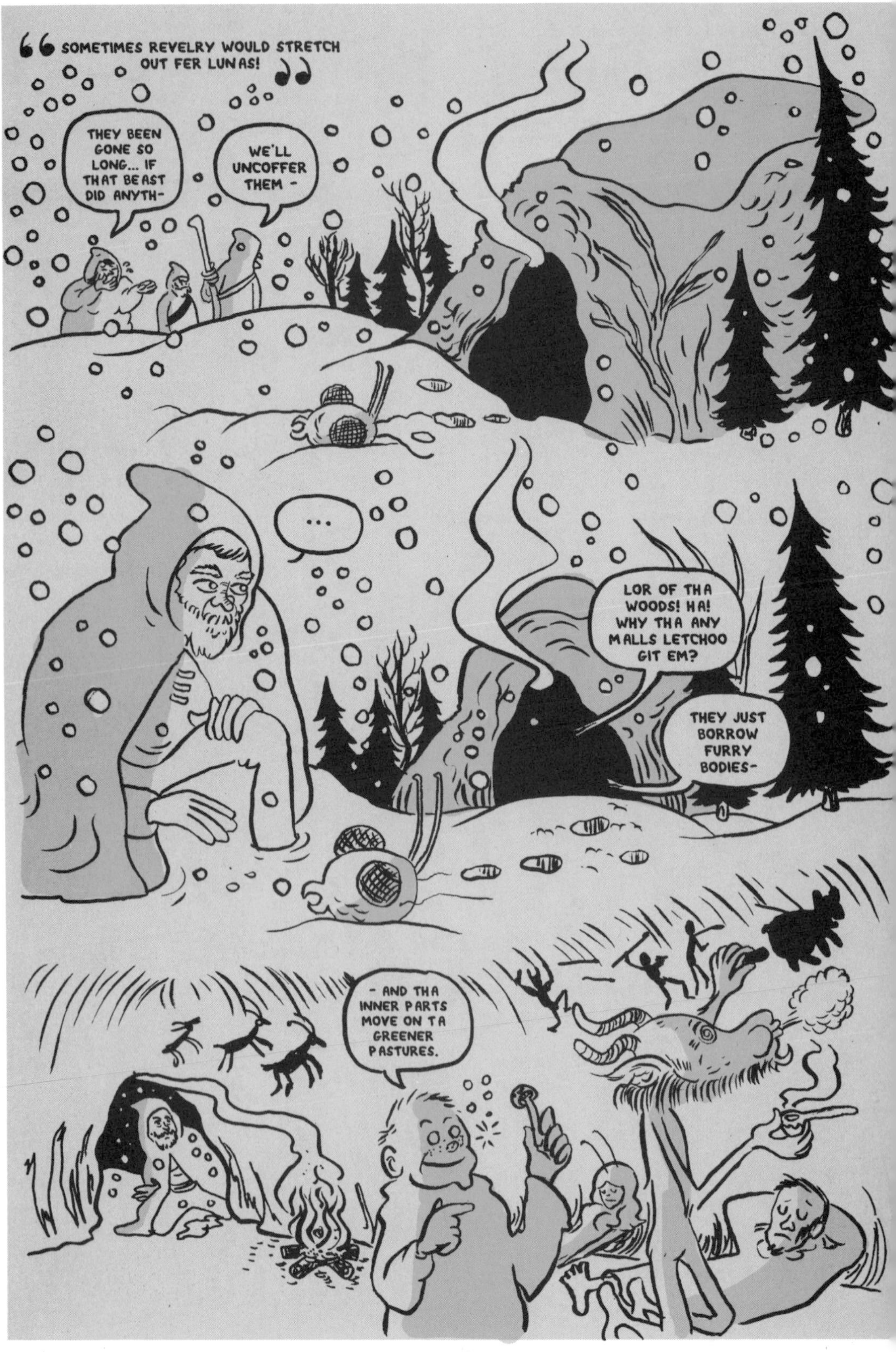
SOMETIMES REVELRY WOULD STRETCH OUT FER LUNAS!
THEY BEEN GONE SO LONG... IF THAT BEAST DID ANYTH-
WE'LL UNCOFFER THEM -
...
LOR OF THA WOODS! HA! WHY THA ANY MALLS LETCHOO GIT EM?
THEY JUST BORROW FURRY BODIES-
- AND THA INNER PARTS MOVE ON TA GREENER PASTURES.

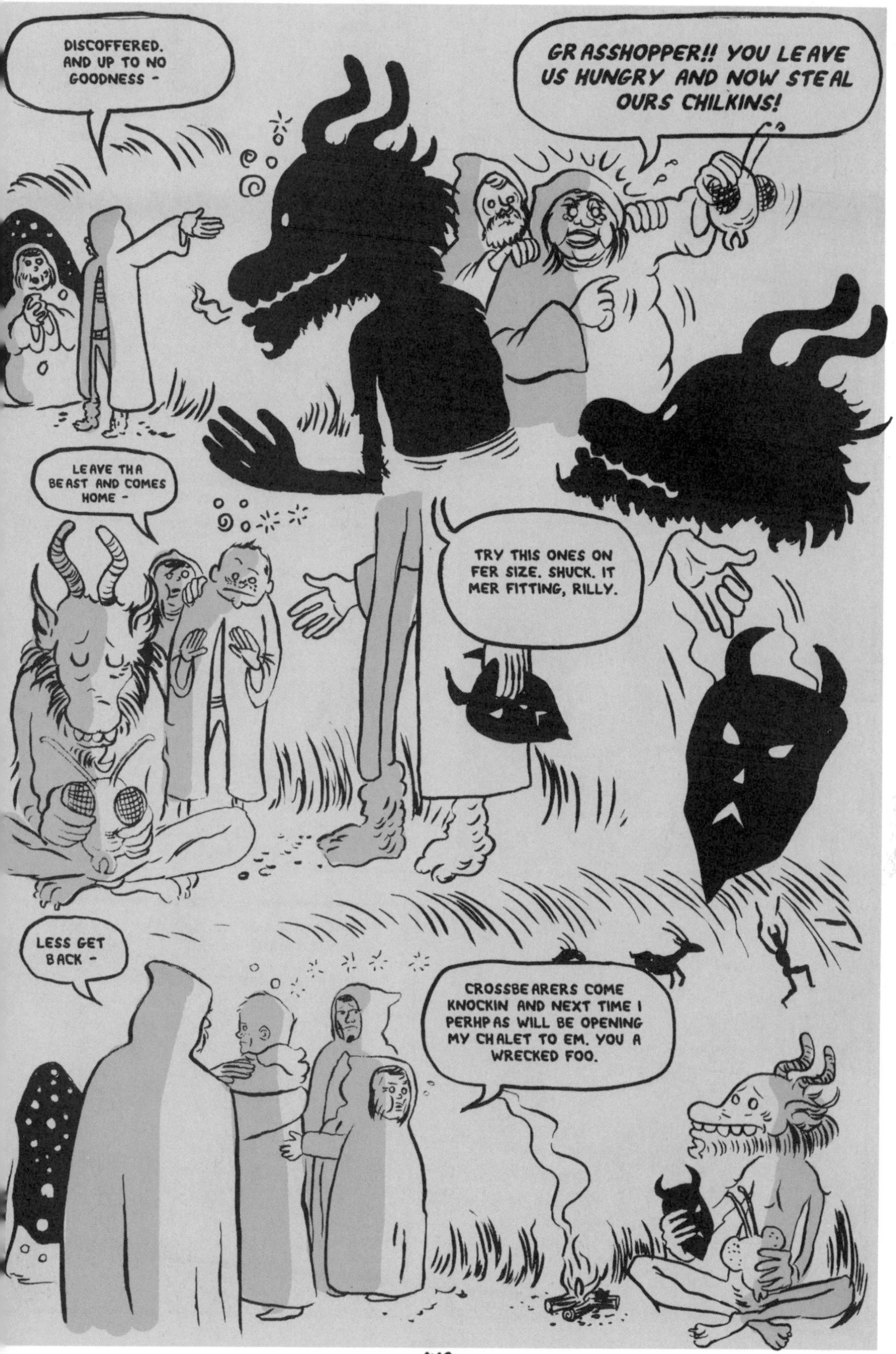
DISCOFFERED. AND UP TO NO GOODNESS -
GRASSHOPPER!! YOU LEAVE US HUNGRY AND NOW STEAL OURS CHILKINS!
LEAVE THA BEAST AND COMES HOME -
TRY THIS ONES ON FER SIZE. SHUCK. IT MER FITTING, RILLY.
LESS GET BACK -
CROSSBEARERS COME KNOCKIN AND NEXT TIME I PERHPAS WILL BE OPENING MY CHALET TO EM. YOU A WRECKED FOO.

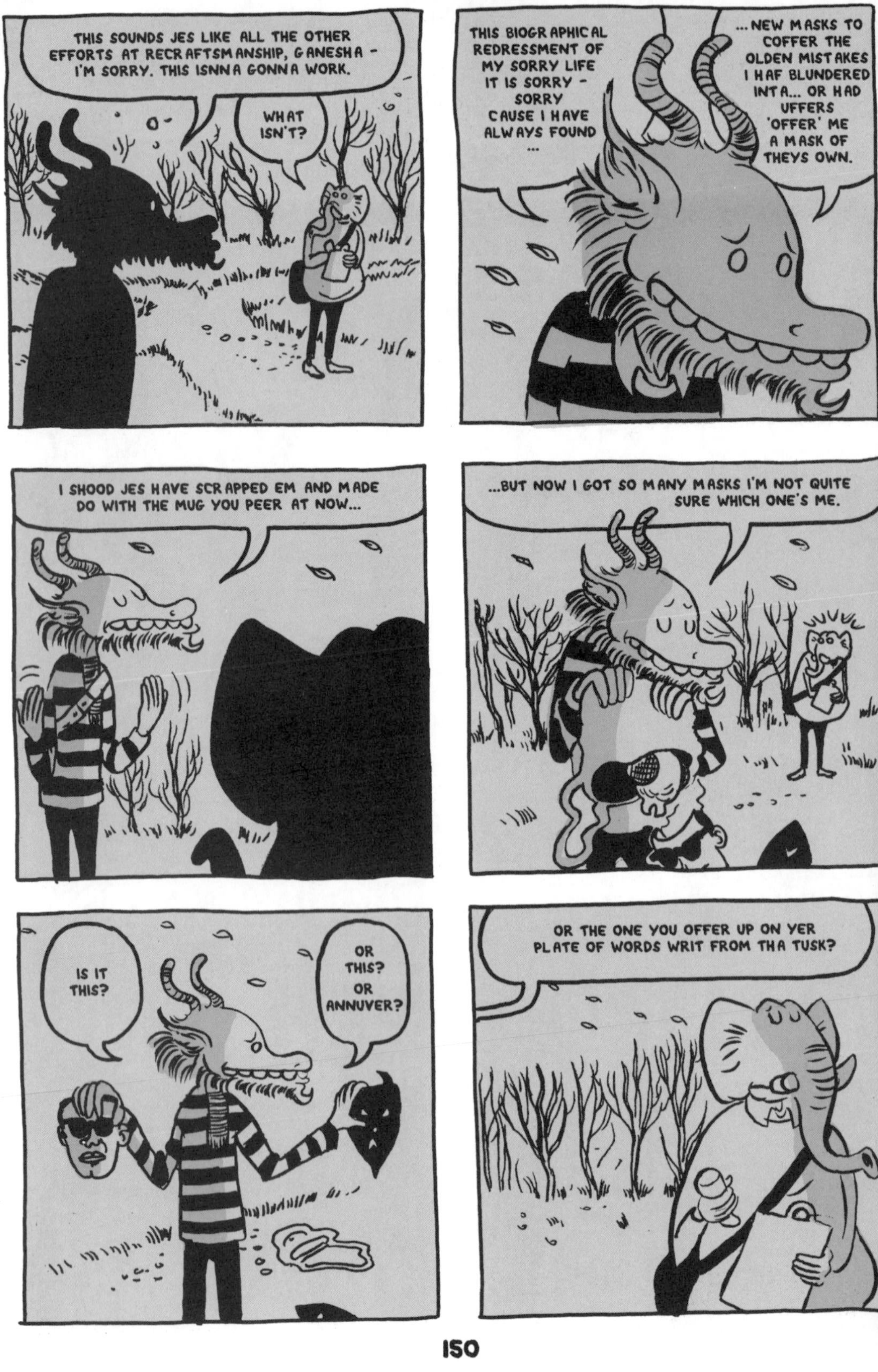
THIS SOUNDS JES LIKE ALL THE OTHER EFFORTS AT RECRAFTSMANSHIP, GANESHA - I'M SORRY. THIS ISNNA GONNA WORK.
WHAT ISN'T?
THIS BIOGRAPHICAL REDRESSMENT OF MY SORRY LIFE IT IS SORRY - SORRY CAUSE I HAVE ALWAYS FOUND ...
... NEW MASKS TO COFFER THE OLDEN MISTAKES I HAF BLUNDERED INTA... OR HAD UFFERS 'OFFER' ME A MASK OF THEYS OWN.
I SHOOD JES HAVE SCRAPPED EM AND MADE DO WITH THE MUG YOU PEER AT NOW...
...BUT NOW I GOT SO MANY MASKS I'M NOT QUITE SURE WHICH ONE'S ME.
IS IT THIS?
OR THIS? OR ANNUVER?
OR THE ONE YOU OFFER UP ON YER PLATE OF WORDS WRIT FROM THA TUSK?

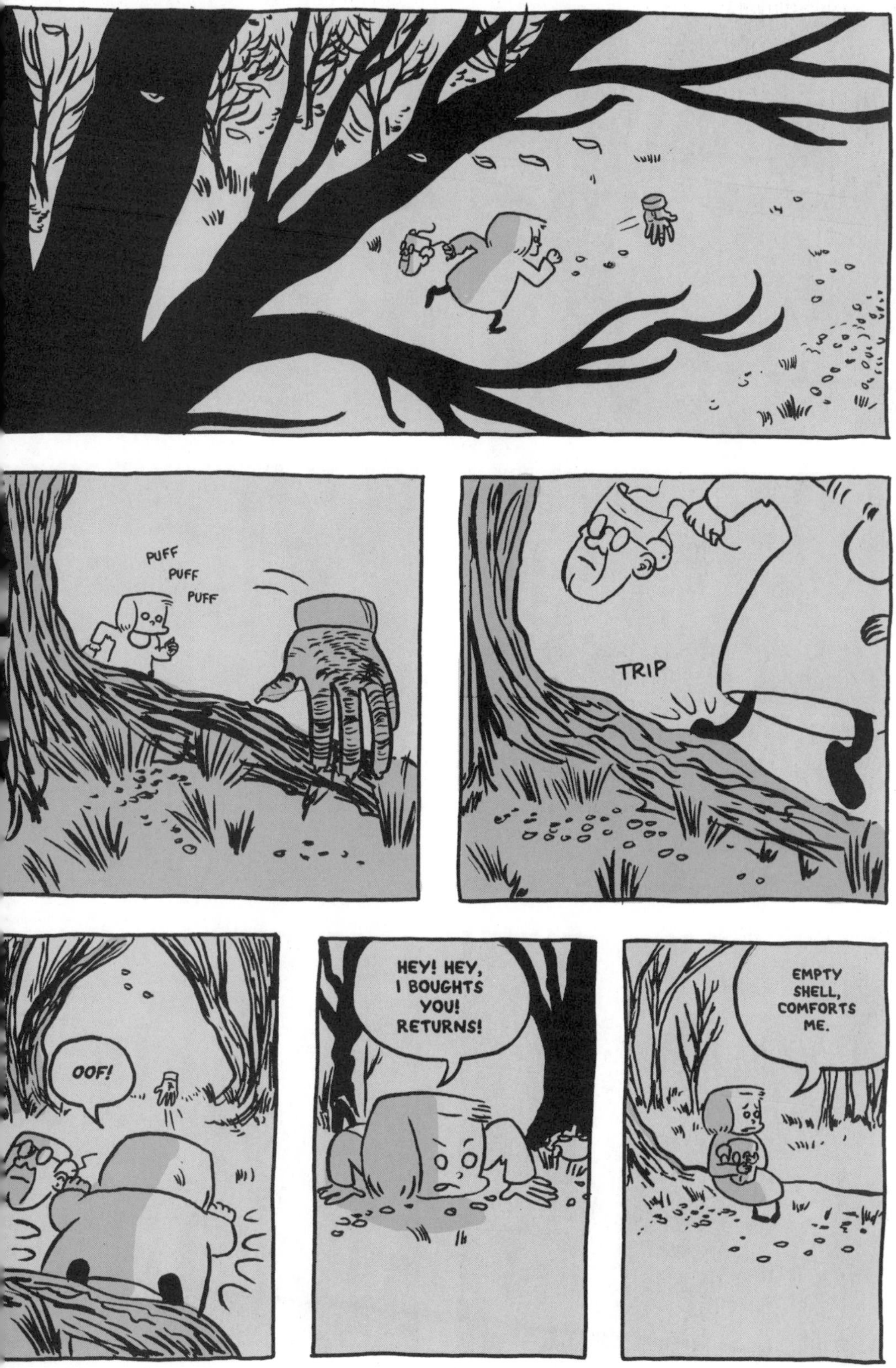
PUFF
PUFF
PUFF
TRIP
OOF!
HEY! HEY, I BOUGHTS YOU! RETURNS!
EMPTY SHELL, COMFORTS ME.

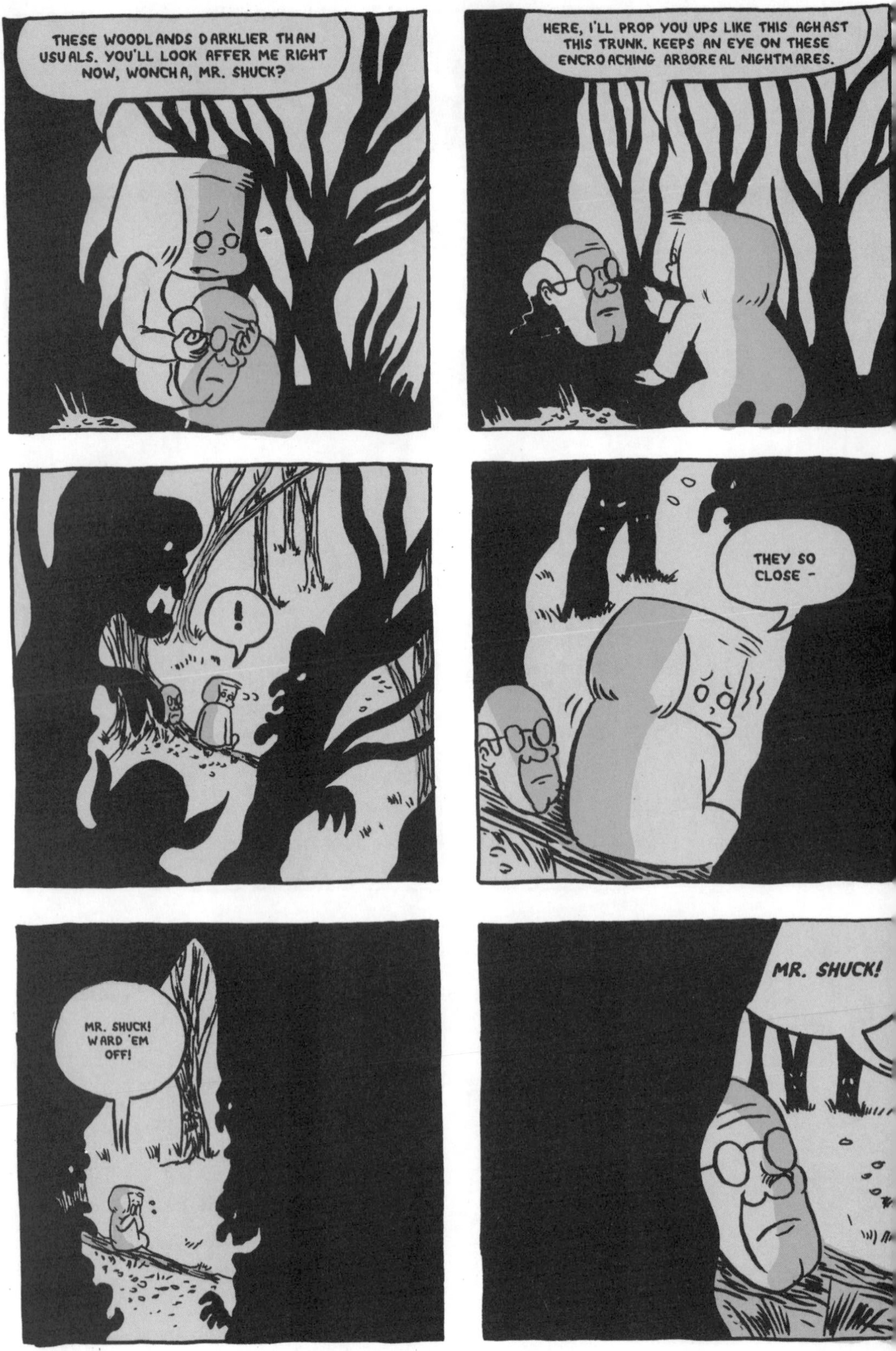
THESE WOODLANDS DARKLIER THAN USUALS. YOU'LL LOOK AFFER ME RIGHT NOW, WONCHA, MR. SHUCK?
HERE, I'LL PROP YOU UPS LIKE THIS AGHAST THIS TRUNK. KEEPS AN EYE ON THESE ENCROACHING ARBOREAL NIGHTMARES.
!
THEY SO CLOSE -
MR. SHUCK! WARD 'EM OFF!
MR. SHUCK!

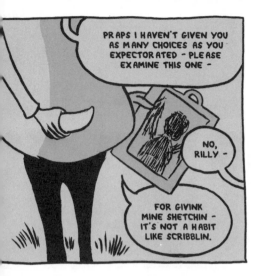

PRAPS I HAVEN'T GIVEN YOU AS MANY CHOICES AS YOU EXPECTORATED - PLEASE EXAMINE THIS ONE -

NO, RILLY -

FOR GIVINK MINE SHETCHIN - IT'S NOT A HABIT LIKE SCRIBBLIN.

OH -HERE'S ONE RIGHT UP WIF THIS NEW SINCERE NATURE OF YERS -

UHUH.

THIS ONE? PRAPS? WIF JES A LIL MORE FUR OFF THE SIDES?

NO! GANESHA - NOTHING WILL SWAY ME FROM MY NEW RESOLVE. I MUST BE THIS HORNED VISAGE YOU EYEBALL.

I FEAR I HAVE LED YOU HERE TO THESE, MY, CROSSROADS ONLY TO LEAVE YOU STRANDED. I WON'T BE RELIEVING YOU OF YOUR SCRIBBLER'S BLOCK, SIR. NOR LIVIN UP TO MY END OF THIS BARGAININK.

NOTHING OF THE SORTS. WE'LL KEEP -

HEY! THA ODDITY JUS ROBBED ME OF MY LIVELIHOODNESS!

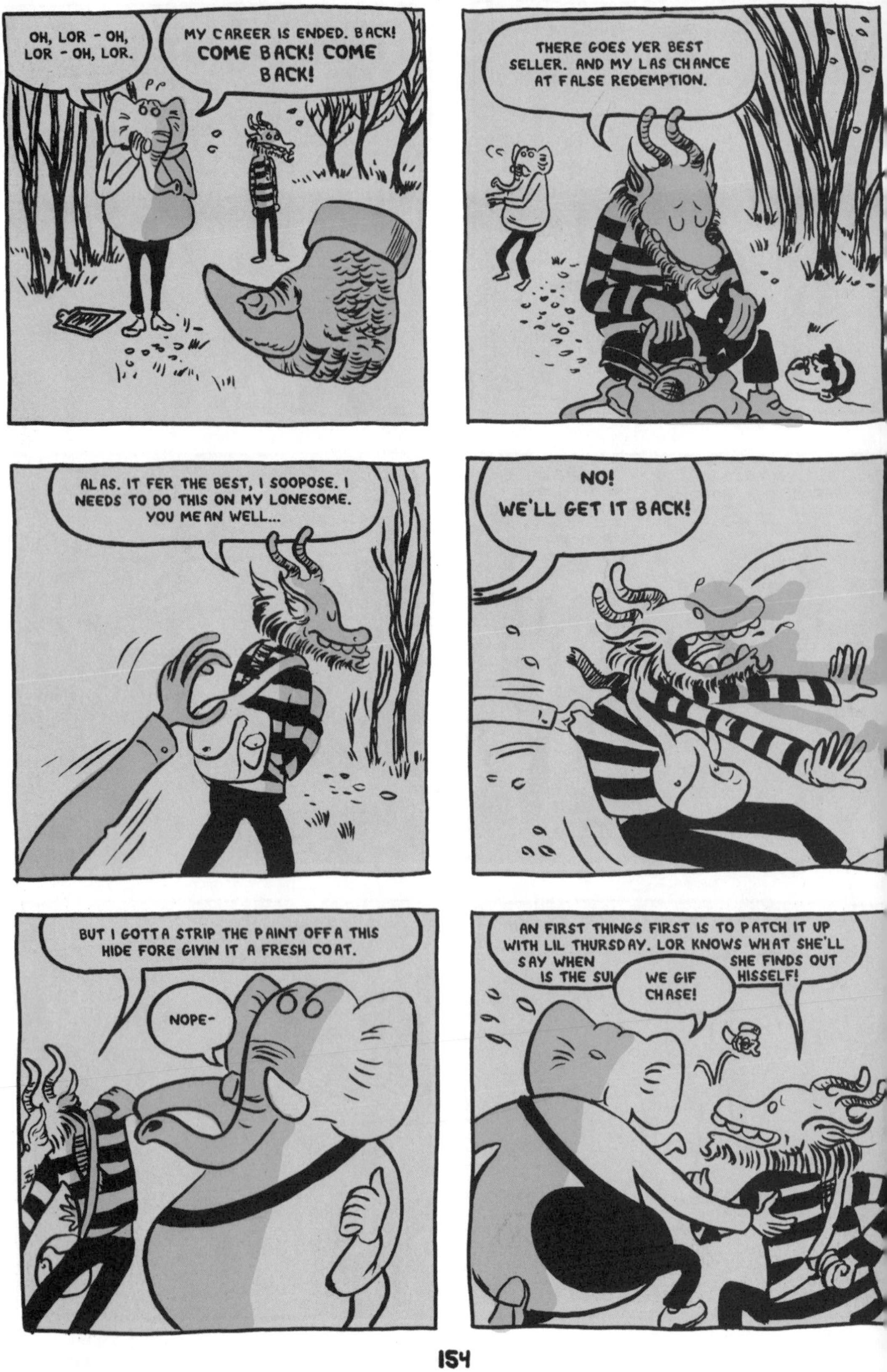
OH, LOR - OH, LOR - OH, LOR.
MY CAREER IS ENDED. BACK! COME BACK! COME BACK!
THERE GOES YER BEST SELLER. AND MY LAS CHANCE AT FALSE REDEMPTION.
ALAS. IT FER THE BEST, I SOOPOSE. I NEEDS TO DO THIS ON MY LONESOME. YOU MEAN WELL...
NO!
WE'LL GET IT BACK!
BUT I GOTTA STRIP THE PAINT OFFA THIS HIDE FORE GIVIN IT A FRESH COAT.
NOPE-
AN FIRST THINGS FIRST IS TO PATCH IT UP WITH LIL THURSDAY. LOR KNOWS WHAT SHE'LL SAY WHEN SHE FINDS OUT IS THE SU HISSELF!
WE GIF CHASE!

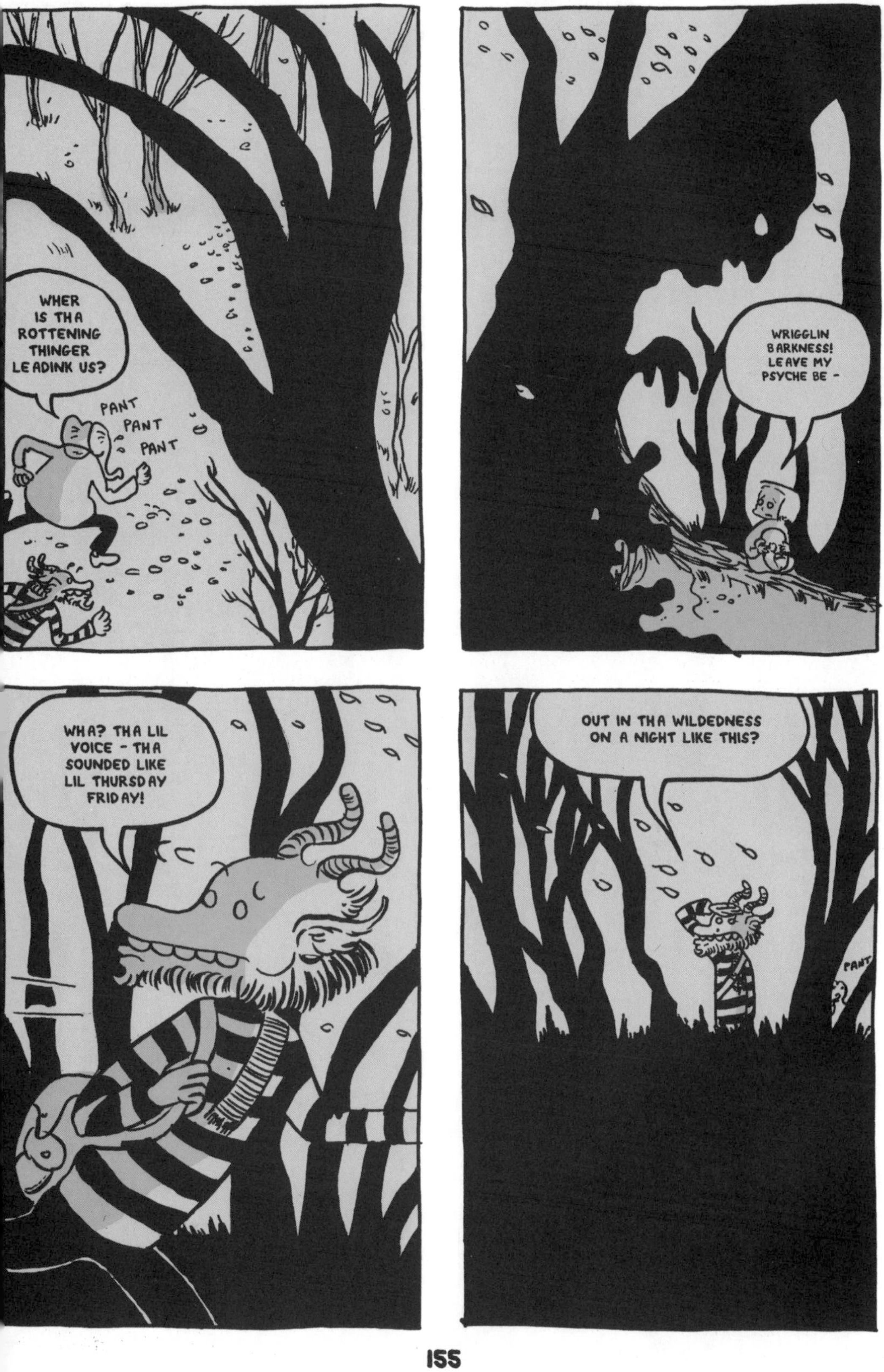
WHER IS THA ROTTENING THINGER LEADINK US?
PANT PANT PANT
WRIGGLIN BARKNESS! LEAVE MY PSYCHE BE -
WHA? THA LIL VOICE - THA SOUNDED LIKE LIL THURSDAY FRIDAY!
OUT IN THA WILDEDNESS ON A NIGHT LIKE THIS?
PANT

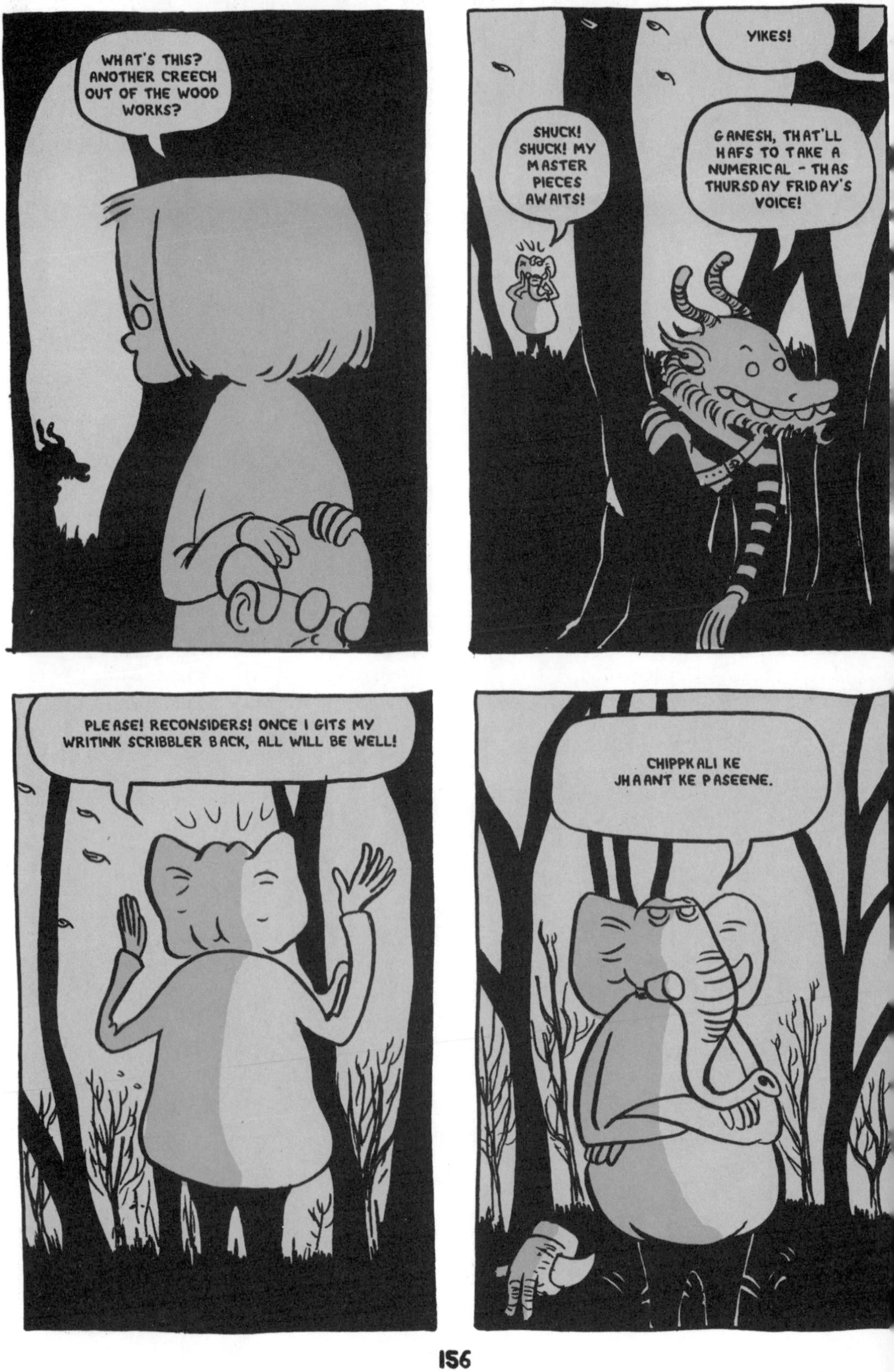
WHAT'S THIS? ANOTHER CREECH OUT OF THE WOOD WORKS?
YIKES!
SHUCK! SHUCK! MY MASTER PIECES AWAITS!
GANESH, THAT'LL HAFS TO TAKE A NUMERICAL - THAS THURSDAY FRIDAY'S VOICE!
PLEASE! RECONSIDERS! ONCE I GITS MY WRITINK SCRIBBLER BACK, ALL WILL BE WELL!
CHIPPKALI KE JHAANT KE PASEENE.

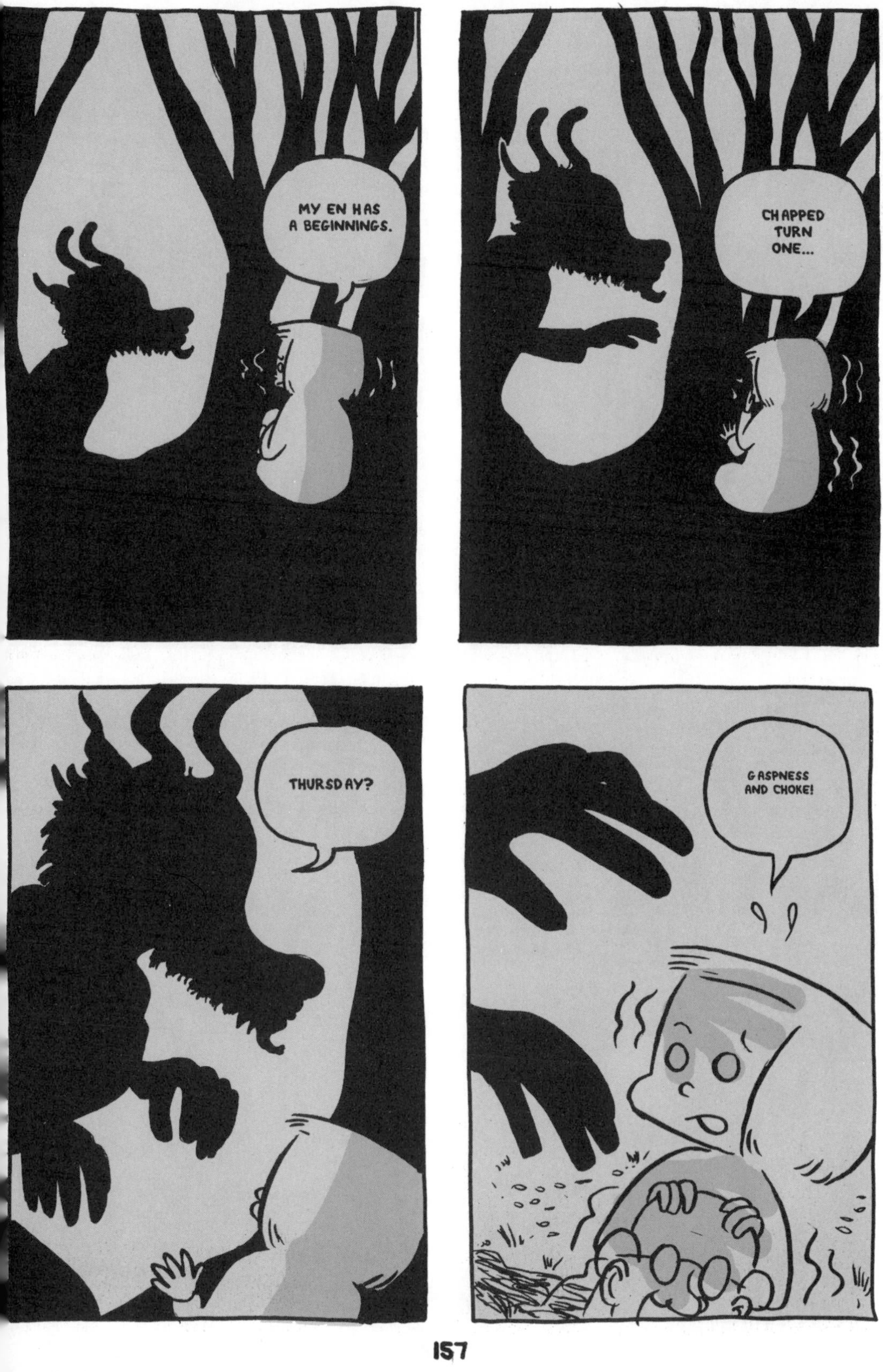
MY EN HAS A BEGINNINGS.
CHAPPED TURN ONE...
THURSDAY?
GASPNESS AND CHOKE!

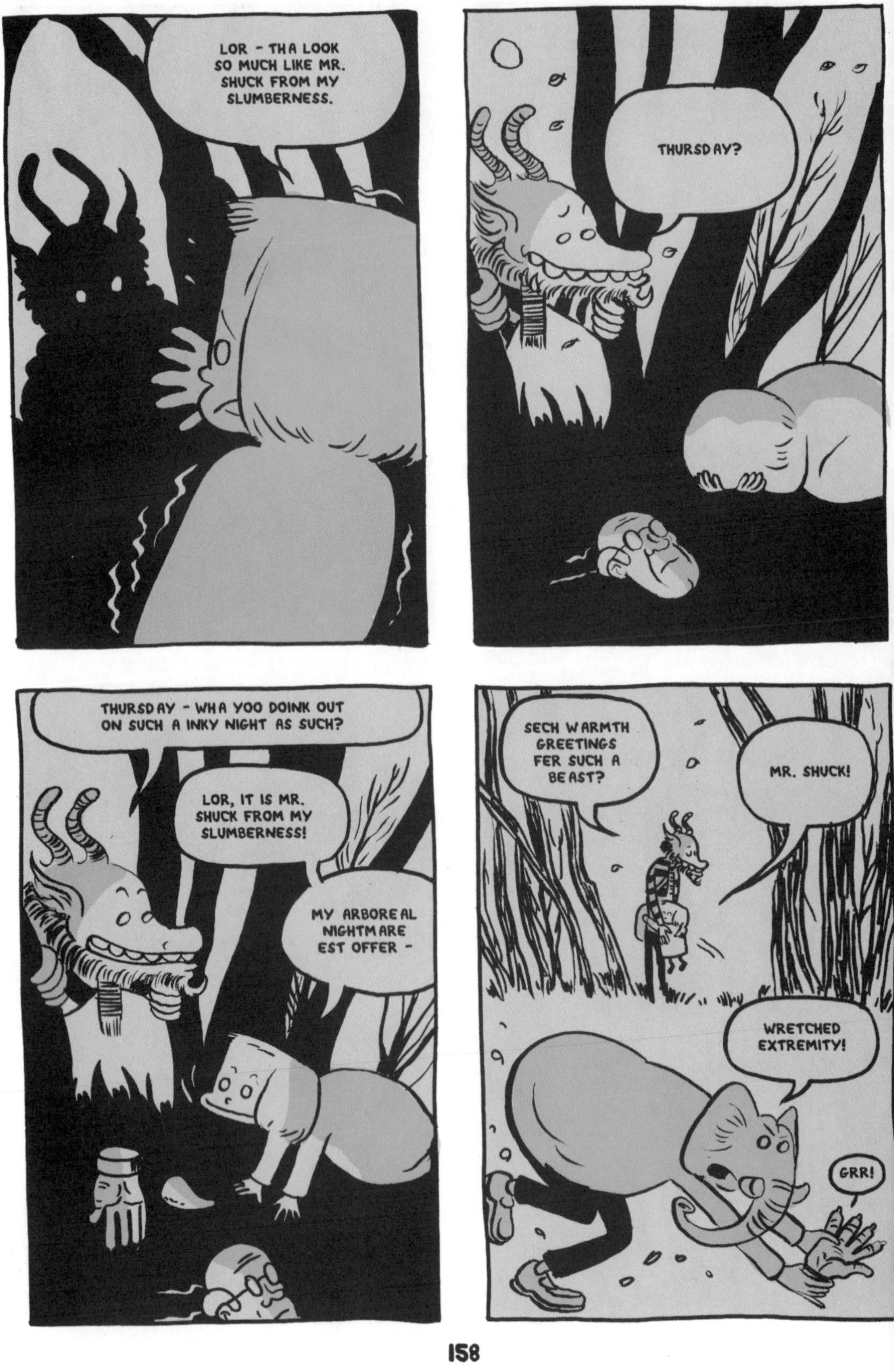
LOR - THA LOOK SO MUCH LIKE MR. SHUCK FROM MY SLUMBERNESS.
THURSDAY?
THURSDAY - WHA YOO DOINK OUT ON SUCH A INKY NIGHT AS SUCH?
LOR, IT IS MR. SHUCK FROM MY SLUMBERNESS!
MY ARBOREAL NIGHTMARE EST OFFER -
SECH WARMTH GREETINGS FER SUCH A BEAST?
MR. SHUCK!
WRETCHED EXTREMITY!
GRR!

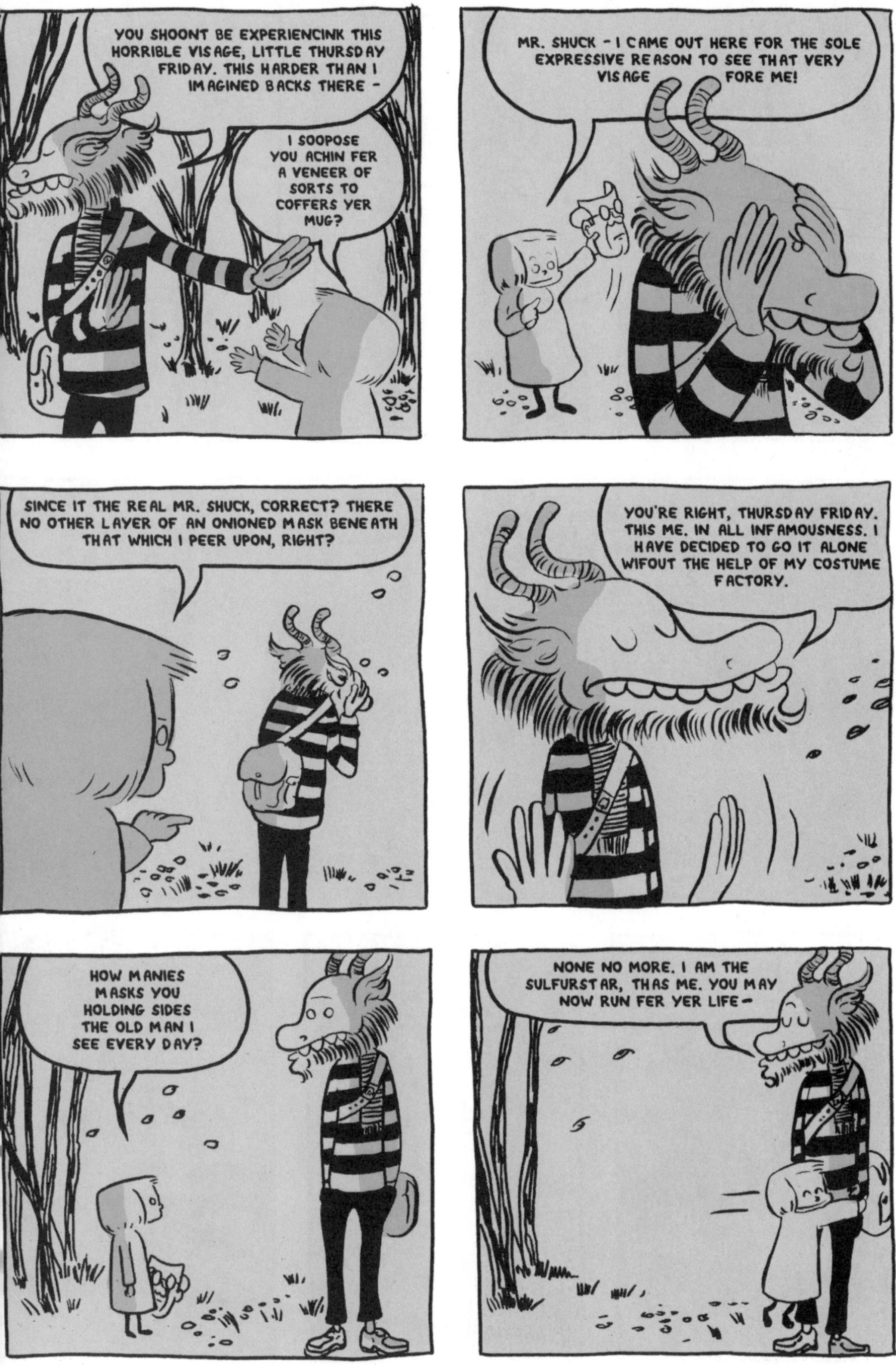
YOU SHOONT BE EXPERIENCINK THIS HORRIBLE VISAGE, LITTLE THURSDAY FRIDAY. THIS HARDER THAN I IMAGINED BACKS THERE -
I SOOPOSE YOU ACHIN FER A VENEER OF SORTS TO COFFERS YER MUG?
MR. SHUCK - I CAME OUT HERE FOR THE SOLE EXPRESSIVE REASON TO SEE THAT VERY VISAGE FORE ME!
SINCE IT THE REAL MR. SHUCK, CORRECT? THERE NO OTHER LAYER OF AN ONIONED MASK BENEATH THAT WHICH I PEER UPON, RIGHT?
YOU'RE RIGHT, THURSDAY FRIDAY. THIS ME. IN ALL INFAMOUSNESS. I HAVE DECIDED TO GO IT ALONE WIFOUT THE HELP OF MY COSTUME FACTORY.
HOW MANIES MASKS YOU HOLDING SIDES THE OLD MAN I SEE EVERY DAY?
NONE NO MORE. I AM THE SULFURSTAR, THAS ME. YOU MAY NOW RUN FER YER LIFE -

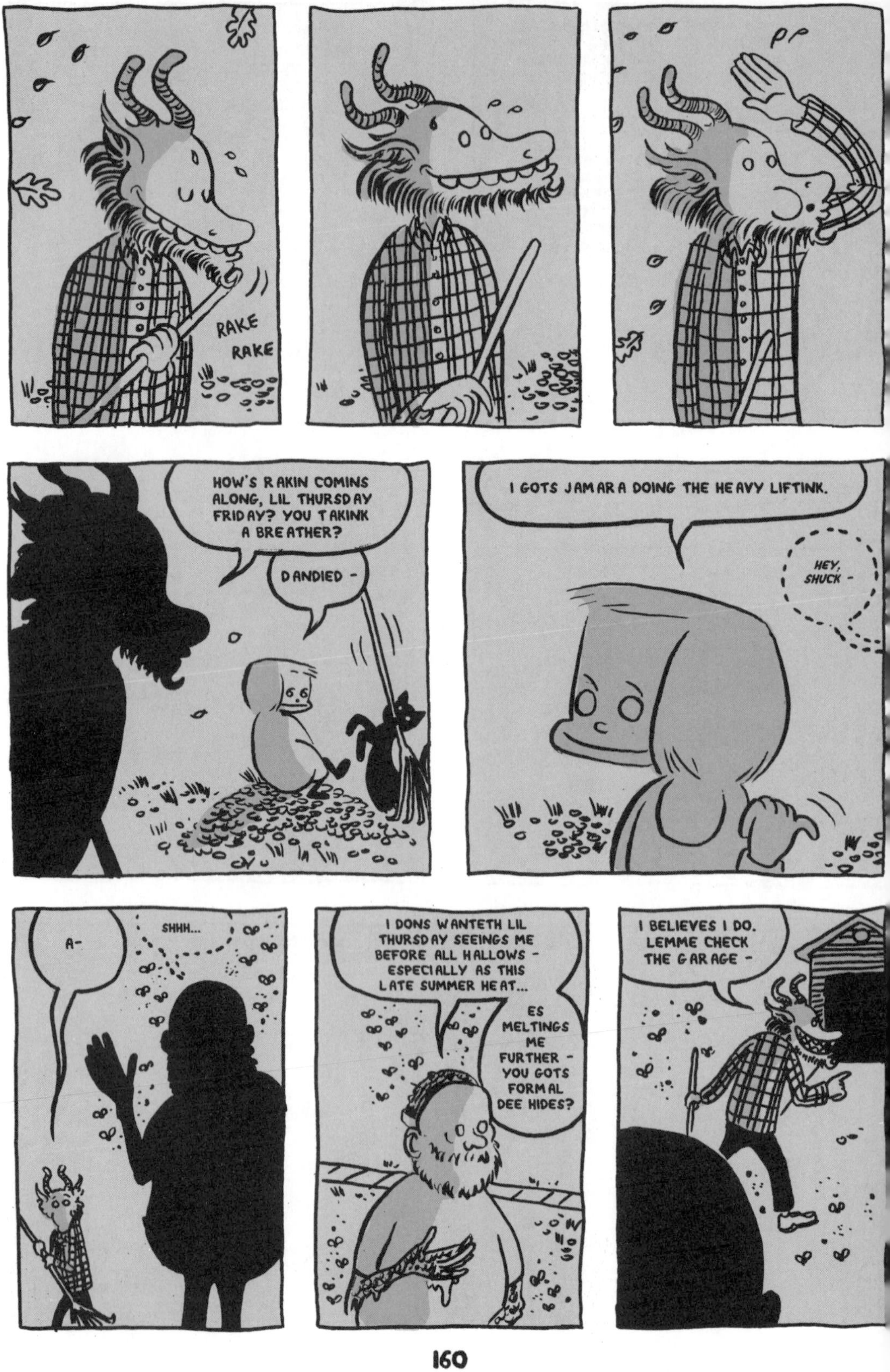
RAKE
RAKE
HOW'S RAKIN COMINS ALONG, LIL THURSDAY FRIDAY? YOU TAKINK A BREATHER?
DANDIED -
I GOTS JAMARA DOING THE HEAVY LIFTINK.
HEY, SHUCK -
A-
SHHH...
I DONS WANTETH LIL THURSDAY SEEINGS ME BEFORE ALL HALLOWS - ESPECIALLY AS THIS LATE SUMMER HEAT...
ES MELTINGS ME FURTHER - YOU GOTS FORMAL DEE HIDES?
I BELIEVES I DO. LEMME CHECK THE GARAGE -

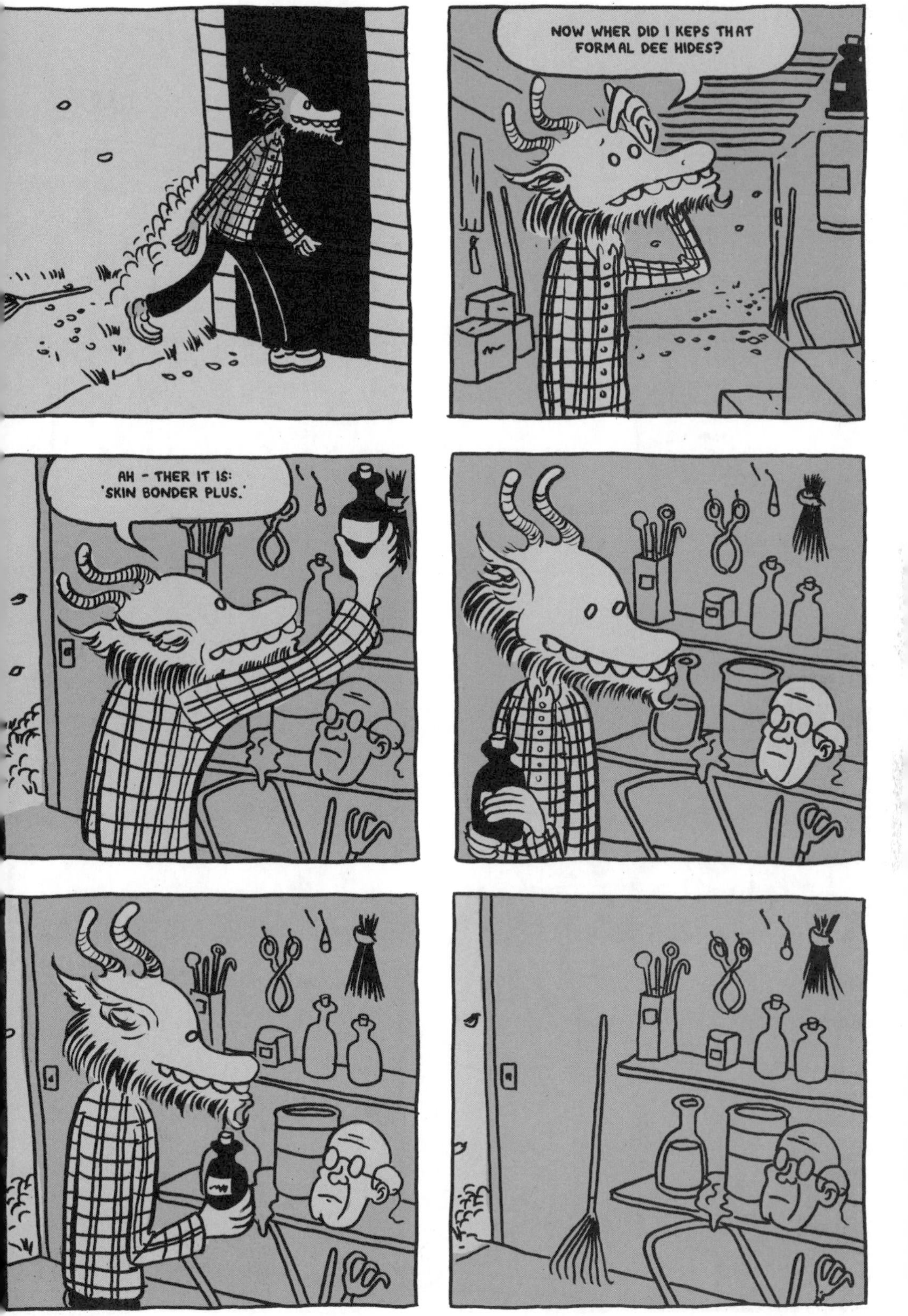
NOW WHER DID I KEPS THAT FORMAL DEE HIDES?
AH - THER IT IS: 'SKIN BONDER PLUS.'

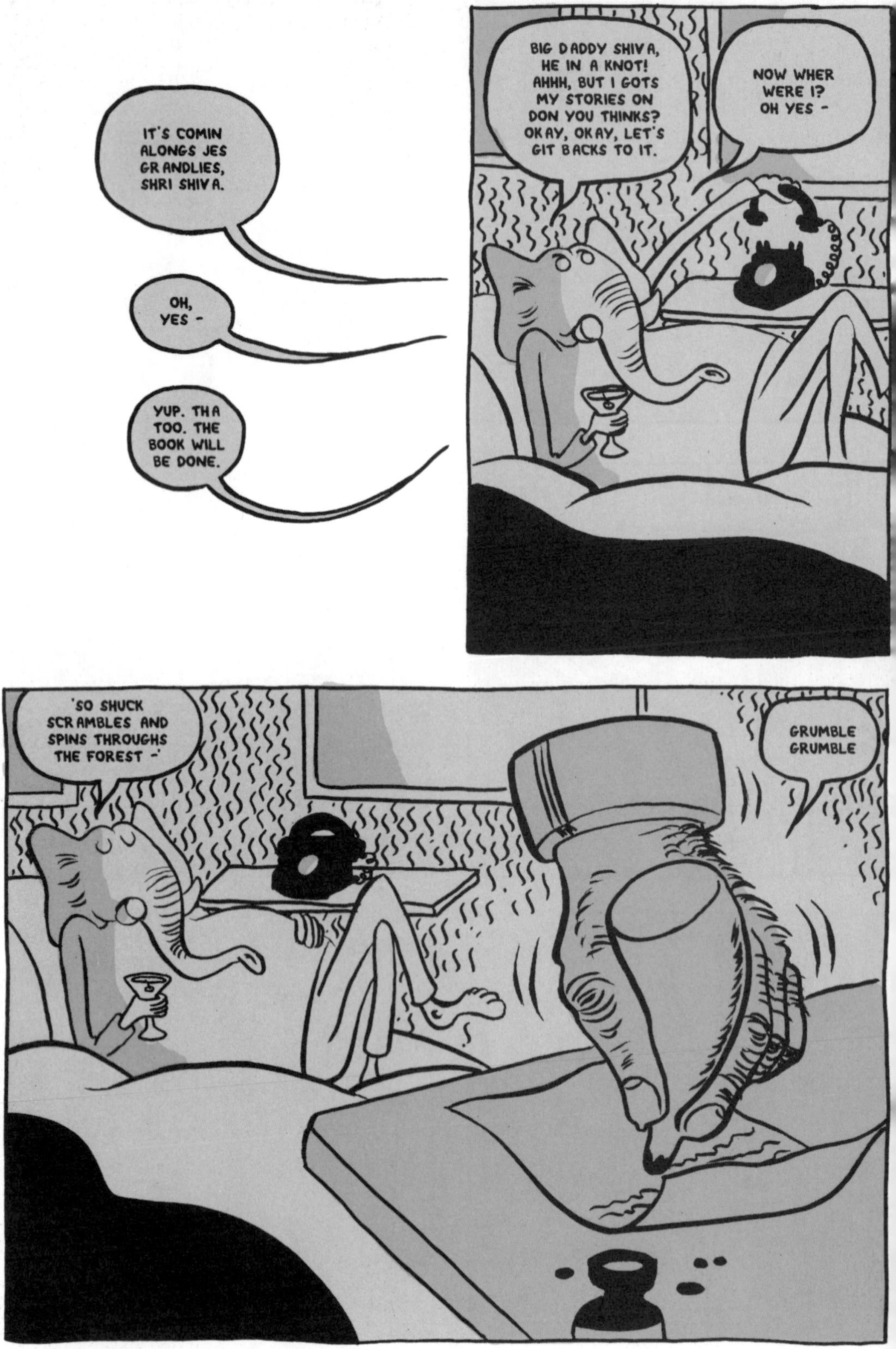
IT'S COMIN ALONGS JES GRANDLIES, SHRI SHIVA.
OH, YES -
YUP. THA TOO. THE BOOK WILL BE DONE.
BIG DADDY SHIVA, HE IN A KNOT! AHHH, BUT I GOTS MY STORIES ON DON YOU THINKS? OKAY, OKAY, LET'S GIT BACKS TO IT.
NOW WHER WERE I? OH YES -
'SO SHUCK SCRAMBLES AND SPINS THROUGHS THE FOREST -'
GRUMBLE GRUMBLE

Acknowledgements

We'd like to thank Jeff Smith for his gracious foreword to this book, Dave Sim for the education in publishing, Damon Hurd for offering half his table at SPX (that got this ball rolling), Scott McCloud for the 24 hour challenge and Brett Warnock and Chris Staros for their patience, help and dedication to the art form.

We'd also like to thank: Mom and Dad for those trips to the art store and Comic Closet, Charles for his daily reading from *Shuck*, Rich for the cornucopia of ideas and support, Matt for helping with expenses, Carrie for reading with a careful eye, Myles for making it all seem real and Ben for always asking 'So what's Shuck up to these days?'

Rick Smith and Tania Menesse

Rick Smith and Tania Menesse live in Denver, Colorado with their daughter Sage and cat Peco.

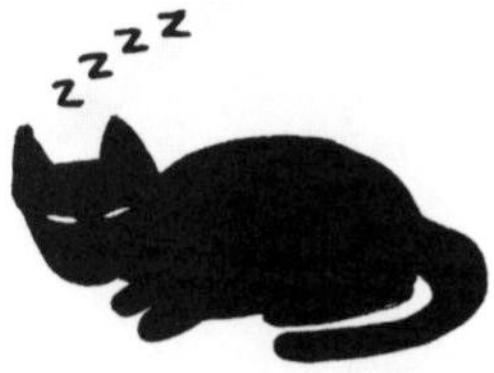

zzzz